T0243844

CRUEL CONFLICT

KATHRYN SPURLING

CRUEL CONFLICT

THE TRIUMPH AND TRAGEDY OF HMAS *PERTH*

Published in 2022 by New Holland Publishers
First published in Australia in 2008 by New Holland Publishers
Sydney • Auckland

Level 1, 178 Fox Valley Road, Wahroonga, NSW 2076, Australia
5/39 Woodside Ave, Northcote, Auckland 0627, New Zealand

newhollandpublishers.com

A record of this book is held at the National Library of Australia.

ISBN 9781760794767

Group Managing Director: Fiona Schultz
Project Editor: Diane Jardine
Designer: Andrew Davies
Production Director: Arlene Gippert
Printed in Australia by SOS Print + Media Group

10 9 8 7 6 5 4 3 2 1

Keep up with New Holland Publishers:

 NewHollandPublishers
 @newhollandpublishers

I dedicate this book to my husband
and best friend.

Nigel Patrick John Spurling
23 December 1944–10 January 2005
WEEO Cdr
HMAS *Perth II*
4 January 1982–21 March 1983

To the Officers and Ship's Company of HMAS Perth I *who were the*
inspiration; may we never forget their story and sacrifice.

FOREWORD

I served in the DDG HMAS *Perth* on two occasions. On the second occasion, I joined the ship in Mackay to take command. As I was settling in to my cabin that evening, I noticed on the bookshelf a small, well-worn book *Out of the Smoke* by Ray Parkin. I was broadly aware of the story of *Perth I*, and particularly the Battle of Sunda Strait, but had never properly read the full history of that magnificent ship, nor fully understood the remarkable stories of her ship's company.

During the remainder of my term in command, I followed up and read voraciously on all and any aspects of *Perth*'s short and illustrious career. In late 1993 I was pleased to welcome Brendan Whiting, the son of Chief Petty Officer Reg Whiting, onboard *Perth* for transit from Langkawi, Malaysia, to Darwin via a short, traditional but emotional service conducted over the site of *Perth* at the northern end of the Sunda Strait. Brendan subsequently published *Ship of Courage* in which he describes his short passage in *Perth II*. He concludes by noting that a specially commissioned *Perth* cap, loaned to him by 'Knocker' White, was blown from his head as he and I climbed to the flag deck after the dawn service. I recall saying to Brendan 'no problems, we'll turn the ship around and pick it up'. He said no, on the basis that he felt the memento was best left in Sunda Strait, *'there in the channel where he and his shipmates made their way from Sangiang into the noble annals of the Royal Australian Navy.'*

Kathryn Spurling has added immeasurably to those 'noble annals' in this monumental and carefully researched story of the cruiser *Perth I*. She recalls the research as being 'something of a marathon' and one can only imagine the extent and depth of the cataloguing, cross referencing, and detailed analysis which has led to this final product. I commend *Cruel Conflict: The Triumph and Tragedy of HMAS Perth* to all who are interested in the short but vibrantly rich history of our navy. Perth is an evocative name in that rich history and Kathryn Spurling's remarkably comprehensive chronology of the ship and her men, and those who loved and supported them, adds immeasurably to our understanding of that critical period in the RAN's history. Her magnificent effort in collecting, collating and articulating these many stories of individual courage and heroism, all of them bound together by that notion of being all of one company – HMAS *Perth* – is greatly appreciated by we who inherit the traditions and values of those who have gone before us.

Vice Admiral Russ Shalders, AO, CSC, RAN
Chief of Navy

CONTENTS

LIST OF ABBREVIATIONS

AB	Able Seaman
ABDA	American, British, Dutch and Australian Command
ACNB	Australian Commonwealth Naval Board
ASDIC	Anti-submarine detection
AWAS	Australian Women's Army Service
BEM	British Empire Medal
Cdr	Commander
CNS	Chief of Naval Staff
CO	Commanding Officer
CPO	Chief Petty Officer
DEMS	Defensively Equipped Merchant Ships
DSC	Distinguished Service Cross
DSM	Distinguished Service Medal
DSO	Distinguished Service Order
EA	Electrical Artificer
ERA	Engine Room Artificer
HMAS	His Majesty's Australian Ship
HMS	His Majesty's Ship
Lieut	Lieutenant
Lieut Cdr	Lieutenant Commander
LSGCM	Long Service and Good Conduct Medal
MBE	Member of the British Empire
MV	Merchant Vessel
OOW	Officer of the Watch
Ord Seam	Ordinary Seaman
PO	Petty Officer
POW	Prisoners of War (s)
PTSD	Post Traumatic Stress Disorder
PUNS	Permanently Unfit for Naval Service
RAAF	Royal Australian Air Force
RAFR	Royal Australian Fleet Reserve
RAN	Royal Australian Navy
RANC	Royal Australian Naval College
RANR	Royal Australian Naval Reserve
RANR(S)	Royal Australian Naval Reserve (Seagoing)
RANVR	Royal Australian Naval Volunteer Reserve
RDF	Radio Direction Finder
RN	Royal Navy
SBA	Sick Berth Attendant
Sig	Signalman
WAAAF	Women's Australian Auxiliary Air Force
WESC	Women's Emergency Signal Corps
WRANS	Women's Royal Australian Naval Service
W/T	Wireless Transmitting Office
XO	Executive Officer

PREFACE

More than 1000 officers and men served in HMAS *Perth I* between 1939 and 1942. It is impossible to do justice to their stories because each is worthy of a book.

I was restricted to what archival material could be found; survivors and families I could trace; and who was willing to discuss often painful memories. The search was long but rewarding, because any historical work is only as good as its primary source material. The many published and unpublished memoirs provided valuable first-hand accounts, interpretations and analysis.

One of the difficulties in writing of another time is to leave the present behind. I can only hope I managed to see and feel enough to achieve this. Another difficulty is how different individuals see, interpret and remember incidents differently. When faced with such variation, I have gone with that most frequently cited. The names of geographic regions have changed since World War II; the Dutch East Indies became Indonesia; Formosa became Taiwan. I have used those of the period with the exception of the name Thailand instead of Siam. Dealing with English, American, French, Dutch, Indonesian and Japanese place names and terminology over a period of 70 years was challenging. The many diaries provide further variation. For example, the Javanese port known to the Dutch as Soerabaja was known by Americans as Surabaja, by the Australians as Surabaya; the name Laboehan is also Labuan or Laubuan; Tanjan Priok is also known as Tandjungpriok or Tanjong Priok; Phonon Phen is also Ponon Phen or Phnom Penh. I have used Australian English given this is an Australian story. The shortened versions of RAN ranks are in keeping with the official 1946 RAN document on repatriated POWs.

Weaving the tapestry was complicated by the non use of recorded first names. Men of the generation were often named after their fathers and to then avoid using the same name for two within a household, families called men by their second given name or another name that did not appear on any official document. Interviewing men of *Perth* was a delightful and inspiring experience, but for the historian who needed to piece together the puzzle, names provided were invariably problematic because, in true navy style, nicknames sufficed. Invariably surnames were not known and first names were vague. Familiarity with naval nicknames, (e.g. men with the name of Kelly tend to be called 'Ned', Miller assumes the name 'Dusty', men with the name Martin tend to be called 'Pincher', Gale becomes 'Windy') helped, but not when there were more than one. Some unique nicknames, such as 'Elmo' and 'Digby' helped but more generalised nicknames like 'Mo', 'Freddie', 'Tich' certainly complicated the quest for the true story.

I also needed to convey the terror, misery and privation suffered by *Perth* I personnel without including what could appear to be gratuitous detail; so, the experiences of the *Perth* men were far worse than even this book described. Hopefully, what is transparent is the power of the human spirit. In other words any inaccuracies or poor interpretations are entirely mine.

When you go home
Tell them of us and say
For your tomorrow
We gave our today

Inscription on Kohima Memorial in the remote mountainous area of Burma.

Acknowledgements

I wish to thank *Perth I* survivors who gave freely of their time and continued to be so patient with me while the months became years. Their empathy and gentleness were pivotal in my own journey through grief and the unchartered waters of life's journey. I would particularly like to thank: Gavin Campbell, Frank Chattaway, Basil Hayler, Frank McGovern, David Manning, Fred Skeels, Gordon Steele, Syd Triffitt and Charlie Wray, who I continued to besiege with text and questions and they unfailingly pulled me back on course and offered such good advice. I marvel at their endurance and the twinkle in their eyes. So many other survivors, like Arthur Bancroft, Norm Fuller, 'Digby' Gray, Syd Harper, Fred Lasslett, 'Spud' Murphy, Jim Nelson, Ray Parkin, 'Robbie' Roberts, Ernie Toovey and John Woods, permitted me to bother them for information. So too Perth I family members, be they many and scattered the length and breadth of Australia, who entrusted to me treasured letters, photographs, diaries and their own recollections and private thoughts. Without such wonderful material this book would have been a hollow volume and indeed would not have materialised.

To my agent Margaret Gee, this book was personal and in parts difficult given that her father Allan held a principal role. Thank you for your support and motivation.

My thanks to my colleagues in the School of Humanities and Social Sciences, University of New South Wales, Australian Defence Force Academy, Canberra, for tremendous support. Dr Eleanor Hancock and Dr Linda Bowman kept nudging me along when I needed it.

I congratulate New Holland for their belief that the stories of people make good naval history.

My family simply believed and that is what I needed most of all.

TIMELINE OF HMAS *PERTH*

1939

13 May	Australian Commissioning crew depart for Portsmouth, England, from Sydney, Australia, onboard Blue Funnel cargo liner *Autolycus*
10 July	HRH The Duchess of Kent, re-names the cruiser HMAS *Perth*
26 July	HMAS *Perth* departs Portsmouth for the New York World Fair
16 August	Departs New York for Kingston, Jamaica, the first leg of its return trip
21 August	Arrives Kingston. Following the declaration of war *Perth* is retained for duty with the America and West Indies Station

1940

29 February	Leaves Kingston for Australia
31 March	Arrives Sydney
24 December	Arrives Alexandria, Egypt.

1941

27–29 Mar	Battle of Matapan
14 July	Departs Alexandria for Australia
6 August	Arrives Fremantle, Western Australia

1942

14 February	Departs Fremantle for East Indies
24 February	Arrives Tanjong Priok, Batavia. Joins ABDA
27 February	Battle of Java Sea
28 February	Battle of Sunda Strait
1 March	HMAS *Perth* sinks. Only 328 of the 681 crew survive.
15 April	*Perth* survivors transferred to POW Camp, Batavia
October	Groups sent to work as slave labour on Burma–Thailand Railway

1943

17 October	Railway completed near Three Pagoda Pass, Konkuita, Thailand.

1944

April	*Perth* survivors chosen for work groups in Japan.
12 September	*Rakuyo Maru* torpedoed by US submarines.

1945

6 & 9 August	Atomic bombs dropped on Hiroshima and Nagasaki, Japan.
2 September	Japan surrenders.
Mid-October	Most *Perth* survivors repatriated to Australia. Only 214 return.

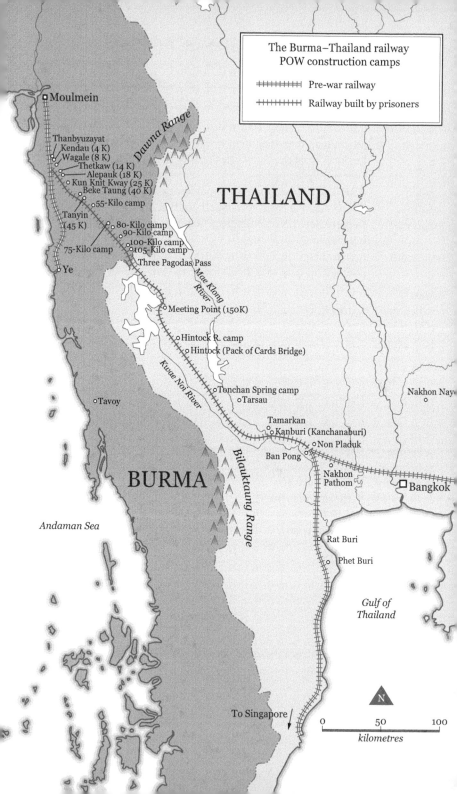

The Burma–Thailand railway
POW construction camps

++++++++ Pre-war railway
++++++++ Railway built by prisoners

Moulmein

THAILAND

Thanbyuzayat
Kendau (4 K)
Wagale (8 K)
Thetkaw (14 K)
Alepauk (18 K)
Kun Knit Kway (25 K)
Beke Taung (40 K)
55-Kilo camp
Tanyin
(45 K)
80-Kilo camp
90-Kilo camp
100-Kilo camp
105-Kilo camp
75-Kilo camp
Three Pagodas Pass

Dawna Range

Mae Klong River

Ye

Meeting Point (150K)

Hintock R. camp
Hintock (Pack of Cards Bridge)

Kwae Noi River

Tonchan Spring camp
Tarsau

Nakhon Nay

Tavoy

Tamarkan
Kanburi (Kanchanaburi)
Non Pladuk
Ban Pong

BURMA

Bilauktaung Range

Nakhon
Pathom

Bangkok

Andaman Sea

Rat Buri

Phet Buri

Gulf of Thailand

To Singapore

N

0   50   100
kilometres

ONE

'For those in peril on the sea.'

Naval hymn

It was a bright autumn morning in Melbourne in May 1939. Family and friends gathered at Station Pier to farewell those assembled on the deck of the Blue Funnel steamer, *Autolycus*. Children were lifted above the crowd, their faces breaking into smiles as they found the familiar face within the sea of Royal Australian Navy uniforms. Adults felt the unsettled sensation in the stomach that comes with goodbyes, and eyes moistened. *Autolycus* cast off, destined for the United Kingdom with crew for a new RAN ship. A 6890-ton cruiser, commissioned in 1934 as HMS *Amphion*, was being re-fitted in the United Kingdom and would be renamed HMAS *Perth*. A return to Australia in September was anticipated. However, a war in Europe would mean HMAS *Perth* reached Australian shores months later. Ultimately the war would have profound consequences for the cruiser, its crew and the many who awaited their return.

Advance parties of RAN Officers and men had departed for England onboard *Stratheden* in February, *Orontes* in March and *Orford* in April. Stores Chief Petty Officer John McMahon was one of the more experienced men in his category and chosen as one of the first to familiarise himself with the Leander-class cruiser. McMahon was promoted quickly as his abilities were recognised. The Geelong-born McMahon had enlisted as an eighteen year old in 1926. Also in the *Stratheden* was McMahon's immediate subordinate, Supply Petty Officer Eric Burton, who hailed from the small New South Wales town of Millthorpe. Burton had been a school teacher before enlisting in 1934. Upon their arrival in England, the two men quickly became involved with the equipment and stores needed to maintain the ship. They needed to be familiar with everything from armaments to steam turbines and liaise carefully with officers like Engineer Commander Robert 'Dolly' Gray. Gray had entered the Royal Australian Naval College as a thirteen-year-old Cadet Midshipman in 1916.

Following completion of their Naval College instruction, it was customary for RAN junior officers to travel to the United Kingdom to spend several years serving in Royal Navy ships. Such a practice, whilst professionally beneficial, increased the social distance between RAN officers and sailors. The gap between the Wardroom (the officer's mess) and Lower Deck was not as significant as that within the British Royal Navy. However, RAN officers, who faithfully absorbed English idiosyncrasies and beliefs and lost contact with their Australian derivations and cultural mores, suffered a loss of respect from the men they commanded. This had long been a contentious issue within the halls of the Australian Parliament. In 1937 politicians were again debating the Royal Naval Admirals who made up the Australian Commonwealth Naval Board and how they favoured a particular type of naval officer, one who did not embrace 'Australian qualities'. It was also felt that the Admiralty sent senior officers to Australia who did not have the best interests of the RAN at heart and treated the RAN as a 'sub service of the RN'. The issue was crucial to ship unification. It was also crucial for a naval doctrine that would not jeopardise Australian strategic interests in favour of the British Empire's wider concerns. For McMahon and Burton the issue was more immediate and personal. Cdr Gray had spent six years with the RN by the time he came in contact with the Australian Supply Chief and PO, but they found him capable and reasonable. The same would not be said of the officer who would command the new ship.

Also on *Orontes* and *Ormonde* were technical sailors like Electrical Artificer Peter Murdoch, a former civilian electrical fitter from Armidale, New South Wales, and shipwrights Don Haddow and Arthur Purkis, who were returning home. Like many of his peers, Murdoch had lost his father in World War I. His mother, Annie, struggled in post-war Australia. It felt at times like her future disappeared with the death of her husband on a foreign battlefield, and her small widow's pension supplied few luxuries. When son Peter entered the RAN in 1936, he allotted part of his pay to his mother, which eased the burden. Annie Murdoch was proud at the ease with which Peter passed his RAN trade and promotion courses, but in other ways her quiet son seemed ill suited for navy life. Shipwrights Arthur Purkis and Don 'Bingle' Haddow, on the other hand, were well suited for RAN service. Born into a navy family in the most naval of communities, Portsmouth, England, Purkis was already a shipwright when he enlisted in the RAN at Sydney in 1922. He was looking forward to catching up with relatives in the United Kingdom although less pleased to leave his wife Lilly in Australia. Haddow was a joiner before he enlisted in 1925. Born in Glasgow his Scottish pride was flamboyantly brandished in the thistle tattooed on his right forearm.

Senior Australian-born ratings (a sailor or non-commissioned officer) in the forward parties included Chief Engine Room Artificer Joseph Hughes, Stoker PO Billy Reece and Chief PO Painter Ed Sandall. Reece was from the New South Wales country town of Goulburn. Small in statue, his 5 foot 4 frame was toughened by hard physical work as a stoker in coal-burning ships. Hughes, a fitter and turner from Sydney, joined the navy in 1924. He was half a foot taller than Reece, with dark piercing eyes and an infectious grin. Both men were recruitment-poster sailors. They had adopted RAN life with enthusiasm, and glowing reports from their superiors followed. Hughes sported three Good Conduct Badges, awarded by the RAN at three, seven and thirteen years satisfactory service.[1] He was expecting his Long Service and Good Conduct Medal in September, awarded to sailors for fifteen years of continuous service with a 'Very Good' conduct rating. Sailors scoffed at the LSGCM, saying it was awarded for 'undetected crime',[2] but the

19

36-year-old Hughes was proud he would soon wear the decoration. The financial stipend accompanying the award would help his family back in Sydney. Reece was only two years junior, and he too took pride in the fact that his third badge would soon be sewn on his sleeve. Ed Sandall entered the RAN in 1923. As a child he had lived through the 'Great War', the war said to be 'the war to end all wars'. He was fourteen when it ended. Many Australian men came back from the war as heroes, but others did not come back at all. It seemed every family Sandall knew had been affected. He grew up in an era of military uniforms and enlisted at eighteen. Sandall felt vaguely unsettled when he farewelled wife Mary and their children, because Europe in 1939 was restless again.

—

Following World War I the misguided beliefs of Australian politicians resulted in severe reductions to the nation's navy. A government paper of 1929, titled 'Economy in Defence' criticised the 'staggering naval expenditure'. In 1931 Australia's Minister for Defence, Senator John Daly, agreed with the recommendation, 'it would be better to pay for the upkeep and maintenance of a unit of the British navy to be stationed in Australian waters', that 'The ideal of an Australian Navy has nothing really to recommend it as a national institution'.[3] The RAN had long suffered from a conceptual straitjacket imposed by the Admiralty in London, which encouraged British imperial naval philosophy and protection. The protestations of the few arguing for a more independent naval doctrine were lost amongst the apathetic majority in Parliament. In the unlikely event of another war they espoused, Australia would be protected by the Royal Navy and the impregnable Singapore forward defence citadel. Implementation of policies of naval reduction and retrenchment drastically reduced ships and personnel.

In 1929 the Australian fleet consisted of eleven vessels. Under the Financial Emergency Act, the fleet was reduced to the cruisers *Australia* and *Canberra*, the seaplane carrier *Albatross* and the destroyer *Anzac*. The 1929 permanent naval force of 4200 was trimmed by 69 officers and 639 men, and the lower deck was further assailed in the ensuing years. Ratings were encouraged to apply for free discharge, regardless of how many years remained on their enlistment. Rowland Roberts joined the RAN in 1924 as a Boy Seaman 2nd class. Boys were recruited as young as thirteen and sent to a hulk commissioned in 1912 as HMAS *Tingira*, and moored off Sydney's Rose Bay. *Tingira* training was demanding, with a strong emphasis on discipline and physical exertion. Roberts was one of 3158 boys to receive initial RAN training onboard *Tingira* in the years 1912 to 1927. At seventeen, Roberts commenced 'man's time' of twelve years from 1927. However, 1930 a 'free' discharge seemed too good an opportunity to miss, so Signalman Roberts walked into 'civvy street'.

When sailor applications for free discharges decreased, officers were encouraged to create lists of 'Ratings who either on medical grounds or as regards Character and/or efficiency would be no particular loss to the service'. The situation became so ridiculous that sailors would return from leave to find they were no longer members of the RAN. One of these was Allan Farley. The twenty-year-old Stoker fell foul of the Naval Discipline Act in 1931 and was assessed as being only of 'Moderate' efficiency, enough for him to be placed on the list and encouraged to leave, which he soon did.

By 1933 the RAN numbered a mere 339 officers and 2483 ratings. A growing appreciation within the halls of government of the rashness of naval degradation was overwhelmed by the lingering effects of the Great Depression. Although by 1936 numbers had increased to 370 officers, 44 midshipmen and 3774 ratings, they still fell short of the numbers the RAN establishment needed.

—

Junior sailors were included in the *Perth* advance parties to the United Kingdom, and the opportunity was not lost on them. For men like Able Seaman Bill Noyce, private travel to the land Australians regarded as the 'Mother Country', was economically unfeasible. Prior to naval service Noyce had worked as a labourer, at least he had tried to find work as a labourer. In 1932 the unemployment rate was 28 per cent and the word 'without' had real meaning. Children joined the long lines outside charity soup kitchens. Men with trades found companies were not hiring, and the queues outside RAN recruiting offices lengthened. Volunteers saw the navy as offering employment security, three square meals a day and free medical and dental care. Unfortunately, it was also difficult to be selected for the RAN. Coppersmith Robert McAuley managed to enlist as an Acting ERA 4th class and appreciated the valuable training he received. He married Edith in 1937, the same year he was promoted to ERA III. By 1939 he was sailing half way round the world.

Naval expenditure was increased as European politicians hunkered down in conference and Nazi military celebrations began to reverberate ever more loudly through the streets of Germany. The new Minister of Defence, Archibald Parkhill, returned to Australia following discussions with the Admiralty in London. The talks imbued him with scepticism and mistrust that the RN fleet to Singapore would actually materialise should Australia be endangered. But the RAN discovered that acquiring ships was easier than those to crew them. Too many highly trained members of the lower deck had been discharged during the previous decade. The decision was made to decommission HMAS *Adelaide* and to use its ship's company for *Perth*.[4] In a cruiser complement of 600, approximately 300 torpedo, gunnery and signal ratings were required, and it was generally believed it took four years for a rating to achieve a high degree of efficiency in these specialised categories. The substitution of eight 4-inch MkXVI guns on high-angle twin mountings on the new cruiser necessitated larger gun crews and more men for ammunition supply.

Stoker Allan Farley persuaded the RAN to offer him a second chance. After drafts to *Australia* and *Sydney*, he was sent to *Adelaide* and *Perth*. Signalman Rowland Roberts was also welcomed back to the RAN. When he had signed on in 1924 as a Boy 2nd class, he was a naïve thirteen year old. In 1934, when the 24 year old signed on the dotted line to enlist for five years and 172 days, he considered himself a wiser man. Time in civilian life was hard and Roberts realised the navy was where his skills were best put to use, given that all he had known as man and boy was the RAN. Roberts would remain in the RAN until the middle of 1945, leaving as a well regarded Yeoman of Signals. His drafts would include HMAS *Perth*, from May 1939 to October 1940.

Even with the 1937 personnel shortfall, when many RAN ships had less than a full complement of sailors, the RAN recruited only ten sailors every two months. Allan Gee was one of the chosen, so too Valentine Savage. Savage was a Belfast Irishman with a quick wit. He was only 5 foot 4 but anyone making fun of that, or his given name, rarely made the same mistake twice. Then they discovered Savage had the nickname 'Tiny'. Nicknames were very much part of naval life. Typically those with the surname Kelly were known as 'Ned', those named Hill became 'Windy', Clarks were 'Nobby', but occasionally a nickname, like 'Elmo', was unique. Allan Gee was a seventeen year old from Beechworth, Victoria, who had always had a 'childhood yearning for the sea and an adventurous spirit'.[5] Life in the navy, he believed, would be a welcome relief from working in a tannery. His parents, strict Salvation Army members, felt some apprehension, but gave their consent. From the first day of recruit training, Ordinary Seaman 2nd class Gee was given the nickname 'Elmo'. No-one really understood why, even some of his lifelong navy friends never knew his given name.

During 1938 the RAN increased its recruiting campaigns, though it would take another war before the short-sightedness of the naval retrenchments was fully appreciated. Australian daily newspapers announced in April that the RAN needed to recruit '2000 men for two cruisers in Britain; ... Recruits were required at 80 to 100 a month'.[6] While there were 4000 men on the waiting list for the Royal Australian Air Force, the RAN, according to the *Argus*, was having trouble 'obtaining sufficient recruits of the right type'.[7] The *Argus* editorial reflected on how much the Australian people had failed to 'realise the importance of the Navy not only to their past but to their future'.[8] But within a few months the recruitment campaigns paid off and the number of volunteers outstripped the RAN's ability to train them. Because the training of sailors was largely dependent on the availability of senior ratings to oversee the process, there was yet another hurdle in the chase for manpower. Not only had the RAN denuded the ranks of the lower deck in the previous eight years, but the RN Admirals who lorded over the RAN had long demonstrated a preference for British-trained senior rates over Australians and, with a war threatening Europe, these men were becoming scarcer.

—

RAN recruits of the 1930s grew up in a climate of economic hardship and celebrated being part of the service. Most developed a dedication to the RAN bred from need, but their appreciation of the opportunities and subsequent loyalty to their nation's navy was strong.

A surprising number of those enlisted and destined for *Perth* were country lads, attracted by the exciting, almost compelling RAN recruiting posters. Seventeen-year-old Queenslander Leon Lohrisch was a station hand; Ray Firmington, a tall, gangly Victorian, was a farm hand. Basil Hayler had grown up in Werribee, Victoria, in a weatherboard four-roomed house, without electricity or running water. His parents, Edward and Grace, had immigrated to Australia under the Soldier Settlement Scheme. It was a hard life trying to scratch out a living on the ten acres awarded under the scheme, but the family fared reasonably well during the Depression years. They grew much of what they needed and sold surplus fruit, flowers and vegetables at market. The Hayler children supplemented the family diet from fishing and rabbiting. Basil went to work in a Melbourne brass finishing works. He did not enjoy the hard, dirty work, and when he saw a 'large advertisement in the newspaper featuring huge battleships ploughing through the sea'[9] raised the subject of joining the navy. His father was initially unenthusiastic, recalling his tough life as a Stoker in the RN, but by July 1938, Basil, at sixteen years and eight months, was an Ordinary Seaman 2nd class.

On their arrival at HMAS *Cerberus*, the RAN training establishment at Westernport, Victoria, new recruits often wondered what they had got themselves into as they commenced training with months of 'total discipline and authority'. Any sailor who had weathered this initial onslaught tended to greet new recruits with the words, 'You'll be sorry'. The first three months concentrated on physical exercise, marching and rifle drill. The first uniform issue was invariably too short, too long or too baggy, but for men unable to afford many clothes in civilian life, the navy kit seemed extravagant. New enlisted men were taken to dormitories and shown how to sling their hammocks between steel bars six foot from the floor and how to occupy this style of bedding. For most it was a comedy of errors; in one side and straight out the other.

The recruits' day began at 0530, and for those too slow to 'lash and stow' their hammocks, instructors would use fire hoses for encouragement. An hour and a half of cleaning followed, before breakfast at 0730. Divisions were for some the highlight of the day. The naval band marched onto the parade ground followed by squads of the newest recruits struggling to synchronise legs and arms and stay in step with the next man. To falter earned the wrath of the Chief or PO in charge of their squad. Worse still was the wrath of gunnery instructors, who never failed to see any infringement or hesitation as a personal affront, and who had mastered the art of accusing the perpetrators of the worst failings possible in language which was novel and inventive at best. 'Jankers', (punishment), commonly consisted of 'doubling' (marching at double time) around a parade ground for two hours wearing a pack and holding a rifle 'at the slope'. Basil Hayler believed his *Cerberus* training changed him from 'a clumsy country bumpkin' to a 'straight well co-ordinated being'.[10]

The remaining months were spent in the classroom and workshops or at the docks for category training. For ordinary seamen there were courses in seamanship, gas, gunnery and torpedoes, and rudimentary instruction in wireless and signals. Two seaman instructors at *Cerberus* in 1938 were included in the commissioning crew of *Perth*. Petty Officer Alf Coyne was a career seaman, having joined as a Boy 2nd class. Before he found himself training new seaman with whom he would join *Perth*, he accumulated a wealth of experience in *Melbourne, Sydney, Adelaide, Canberra, Australia, Voyager* and *Vendetta*. Onboard *Perth* Coyne would assume the responsibilities of 'Captain of the Quarter Deck'. Ray Parkin joined the RAN in 1928, the day after he turned eighteen. He did not have the seagoing experience of Coyne; his abilities were different. He was a born teacher, a man of books, 'a genuine intellectual, a thinker and a philosopher'.[11] PO Parkin would assume the position of 'Captain of Foretop' and later quartermaster in the new Australian cruiser.

Another *Cerberus* instructor to join his 1938 trainees was Yeoman of Signals Percy Stokan. Training for signalmen and telegraphists was longer than for any other RAN new entry. The course of roughly eighteen months involved absolute knowledge of the *Fleet Signal Book*; cyphers and codes; and fleet manoeuvring formations. To learn the latter, new signals recruits spent hours marching as if they were warships steaming in line ahead, line abreast and quarter line formations. With small flags they simulated signals received and executed, turning in succession with as little hesitation as possible. Repetition after repetition was needed to attain the self-assurance necessary to operate under war conditions on a blacked-out bridge. The Yeoman did his utmost to draw on his service in *Anzac, Albatross, Tattoo, Canberra, Brisbane, Australia* and *Sydney* to instil the work ethic he believed necessary for the RAN communications branch. Stokan, from Toowoomba, Queensland, had been a little foolhardy in the early years of his RAN career. He hoped he had impressed upon the class of 1938 that in war the likely repercussions of typically adolescent behaviour would be more dangerous than when he was their age.

John 'Macca' McQuade, from Western Australia, was another who had worked as a farmhand before he entered the RAN in 1938 as a Stoker 2nd class. Two other 1938 Stokers 2nd class destined for *Perth* were Norm King and Cecil Doggett. Stokers were known as the hard men of the navy, and their duties contributed to this. Two months of classes on steam boilers, turbines and other forms of ship propulsion did not prepare a young stoker for the deplorable working conditions they faced on navy ships, and time spent boiler-cleaning, scraping soot from the inside of the funnels, and cleaning and red-leading the smelly, dirty bilges. Whatever the duty, they finished up covered in filth. It was an occupation that tested men to extremes and they, in turn, sometimes tested RAN discipline to extremes.

By the time they were due to join their first sea draft, the newest sailors were full of confidence. They wore their caps with panache, flat aback whenever they could get away with it. They preferred their uniforms tighter fitting and invariably sported a new tattoo. Stoker Norm King described how:

> In a surge of patriotism we tattooed ourselves with slogans. First the design was painted on the approved area, then with four needles wrapped around a match and dipped in Indian ink the art work was followed. It was torture but who could refuse such noble sentiments like 'For King and Country'. My tattoo had an anchor with the words, 'Death before Dishonour'. Fortunately for me it faded before being put to the test.[12]

—

Those who crowded the guard rails of *Autolycus*, watching the colourful streamers stretch and break their earthly bonds that bright 19 May 1939, represented a microcosm of Australian middle and working classes. Two were brothers in every sense of the word. Phillip and Rose Ryan had had their sons 21 months apart, and their boys grew up good mates. Richard Ryan emulated elder brother Charles Ryan, so it came as no surprise when he followed him into the RAN as an Ordinary Seaman. The brothers asked to serve together and were pleased when they found themselves off on a grand adventure to the United Kingdom. These *Perth*-bound men who wore the square rig were also the most educated group of men assembled under the white ensign. Prior to enlistment in 1938, Ken Kite, from Bombala, New South Wales, was a shop assistant; Ed Burley from Sydney was an electrical fitter; Sydneysider Bob Collins was a clerk; Tasmanian Herb Langdon was a salesman.

The newest members of the RAN were both wary and respectful of the most senior rating onboard, Master at Arms Herbert Creber. Born in England in 1899, Creber commenced his navy career in the RN as a Boy Seaman. He was loaned to the RAN until he finally decided to call Australia home and transferred to the junior navy. A tall, solidly built man, Creber had the physical bearing of a master at arms and he looked forward to this responsibility in the new ship. He encouraged older rates in *Autolycus* to use the weeks ahead to discuss with their subordinates what their duties would entail.

Whilst time would tell regarding the quality of the younger men, Creber was impressed with many of the senior rates he found within the 500-strong contingent. He hoped that with their help over the five-week journey to the United Kingdom, the ship's company would begin to bond. Much of the early influence on junior sailors came first from Leading Hands. Two of these were Leading Seamen Roy Carter from Hobart, Tasmania, and Len Branford from Exeter, South Australia, who had entered the RAN at seventeen, straight from school. Acting Leading Stoker Patrick 'Chopper' Sands talked with eighteen-year-old Stoker 2nd class Leo Burgess about their duties in the cruiser's 'A' boiler room. The modified Leander-class ship had two separate boiler rooms and two separate engine rooms. In the event of an explosion disabling one, the second should enable the ship to maintain some momentum.

Two of the more impressive senior rates, who coincidentally were both involved with the ship's propulsion systems, were George Giles and Reg Whiting. Giles, a PO, came from Wyalong, New South Wales, and had joined the RAN at 21, in 1922. He excelled at the tough life of a stoker and by 1939 had been recommended for promotion each year bar two. Whiting was born in 1901, the only son of a couple from Launceston, Tasmania. Having joined the RAN at nineteen, he received a valuable navy apprenticeship as an Electrical Artificer. He married Alice in 1926 in Brighton, Victoria, and sons John and Brendan were born in 1928 and 1935. Whiting spent three years at Sydney's Garden Island Dockyard, specialising as a Gyro compass artificer, and as Chief EA would take charge of *Perth*'s electrical power systems.

Creber was also aware that his sailors included a few colourful characters, on whom he would need to keep his eye. One of these was George 'Moggy' Catmull. 'Moggy' had joined the RAN as a fourteen-year-old Boy Seaman in 1924, as his parents believed that his regular salary could assist the needs of their large family and keep him on the straight and narrow. His salary did help, but staying within the bounds of navy discipline proved another thing. As he circumnavigated the RAN fleet, in *Brisbane, Melbourne, Sydney, Canberra, Australia* and *Albatross*, his service included a lot of promotions and dis-ratings – the awarding of good conduct badges and their removal. When he joined the commissioning crew, 'Moggy' was again an AB, and had sewn on his 1st Good Conduct Badge, for the third time.

Few on *Autolycus* were as colourful as Moggy or as stereotypically 'pusser' (navy) as Creber. Perce Partington turned nineteen a week out of harbour. He was the seventh and last child of Percival and Ethel. The Partingtons were a musical family who had regularly played together at local dances. Opportunities to make music a full-time profession were very limited, so Leslie, Arnold and Perce all enlisted in the RAN as Bandsmen in 1938.

The first Australian Navy band, a mixture of Australian, former Royal Marine and British Army musicians, arrived in Sydney in 1913 in the new Australian flagship, HMAS *Australia*. A second band was organised at HMAS *Cerberus* in 1927, and in the late 1930s there was rapid expansion to recruit musicians for bands for each of the RAN cruisers, as well as some shore establishments. Members of RAN bands wore the uniform of the British Royal Marines.[13] The ship band usually had one trombonist, and on *Perth* that was to be Perce Partington. Brother Leslie, eleven years senior to Perce, filled the same position on *Sydney*. Arnold, 'a very fine trumpeter'[14] was a member of the *Canberra* band. Important in maintaining morale, during normal daily routine the band played on the quarter deck, at colours, during the Sunday Church Parade and occasionally outside the wardroom. The band was integral to ship port visits and parades. In addition to musical duties, bandsmen worked in first aid parties, as lookouts, in transmitting stations and as shell bearers in ammunition supply parties.

'Bandies' were a very mixed, some would say 'odd', bunch of men. Perce Partington, a professional musician, represented one end of the spectrum. Bandsman John 'Tubby' Grant, the other. 'Tubby' was the youngest of eight children from Koondrock, Victoria.[15] He was a tiny 4 foot 5 when he entered the RAN in 1923 at sixteen as a Boy 2nd class. His civilian occupation was listed as 'Leather Worker'. His first naval career was as a Seaman. In 1927 he delighted in becoming a Bandsman. Sea service in many RAN ships occurred, along with the tattoos, a battleship on the right forearm and a flag and ship on the left upper arm. He did not grow as tall as he would have liked, at 32 he stood a mere 5 foot 2. Bandsman Alf Brown, at 5 foot 10, was a good bit taller and approaching his thirty-eighth birthday. From London, England, he served with the British Army during World War I. Bandsman Henry 'Ned' Kelly was also an Englishman who had enlisted in the RAN in 1929. These bandsmen were aware of how diverse their backgrounds were, but none could have imagined how different their destinies would be.

—

Many of the younger sailors in *Autolycus* had never been to sea, and there was some discontent with sailor's quarters. The RAN had chosen economy before comfort – not unusual but this time it was fairly grim. A Melbourne newspaper reported 'Luxury Trip for Sailors', but the newspaper's reporter had interviewed the six RAN officers, who were accommodated in the passenger quarters and only two of whom, Lieutenant William Frank Cook, and Cdr Charles Anthony Downward, were destined for *Perth*.[16] Officer accommodation was described as 'clean but adequate'. Ratings slung their hammocks and ate their meals in the ship's forward cargo holds, which had formerly carried horses. Whilst this was a familiar scent from home for country lads, Stoker Norm King was unimpressed: 'no amount of scrubbing with carbolic could get rid of the stink'. When *Autolycus* made an unscheduled port call at Albany, Western Australia, to land stowaway 'Curly' Sutton (dropped from the commissioning crew because of illness) Norm King believed that, had they been allowed, many fellow sailors 'would have liked to have gone [ashore] with him'.

Lieut Bill Cook sympathised with the ratings on sailor accommodation in *Autolycus*, 'I was full of admiration for the morale and spirit of the sailors, who accepted the situation with unusual sangfroid, and made the best of it'.[17] Born in Numurkah, Victoria, 22-year-old Cook had joined the Naval College in 1930 – one of only twelve Midshipmen selected that year. That was a tumultuous year for RAN retrenchments and cost-cutting. In the middle of 1930, the Naval College was moved from (*Creswell*) Jervis Bay to Flinders Naval Depot (*Cerberus*) in Victoria to centralise all RAN training and reduce expenditure. No midshipmen intakes took place in 1931 and 1932, although a special entry occurred in September 1932. Whether the scheme of moving to Flinders and training the sailors and officers at the same establishment helped to close the distance between RAN officers and sailors of the era is open to debate, but Cook would demonstrate a good understanding of the Australian lower deck which would make him a popular junior officer and, in time, Commanding Officer.

So too, Cdr Downward quickly attained the respect of the men. He had joined the RAN as a Surgeon Lieutenant in 1925 but felt marginalised in wardrooms, being a medical man foremost and a Roman Catholic, when it was preferred that proper naval officers were neither. He felt more highly regarded by sailors. They noted how well spoken and knowledgeable he was, how he was a voracious reader, and how he paid his way through his University of Sydney medical studies with billiards and snooker winnings – not exactly the gentlemanly way.

The Australian coastline was soon lost from view as the steamer made for South Africa. Ordinary Seaman 2nd class Basil Hayler found compensation for the ship's lack of comfort in the sights that could only be appreciated by those on the open seas, 'I marvelled at the gracefulness of the huge wandering Albatross seabird as its wing tips skimmed the tops of the waves; then in the warm tropical waters were brightly coloured flying fish fanning out from the bow of the ship in their thousands'.[18] Even Stoker Norm King delighted in the many dolphins that swam with the ship, effortlessly surfing the wake. He found it wonderful 'to relax on the upper deck and watch the ocean roll past', while whale sightings were 'breathtaking'. Relaxation ended abruptly when the roaring forties wreaked havoc, forcing the ship to reduce its speed to seven knots for several days and delaying their arrival at Durban until 8 June. Some very green sailors, in nautical terms and in facial colour, were well pleased to have 36 hours in port. Once on dry land they needed to overcome the strange sensation of their bodies, accustomed to the roll of a ship, accepting that the ground remained in the same place for both feet.

Durban was an eye-opener for young Australians who had previously not ventured far from home. Most noticeable was the treatment of blacks. Sailors watched as blacks were assaulted and abused, Allan Gee was 'shocked at the way the whites treated the black people'.[19] The most sobering experience was the public hanging of three black men whose bodies were strung up from a gibbet behind a warehouse. A placard attached to their corpses condemned them as revolutionaries, but they were only guilty of involvement in a tram strike. The *Perth* crew was pleased when their 'Blue Funnel' (merchant ship) transport pushed on for the United Kingdom.

On 28 June the crew gathered on deck as it entered Portsmouth harbour to catch the first glimpse of their new ship. The elegant lines of the cruiser were instantly appealing and the general excitement within the RAN group palpable. Steward Robert Smith was a dark-haired, blue-eyed seventeen year old from Toowoomba, Queensland. He shook his head when he reviewed his situation. He had had a very uninspiring factory job before he enlisted in 1936. Even Brisbane was seen as 'the big smoke', and yet here he stood on the misty docks of Portsmouth, England. Preparations were underway for the renaming ceremony on 10 July. Navy folklore is steeped in superstition concerning such occasions. Time would tell if this renaming would add weight to the superstition.

TWO

*'One is amazed at, and somewhat ashamed of, the
lack of foresight any of us had.'*

Lieutenant Bill Cook

Advance parties had been heavily involved in the ship's refit. Acting Petty Officer 'Horrie' Abbott who had left Australia for England in late 1938 to undergo courses with the RN, was pleased to welcome an Aussie crew onboard. Their Commanding Officer, Captain Harold Bruce Farncomb, MVO, RAN, addressed the new arrivals in a less welcoming tone. Farncomb, born in February 1899, had joined the Australian Naval College in 1912. He had spent much of his naval service attached to the Royal Navy and had misgivings concerning this young Australian crew. More than 50 per cent of the ship's company of 600, including 47 per cent of the ordinary seamen, were below the age of 21, and a large proportion of the remainder were under the age of 24. The official *Perth* log included the comment: 'As for efficiency, as the ratings are mostly young, time alone will tell'.

Farncomb believed the answer lay in hard work and hard discipline. If the *Autolycus* passengers believed they would have a few days to stretch their legs, they were mistaken. No sooner had they moved from *Autolycus* to their new messdecks, than they were caught up in a cleaning and painting frenzy. There was much washing of paintwork, chipping of rust, repainting and polishing to be done in preparation for the renaming ceremony.

An excited hum permeated the ship on the morning of 10 July 1939 as royalty was due for the official renaming ceremony. The lower deck was cleared at 1315 and dignitaries began to arrive. At 1415 Allan Gee blew his new bugle as Her Royal Highness, The Duchess of Kent, Princess Marina, alighted from her car. Ord Seam 2nd class Basil Hayler was a member of the Royal Guard of Honour and, standing proudly to attention, the young seaman was duly impressed with the young Princess who passed by gracefully, 'I can still smell her perfume' he recalled half a century later. The Hon. Stanley Bruce, the Australian High Commissioner, delivered what one sailor referred to as, 'a rather lengthy address, in which was embodied the part Australia was playing in this great National Defence rally of our great Empire'.[1] At 1455 Princess Marina pulled on a silken bell rope, and, as the White Ensign and Union Jack unfurled and the HMAS *Perth*'s Coat of Arms was revealed for the first time, the Princess officially renamed the cruiser and wished all those who would sail on the newest Australian ship the best of luck. Three lusty cheers erupted from the ship's company, with most feeling a sense of pride in their demonstration to 'the British people that we, in Australia, were doing our bit towards Empire security. ... we hoped we had impressed our English cousins with our willingness to help them ... in this hour of need'.[2]

—

The youthful Australian crew was enthusiastic, but on a warship there could be no substitution for experience, so a number of Royal Navy loan personnel joined, including four radar operators and two coders. Coders were needed for the increasing secret wireless traffic. RN PO Geoffrey Balshaw, from Blackpool, agreed to be loaned to the RAN for two years, and took charge of *Perth*'s anti-submarine detection system (ASDIC). It would take a little time to adjust to being one of the few RN'ers in a large Australian ship's company, particularly as some of the Australian sailors had reservations about Englishmen. AB Bill Bracht noted, 'I was not too enamoured of the majority of Englanders I came in contact with at Portsmouth. Even the British ratings would refer to us as "Colonials".[3]

The wardroom of 35, on the other hand, appeared to consist predominantly of RN officers. Lieut Guy Clarke, from Kent, soon to be promoted to Lieut Cdr, would have his short stint on the Australian ship extended until March 1942. So too 22-year-old Lieut Michael Highton, from Buckinghamshire; his wife, Clothiede, would follow him to Australia. Lieut Cdr John Johnson, from Yorkshire, and Devon-born Lieut Cyril Palairet would stay longer than the initial two-year loan period designated when they joined *Perth*. RN-commissioned lower deck men included Portsmouth's own Warrant Engineer James Tuersley and the colourful Commissioned Gunner with the Scot's brogue, George Ross.

Acceptance trials were held to ensure the ship was ready for sea before the cruiser and crew began their trip home the long way, with what promised to be an exciting stopover in the United States. *Perth*'s departure at 1130 on 25 July was cancelled when a defect was found. It took little to stir the suspicions of seafarers and one wrote: 'There seems to be a slight Hoodoo on the ship and it is hoped we can shake it off on our way to New York'.[4] Finally the ship sailed for New York on 26 July, with the crew excited about representing their country at the 1939 World Fair.

The possibility of icebergs resulted in a southerly diversion. Nearing their destination they encountered thick fog, finally out of the mist loomed the breathtaking Manhattan skyscrapers, the most noticeable amongst them being the needle-pointed Empire State Building. As the Australian ship glided past the majestic Statue of Liberty that held forth her light for democracy, a 21-gun salute was fired. Shore batteries thundered back the same honour as *Perth* secured alongside Pier 53 at 0830 on 4 August 1939.

—

The program was tight and busy, and, as is typical of July in New York, the weather was hot and humid. Sailors were disenchanted with the uniform stipulated for shore leave. Dress for libertymen (men granted leave) was No.7s (full long, white uniforms) until 1800, after that time the uniform would be No.1s or No.2s. (blue uniforms). Although it was customary for 'blues' to be worn in Australian cities in hot weather, Captain Farncomb decided to abide by Admiralty orders for the America and West Indies Station (region), which stipulated whites.

Regulating (administrative) staff quickly surmised there was dissatisfaction within the lower deck. The lack of adequate laundry facilities onboard, combined with the inclement weather during the passage across the North Atlantic, meant that their kit of 'whites' was not up to the standard of their blues. This, the men suggested, would not do credit to the RAN. The fact that sailors would be required to return to the ship by 1800 to change uniforms undoubtedly added to their annoyance.

Upon arrival in New York, Captain Farncomb left the ship in order to be received by city leaders. Master at Arms Herb Creber attempted to report the unrest to the next in charge, but Cdr W.L.G. Adams, RN, was 'turned in', having retired to his cabin suffering the after-effects of an inoculation. Creber then reported the matter to the Duty Officer, who dismissed the grievance because sailors had not pursued their complaints through official channels, via their Divisional Officers. Farncomb later conceded in his letter to the Admiralty and Naval Board that general discontent lay beneath the incident. He considered, however, that the 'strenuous work' involved since *Perth*'s commissioning was not a factor in the dispute. His interpretation was wrong. AB Keith Baker wrote in his diary, 'the ship's company have worked like slaves since commissioning', and the following day, 'the discontent seems to be worse this morning and if something is not done it may turn out serious'.[5] Sailors had wearied of what they referred to as the 'bullshit routine'. The type of duty that had concerned them most was when sailors were lowered over the side of the ship in the cold and foggy North Atlantic to paint.

In his ACNB report, Farncomb also dismissed discipline as a cause. On this he was also incorrect. Members of *Perth*'s ship's company did not react favourably to the officious nature of their Commanding Officer or his Second-in-Command, who seemed intent on imposing the same discipline and relationship between officers and men as was pursued in the Royal Navy. Commander Adams was described as a rather 'pompous little man known as "Flip the Frog" to the sailors' who was very '"Royal Navy" in his demeanour' and had not previously served with an Australian crew.[6] One sailor wrote, '*Perth* should have been a happy ship but it wasn't'.[7] Captain Farncomb was a 'very autocratic man and his attitude towards the crew worked its way down through his officers'.[8] Ratings believed some junior officers were deliberately antagonising them with frequent visits to their messdecks. The entry of an officer required ratings, even those sleeping after night watches, to stand to attention until otherwise ordered.

The incident quickly escalated. Although not as incendiary as depicted in the *New York Times* headline, 'Aussie Mutiny Here – Officers Too British', it was worse than Farncomb would have Naval Board believe in his communication of 21 August 1939. Lieut Bill Cook noted that it was a 'small but nevertheless regrettable incident'.[9] Approximately a third of the ship's company failed to fall in for work at 1315 as 'All Watches for Exercise' was sounded, instead, they gathered in the foc's'le (the fore part of the ship). The group included three leading seamen and eight leading stokers, but no-one higher than leading rate. The group was informed that their behaviour constituted mutiny and they would receive the full severe punishment for that crime if they did not answer a call to 'Clear Lower Deck'. It is difficult to elicit from official and rating diaries exactly what occurred. Whilst official reports tended to minimise the situation, sailor renditions embellished it. According to one, the incident was 'grossly exaggerated'.[10] Another version suggested *Perth* officers arrived wearing side arms and proceeded to order individuals below but no one moved. The Naval Board reported to the Australian Prime Minister that there was no truth in American newspaper reports. Finally it was admitted in the Australian Parliament on 7 August 1939 that a 'Minor Strike' had taken place, but that it had been 'amicably settled' after sailors were allowed to proceed ashore in blue uniforms when they made individual requests to do so. Stoker Norm King, in his notes, offered the most humorous version of the culmination of the so-called 'mutiny': 'Several car loads of New York police arrived armed to the teeth. They carried enough weapons to start a major war and nobody knew whose side they were on, [so] the fiasco was called off'.

Perth's officers needed to quash the situation as quickly as possible, given the fact that official parties of dignitaries were due to arrive. Later Farncomb informed the men that had he been onboard, 'I would have shot the lot of you'. As punishment, no additional leave concessions at ports visited on the remainder of the trip to Australia would be granted, nor did he intend to arrange any lower deck entertainment at these ports. He wrote to ACNB that he spoke 'forcibly to the leading hands'. Farncomb believed that the ship's company had demonstrated a 'lack of confidence' in its divisional officers, but refused to believe he or his officers, and their pursuit of another navy's discipline regime, were responsible. Instead he blamed the 'poor state' of the *Perth's* lower deck, and the, 'deterioration ... in the quality and morale of the men' onboard. He reported to ACNB that the blame lay with some 'unpleasant individuals of the petty agitator type in this ship', whom he would discover and punish. Farncomb believed one such man was Charles Essex. Essex had been awarded a 'Very Good Conduct and Superior Efficiency' rating the previous three years and was duly promoted to Leading Seaman in January 1939. Farncomb ordered his dis-rating. Essex 'lost his hook' immediately and was dropped to a 'Good' character assessment, meaning that he would need to wait at least another eighteen months before his Leading Seaman rank could be restored.

Farncomb complained to the Naval Board about the 'poor quality of recruit' being enlisted. Too many, he believed, had worked in a 'trades union atmosphere' and 'until their early habits and mentality are eradicated', they would continue to cause problems within the RAN.[11] To eradicate this, Farncomb thought closer scrutiny should be given to those applying for RAN entry, and new recruits must then be subjected to severer discipline at HMAS *Cerberus*. As other senior officers had done throughout the decade, Farncomb refused to entertain the notion that overall responsibility lay with himself or his officers.

Despite the uniform incident, New York City was exciting. The Americans showered hospitality on officer and sailor alike. Officers were wined and dined and associated with Hollywood celebrities, like Johnny Weissmuller (who played Tarzan) and Esther Williams. Free admission was given at theatres like Radio City Music Hall, Roxy Theatre and the Paramount Theatres. However, demarcation between officers and other ranks was clearly evident. Officers were given honorary membership to clubs such as The British Club and the New York Yacht Club, while sailors were restricted to organisations like the YMCA and the Soldiers and Sailors Club, but there were no complaints.

With free tickets to the World Fair and reduced rates to amusement centres, the ratings had a lot to occupy them. Stoker Joe Hartley and Leading Stoker Jock Lawrance were given tickets to the Red Sox versus New York Yankees baseball game. During a break in the game, Hartley agreed to play a mock cricket match against some Americans. To the delight of the capacity crowd of nearly 80,000, Hartley hit the ball out of the stadium.

Much was crammed into the eleven-day stay, its highlights amazing *Perth* crew who had previously only seen such attractions on cinema screens. With clubs open 24 hours a day, Stoker John 'Macca' McQuade and Ord Seam Allan Gee favoured drinking and dancing with the 'gorgeous' local girls over sleep – it was 'an endless party'.[12] Perhaps the apprehension felt by Allan's Salvation Army parents had been justified, and he conceded, 'Mum would not have approved of any of it'. On 11 August a special 'Australian Day' was celebrated at the World Fair. Five buses carrying 150 *Perth* officers and ship's company were given a police escort, so they could proudly parade outside the Australian pavilion. There were more political speeches to suffer, but the representative for the Mayor of New York unwittingly caused laughter when he referred to the toy koala gift as a toy bunny.

There was a clamour to return to the ship before 0600 on 16 August. Signalman Rowland Roberts noted, 'By the look of the ship's company, I think the pace these New Yorkers set them, and the night life was just a bit too much for them'. Several sailors did not make it back onboard before the ship sailed. Two ratings quickly presented themselves to the Australian Consul General and were put on transport to rejoin *Perth*. The third, Ord Seam Edwards, did not, and his Commanding Officer signalled Navy Office recommending RAN dismissal. Chief PO Painter Donald Kinsella was left in Brooklyn Hospital. Born in Queenstown, Tasmania, in 1901, Kinsella had been a house painter in civilian life and asked the RAN to take advantage of his experience. Instead the navy enlisted him as an Officers Cook. Kinsella continued to submit his request for a rating change until after five years, in 1930, the RAN agreed. He was later moved to England, suffering from iridocyclitis. The link between lead-based paint and poor health had not been made in 1940.

The Australian cruiser departed, and sore heads and stomachs mended on the leisurely trip south to Jamaica. The ship and crew were returning home, but shadows of war intervened. A *Perth* diarist, in righteous tone, wrote, 'Why must these power-drunk fools gain their ends by slaughtering women and children, it is hoped this "Freak" Hitler will come to his senses'.[13] After five days visiting Kingston, *Perth* weighed anchor and proceeded to sea. Thoughts of the next leg were dispelled when Farncomb addressed his crew on the evening of 26 August. The solemn Commanding Officer advised that the Commonwealth Government had placed the ship under Admiralty jurisdiction and that *Perth* was ordered to patrol the northern part of South America and the Caribbean. Disappointment was muted by excitement of the game at hand, to challenge shipping and impound any cargo destined for Germany or German-occupied territory. However, the Admiralty assumed command of *Perth* without the approval of the Australian Government. Prime Minister Menzies had agreed in principle without first securing the consent of his Cabinet or the Australian Parliament. Whilst this finer point was not appreciated by those onboard, one sailor saw the irony in their being in the lackadaisical Caribbean, 'To think that these so-called savages were living in such peacefulness and happiness, whilst we civilised races of this earth were awaiting the word to blast each other into eternity'.[14] The ship's name was removed from boats, lifebuoys and sailors caps, and the crew was placed in a state of 'immediate readiness to go into action'.

On the forenoon of 3 September, Farncomb again addressed the crew with the news that 'total war' now existed with Germany and called for three cheers for 'His Majesty the King'. From those who stood on the decks of *Perth* came 'such a rousing response, and it can be said that it came from the bottom of their hearts with the will to serve'.[15] The younger members of the crew were unrestrained in their enthusiasm to be part of this wonderful adventure, 'We imagined ourselves as heroes'.[16] Lieut Bill Cook would admit much later, 'one is amazed at, and somewhat ashamed of, the lack of foresight any of us had'.[17] Ord Seam Basil Hayler was hit by, 'a strange feeling of apprehension'[18], because he was at war as his father had been a quarter of a century before. For Sig Rowland Roberts came the realisation that 'our dream cruise was over: when we would see our sunny shores again, we did not know'.[19] Thoughts returned to those at home.

—

In Sydney, Isabel Justelius was woken by knocking at the front door. As she struggled into her dressing gown, she peered with bleary eyes at the bedside clock, it was 2 a.m. the morning after Australia had declared war on Germany. She opened the door to reveal two uniformed men. They asked to see her brother Eric for whom they had a navy call-up notice. The 26 year old indignantly informed authorities she would take the notice but given the ridiculous hour she had no intention of waking her brother or any other member of her family, 'it could wait till morning'.[20] Returning to bed it was difficult to sleep. Foreboding thoughts intruded as Isabel realised that life as Australians knew it was about to change forever. Eric was not surprised by the official letter his sister handed him at breakfast. He had finished his education with qualifications in accountancy but quickly became bored with the vocation and yearned for adventure, and his family had been surprised when Eric returned home one afternoon in 1925 to tell them he was enlisting in the RAN for twelve years. Eric had enjoyed his navy service as an Ordinary Seaman on the 'big' ships, *Sydney, Melbourne, Brisbane* and *Australia*, but by

1929 the navy was suffering budget restraints and Eric had been just one of many sailors encouraged to leave with a free discharge. Reporting for duty in September 1939, Eric Justelius was entered into the Royal Auxiliary Fleet Reserve as an AB and sent to serve on *Doomba,* until he joined HMAS *Perth.*

Another recalled for duty was AB Harold 'Ben' Athol Chaffey. Like Eric Justelius, Ben Chaffey had joined the RAN in 1925 at the age of 18. He was born in Hobart, Tasmania, in November 1907 and entered the RAN as a 5 foot 6, fair-haired, blue-eyed youth with a fresh complexion. Over his years of naval service his hair would change to brown, then grey and his height lengthen to 5 foot 9. He would also add tattoos to both arms. During his early years 'Ben' had had a few wild oats to sow and more than a couple of run-ins with naval discipline. He had been earmarked as one the RAN would deem 'of no particular loss to the service' and left the RAN in May 1930. However, in 1939 'Ben' Chaffey reported for duty as Australians struggled to appreciate the gravity of events overseas.

—

Perth stayed on patrol for the next five months, navigating the waters between Venezuela and the Caribbean as well as escorting convoys of merchant ships across the Atlantic. The sea patrols developed a monotonous pattern, as *Perth* chased shadows and authenticated merchantmen, but the crew were ever hopeful they would encounter German ships straying outside the three-mile (five-kilometre) zone of neutral ports. As relief from the onboard tedium, an 'Amateur Hour' was organised. Twenty-four contestants, some attempting to sound as suave as Bing Crosby but most sounding more like Gracie Fields, monopolised the ship's loudspeaker system. As pretenders competed for the winner's prize of £1, with each recital humour was encouraged, and for some it was a prerequisite. So popular was the contest, that it became a monthly fixture.

Such recreational time-out was nonetheless minimal. The Australian cruiser was senior ship of the 8th Cruiser Squadron, operating with French, Canadian and other British ships. On one occasion a dummy third funnel was added to *Perth* to convey the impression that there were two cruisers in the vicinity. The crew was amused and pleased when an American radio broadcast referred to *Perth* as the 'Terror of the Caribbean'.

Each day officers and men continued to hone skills for saving the cruiser should false sightings become real enemy encounters. Leading Seaman Bill Bracht had joined the RAN as a seventeen year old rather than go down the coal mines in his home town of Cessnock, New South Wales. He thrived in his duties and felt that he was an important member of the cruiser crew. Bracht was Director Trainer in the high-angle gun crew, which controlled the twin, 4-inch anti-aircraft guns. Bracht believed he had the best station on the ship, situated in front of the foremast and above the bridge. It was the highest point of the ship other than the crows nest lookout. He was an integral part of his ship's air defence and was in telephone contact with the Air Defence Officer on the bridge.[21] Bracht was not alone in his belief that his duties were of the utmost importance; the ship's safety depended on each member of the crew feeling this sense of responsibility.

Perth's new base was Kingston, Jamaica, and the cruiser crew quickly warmed to the locals who happily adopted the visitors. The brilliant colours and garish lifestyle of the Caribbean continued virtually untouched by war. Smuggling cheap rum aboard was a popular pastime with some sailors. One method involved replacing the contents of a Coca-Cola bottle with something rather more potent. However, as young sailors ventured ashore they were given the warning 'beware of rum and syphilis', because both were inexpensive and easy to find: 'Sex was very cheap for those who wanted it, and I guess that covered every sailor on the ship'.[22] Crew became familiar and popular visitors in various parts of the Caribbean and they in turn enjoyed the white beaches with crystal-clear water. The wonderful scenery of unspoiled coastlines and mountainous hinterland in countries like Dominican Republic, Venezuela, Haiti, Trinidad and Tobago, made the war seem remote.

Monotonous routine was broken by occasional excitement. During October escorting convoys proved an interesting task, although the 'break neck' top speed of eight knots that some ships used caused angst. On 4 October *Perth* left to escort 46 French and British ships across the North Atlantic. From the balmy weather to the bitter cold, where ice formed on rigging, Ord Seam 2nd Class Basil Hayler spent his duty hours as starboard lookout, perched in a box on the side of the bridge. With powerful binoculars he searched the surface of the sea for submarine periscopes, torpedo tracks or the masts of approaching ships. On the return trip they encountered huge seas, which smashed sea boats and rigging and washed overboard anything not tightly fastened. This, combined with the blinding rain, meant that the cruiser's decks were awash from bow to stern and areas below decks became flooded. Winds reached 120 miles per hour (200 kilometres per hour), and the ship tossed and rolled throughout the night. Those clinging within prayed for it all to end, then the cruiser rolled 30 degrees and they wondered if it was about to. There were a few minor injuries, including Steward Tom McKenzie who fractured his big toe. He was issued a 'hurt certificate' in case he wished to seek restitution after the war. A crueller twist later meant he would never have that opportunity.

Reaching tranquil green waters again off Bermuda was a welcome relief from the Atlantic. On 22 October Basil Hayler turned eighteen, which meant that his rank rose to Ord Seam and, more importantly, his wage increased dramatically from £1/16/- to £3/4/-. Bandsman Walter Douglass also celebrated, as he was promoted to Bandmaster. For another member of the crew, celebrations were not in order. ERA 'Bill' Barnes was informed that his father had died. It was at times like this that family separation proved most difficult. Barnes had watched his father's health deteriorate, a legacy of service in the previous war. Just a month before Barnes had received birthday greetings from his parents; now the 25 year old took some quiet time to think of someone who was no more, and of his mother, Margaret, in Sydney.

The ship sailed to Halifax, Canada, on 22 October, arriving on 28 October to collect additional crew to swell their ranks to a war complement of 680. These newest members had had a long journey to meet *Perth*. Stoker Alf Hansen from Fremantle had had scarcely time to become accustomed to naval uniform. He had enlisted in May 1939, and no sooner had he completed his *Cerberus* training, than he found himself on a sea voyage from Sydney to New Zealand and another to Canada. So too Ord Seam Ross Birbeck and Vincent McGovern, an ERA from Sydney. Vincent's brother, Frank, was in the process of joining the RAN and the brothers were keen to serve in the same ship. Birbeck would prove indispensable, and not just for his naval skills. He was a hairdresser, always useful in a ship requiring hundreds of short back and sides, and later his singing voice would be invaluable in maintaining morale. One AB joining had the impressively long name of Willoughby Hamilton Harry Smith. Smith was a nineteen year old from Melbourne, who had been in the navy only three months. The new arrivals found an unusually integrated ship with a 'great esprit de corp between all branches ... It was unique because people on most ships tended to stick to their own areas and mates, but *Perth* was different'.[23]

Like Smith, Blacksmith II Alfred 'Sandy' Albert Saunders had joined the RAN at nineteen. Previously life had been tough and he had toiled as a labourer for very little pay and few prospects. The RAN offered both, and he enlisted as an Ord Seam in 1927. His first sea draft was *Sydney*, a coal-burning Town Class Light Cruiser. He preferred his next ship, the more modern 10,000-ton Kent Class Cruiser, *Canberra*. As an AB, Saunders was sent to the Seaplane Carrier *Albatross*. It was an interesting few months, and he had no problem when he was drafted back to *Canberra*. The opportunity arose for trade training, which he gladly accepted even if it did involve a sort of demotion.

Training to be a blacksmith in the navy seemed odd to many, but they were needed to maintain cables and anchors. For Saunders the worst part was being sent to the 24 Class Convoy Sloop HMAS *Moresby* in April 1935. The former Royal Navy hydrographic vessel HMS *Silvio*, had an unhappy history and was horrible to serve in. Just the year before there had been a mutiny onboard, when sailors had tired of arduous duty and a particularly ill-tempered PO. Seven ratings were singled out as the 'possible ringleaders' and discharged. Conditions did not improve. Saunders struggled through nearly two years service on the old tub before being rated Blacksmith IV and drafted to another Kent Class, HMAS *Australia*. By the time Saunders left Sydney bound for Canada and his new ship, the former labourer had already seen more of the world than his mates back in Kyabram, Victoria.

—

At the beginning of November clandestine bookies on *Perth* did a brisk trade on the pending Melbourne Cup. Even in a war situation on the high seas, sailors wished to have a 'flutter' on one of their nation's most iconic sporting events. On the morning of 7 November, the news that 'Rivette' had won gave more joviality to punters than those who took their bets. However, for Chief Ed Sandall the running of the race that stopped a nation was of minor importance. Sandall had struggled in the cold weather of the Atlantic and his persistent respiratory system infections caused concern for Surgeon Cdr Downward. The ship could ill afford to lose such an experienced Chief at this time, particularly one who had been a member of the forward commissioning crew and knew the ship so well. Another medical survey convinced Downward that Sandall was 'unfit for service in climate'. There being no guarantee the ship would not undertake more Atlantic service, plans were made to return the him home to Australia. When his illness worsened, he was sent instead to hospital in England. Still in an English hospital in February the following year, the RAN and his family were advised he would be fit enough to leave the United Kingdom by the end of the month. Chief Ed Sandall died on 3 March 1940 and his wife was simply notified that he had been buried in England. *Perth* had lost its first crewmember.

By the end of the year, the ship had steamed 29,000 miles (46,600 kilometres) and spent 99 out of 118 days at sea. Most of the crew were missing their families as they faced a Christmas about as far away from Australia as they could be. Chief EA Reg Whiting took time to write a letter to his four-year-old son Brendan, 'Jove! Bren, it is too bad I cannot get home on account of this War business, for I have some good toys for you, especially a bonza motor car'.[24] However, Christmas Day on RAN ships was always memorable as all participated vigorously in the festivities. The war was forgotten as the day commenced with the playing of the hymn 'Christians Awake' over the cruiser's PA system.

Perth cooks produced a wonderful spread of food, and the men enjoyed their beer issue. Breakfast consisted of grapefruit, fried eggs and bacon, bread rolls and coffee. The large meal of any day in navy ships was dinner (lunch), and on 25 December 1939 it was cream of tomato soup, roast turkey and seasoning, York ham, French beans, green peas, roast and boiled potatoes, followed by Christmas pudding and brandy sauce with fresh fruit and nuts. There was an afternoon tea of Christmas cake. For those who were still hungry, supper (evening meal) was cold roast turkey, cold roast pork with apple sauce, salads and mayonnaise dressing, and jellied fruit. A sailor held in the ship's cells was released for the day on the proviso he returned himself before Commander's inspection. The miscreant smiled broadly at the inspecting officer from behind bars at 2100. If the officer was puzzled by the sailor's joviality, he passed no comment.

—

Perth traversed the Panama Canal on 2 March 1940. Unlike the previous two occasions, those onboard were optimistic that surely this time their ship would continue south-west, and it did. The cruiser's course was set for Tahiti and Fiji. As the first Australian warship to visit the French colony, crew members were again feted. Prior to leave being granted, Farncomb addressed the ship's company: 'you are cautioned to conduct yourselves in a proper manner as the Tahitians have the reputation of being overly-friendly and remember Tahiti is reputed to be "The Island of Free Love"'.[25] Clearly from the number of winks and nudges, members of *Perth*'s lower deck had no intention of adhering to their commanding officer's directive and every intention of investigating the claim. Leading Seaman Bill Bracht soon realised how 'beautiful' the Polynesian girls were, and never had he seen 'so many girls in such a small town'. Sailors quickly picked up on the fact that 'a white flower worn in the hair above the left ear meant that they were unattached'.[26] There were plenty of places to meet and enjoy the company of female inhabitants, and not speaking the language never proved an obstacle. Papeete offered many delights, not least of all the best French champagne for only 1/6d a bottle, and there were many sailors who arrived at their ship's gangway late, happier than usual and intent on bringing female companions onboard.

An excess of champagne encouraged some of the Australian sailors into further waywardness. A group that included Range Finder Leading Seam Arthur 'Olga' Close misappropriated an icon belonging to an indigenous chief. As the ship was about to leave, the chief came onboard to demand the return of the icon. He allegedly threatened that if the icon was not returned, 'this ship will sink'.[27] Nobody owned up, but when the ship finally sailed the icon was thrown out a porthole into the ocean. This may have prompted the pact between Close and Leading Seam Jock Lawrance that if anything happened to either of them, the remaining sailor would care for the other's children. Time would test the curse, but there was a more immediate price to pay – their Captain, angry with the blatant disregard of his order, 'I was dismayed at the performance of some of you', ensured that few of the ship's company were granted leave in their next stop, Suva, Fiji.

—

As *Perth* entered Sydney Harbour on 31 March 1940, there were emotional scenes. The splendour of the setting was enhanced by a flotilla of small boats and ferries, their decks crowded with waving and cheering people. Garden Island wharf looked almost ready to give way under the assembled multitude of relatives and friends, navy personnel, dignitaries and media. Crew members lining the cruiser's railings felt the swell of emotion born of relief and pride. The majority of the cruiser's crew had circumnavigated the globe. Many had left as raw recruits in a peacetime navy, and returned more seasoned to a nation at war. So much had taken place in less than a year and it was difficult to fathom that, since boarding *Autolycus,* they had travelled 73,000 miles (117,500 kilometres).

Some were embarrassed at being treated as men returning from war, confided Lieut Bill Cook, because their duty had been, 'pleasant and non-arduous'.[28] However, the crew of *Perth* marched proudly through Sydney, looking transformed from the groups of RAN personnel who had departed Australian shores in the middle of 1939. Although some men would transfer in the months ahead, the men had united as a crew and could indoctrinate 'new chums' into the ways of the cruiser. However, the next chapter would definitely not be 'pleasant and non-arduous'.

THREE

'We soon came to realise that we were now in a real war.'

Ordinary Seaman Basil Hayler

With the cruiser in refit in Sydney, *Perth* crew enjoyed leave, returning to homes adjusting to war. Australians were still largely unaffected, so their mood in early 1940 remained buoyant. Chief EA Reg Whiting took the opportunity to secure his family's future and purchased a small, two-bedroom brick cottage not far from the Garden Island Dockyard. He busied himself over the following months making small improvements, so his wife Alice and their sons would be comfortable. Bernice Saunders was pleased to have husband Alf back and hoped the blacksmith would fix a few things around their home. May Hughes also had a 'to do' list for her husband, although she valued their free time together. She had been married to Chief ERA Joseph Hughes for several years and had never known her husband out of the RAN, but naval marriages held stresses few outside the service understood.

For most Australians geographic mobility was uncommon, and newly married couples remained close to their extended family. For navy families this was invariably not the case. Sea duty meant long absences, and wives and children learned to cope. Assistance and all-important understanding flowed within small naval communities, but life was never easy. Wives struggled to reconcile their loneliness with the knowledge that their husbands were part of a close-knit crew and doing what they loved. There was little comfort for wives during peacetime in the 'for king and country' sentiment, when it seemed that civilian neighbours failed to appreciate the sacrifices involved. And with the nation at war, navy wives had to endure the added trepidation intrinsic to their husbands' service in the defence forces.

George Hatfield took full advantage of shore time and was feeling pretty pleased with himself. He was promoted to Leading Seaman in January and during this interlude he married his sweetheart, Amelia. Auburn-haired Arthur Lewis had also been promoted in January, to ERA IV. Like Hatfield, he decided he wouldn't leave Australian waters again without marrying his girl Joan and settling in Sydney. The ship's programme during May meant sea trials off the east coast, so those with families in the region were grateful for precious shore leave each time *Perth* moored in Sydney Harbour.

—

On 6 June Captain Sir Phillip Bowyer-Smyth RN, assumed command of the ship. There were few onboard sorry to see the change in command. Farncomb was not well liked by those who served in the lower deck. His officious nature, his belief in stern, unrelenting discipline, and his perceived arrogance towards the ship's company had earned him little esteem. Even a Naval Board dominated by Royal Navy Admirals could not have failed to note that Farncomb had initiated 50 disciplinary warrants against *Perth* sailors, when a fifth of that number was more common. However, the *Perth* sailors viewed Farncomb's replacement with some ill ease. Their new Captain was a British Baronet, a member of the Royal Navy and prior to the war had been British Naval Attaché at Rome. These were not the greatest qualifications for a cruiser captain of a primarily Australian crew that was likely to be thrown into enemy action. He would need to prove himself before this crew showed him genuine respect.

When Australia entered the war in support of the British Empire, the permanent RAN had been made up of 6340 officers and men.

Recruiting campaigns were launched, but lack of foresight in previous decades meant the RAN would struggle to enlist and train the large numbers of personnel it urgently needed. Almost reluctantly, RAN flag officers consented to the commissioning of officers who were not vetted and trained as carefully as they had been into the ways of the Admiralty. The majority of hostilities-only officers and sailors came from the Royal Australian Naval Reserve. Recruited directly from shore, their training was greatly accelerated. Marginally more valued were Royal Australian Naval Reserve (Seagoing) and Royal Australian Naval Volunteer Reserve personnel. RANR(S) officers possessed Mercantile Marine accreditation with sea experience. RANVR consisted of personnel 'with the habit of the sea and especially those who possess experience as yachtsmen, marine and civil engineers etc'.[1]

RANVR personnel were often given specialist duties within the RAN, such as anti-submarine work. Morse code operators were particularly valued and entered at a higher rank than if they had they entered the RAN or RANR. Sailors with previous naval service were also entered as members of the Royal Australian Fleet Reserve. At the outbreak of war, there were 244 RANR officers, 75 RANR(S) and 163 RANVR, a total of 482. By October 1943 this number had increased to 421 RANR, 485 RANR(S), and 1473 RANVR, a total of 2379. The increase of sailors was even more dramatic. The number of 3869 RANR rose to 17,110 by October 1943. In the RANVR enlistments rose from none to 1248, and in the RAFR 460 to 594. With rating numbers increasing from 4229 to 18,952, enormous strains were placed on RAN training regimes. *Cerberus* recruit training was shaved and category (specialist) training reduced to the bare essentials.

Chief Yeoman of Signals Herbert Hatwell arrived onboard *Perth* just two days before the new Captain. He was known as a hard taskmaster, but few could discount the wealth of experience he brought with him. Born in 1905 in Peterborough, South Australia, Hatwell was another who had joined as a Boy Seaman and survived the harsh *Tingira* training. He realised very early in his RAN service he wished to be a Signalman, and as a Signal Boy saw service on the old Town Class Light Cruiser *Brisbane*. In 1923 he was promoted to Ordinary

Signalman 2nd class. Ensuing years on *Melbourne, Swordsman, Australia* and *Canberra* came with promotions and, a month after war was declared, he was made Chief. He struck fear into the hearts of juniors like Ordinary Signalman 2nd class Ron Hill, and Hatwell knew youngsters like seventeen-year-old Hill meant a significant increase in his own responsibilities. Gone were the days of extended training for new signalmen. Hill's training had been less than seven months.

Nineteen-year-old Tasmanian Ken 'Mo' Ikin was a new addition to *Perth*'s ship's company and typical of the naval volunteers who enlisted following the declaration of war. The lower deck had never before seen the like of these new men. From Brisbane, Queensland, came Socrates Likiardopoulos, his 'Trade' inscribed as 'Scholar'. With his surname shortened to Likiard, he assumed duties as a Supply Assistant. The same sense of duty to one's country and king, infused with a sense of adventure, had lured another generation to war. The vast majority of the 'hostilities only' personnel signed on for two or three years 'or duration of war and six months, whichever the longer' – none who signed the form in the early months of the war could fully appreciate this latter clause. This most dangerous of adventures would not be over by Christmas as many believed. Don Kirkmoe was another young and enthusiastic edition to *Perth*. The good-looking, brown-eyed, seventeen-year-old South Australian joined the navy for the simple reason that the navy accepted him sooner than the army. He already had brothers in the army and mother Blanche had only to give her permission and the former message boy was in the RAN. Less than six months later he was a Stoker 3rd class in *Perth*.

Other men chose the navy over the army or air force, because they had personal links to the sea. Henry Straker was a Methodist from Lake Macquarie, New South Wales. When he could escape chores, he had watched boats entering the lake from the ocean and spent time fishing there. The navy was for him and he joined Kirkmoe in *Perth*'s stokers' messdeck. Douglas Sackfield Asplin was born in Alberton, South Australia, on 24 August 1921. He and his sister Joan, four years his junior, were educated at Largs Primary School and Woodville High School. Doug was an energetic child and joined the local cub and scout troop. He was not a 'willing student', but it took some convincing and a job offer at Goode, Durrant and Murray Wholesalers, before his parents, Joseph and Florence, agreed that he could leave school at fifteen. Living near the ocean, he delighted in anything to do with the water. He grew up listening to stories told by his grandfather, who had served as a seaman on a sister ship of the legendary *Cutty Sark*. They were exciting tales of tea clippers racing each other from China to England. Doug was an excellent swimmer and had inherited his grandfather's love of boats. He joined the Largs Bay Yacht Club but, unable to afford a boat of his own, he set about building one in the family garage. By the time he completed the yacht, he was a member of his nation's navy.

As willing as this new breed of sailor was, nothing could compare to experience. It was left to senior rates to ensure that their subordinates learnt rapidly on the job. Discussion within *Perth's* chiefs' mess demonstrated concern over the accelerated RAN training. Chief PO Roland Hubbard, with seventeen years of service, faced the task of turning young men who had just been born when he entered the navy, into seaman – and under emergency conditions. He conferred with fellow Chief, Andrew Hudson, about this regularly. The men shared the same mess, rank and responsibilities, but were very different men. Hubbard was a typical Aussie from working-class Deniliquin, New South Wales. A little rough around the edges, he was imbued with the Presbyterian hard work ethic. Hudson was a Catholic, a true Irishman from the small town of Wexford. A member of the commissioning crew, the 39 year old wore Royal Navy ribbons from the previous war, and, if these did not attain respect, his no-nonsense attitude soon did.

The cruiser's crew continued to alter over the ensuing months, some of those leaving would be more missed than others. Surgeon Cdr Charles Downward was posted to *Canberra*. He looked after the welfare of the crew well and was a character in his own right. His future career would be chequered. In 1943 he would be awarded a Distinguished Service Cross for 'skill, resolution and coolness during operations in the Solomon Islands'. In 1946 he became Honorary Surgeon to the Governor General of Australia. Downward would transfer to the retired list in 1958 as a Surgeon Captain. He retained fond memories of his time on *Perth*. One member of the crew who would have stayed in the cruiser but was removed was Victor Zamit, a Maltese-born sailor attached to the ship's canteen. When Victor had joined, he had spoken very little English, and the sailors took it upon themselves to teach him the language. Unfortunately, the language he was exposed to was liberally accentuated with Aussie swear words, best avoided except within the messdecks of RAN ships. Once he had to speak to some Sydney suppliers to replenish stocks. The suppliers were unimpressed with the hapless Zamit's use of English and called the police. After a police interview the RAN decided it was in Victor's best interests to send him to a shore canteen and give him corrective English classes.

—

Captain Bowyer-Smyth familiarised himself with his new command and crew during convoy and patrol work and gunnery exercises. One convoy *Perth* protected included the huge *Queen Mary*. Laden with Australian soldiers and supplies, she was part of a the third convoy of Australians to the Middle East. The convoy hit fierce weather in the Great Australian Bight, and those in *Perth* were amazed to see waves breaking over the bows of *Queen Mary*. Buffeted below in the boiler and engine rooms, *Perth*'s newest stokers struggled to continue their duties and contain their stomach contents. The service cards of two, Gordon Steele and Syd Triffitt, were so similar, that they could easily confuse those responsible for *Perth*'s personnel records. The Sydneysiders had enlisted the same day, 17 June 1940. When they reported for duties, the new enlistees were lined up in alphabetical order and the presiding Petty Officer remarked, 'We don't want you lot to struggle with choice, so this half of the line will be Seamen and this half of the line will be Stokers'.[2] Steele and Triffitt were in the second half of the line, so Stoker 2nd class they became, and both arrived at HMAS *Cerberus* for training a month later. Training was brief before they joined *Perth* together on 15 October 1940. By the end of the year their Divisional Officer marked their cards, 'VG Character' and 'Satisfactory Efficiency' and their war had begun.

As the 1940 training exercises continued, further excitement was initiated by Rear Admiral John Crace, the RN Flag Officer who was Commanding the Australian Squadron. Without informing the ship's Gunnery Officer, Lieut Warwick Bracegirdle, Crace decided to test the 4-inch gun deck crew, commanded by Lieut Edward Sweetman. Sweetman was a member of the RANR(S). The efficiency of officers who were not products of the RAN naval college and had not spent years at sea as junior officers was obvious, and not just to those with whom they shared the wardroom. Sailors, particularly members of the permanent RAN, referred disparagingly to hostilities-only officers as 'ninety-day wonders'. One recorded his thoughts in harsher tones, 'RANVR officers were quite ineffectual in a seagoing capacity ... some constituted a dangerous hazard to ships and ship's company ... some were excellent, most were better left ashore ... it was an appalling thought that into the hands of such incompetents lives of men depended'.[3] When *Perth* had returned to Australian waters at the beginning of 1940, the wardroom had been made up of permanent officers; now half the cruiser's officers were reservists.

A 24-year-old Victorian, Sweetman had commenced life in the navy as a Midshipman in 1934. His only previous sea posting was in *Canberra*. Sweetman, known to members of the lower deck by the nickname 'Sweetie Pie', struggled with his confidence. Somewhat overcome by his important audience and anxious to prove his expertise at his station, Sweetman ordered a short barrage at 30-degree elevation. Rear Admiral Crace failed to countermand the order, which he should have realised was unsafe and against procedure given that there was an aircraft onboard. When the shots were fired, *Perth*'s Walrus aircraft, which was stowed ahead of the crane, was jolted and its wing crumpled. Sweetman and Bracegirdle were both reprimanded as a result of a Naval Board of Enquiry into the incident; Rear Admiral Crace was not. Sweetman would unhappily remain in *Perth* during what evolved into a most difficult year. After several months struggling with ill health, he would join *Brisbane* in mid 1942 as, ironically, the Air Lieutenant. His adverse report in *Perth* would not be his last, but although he seemed ill-suited for naval service he did not transfer to the Retired List until 1956, as a Lieutenant Commander.

The unfairness of the reprimand was not lost on Bracegirdle, given that he had been completely unaware of Admiral Crace's reckless supervision. The Bracegirdle name stood proudly in RAN tradition. Lieut Warwick Seymour Bracegirdle was the son of the legendary Rear Admiral Sir Leighton Bracegirdle. Bracegirdle the elder had established an enviable reputation during World War I, particularly as the Commanding Officer of the 1st Royal Australian Naval Bridging Train, a naval engineering unit deployed initially at Gallipoli. It seemed pre-ordained that Warwick Bracegirdle would be appointed a Cadet Midshipman at thirteen at the beginning of 1925. He had a large pair of shoes to fill and perhaps because of his name or perhaps despite of it, he was awarded the Kings Medal as the Outstanding Midshipman of his graduating class. In keeping with RAN protocol, he had spent six years as a junior officer attached to the RN, and he had struggled a little in this environment. He failed his Navigation Qualification and his first attempt at being promoted to Lieutenant. Gunnery became his chosen speciality, and after service on a number of RN ships he joined *Amphion*.[4]

—

After the Crace fiasco, those who sailed in *Perth* settled down to more weeks of convoy escort duties and gunnery training, ever vigilant now of blast damage to the ship's aircraft. From 1935 all RAN cruisers, except for the old *Adelaide*, had been fitted with aircraft catapults and Seagull V aircraft. *Perth* was supposed to have had a catapult installed in England, but due to the war in Europe this had been included as part of the Australian refit. Although described as a 'sturdy little aircraft, even aerobatic',[5] the Seagull was vulnerable to damage, as *Perth*'s crew had witnessed first hand, and was too big and cumbersome for the Leander Class. The aircraft was intended for reconnaissance, but the best use of the 'Pusser's Duck', as far as crew were concerned, was for it to be despatched ashore for bags of mail. The laborious job of hauling the aircraft from the ocean back onboard was much less popular with the ship's company. Six members of the Royal Australian Air Force No.9 Squadron, posted to *Perth* were responsible for the aircraft – six men dressed in khaki and royal blue, in a sea of navy and white uniforms.

In October *Perth* sailed from Sydney to escort yet another convoy to the west. After Fremantle there was a rendezvous with HMAS *Canberra* off the Cocos Islands, then a return to Fremantle at the end of November. By then the crew had been informed that it was likely that *Perth* was bound for overseas duty. The news was not universally well received. The men were granted leave.

Two nights later mines blew up two merchant ships in the Bass Strait and *Perth* was despatched to investigate. Such was the urgency of the ship's departure, a third of the ship's company did not make it back onboard. Alec 'Spud' Murphy was one such sailor. A West Australian who had signed on for twelve years because he was 'sick of farming',[6] Alec had somewhat romantic ideas of navy life. Duty as an Ordinary Seaman in the Kent Class cruiser *Canberra* quickly erased any such inclination. Life on *Canberra* had been fairly 'harsh'. Able Seaman Murphy was concerned he may not have got off to a good start being 'adrift'. He was relieved when he was allowed to rejoin *Perth* and escape punishment. Ratings from Alec's old ship, *Canberra,* were drafted in to replace sailors who chose not to return.

Some sailors deliberately chose not to return to ship, although it often took a trip ashore and a few beers to summon up the courage to do this. Other sailors found that they had accidentally missed the ship when they sobered up after a particularly heavy run ashore. Stoker Alf Hansen, who joined in Canada, was one of the latter, and he spent 28 days in detention at HMAS *Leeuwin* paying for his lapse of judgement. Another was Jeff Latch, a twenty-year-old Stoker from Victoria and member of the commissioning crew. The former brass finisher had hoped to be drafted off *Perth* when it returned from the round the world trip, but he was not and had been unsettled by the news that his ship would likely redeploy. Regardless that there was a war on, or perhaps because there was, Latch did not wish another long stay out of Australian waters. Another sailor who did not return to his ship was Able Seaman Cliff Langford. He too was unimpressed by rumours of overseas service with no finish date. Langford's father, a policeman in Hobart, struggled to understand how there could be a warrant out for his son's arrest but as far as he was concerned Cliff had acted not only unlawfully but unpatriotically.

On 28 November the cruiser and its crew left to escort a convoy north. On 29 November both twenty year olds were sentenced to detention, Langford to fourteen days, Latch, who was still at large, to a harsher sentence of 90 days. Impetuous Irishman Stoker 'Tiny' Savage was designated absent without leave. His actions had nothing to do with bravery but love. Whilst on leave he had met a girl in Western Australia, decided she was the one and could not bear to leave. He married the girl, Norma Betty, then turned himself into authorities. After their incarceration Hansen, Langford and Savage rejoined *Perth*.

—

By 5 December the ship was in Colombo, Ceylon (Sri Lanka). With the ship secured alongside, crew were introduced to the distinctive charms of Asia. PO Roy Norris was immediately impressed by a sunset which almost defied description, 'an artist's palette run mad – a thing of flames shot with all colours of the spectrum'.[7] He was less impressed with 'the smell' and 'highlights' of Colombo.

Bandsman George Vanselow explored the streets, observing 'the palatial residential quarter and also the dingy but colourful native villages'.[8] Vanselow had an artistic eye. Unlike a good many of his peers in the cruiser, the Victorian had enjoyed his education, at Gnotuk School and Camperdown Higher Elementary, and could lose himself in books and his own imagination. He loved boats and spent his leisure time on Lake Bullen in his canoe. Poetry was another love and his verse was published under the name George Davies because at this time many Australians were not too sure if poetry was a suitably blokey pastime. Prior to his enlistment in May 1939, George had been an advertising manager for Manton & Sons Ltd, Melbourne. The position had been stressful and taken its toll on his health. At the age of 25 he had joined the RAN as a musician and *Perth* in July 1940.

The exotic pleasures of the East were tempered by confirmation that the ship would not return to Australian waters but sail two days later for the Middle East to relieve *Sydney*. Nonetheless morale was high. The more adventurous in *Perth* had wearied of convoy duties and complained about not being involved in 'real war'. They firmly believed that if given the chance they and their ship would demonstrate great skill as a fighting unit. The crew of *Sydney* had been given such an opportunity in the Mediterranean and had excelled, sinking the Italian cruiser *Bartolomeo Colleoni* on 19 July 1940.

As *Perth* shepherded the convoy of Australian troops and supplies into the Red Sea, the crew was introduced to the intense heat of the Middle East, which was exacerbated by the need to keep a darkened ship. When its convoy duties were completed, the cruiser turned towards the port of Aden in Yemen, the crew mindful that they were entering a more dangerous chapter of their service. The level of tension rose, as nights were marred by a full moon. Bill Bracht considered himself a seasoned sailor but during his evening watch as Director, Control Tower, he panicked at a shooting star, believing it to be a flare from enemy aircraft. Bracht sounded the alarm and his shipmates rallied to action stations. It was a useful drill for later events, but for Bill Bracht it meant humiliation.[9]

On 23 December, with most staying on deck watching, the ship passed through one of the manmade wonders of the world, the Suez Canal. Seventeen-year-old Stoker Don Kirkmoe spent non-duty time on the upper deck enthralled by the world unfolding in front of him, 'The scenery is very picturesque. The town of Suez is very nice as it has a background of high rugged mountains ... we have now arrived at the irrigated part of Egypt with all tea trees lining the waters edge ... Just passed AIF camp [the Australian army base] and they gave us a good welcome'.[10] The following day *Perth* moored off Alexandria, Egypt. The ship was now part of the Royal Navy Eastern Mediterranean Fleet, and the assembled ships were inspiring. Youthful *Perth* sailors believed that they were ready to defend 'democracy' and that their training and enthusiasm would be enough, 'Oh the wonderful battle, how we looked forward to it ... Fear did not enter our thoughts, we were unafraid'.[11]

Thoughts of glorious battles were put aside the following day as Christmas dinner with all the trimmings and a bottle of beer issue were consumed with relish. The cooks, ably led by Chief Cook Bob Bland, excelled themselves yet again, particularly with the 'Pusser's Plum Duff' with brandy sauce. The 37-year-old Bland, from Sydney's Balmain, had entered the RAN in 1921. The sixth child of Thomas and Mary Bland, he had been apprenticed to a blacksmith but felt strange in the profession and persuaded his parents to allow him to join the navy as a cook. He had adapted to life as a sailor quickly and sought RAN-sponsored general education to improve his prospects. His personal and professional life flourished during a difficult period of RAN budget cutbacks and retrenchments, and he avoided the fate of many of his lower deck peers. He chose the category of Cook (Ships) because he preferred duties in the large galley catering for sailors rather than for the wardroom. His enthusiasm for his life and duties resulted in acceleration through the ranks, and by 1935 he was a Chief. Even when home on leave, Bland enjoyed cooking for wife, Florence, and their two sons. In *Perth* he became well known for his 'tiddyhoggies' (pasties), but on Christmas Day 1940 he and his staff conjured up a feast. Food was crucial to morale within RAN ships and Christmas Day was particularly important, because this day more than any, thoughts of loved ones were never far away. Able Seaman James Cooper felt 'very homesick' and thought of his wife and daughter, 'How I wish I was home this day ... this trip has made me realise just what Etty and Joan mean to me'. Cooper from Yatala, South Australia, had joined *Perth* in November 1940. His solution for homesickness, and whatever else that ailed him, was to get drunk, which he justified as 'the only thing I do when I go ashore and I never go with women'.

The more fortunate managed to gain leave during the next days to savour the ancient wonders of Egypt. Those less fortunate had the pleasure of painting *Perth* in camouflage colours. To encourage ship morale Bowyer-Smyth had promoted a competition for the best camouflage design. The multi-talented AB Ross Birbeck won the prize of two bottles of beer; the cruiser, sporting its unique Australian-conceived, dark rainbow-shaped shading, was ready for combat.

On 30 December *Perth,* along with HM Ships *Ajax* and *Orion,* were formed into the 7th Cruiser Squadron. December was challenging, with the ship steaming a total of 10,515 miles (17,000 kilometres) between 28 November and 31 December, with 29 days out of 34 spent at sea,[12] but it would be nothing compared to the demands of the next six months. One night *Perth* was duty ship. Able Seaman Jim Nelson, was given the responsibility of playing 'The Last Post' to close down the Eastern Mediterranean fleet at 2100. Nelson, from Sydney, was one of the 'hostilities' youngsters, who had joined the cruiser during the middle of 1940, one of those referred to by Chief EA Reg Whiting as, 'wide-eyed and looking forward to their first trip overseas and the experience of a lifetime'.[13] It was with some trepidation the eighteen year old approached the quarter deck with bugle in hand, 'It is a haunting tune, spirited yet deeply melancholy ... I put my heart into it, something that went out as an undercurrent that whispered to the seamen who could understand'.[14] Through the final years of the war *Perth* seamen would shudder when the all-too-frequent and mournful sounds of 'The Last Post' were played in a different context and a different land.

—

One of the congregation points in *Perth* was the canteen, and one of the more popular individuals on board was Alfred Hawkins, who ran it. Along with a staff of three other civilians, he sold items of non-RAN issue, from shaving cream to toothbrushes, postage stamps to cigarettes, which those onboard greatly appreciated. Born in 1900, Hawkins had enlisted in the RAN as an Engine Room Artificer in 1921. In June that year he had joined the ship's company of the RAN flagship *Australia* but had scarcely had enough time to acquaint himself with the ship before he was sent to *Brisbane* six months later, then six months later to *Melbourne.* Additional trade training involved shore time and a draft to *Platypus* and *Swordsman.* He did not enjoy his term on either ship and, although he qualified as an ERA II by 1928, he began to wonder about his chosen career path. Alf had also married, and he and wife Florence had a three-year-old son Alfred, named after his father and grandfather. The ERA had applied for a discharge ten months prior to the end of his twelve-year service, and the RAN had agreed on condition that he gain selection as the Canteen Manager of HMAS *Albatross*. Three years later he was Canteen Manager of *Moresby* then *Adelaide*. There was some irony in the fact that life as a Canteen Manager meant as much sea time as his life as a sailor. Recognised as one of the most experienced and capable Canteen Managers, he joined the new cruiser in July 1939. At least there was an added dimension to service on *Perth* now, his sixteen-year-old son Alfred joined him on staff, along with John McCulla and Ken Borough. Two Alfred Hawkins was confusing so the ship's company referred to the ever-cheerful senior Alfred as 'Happy'.

In company with the 6-inch cruiser, HMS *Ajax*, the Australian ship, now known as 'Ship 3' departed on New Year's Eve to patrol the Kaso Strait, east of Crete, an area subjected to a great deal of enemy activity. Able Seaman Jim Nelson wrote in his diary, 'we are all very keen and excited hoping to get a share of it'. The following day he and others received their baptism of fire when Italian aircraft, from their characteristic high-altitude formation, attacked. Nelson thought it incongruous that the ship should be straddled by bombs in front of the beautiful backdrop of the snow-capped mountains of Crete. This first attack revealed an element of panic within *Perth*'s gun crews, particularly the 4-inch crews. Clearly there was more to be done to safeguard the cruiser. The Captain and Gunnery Officer Bracegirdle had a conversation on the need to raise the expertise of the ship's gun crews. Within a month dire necessity increased their proficiency to expert level.

On 3 January *Perth* sailed into the splendid harbour off Athens, and moored alongside the port of Piraeus. The breathtaking mountainous background was only surpassed by the ancient ruins of Greece. Libertymen marvelled as they explored the Acropolis. Bandsman George Vanselow savoured 'the novel experience of running on the track at the Olympic stadium', the first Olympic track. He 'revelled' in what he saw, the books he had consumed as a young adult on the Golden Age of Greek civilisation were coming to life.

PO Roy Norris too was captivated: 'The sheer beauty of the Acropolis has to be seen to be appreciated – there are indeed sermons in stone. I went to see it as a matter of course but the place soon captured me entirely'.15 Athens was 'a joy forever', Norris wrote in his diary, and yet the situation in which he found himself caused sad deliberation:

> I wondered at all the history of this place and the achievements
> of that humble creature man. How has it happened that his
> solitude has been destroyed, his godliness destroyed and herded
> into a hideous riot of murder and destruction.[16]

The cruiser crew gave themselves to the evening delights, and for Bandsman Vanselow, this included 'the beautiful dark-eyed girls'. While he may not have succumbed to those dark-eyed girls who could be found in 'houses of ill fame', who could 'fulfil man's desires' and 'satisfy their biological urges',17 others did. Some remembered their initiation, but more woke the next morning with little recollection of the night before – champagne and cognac were very cheap to buy and wonderful to consume.

Perth's departure on 6 January, in company with HMS *Ajax,* meant a return to reality on a three-day patrol of the sea lanes between Greece and Crete. Enemy aircraft were sighted on arrival in Suda Bay in Crete, which was already being referred to as 'Suicide Bay'. On 8 January the cruiser crew was impressed by the sight of the Eastern Mediterranean Battle Squadron, 'in a fan-shaped spearhead formation spread over the ocean'.18 The next day they were pleased to see HMAS *Sydney* and *Stuart.* There was no opportunity for crew to meet and greet. *Perth* relieved its sister cruiser *Sydney*, and with muddled emotions *Perth's* crew watched *Sydney* disappear over the horizon to return home.

Off Malta on 11 January *Perth* fell into company with the West Mediterranean Fleet and received the news that the 10,000-ton cruiser HMS *Southhampton* had been severely damaged during an air attack. The Australian cruiser steamed to the scene. For an hour *Perth* circled the flaming British ship, and crew members watched in horror as those onboard *Southhampton* leapt for their lives, until a sickening explosion sent a violent orange plume of flame skywards and reduced the RN cruiser to rubble. Any romantic visions of war were blown away as they witnessed the, 'dawning of the carnage ... It was a horrible and terrifying sight and our crew were very sombre and more resolute after witnessing it first hand'.19

FOUR

'Who can sleep, our nerves are just about going ...
I cannot stand much more of it without a rest.'

Able Seaman James Cooper

Patrol and escort duty brought with it more air attacks. HMS *Ajax* and *Perth* were nicknamed 'The Hair Trigger Twins' because of the 4-inch gunfire cross barrage they adopted to protect each other. On 14 January *Perth* steamed into the Grand Harbour, Malta. Those onboard were surprised by the welcome they received. Maltese lining the waterfront cheered while others waved from windows. The Australians warmed to the people and enjoyed the hospitality they extended. It was an amazing experience to visit the catacombs and 'Zitta Zechia'. But those who made war in 1941 had little appreciation for natural and architectural marvels. The German Luftwaffe was now supreme in the skies over the Mediterranean and air raids on Malta were constant.

There was a sense of vulnerability that came with being tied alongside the Valletta dockyard concrete wharf in the dock basin. It was the most heavily bombed spot in the world. On *Perth*'s starboard side a 100-foot (30-metre) cliff blanketed the starboard 4-inch guns. Within sight lay the battle-scarred RN aircraft carrier *Illustrious,* which looked to Stoker Don Kirkmoe 'just a mass of gaping holes. It seems a miracle how she ever reached port'. HMS *Gallant* was also there with its 'bows blown right away'.[1] Astern of the Australian cruiser, was the merchant vessel *Essex*, loaded with tons of explosives.

On 16 January sirens sounded their shrill alarm, and naval gun crews did their utmost to protect ships against a sky thick with aircraft. AB James Cooper muttered a prayer as he gazed skyward and his *Perth* gun crew opened fire. They fired 50 rounds before they scored a hit, 'a plane right in the middle, it was a beautiful hit'.[2] Those not directly involved with the guns prayed that such success against the German Junkers 87 dive bombers would continue because, as PO Roy Norris admitted, 'All that stood between us and total extinction was the resolute guns' crews who continued to pour an unending stream of steel into the air'.[3] Kirkmoe wrote: the 'din is deafening ... it certainly tells me that there is no place like home'.[4]

It was looking as though the lucky ship *Perth* would survive unscathed yet another day, when a 1000-pound bomb landed between the Australian ship and the wharf. *Perth*'s stern rose out of the water, and steel plates and a propeller shaft groaned and buckled. Below decks, the aft section was a mess, one of the oil fuel tanks was holed, and two compartments flooded. Worse still *Essex,* with 4000 tons of ammunition onboard, took a direct hit and was set alight. *Perth*'s fire party, led by Lieut Claude Guille, RANR, rapidly deployed to the blazing merchantman. Guille quickly assessed that the dockyard pump's water pressure was insufficient to quell the flames, so he ordered the hoses attached to *Perth*'s own fire mains to extract water from the harbour. Leading Stoker Peter Allom realised the fire was inaccessible from the first angle of attack and struggled with an unwieldy hose until the water was directed through smashed square ports. One sailor described it as 'a terrifying job that, with the red tongues roaring through the fumes, licking out towards the magazines. If the ship had gone up none of us would have known anything about it'.[5] The *Perth* party successfully extinguished the flames before the dangerous cargo could ignite. Stoker 2nd class Jimmy Millerick, a 21-year-old Victorian, suffered smoke inhalation and slight burns. An exhausted Allom pushed himself on to assist in clearing smoldering debris and help members of *Perth's* medical party remove the wounded and the bodies of 30 *Essex* sailors.

Pete Allom had perhaps the most unusual birthplace of those in *Perth* – Tampin in the Federal Malayan States. He had enlisted in Sydney in 1934 at eighteen and travelled to the UK in *Autolycus*. He was awarded a British Empire Medal for his bravery and effort at Valletta. Other fire party members awarded BEMs were Canteen Manager 'Happy' Hawkins and Stoker Percy 'Bluey' Larmer. Hawkins was the first RAN Canteen Manager so recognised. For the 33-year-old, red-haired Larmer, it was a long way from life as a dairy worker in Toowoomba, Queensland, to being a hero in a war in the Mediterranean. He had struggled to gain favourable recognition in the RAN after three drafts to the troubled *Moresby*. Being a stoker onboard the old hydrographic vessel was akin to guilt by association. Even though his divisional officers repeatedly awarded him favourable reports and promotion recommendations, he was only a three-badge Stoker when he became a member of the *Perth* commissioning crew, which travelled to the United Kingdom in *Autolycus*. His promotion to Leading Stoker was not confirmed until the same month he was awarded his LSGCM medal, and three months after he fought the fiery *Essex*. Larmer was nonplussed when told he would be given the bravery award but knew his wife Thelma, in Sydney, would be pretty proud.

Claude James Poingdestre Guille was awarded an Order of the British Empire. Born in Southampton, England, Guille had reached the rank of Lieutenant in the Royal Navy Reserve before retiring in 1933. He was granted a commission as a Lieutenant in the RANR(S) in 1940, and the 32 year old was posted to *Perth*. His charge of the fire party was the high point of his career. His OBE citation read: 'he became the moving spirit of the party' and this behaviour was 'entirely consistent with his general character and outstanding ability as a practiced seaman'. Men could excel under extraordinary circumstances. Guille was posted off *Perth* towards the end of 1941, to *Mildura* – from a cruiser to an 815-ton Bathurst class minesweeper – but this was his own command and his abilities as a seafarer could come to the fore. His promotion to Acting Lieutenant Commander at the end of 1943 suggested a positive change in his RANR fortunes. Guille's seafaring was his strength but other skills were deemed necessary for the well-rounded naval officer.

Later, he was reprimanded for 'discrepancies in victualling and stores in *Mildura'* and told he must, 'exercise more supervision in capacity as Captain'. Guille was not substantiated as a Lieutenant Commander and, after spending an unhappy period on land at the Port Moresby shore establishment, *Basilisk,* he was demobilised in January 1946.

—

AB Jim Nelson had been ashore when the Malta port area came under attack. Running for his ship, he dived for cover as the world around him disintegrated. Nelson eventually boarded concussed, bruised and with blood coming from his ears. He wondered if split ear drums would be a handicap for a ship's bugler. A *Perth* cook in the ship's galley was scalded on both legs, but dismissed the mishap until he finished his duties. Many of those on *Perth*'s upper deck were showered with debris, but unlike those in *Essex*, their injuries were minor. AB Bishop on the gun deck was struck by a piece of flying metal, which caused more laughter than sympathy when the size of the bruise on his buttock was revealed. The laughter was not solely due to Bishop's blackened butt – it was more due to general relief at having survived another day. As the Australians scanned the damaged dock area, they observed demolished buildings and walls collapsed or shattered, except for one wall that continued to stand alone, 'on it was a life-sized painting of the Christ'.[6]

Rather than physical injury, nerves became more of a concern for those in *Perth*. However, men of this generation were reluctant to discuss emotions and they would only confide in the non-judgemental form of a diary. This inability to discuss their fears freely would have dire consequences for many. AB James Cooper considered himself a seasoned sailor, a tough man, until he encountered air attacks. Born in Yatala, South Australia, Cooper already had twelve years' service under his belt when 1940 came around, but with a war on he had little choice but to continue serving. Cooper transferred to the RAFR for five years, but with the manpower shortage this made no difference and the 33 year old found himself in *Perth* in the 'Med' as dive bombers rained havoc. After the attack of 16 January he wrote, 'I was never so frightened in all my life'. PO Cook Roy Norris confided in his diary that the only worse experience he could imagine would be 'getting blown to atoms', but then again that wouldn't be worse because, 'then we'll be beyond caring'.[7]

There was little respite whatever duties were set the cruiser and its crew; in harbour or at sea, attack from the air or from the depths was always anticipated. Ordinary Seaman Basil Hayler lay awake desperately trying to rest, but his mind worked overtime, and he wondered which would be the worst death, from a torpedo or a bomb, 'The stress on mind and body was enormous ... The most frightening time seemed to be the waiting'.[8] In friendly waters the ship's company was divided into three watches, Red, White and Blue, with one on duty (closed up). In dangerous times, the ship's company was divided into two watches, Port and Starboard, or 2nd Degree Readiness when some personnel were closed up and the guns partly manned; then Action Stations or 1st Degree Readiness. The tension, as the enemy was sighted but not yet in range, was palpable. Air raid yellow was sounded when unidentified aircraft or shipping was sighted, and the Duty Watch manned the guns, and waited, and waited. Air raid red when the enemy prepared to attack and *Perth*'s guns commenced their deafening roar. Air raid green meant you were still alive and would fight another day.

Night patrols were hazardous. A Radio Direction Finder was fitted to *Perth* in February 1941, but it was only effective over short distances and frequently broke down, hence 'seek and destroy' missions were also exercises in 'staying alive'. Daylight arrived with the sight of mines brought up by destroyers towing paravanes (minesweepers) bobbing around too close for comfort until they were destroyed by other destroyers. The manmade hazards were made even more dangerous by nature itself. The Mediterranean was renowned for its extremes – heavy weather, gale force winds and blinding sandstorms. Sleep was difficult after adrenalin-charged days and, in the stillness of a Mediterranean night, the demons emerged: 'I had little sleep ... I was wet through all night ... I had a terrible dream and woke up crying', wrote AB Cooper. A *Perth* Steward broke down and was placed in sickbay. *Perth* limped to Alexandria for repairs. The ship had another five-and-a-half months service in the Mediterranean to go.

The crew empathised with the plight of civilian populations of the Mediterranean, for the people were virtually defenceless against the full wrath of the Luftwaffe. During the first month of 1941, the cruiser *Perth* spent 24 days at sea and covered 8370 miles (13,471 kilometres). Sailors adopted tactics reminiscent of a Hollywood Western, mentally adding a notch for every air attack they survived. Roy Norris, fascinated by a Mediterranean sunset featuring 'coloured fires and phantasmic shapes', fancied the specks he saw on the horizon could be ships vanishing into, 'the very gates of heaven over these burnished jaws of Hell, leaving behind a sky resembling black crumpled paper'.[9] He tried to ignore the 'buzz' that his ship would return to Australian waters, but agreed on a wager with a messmate that *Perth* would remain until at least the end of June. It was a wager about which he said: 'I hope I lose'.[10]

The first day of February was spent standing by a torpedoed, but still afloat, oil tanker. On arriving in Alexandria on 7 February, the Australian Prime Minister Robert Menzies came aboard. The consummate politician, Menzies mingled with the men, and Stoker Gordon Steele was duly impressed when his Prime Minister shook his hand. The ship's company nonetheless was not really in the mood for such a visit, all they wanted to do was to get ashore to unwind. Instead there had been a frantic 'make and mend' to tidy the ship and then line up for inspection: 'this we did not need! Dutifully we stood there while he rambled on with a long politically inspired speech'.[11] They were under no illusion that, should their Prime Minister ask after their well-being, they had no alternative but to answer positively and enthusiastically. There could be no riposte such as: 'This is a bloody mess you politicians have got us into, and we don't see any of you blokes when the bombs are falling'. While dockyard personnel assisted with bomb damage repairs, *Perth* crew took full advantage to explore Egyptian monuments of pharaohs and slaves.

Yet, as invariably happened after a period of exacting and dangerous days, the tension could not be dispelled. The knowledge that they must return to the dangers of duty made any interlude almost as excruciating as the danger itself. There was a palpable sense of relief as the cruiser again slipped mooring lines and resumed the duty regime. *Perth*'s Executive Officer had left the ship in Alexandria and few within the ship's company were sad to see the departure of Commander Adams, the RN officer known as 'Flip the Frog'. However, his parting gesture surprised a few, because the aloof XO insisted on shaking hands with everyone onboard. Time would tell how Lieutenant Commander Charles Reid, already referred to by sailors as 'Pricky', would do following his promotion to Commander and appointment as 'Jimmy' (Executive Officer). Charles Rupert Reid had entered RANC as a thirteen-year-old Cadet Midshipman in January 1918. Many of his early years as a RAN officer had been spent in England and attached to the RN. Reid chose signals as his specialisation, but after suffering a leg injury in 1929 his career took a downturn. On his next exchange service with the RN, he again ended up in an RN hospital. He was on a third RN exchange when he was posted to help transform *Amphion* into *Perth*. A combination of factors meant his first years on *Perth* were not happy or easy. Reid was a 'strict disciplinarian which did not initially endear him to the sailors ... Farncomb ... no doubt endorsed this attitude'.[12] Already not held in high regard by the ship's company, few believed Reid's temper would improve.

With entry to a floating dock completed on 9 February, the cruiser's hull and the extent of the damage that had occurred at Malta were fully exposed; repairs would take more than a couple of days. *Perth* was in dock until 20 February. Captured Italian Breda guns were fitted on 22 February and quickly put to use on the enemy. Back in action it seemed that the days blended together – sleep, eat, action stations, pray like hell that you would be delivered safely by the efficiency of your Captain and shipmates and that the lucky *Perth* would endure. All around them ships fell to the enemy. On 1 March HMS *Mohawk* was sunk, the aircraft carrier HMS *Illustrious* was again damaged severely and the bow of HMS *Gallant* was blown off when it struck a mine. It was almost a routine day, although AB Nelson did use bold print in his diary to write: 'WHAT A HELL OF A DAY'.[13]

Of his first night air attack on *Perth* Stoker Gordon Steele wrote in a shaky hand, 'Boy, did I have the wind up'. When not on duty in the boiler room, Steele's action station was as a member of the aft 6-inch magazine ammunition party. The six to eight man magazine party, with Chief Cook Bob Bland often in charge, worked four levels down, behind locked doors, with volatile cordite shells, in oppressive conditions. As action stations concluded, relieved men would 'scurry out of our little holes'[14] pleased to see the sky. February seemed a blur, with 3323 miles (5350 kilometres) travelled, at an average speed of 20 knots. A German broadcast announced that HMAS *Perth* had been sunk – this was the third time *Perth* had been 'sunk'.

—

As March progressed fatigue took prominence. Gun crews were exhausted, but still the air attacks came. AB Jim Cooper confided: 'I will sure be glad when this war is over ... I thought of Etty and Joan at home and what they would do without me'. Like others he struggled to keep going and doubted his ability to do so. He was brutal on himself for failing to be as professional in combat as others, particularly Leading Seaman Bob East. East had joined the RAN through the boy training scheme in 1918, but left the RAN in the 1920s. At the outbreak of war, East enlisted in the RAFR and joined *Perth* towards the end of 1940. As far as Cooper was concerned, East epitomised coolness in battle, he appeared untouched by nerves. In reality East was simply better at disguising his fear. Bob East returned to Australia in September 1941. Although promoted to Acting PO in April 1942, he was diagnosed as 'Suffering from Anxiety State'. His health deteriorated further, and by September he was admitted to the hospital at HMAS *Cerberus* for two months' treatment. Too little was known about 'war neurosis' or Post Traumatic Stress Disorder, as it would later be known, and the diagnosis of 'Anxiety' resulted in poor medical treatment. Invariably the sufferer was made to feel he should be able to overcome the ailment himself. East struggled to fulfil naval duties at a shore establishment, and in June 1943 his record was again notated with the word 'Anxiety'. He was drafted to several shore establishments, but continued to seek medical attention on a regular basis. In May 1946 East was discharged as medically unfit. Anxiety would blight the rest of his life and would affect many others who served in *Perth*.

The winds that came into the Mediterranean had names of their own. Those emanating from Europe were called Meltemi and Sirocco. Those blowing up from Egypt and Libya were given the name Khamsin, Arabic for 'fifty'. Seamen knew to fear a Khamsin wind, a hot south-easterly, which blew for 50 days from mid March and brought with it terrible sandstorms that defied all human activities. The Seventh Cruiser Squadron was off the Egyptian coast steaming in 'line ahead' formation, 250 yards apart, when hit by a Khamsin, and they lost sight of each other. *Perth* signalmen turned on the 18-inch signal lamps on port and starboard sides of the flag deck. Under normal circumstances the 40 million candlepower lamp could transmit Morse signals 20 miles (32 kilometres). Struggling against the blinding sand, signalmen could only see the next cruiser's signal lamps as tiny purple eyes. Other crewmen on the flag deck were but vague red shapes. The brick-red dust coated all before it, and, even when wearing protective balaclava-like flash hoods, men struggled to breathe. At the end of the day, 'a mantle of orange dust' was 'inches thick everywhere; one feels it thick in hair, eyes, teeth and skin.'[15] It was a case of 'all hands' to remove the coating from the ship.

On 6 March, 47 army officers and 610 troops, mostly New Zealanders, were embarked for the voyage across the Mediterranean to Greece, and for the first time, 'amid much cheering the Australian Flag was hoisted'.[16] Winds, this time from Europe, buffeted the ship and many of the soldiers suffered sea sickness. So often closed up at first- and second-degree readiness for thirteen, sometimes eighteen hours, the crew struggled with fatigue and the weather, 'we are all tired, cold and hungry'.[17] The gale-force winds continued to batter the cruiser and upper deck personnel shivered in temperatures in the low 40 degrees Fahrenheit (5–7 degrees Celsius).

On 10 March the mission was to evacuate sick soldiers from Crete and take them to Alexandria. In the skies above, fighters from both sides were engaged in a dogfight. Stoker 2 Don Kirkmoe was off duty and on deck watching, he noted in his diary, 'It has an entertaining side but one cannot forget that men are trying to kill each other'. Nonetheless crew morale continued to soar when Allied warships steamed 'line ahead', as HM ships *Orion, Ajax* and *Gloucester* in company with four destroyers did on 27 March. With a strict regime of radio silence observed by the Allied fleet, signalmen were kept busy passing messages by flag and light, their counterparts in ship wireless rooms intent on listening to enemy or shore transmissions but not touching their own keys. The message relayed from the flagship was 'enemy offensive action in these waters in the next few days'. Early the following morning, visual contact was made on the port quarter shortly before three 8-inch Italian cruisers opened fire. As the fleet went into action, radio silence ceased and signalmen on the upper deck assumed the position of bystanders at the ensuing light and noise show.

With the Allied warships hopelessly out-ranged by larger Italian cruisers, there was little option but to make smoke to conceal the ship and withdraw. But the withdrawal had a further purpose, to entice the Italian ships closer to the main Allied battle fleet. Over the following half hour, *Perth* was straddled by shells. One Australian seaman wrote, 'We charge out of our screens, fire a salvo, thumb our noses at the 'Ities' and duck back into the screen, always heading south'.[18] Another suggested that *Perth* did not fire a shot and bravado was superficial, 'We were the baited trap and now I know just what it feels like to be a piece of cheese'.[19] The Italians gave chase and realised too late they had been duped. It was a relief for those in *Perth* when their enemy came under attack from aircraft off the British carrier *Formidable*. The battle that raged between 27 and 29 March 1941 was named The Battle of Matapan. During the bedlam the ship's Chief Petty Physical Training Instructor, Don Viney, became preoccupied with saving life. It was not his own, or even those of his shipmates, but two small birds that had alighted on the ship exhausted and confused. He placed a cup of water beside them, crumbling tiny pieces of bread in the container to entice them to drink. It seemed bizarre, the solidly built, heavily tattooed, 35-year-old Tasmanian, a navy veteran of twenty years, whose voice made subordinates jump to attention, gently coaxing two small birds to drink while enemy shells threatened his ship and all who sailed in it. In their struggle to maintain the fragile bond with life, men assumed uncharacteristic behaviour. The huge ship losses and the death of some 2400 seamen during the Battle of Matapan virtually ended the World War II participation of the Italian navy.

There was no downtime for *Perth*'s crew, and the following day the ship escorted a 26-strong convoy to Suda Bay. *Perth* suffered repeated air attacks, the most terrifying to date, and it seemed on 30 and 31 March 1941 that enemy planes were immune to the barrage from *Perth*'s guns. For two hours the world was permeated with the scream of aircraft audaciously skimming the ship's superstructure. Those on the upper deck were transfixed by the potentially lethal ballet enveloping them. A signalman struggled with the effects:

> When our twin four-inch high angle guns fired directly astern
> ... the flames from the guns seemed to reach (our) position ...
> The noise was very severe; we were virtually standing in front
> of the guns. The Doppler effect made us deaf ... The twin four-
> inch guns were possibly the loudest piece of ordnance. Six-inch
> gunfire was more a puffing explosion, the four-inch a harsh
> cracking with a fierce concussion of air that physically struck
> the flesh of one's body. We were like boxers subjected to body
> pummelling.[20]

The lives of those below decks were no less frightening. At action stations almost 90 per cent of the crew were sealed in compartments behind watertight doors, cocooned behind steel. Ord Seam Basil Hayler was now a torpedoman, spending more time below decks performing electrical maintenance, and he was not enamoured, 'the ship is rocking, rolling and swerving violently' and 'with all the noise of guns going off and bombs exploding and not being able to see what is going on ... it is not the most pleasant place to be'. Men below could hear the gun blasts, could feel the ship beneath them urgently heeling to port and starboard as their Captain endeavoured to evade the enemy. Stokers particularly struggled with their duty. Four hours in boiler or engine rooms were universally dreaded. In the boiler room the hammering of the guns and smell of cordite drawn down by turbine fans just made arduous duty even harder. Stokers knew that a fracture of a superheated steam pipe would result in them being pressure cooked. Below decks duty men felt the distressed vibration of the engines, yet they could only hold on, hope their side was winning and pray to whatever superior power they believed in.

Electrical Artificer Peter Murdoch, who had travelled to England on *Ormonde* in what seemed a lifetime ago, was 'lost overboard' on 31 March 1941. His mother Annie had been right to worry about the sensitivity of her son. He may well have thrived in a peacetime navy, but this war wreaked havoc on the strongest of men and Peter was not one of these. Beneath decks he was subjected to unrelenting noise, pummelled as the ship lurched and wished desperately it would stop. His fear escalated as the air attack intensified, and Murdoch escaped to the upper deck. But there was no escape, and arriving topside he witnessed the fiery mayhem. Overwhelmed there seemed nowhere to find absolution but to jump overboard and end it all. The RAN advised Annie Murdoch that he was 'lost overboard', and he was just as much a fatality of combat as any other man.

Those in *Perth* understood the situation and did not judge Murdoch severely. However, authorities in Australia marked Murdoch's file 'deserted in the face of the enemy',[21] which meant that his mother, whom he had been supporting since she had lost her husband to World War I, was unable to claim his Deferred Pay and War Gratuity. It would take years of agitation on the part of crew mates before this ruling was overturned. Reports of Matapan in the sanitised, Australian wartime media were dominated by the words 'magnificent' and 'glorious victory'. Nowhere did they feature the words 'fear' and 'fatigue'. Truth was the first victim of war.

—

Perth spent 26 days of March at sea. The ship covered 8891 nautical miles (14,300 kilometres) but this was irrelevant. For the crew the most important thing was that they had survived. They prayed the ensuing miles would not be as perilous, but April started badly when the Axis powers invaded Greece and Yugoslavia; immediately the cruiser and crew were embroiled.

Perth was alongside Piraeus, with men ashore for a well-deserved opportunity to enjoy Greek hospitality, when the port area was targeted from the air. AB Jim Nelson and AB Jack Cox were enjoying glasses of ouzo at the *Kit Kat Cabaret* in Athens, when the air-raid siren sounded. Securing transport to the port 'with bombs raining down all around',[22] they found their ship had slipped moorings and escaped. Without hesitation Nelson and Cox offered their gunnery skills to a Greek officer. He took them to the top of a building where a Breda machine gun crew lay slumped over the gun mounting. Removing the bodies, the Australian sailors assumed the positions of the Greek soldiers. Nelson picked up the gunner's glove and flinched when he found the previous wearer's hand in it. The *Perth* gunners proceeded to fire at lights set up on the roofs of surrounding buildings by German 5th Columnists to guide German forces in.[23] They were strafed a number of times, but survived their stint with the Greek military and returned to the harbour hours later.

Some 200 members of the crew struggled to return to their ship. PO Roy Norris was enjoying the Acropolis by moonlight when the sky erupted. No transport was available until the all-clear was sounded, and when he reached the port area many ships were alight. *Perth* crew were instructed to congregate onboard HMS *Calcutta* until such time as it was safe for their ship to retrieve them. There was little room to rest and, with smouldering ships all around, it was not a scenario that encouraged sleep. Ord Seam Basil Hayler had managed to drift into restless slumber but was jolted back to consciousness at 0315 by a huge explosion. Norris, unable to find space below decks, had settled down in a whaler (boat) on *Calcutta*'s port side. He was uncertain if he physically moved out of the boat or was blown out when the ammunition ship *Clan Fraser* blew up, he just remembered, 'the most ear-splitting detonation ringing in my ears; the sky a lurid mass of flying white-hot metal'.[24] Arriving topside other *Perth* crew members were met by fires bursting out all over the harbour, as red-hot shrapnel from the munition ship rained down from above. *Calcutta* was caught in the violent chain reaction as some eighteen ships were set alight, many sinking. Several of *Calcutta*'s crew were killed and a number of *Perth* sailors injured. Jim Nelson, still coming to grips with his previous evening fighting on a Greek rooftop, struggled to take it all in, 'I will never forget the destruction. It is impossible to describe the scene ... it was horrible'.[25]

Ajax, *Perth*'s 'twin', was burning, and as *Perth* crew ran onto the wharf area to assist where they could, another huge explosion sent them sprawling. It was decided personnel needed to be removed for their own safety, and the Australian sailors were mustered and marched through Pireaus to the relative safety of the outer harbour.

Meanwhile other personnel were having adventures of their own. The ship's motorboat was sent in to the inner harbour to collect personnel. With *Perth*'s Gunnery Officer Lieut Warwick Bracegirdle aboard, the boat ventured back to its cruiser. However, while they were traversing pools of burning oil, the boat's engine stopped and could not be restarted. With their dead craft drifting towards a burning wreck, those onboard hastily abandoned boat and swam ashore. The following morning Bracegirdle and another *Perth* officer, Lieut Richard Power, managed to acquire a skiff to row to their ship. Their journey coincided with the ignition of *Clan Fraser*. Bracegirdle and Power attempted to pull a fuel-loaded barge away from the ammunition ship, but the *Clan Fraser* disintegrated. Roughly ejected from their own boat into the water, they resurfaced only to be showered with pieces of hot metal. Both suffered superficial injuries and Bracegirdle was concussed and had a split eardrum. The officers were taken to hospital, objecting strongly, until they were released and allowed to return to their ship.

It had been a very wise decision to remove the Australian cruiser from the harbour when the bombing commenced, even with a third of the crew missing. The ship was attacked during the night and one near miss sank the *Cyprian Prince* anchored close by. *Perth* seamen were involved in the rescue of survivors. However, by 0900 the crew and *Perth* were reunited. With the steel decks of their cruiser beneath them, the RAN officers and men cast their eyes over the apocalyptic scene and counted their blessings. One diarist wrote, 'It was a long, hard, terrifying night, one I do not ever want to go through again!'[26] Another hoped, 'God guard us as well in the future'.[27] This war was terrifying, but there was comfort and familiarity in the ship.

—

Everyone was pleased to be in open sea again, there was always pleasure in feeling the ship underway and the sensation that they could outpace the danger and horror, even if they couldn't. On arrival in Suda Bay, 52 bags of mail from Australia were taken onboard. It was not unusual for a crewman to receive two dozen letters or more from home at once during a rare mail delivery. It was the happiest of occasions. For Bandsman Perce Partington, one of those who had started the 'grand adventure' on *Autolycus* so long ago, the news was not good, his brother Arnold, a bandsman in *Canberra*, had died. Perce and Arnold had been close, and now the fine trumpeter lay in a grave in a Mauritius Military Cemetery, dead from acute appendicitis four days after his twenty-fifth birthday. By the time the Partington family in Australia was informed of Arnold's death, he had already been buried on the other side of the world.

Noel Smith was a nineteen year old who believed he should do his duty so enlisted in the RAN in November 1939. He then found that some of those who enlisted immediately following the declaration of war referred to 'his kind' as 'slow learners' for waiting two additional months. Smith entered as an Ordinary Seaman, but because he had picked up some basic culinary knowledge as a station hand, on the family property outside Orange, New South Wales, he applied to transfer to cookery school. By March 1941 he was a Ship's Company Cook and off to the Mediterranean to join *Perth*. He arrived onboard *Perth* the same day as the 52 bags of mail, and consequently was barely noticed by a crew engrossed in letters from home. Unbeknown to Smith he had joined the crew and the cruiser when they were about to be involved in some of their most perilous missions. By the end of the following month, the young cook was dead.

FIVE

'I am only nineteen years old!
What is expected of me?
How much more can I give?'

Able Seaman James Nelson

More troops, more hazardous trips across the Mediterranean, more air raids, more time spent closed up at action stations, more war; but the crew and the cruiser *Perth* remained lucky, as ships disappeared all around them. Hostilities were going badly for the Allies in the first months of 1941 with defeat in France, the massive evacuation of Allied troops from Dunkirk, as well as further retreats in North Africa. For naval forces in the Med, the situation was no less dire. On 21 and 22 April 1941 alone, enemy aircraft sank 23 Allied ships, while others were deemed 'unseaworthy'. The days seemed to congeal into one. *Perth* gun crews remained closed up on rations of bread and tinned beef. AB Cooper admitted that he said his rosary more often on 21 April than he had the rest of his life or was likely to again. Then another even more awful day arrived.

AB Nelson noted in his diary on 22 April, 'How long can we keep this up? ... Our crews are battle weary, tired and exhausted. With the Luftwaffe controlling the air and yet today we are being called upon to again proceed into the major action'.[1] The following day the cruiser once more arrived in Suda Bay. 'The Harbour is starting to fill up with sunken ships, altogether there are HMS *York*, one Greek destroyer, three tankers and 2 merchant ships resting on the bottom'.[2]

Work parties from *Perth* and other ships combined to transform the partially sunken hulk of HMS *York* into a decoy. A sudden air attack caught them exposed and undefended; *Perth*'s Shipwright Don 'Bingle' Haddow was killed. Donald McEachan Haddow was born in Glasgow in January 1904. He would later brandish his Scottish pride flamboyantly with a thistle tattooed on his right forearm. Haddow had enlisted in the RAN as a Joiner in 1925, but was one of those discharged 'free' in 1930. Whether this was his choice or that of his employer is not known, but he had re-enlisted in 1935 and was promoted to Shipwright two years later. Haddow had been a member of the forward *Ormonde* commissioning group and had qualified as a Diver.

On 22 April he resurfaced from *York's* submerged hull and was hauled into the work boat. Garbed in his heavy diver's suit and lead boots, Haddow had just removed the copper helmet when a bomb landed nearby, swamping the boat, and sending the helplessly weighed-down diver plummeting to the depths below. Edith Haddow now faced the task of raising their two children alone. A more sombre tone settled over his ship's crew, 'Vale number two of our ships company'.[3]

—

At 1800 on the 23 April, *Perth* sped to Porto Rafti, east of Athens, to assist with the evacuation of troops. AXIS aircraft dropped flares to illuminate ships that were perilously close to the coastline. Enemy machine guns strafed the Australian cruiser, and gun crews returned fire until those responsible were 'blown to bits'.[4] There was the constant need to remain keenly alert to the dangers at hand. Accurate information on rendezvous points was as scarce as up-to-date coastal navigational information. The naval force continued to manoeuvre into inlets trying to avoid mines, submarines and bombs to collect the valuable cargo, in what was a 'hair-raising experience'[5] to say the least. As another night passed and the fires burning on the Greek shore multiplied, someone mentioned it was 25 April, ANZAC Day. Funny that, how a nationalistic icon symbolising a particular notion of Australian identity had emanated from a poorly planned military campaign at Gallipoli, not far from where they now found themselves endangered, in another poorly planned military campaign with their forces in retreat. The realisation that Australian soldiers were likely to be left to the mercy of an opposing army once more made the day even more solemn.

The following days were spent racing against an advancing enemy, and the Australian cruiser and crew tried desperately to protect those on the beaches and to evacuate whom they could: 'We are all aware and conscious of the responsibility of getting our troops off and surviving the dangers of the return trip but our ship's morale is high'.[6] Ord Seam Basil Hayler watched the grateful Imperial troops struggle up the scrambling nets draped over the side of the ship and thought they 'were a pitiful sight'. Sailors did their utmost to drag men onboard, but some were so weak they fell back into the water and drowned. There was no time to mourn the dead; compassion could only be afforded the living. 'I never wish to see such a ragged, exhausted, battle-weary crowd of men'.[7] One Lieutenant came onboard, proudly moving under his own power until a sailor went to take him by the elbow, and the soldier recoiled with the request, 'Don't squeeze too hard, Jack' – his arm had been shot off.[8] When evacuees realised they were in an Australian ship their emotion was enough to rally the most tired crew member. *Perth* cooks worked tirelessly to ensure all were fed and supplied with hot coffee and cocoa, and sailors emptied their lockers so Australian soldiers were adequately clothed. A twist of fate would see the favour reciprocated in 1942.

—

With the latest batch of evacuees offloaded in Crete, *Perth* returned rapidly to the waters of southern Greece on a mercy mission to Kalamata to collect troops, political refugees and their wives and children. With meagre intelligence the cruiser and accompanying destroyers were closing in on the port when the operation was suddenly curtailed. The speed of the German advance ended any hope of further evacuations, 'all we could see was a blazing town'.[9] Crew felt helpless as they watched the fighting ashore intensify, and their ship turned away.[10] 'We were bitterly sorry for Greece. Greece was the most lovable place we ever went to in the Middle East',[11] Bandsman George Vanselow wrote.

For what seemed an eternity, the Australian cruiser was subjected to unrelenting aerial assault, with countless near misses. One crew member wrote home, 'the good ship *Perth* seems to have a patron saint watching over her'.[12] An AB known for his rough nature was seen to drop to his knees during a short lull and when asked what he was doing he replied, 'I'm praying! And I'm praying harder and faster than I ever have in my life'.[13] Members of the crew had been rattled during the Malta air raids, but in the midst of this April maelstrom, Malta seemed a distant and easier experience. On 24 April the onslaught continued, and, as aircraft released their fury, AB Cooper, said his prayers and made up his mind that his 'end would come very quick'. But it didn't, at least for *Perth*; the cruiser's 'Pusser's Duck' was not so fortunate.

On 28 April the Seagull took off on a dawn patrol across the 50-kilometre wide strait towards Antikithera and was soon attacked by German Dornier Light Bombers. PO Telegraphist Dan Bowden opened fire with the machine gun, whilst the pilot, Flight Lieut Beaumont, attempted to evade the enemy. Bowden had never anticipated shooting at enemy aircraft from a twisting, turning plane, when he had enlisted in the RAN as a Boy Seaman in 1925. How he progressed from that to this point was a bit of a blur for Bowden.[14] As Beaumont banked the aircraft one way then another, the men heard 'the explosive pops of the cannon shells above our engine noise as the shells hit and exploded'.[15] Flares caught fire and Bowden let go of the gun to hurl them from the aircraft. Together with the Observer, Sub Lieut Brian, Beaumont and Bowden gained confidence as the enemy planes 'frequently aborted their attack'.

Had they been battling one aircraft, it is possible their fortunes may have been better, but 'as we dodged one, the other was on us and I could see pieces flying off our tail and holes appearing in our aircraft'.[16] Eventually the starboard petrol tank took a shell, burst into flames and the Seagull plummeted to the water. The three had time only to grab a signal pistol and cartridges before abandoning the blazing aircraft for the rubber dinghy. They watched the hulk sink, as their dinghy drifted.

They had been fortunate. Bowden had only a broken bone in his hand and Beaumont, a grazed right wrist. During the afternoon they were picked up by a British warship.

Although the aircraft had been the brunt of many a disparaging comment from members of the *Perth*'s ship's company, its loss affected the crew, and they were relieved to hear those inside had escaped with minor injuries. It was difficult not to harbour some doubts that their luck might not be wearing a little thin after all, particularly when everyone was, 'physically and mentally worn out'.[17]

April was nearing its end, and *Perth* had now ventured 9463 miles (15,225 kilometres) and spent 26 days at sea. She had lost one crew member, and the Pusser's Duck was no more.

—

By the beginning of 1941, Alexandria provided a brief reprieve, a welcome 'break from routine',[18] except that with the city itself under attack from the air, there was 'no rest anywhere now'.[19] This sometimes induced a reluctance to go ashore. Chief EA Reg Whiting remained onboard, complete in the enjoyment of mail, 'parcels, books, papers and eats, what manna from heaven'.[20] Seafarers felt safest in their own ship. Non-seafarers failed to understand, particularly given the recent onslaught *Perth* had suffered, and perhaps the emotions were not always clear to the seafarer either. However, this was more than just a ship, more than just a place of duty, this ship was home and provided its own sense of self, of comfort. To the crew, land felt foreign. There were, though, disadvantages to being in harbour; at sea they were a moving target and could quickly alter the angle of guns for the best defence. Fortunately this particular ship had given them a degree of safety, defying the law of averages in the mayhem of the last months.

Shore leave did offer indulgences, excitement and hazards, and living on the edge tempted men to cast caution and inhibitions to the wind. The Fleet Club, with its sawdust floor and good beer, was a favourite haunt. AB Cooper admitted he 'got drunk' whenever he got ashore. He was not alone; it seemed the best remedy for obliterating the fear and sense of foreboding, for a short time at least.

Visiting brothels was another way of coping. For some, the lack of normal relationships was justification enough. For others, having a first sexual encounter in a brothel was justified by the war and their treacherous service conditions. However, such sexual adventure came with consequences. During the quarter ending 30 June 1941, 29 members of Perth's ship's company were treated for venereal disease. Such a diagnosis brought penalties: apart from the physical discomfort, it had a degree of stigma attached and, in the RAN, acquiring VD was a chargeable offence. The afflicted soon found that he faced financial retribution, the size of which was calculated on his pay. Leniency could be given if the sailor was young and it was believed he had been led astray; blatant disregard resulted in the opposite. In the case of one AB first-time offender who was fined 9 shillings (daily pay was 7 shillings), when he again visited an Egyptian brothel and suffered a second dose of VD, another charge was filed on his service record and he was fined £3/3/-. Official *Perth* records do not indicate if any officers were plagued with such an aliment, but this does not mean they did not suffer it, only that it wasn't noted.

Drunkenness often led to other offences. Twenty-year-old Stoker Alf Hansen had not learnt from his 28-day detention for recalcitrant shore behaviour the previous November, and in April he was sentenced to a further 42 days detention. AB Richard Killalea was given 14 days cells for repeatedly being absent without leave. Other members of the ship's company faced reprimand, stoppage of pay, reduction in conduct and extra duty for becoming involved in altercations ashore.

Lack of understanding between sailors and non-sailors was not unusual, and in Alexandria the situation was exacerbated by frayed nerves and alcohol. Australian sailors would not tolerate disparaging assertions from soldiers about the 'pampered lives' they led, particularly from English soldiers. A stoker wrote, 'these kipper soldiers couldn't fight my girl, I don't know where England would be today if it wasn't for the dominion troops'.[21] It was not uncommon for a member of the ship's company to return dishevelled and sporting facial lacerations. There had always been rivalry between soldiers and sailors, and they would compare their combat service. Soldiers taunted sailors on what they perceived as a lack of service hardship and used the differences in the numbers of army and navy war injured as a basis for their argument. They failed to appreciate that the injured were less likely to survive a sinking ship.

During this brief interlude ashore, RAN ranks were strengthened by the arrival of Australian destroyers *Nizam* and *Napier*. It was great to catch up with more RAN operatives, even if the men could not answer their questions about war service in the Med honestly – it needed to be witnessed first hand.

—

Where April had seen the loss of Greece, the Battle for Crete started in May. When those in *Perth* thought it couldn't get worse, it got worse. When they believed it was impossible for the assault from the air to intensify, it did. Patrols and protection of convoys to re-enforce Crete defences took much of the month. Duty was almost mundane; enemy aircraft were sighted, guns offered their barrage, Captain Bowyer-Smyth issued rapid course and speed changes – bombs evaded. The episode was repeated again and again. Gunnery Officer Warwick Bracegirdle observed how his Captain developed with the Navigator, Lieut Gerard Talbot-Smith, 'a very cunning ruse during air attacks. Of never keeping the ship steady on the one course, but just weaving a little', thus ensuring dive bombers did not have a straight wake to aim for.[22] There was still opportunity to appreciate the 'formidable array of sea power' the Mediterranean Fleet presented, the 'magnificent panorama of ships spread across from horizon to horizon. The sensation of 'pride, power and confidence one gets … is amazing'[23] wrote AB Jim Nelson. What was harder to accept was that the Allied fleet was diminishing, each day another ship and its men ceased to exist.

On 20 May *Perth* was ordered to take up position off northern Crete. Seamen knew the waters as 'E-Boat alley' and within three hours the Australian cruiser withstood attacks from several submarines. Further torment came from above and the night was another spent closed up, attempting to repel superior forces. During the morning of 21 May, destroyers from the 1st Battle Squadron steamed to the Kithera

Channel to support *Perth,* which one RN officer observed to be 'under heavy air attack'.[24] Some 1330 German aircraft took part in the Battle of Crete, and the Australian ship suffered many near misses during air strikes, which came at 0830, 1000, 1020, 1035, 1050, 1115, 1230 and 1300. The destroyer HMS *Juno* steaming alongside was hit amidships; it took but a minute and a half to disappear. *Perth* needed to stay under power to avoid the same demise. There could be no stopping to save *Juno* survivors, who bobbed with the flotsam in the inhospitable waters, 'It was horrible ... there was nothing we could do ... fighting for our own survival ... I can not find words to express my feelings of horror at the carnage',[25] wrote AB Nelson. The horror turned to anger as enemy aircraft machine gunned the hapless survivors. There was no relief: 'It is dark now but there is no rest for the weary as we are to remain closed up all night', wrote Don Kirkmoe.

On 22 May *Perth* was part of the naval force despatched to the waters north of Crete, to prevent German seaborne troops reinforcing their paratroopers who had landed in Crete. The Australian crew and their cruiser were subjected to unrelenting air assault for thirteen hours. As one caique came under fire from *Perth*, German troops ran up a white flag and began climbing into them; but no quarter could be given. Although the Allied squadron sank many caiques, without fighter protection Allied ships and those who manned them were completely at the mercy of overwhelming attack from the air: 'The sky was swarming with planes, they droned overhead like a nest of angry bees'.[26] At one point seventeen JU87 aircraft circled above before peeling off, then diving down with their characteristic high-pitched scream as they released their bombs, bombs too numerous to count. It was a scream that would reverberate in the consciousness of *Perth* veterans forever. Crew in the Director Tower, some 60 feet (18 metres) above water level, were at times thigh deep in water, from waterspouts created by bombs hitting the ocean.

With 4-inch, Pom Pom and Breda ammunition expended, squads of sailors with Lee Enfield .303 rifles hunkered down on the upper deck, firing at will using colour tracers mixed in with normal bullets. The colourful pattern flaring into the sky confused pilots, and they eventually broke off their attack but not before three Stukas flew across *Perth*'s quarterdeck, machine guns blazing. Five of *Perth*'s crew suffered minor injuries. One *Perth* Officer felt it curious that the experience seemed worse in hindsight: 'my nerves seemed numb while the attacks were on. I felt like a spectator rather than a participant'.[27]

Late in the day HMS *Greyhound* was struck aft and the magazine blew up. When the smoke cleared the warship was lying on its side and swiftly sinking. HMS *Warspite* was aflame, the Allied fleet withdrew, Crete was lost.[28] *Perth* had again been fortunate. Bomb splinters and bullets scarred the superstructure and so too its ensign. Wireless aerials had been blown off; machine cannon holes punctured the main mast; degaussing gear was damaged and other parts of the ship were now marked and holed. But the ship had not been set alight, and that meant Leading Stoker 'Bluey' Larmer, a member of the infamous Malta Fire Party, had been able to sit coolly on a hatch and read his book throughout the action. Others hanging on for grim death shook their heads and wondered if 'Bluey' was insane or just very brave. Captain Bowyer-Smyth remarked, 'It was the liveliest day I have ever spent and I do not particularly want to repeat it'.[29] His crew fully realised that but for the skill of their Captain who manoeuvred the cruiser as if it was a destroyer, their fate would have been different. 'He is a man loved by all our crew, we will follow him anywhere for he has our full confidence'[30] wrote AB Jim Nelson. His cruiser retreated to Alexandria for hasty repairs. The 4-inch gun barrels were worn out and needed to be replaced. The city's harbour was looking more and more forlorn each time *Perth* returned. The waters increasingly littered with ships with 'their bows or sterns blown off, or half sunken',[31] stark reminders of what they had once proudly been; the vacant moorings, stark reminders of ships and men that would not return.

—

On 29 May Captain Bowyer-Smyth addressed his crew. He warned them the mission they were about to undertake would be very dangerous and wished them 'Good Luck'. Whilst his officers and sailors appreciated the honesty and sentiment delivered by a Captain they trusted and admired, they would never shirk the responsibility of rescuing Allied troops from a lost campaign. It was with a sense of deja vu that the cruiser and crew left port for a perilous rendezvous with a spent military force. Under the cover of darkness, *Perth* and HM Ships *Phoebe* and *Glengyle* anchored and embarked exhausted and ill men. Boats hurriedly ferried soldiers from shore to ship. Some evacuees, anxious to escape Crete's beaches, swam to *Perth* and sailors hauled them up scrambling nets. Wounded were brought aboard on stretchers to be tended by the ship's medical parties, the relief visible in their dark, hollow faces. Sixteen-year-old Canteen Assistant Alf Hawkins was a stretcher bearer. Each time he and another ferried an injured soldier down to sick bay, he would return topside to find more and more waiting. Chief ERA Reg Whiting observed a 'pitiful scene as the second generation of Anzacs, ragged, weary and hungry' boarded.[32]

As enemy planes dropped flares to illuminate the Allied ships, *Perth* weighed anchor and set course for Alexandria with an additional 1200 souls onboard, occupying every deck space. The majority were New Zealanders, and this seemed to further validate the inherent dangers of this mission. It was an unusual pact Australians shared with New Zealanders. Mostly it was a relationship born of fierce rivalry, but should another nationality threaten or deride one, they would face the wrath of the other. Both these nationalities were born of similar ilk, developed under the same limitations of a tyranny of distance, transposed cultures struggling to comfortably align with very different indigenous populations. Perhaps it was simply a bond forged again in 1941 as it had been in 1915, between military and naval forces from the Antipodes placed in jeopardy by higher authority from another hemisphere. During the small hours of 30 May the New Zealanders were given gentle treatment, crew not closed up rallied around to ensure their visitors were given food and drink, and again sailors rummaged through their lockers to make certain soldiers were adequately clothed and sheltered.

At 0800 German dive bombers arrived and commenced their attacks. At 0935 a 1000-pound bomb, from a high level JU88 bomber, landed behind *Perth*'s bridge, at the base of the foremast. Those on the bridge were just breathing a sigh of relief as their ship had dodged a stick of bombs, when one that did not drop with the rest smashed through the upper-deck blacksmith shop, then the galley and exploded in the 'A' Boiler Room. The crows nest lookout on the masthead heard the scream of the bomb during its rapid descent and felt its heat as it destroyed the Directional Finding equipment fastened to the mast. The speed of events left him helplessly suspended 140 feet (43 metres) above sea level. Whereas his normal view of the ship was that it resembled 'a long, thin cigar', on 30 May he watched the explosion below, then smoke obliterated the ship. Terrified he, 'momentarily likened himself to a witch riding a broomstick' and wondered if *Perth* remained beneath him.[33]

PO Roy Norris was working in the galley with three other cooks. He raised his head when the bomb hit and asked Leading Cook Bill Fraser, 'What was that?' The 23-year-old Fraser who had escaped a career in the coal mines of Lithgow, New South Wales, to join the RAN and become a member of *Perth*'s commissioning crew, replied it was just likely reverberation from the 4-inch guns. Norris was unconvinced, 'like hell that sounds like a bomb to me'. He turned and walked away, intent on donning his anti-flash gear. A blinding flash and explosion stunned him. As the lights went out, the space was filled with steam and dust. Soldiers in the vicinity panicked, causing Norris to react with a 'fierce rage'. He was none too gentle this time with the stampeding troops, then finally was able to communicate with the engine room to switch off the steam to the galley. Re-entering the galley he found a mass of twisted debris and Cook Noel Smith, the nineteen-year-old former station hand from Orange, New South Wales, who had unceremoniously arrived onboard *Perth* the previous month with 52 bags of mail. It was clear to Norris the young Cook was dead. Norris saw Fraser underneath the wreckage, 'a mass of mangled flesh but still breathing and smothered in oil fuel'. He died shortly after. There was initially no sign of Cook Brown; he had been blown out of the galley, and sustained a head injury and leg wound.[34]

Newly made up Stoker Syd Triffitt was at the steam pipe position in the forward engine room. Since he and his Stoker classmates, Gordon

Steele and Harry Smith, had enlisted less than a year earlier, their world had been turned upside down. There was no 'normal' anymore: 'There was a dull boom and Leading Stoker John Poulter said to 'Dolly' Gray, "I have lost my steam"'.[35] Gray replied almost laconically, 'We have been hit'. Triffitt and Poulter diverted the steam to slow turn the forward screws, 'otherwise they would have acted like an anchor'.

The scene in 'A' boiler room was no less chaotic. All hell had broken loose, first with the noise of the bomb, then the bomb had burst and the main boiler steam pipe had erupted, enveloping the boiler room in scalding steam, and everything had gone black. Stoker 2nd Class Harry Smith was a member of the large October *Perth* intake. In the RAN less than a year, the dark curly-haired Smith had heard the command to leave the boiler room, but confused by the noise, steam and darkness, he had rushed to the starboard instead of the port ladder and died in a fury of steam. The 20-year-old Smith had been using his navy wage to support his mother May, back in Melbourne. On 1 June, May Smith received the news she dreaded most, Harry had been 'Killed at sea by enemy action, direct bomb hit 30 May'.[36] In time she would receive a War Gratuity payment of £71/5/- and £6/11/3 in lieu of leave Harry had been unable to take. May Smith was left to ponder the awkwardly delivered, sympathetic platitudes and how the sum of £76/16/3 was assessed to be the value of her son's life.

Acting Warrant Mechanician Henry Hill, a native of Devonport, England, had drafted in just seven weeks before, joining *Perth* the same day as young Cook Noel Smith. He had had no opportunity to familiarise himself in a timely manner with his duties as officer in charge of the forward damage control headquarters. Then, as now, he had hit the deck running, and when he reached the forward boiler room and wrenched open the watertight door he found Stoker PO Bill Reece trying to quell the panic of junior stokers and evacuate the area as quickly as possible. Hill and Reece removed two scalded stokers and set about turning off steam valves and isolating the boiler. The two senior men then returned to the black, steam-filled space to look for the missing man. They could see him on a grating beneath the fractured steam line and suffered burns themselves to retrieve the badly scalded body of Harry Smith. Bill Reece, his 5ft 4 frame toughened by hard physical work as a Stoker in coal-burning ships, was a recruiting-poster sailor and member of *Perth*'s forwarding commissioning party. For these acts Henry Hill would be awarded a Distinguished Service Cross for his 'outstanding gallantry, fortitude and resolution and for coolness and determination in dealing with a difficult situation', and Reece would be awarded a Distinguished Service Medal for 'outstanding gallantry, fortitude and resolution'. Lieut Cdr Eric Tymms struggled to keep up with the badly injured. Tymms was born in the Queensland town of Rockhampton. He was a diligent student and left the town of his birth to become a doctor. He had joined the RAN as a Surgeon Lieutenant in 1935. After serving on two very different ships, the Kent class cruiser *Canberra* and the Grimsby class sloop *Swan*, he joined *Perth* just prior to the cruiser's deployment to the Med and was promoted to Surgeon Lieutenant Commander in January 1941. He continued tending injuries through the day and night despite his own fatigue and for this would be awarded a DSC, for 'untiring energy and conspicuous devotion of duty in his care of wounded'.

Chief Cook Bob Bland had been mentioned in despatches during the Greek campaign for working 'untiringly and cheerfully' throughout the night, ensuring all evacuees were well fed. During the Crete campaign he supervised the restoration of the bomb-damaged main ship galley and rallied the remaining cooks to provide evacuees and crew alike with hot food. For his 'zeal, patience and cheerfulness' he was awarded the BEM. This man who considered himself an ordinary member of the RAN just doing his duty, would be mentioned in despatches again in another year, in another region of the world, when 'just doing his duty' directly resulted in saving the lives of *Perth* crew. War led to ordinary men performing less than ordinary deeds.

Blacksmith Alfred 'Sandy' Saunders was one of the injured, but he felt grateful his injuries were slight. He was working in the blacksmith's shop, busy with hammers, tongs and fire, when the bomb tore through the structure and continued downwards. His shock was worse than his burns. For some members of the fire and repair party it was the first time they had seen what a blast could do to human bodies; bodies so mutilated they were beyond recognition. Stoker Norm King and Leading Stoker 'Bluey' Larmer carried bodies to a location near the gangway, there were four sailors and nine troops. King was dazed, having himself suffered a slight concussion and superficial wounds from bomb splinters. He and his mate Stoker Henry 'Bluey' Straker had been on the upper deck nervously puffing on cigarettes, watching their ship dodge and weave in action. Straker was the bloke who had grown up in Lake Macquarie, New South Wales, watching the boats entering the lake from the ocean. Joining the navy seemed second nature. When the bomb hit Perth, 'Henry was standing alongside an access ladder. He took the full blast, it pushed him through the rungs of the ladder',[37] King recalled. Straker was killed.

The death and damage caused by the bomb was bad, but it could have been worse, it could always be worse. Bowyer-Smith later apologised to the crew, 'Sorry boys, I never saw it coming'. When the aerial assault finally abated, AB Jim Nelson and AB Alex Creasy were delegated to prepare the bodies for evening burial. They stitched them in canvas and weighted each at the feet to ensure those who were once men would plunge to the depths. The quarterdeck was full that evening, crew and troops gathered beneath a 'crescent moon', which highlighted the cruiser's 'zig zag wake of phosphorescence'.[38] Syd Triffitt later reflected on a conversation he had with Harry Smith as they watched the Australian mainland disappear just half a year earlier 'I said, "it will be a long time before we see that again". Harry replied, "I will never see it again Syd". I poo-pooed his remark and said, "Mate, we are going on a great adventure, not a death run". How wrong I was.'[39] As Chaplain Ron Bevington concluded the service and the bodies were committed to the sea, it fell to Duty Bugler Nelson, to play the Last Post and Reveille. Nelson struggled to raise a note, then closed his eyes and played 'as I had never played before. Every feeling in my body went through that instrument. I made the strident bugle tones as mellow and sweet as I could'.[40] Norm King, struggling to reconcile his shipmate's larger than life personality with the simple, rapid naval burial wrote, 'My mate Henry Straker didn't rate more than a canvas bag'.

The horror was not yet over for Nelson. The following day he and AB Creasy were detailed to clean the starboard well deck after engineers had cleared some of the wreckage: 'Hosing down the deck under the loading simulator I washed out a head. It was a friend of mine ... I am only nineteen years old! What is expected of me? How much more can I give?' All the bodies had not been committed to the depths in their entirety the previous evening. Too many young men like Jim Nelson were being asked to witness things no one should. During such grim times younger men often challenged themselves on what they believed were shortcomings in their 'moral fibre'. They looked to older men to offer leadership and testament that they too would become stronger and capable of undertaking the seemingly impossible duties they were being called upon to perform. Nelson looked up to men like Creasy, who he observed going about these most demanding duties in a seemingly 'well controlled manner'. Youngsters like Nelson failed to appreciate that older men too were struggling with these terrible days. AB Alex Creasy was 38 years old, a man of ten years' RAN service on *Australia*, *Tattoo*, *Vampire*, *Waterhen*, *Vendetta*, *Brisbane* and *Sydney*. He had been one of the *Perth*'s commissioning crew, but Creasy had never endured combat prior to the Med, and he too doubted his own fortitude. As soon as *Perth* returned to Australia, AB Alexander Creasy left the ship and never returned. His service card was marked 'RUN' (desertion) and later when RAN investigations failed to discover his whereabouts, it was marked, 'not to be claimed for further service'. Undoubtedly, wherever he was and for however long he was there, Creasy would continue to harbour doubts about his own 'moral fibre'.

—

The Mediterranean campaign exacted a heavy toll. During May alone some 2000 naval officers and sailors were killed. Regardless of the Herculean efforts of ship crews, operations in the Med further underlined the vulnerability of thinly armoured ships to aerial attack. HM cruisers *Fiji* and *Gloucester* and destroyers *Kelly*, *Kashmir*, *Juno*, *Greyhound*, *Hereward* and *Imperial* were sunk; *Kipling* was holed, the battleship *Warspite* damaged, the cruisers *Carlisle*, *Ajax*, *Dido* and

Niad in need of urgent repairs, and *Orion* hit with 260 of its crew killed and another 280 wounded. Admiral Cunningham made no secret of the reason for the costly campaign, 'In my opinion three squadrons of long-range fighters and a few heavy bomber squadrons would have saved Crete'.[41] Those who had suffered the ridiculous odds concurred, Chief EA Reg Whiting, believed 'You cannot fight against dive bombers'. It was beyond his comprehension how *Perth* and those onboard survived the 30 May attack, 'God is with us. I am feeling very forlorn and like everyone else, just about done in'.[42] Admiral Cunningham advised Britain's Prime Minister Winston Churchill that his decimated fleet was no longer capable of major exercise.

With the cruiser secured at No.46 shed on the Alexandria dock, an additional 25 ERAs boarded to assess and commence repairs. It would be a lengthy period. For those members of the crew not involved in maintenance, it was time for replenishment of the body even if the mind continued to struggle. AB Cooper confided to his diary, 'when you see ships with boys on you know blown to the bottom, well it makes you think what it is all about'. He had watched flesh and bone reduced to nothing and was revolted at what he saw: 'God will I ever forget it as long as I live?' Air raids continued in the Alexandria area, killing hundreds of civilians and military personnel. It was difficult to find humour in the situation, but when bombs fell on the brothel district, sailors wondered if military clientele who died would be listed as 'killed in action'.

—

The original estimate of a fortnight for repairs extended again and again. Finally on 24 June *Perth* was ready for departure. Rumours circulated between decks that the ship was returning home. The men were overjoyed. Their duty in the Mediterranean had been physically and emotionally taxing, it was time to go home. Another rumour circulating concerned their Captain. He was highly regarded by most, but some believed he wished to delay the departure of *Perth* for home waters in the hope that he and his ship could achieve greater glory. Bandsman George Vanselow penned a poem:

When 'Cappy' all excited like
Came rushing through the door
The Admiral nice and friendly, sez
'You'll soon see Sydney's shore'.
'Like Hell I will' the Capt'n says
'You can't do this to me!
I'm Blood and Thunder Bowyang-Smith
In search of Victoree'.
'Oh Andy, Please! Just one more chance
To win my way to fame!
What Sydney's done so we can do
To vindicate our name'.
The Admiral's eyes were moist with tears
His voice began to falter
He hunted fleet's appointments up
To see what he could do –
'Ah Bowyang lad! Here's just the job
To suit you through and through.
You'll land some troops not far from here
To snatch an Isle from Rome
And then I'll wash my hands of you
Because you MUST GO HOME!'

So the ship sailed to Haifa, Palestine, to take part in the Syrian campaign. The campaign against the Vichy French emplacements in the Wadi Damour region commenced on 8 June, so the bombardment routine was well rehearsed by the time *Perth* arrived on 25 June. For five nights the guns of the Australian cruiser joined others in a symphony of light and noise, unlikely to be enjoyed by enemy troops ashore.

Perth returned to Haifa on the evening of Saturday 28 June. The following day Warrant Supply Officer Claude Woodley had a good and a bad experience. The crew of a RN destroyer was evacuated from their ship due to mines. *Perth* was required to billet them for the day and Woodley ensured there were enough stores readily available. The 40-year-old Woodley was born in Torquay, England, but now called

Australia home. He enjoyed catching up with 'RNers' and was pleased when they highly praised the meals they were given, 'they reckoned they had joined the wrong Navy'.[43] That was the pleasant experience. The opposite was when an order of onions arrived. An error in translation resulted in the delivery of three ton, an entire barge-load of onions. Many sarcastic comments followed in the ensuing weeks as cooks endeavoured to come up with a hundred and one different ways to serve an onion.

More serious than onion overload were attacks from the sky. With the surrender of the Vichy French imminent, German aircraft defiantly dropped bombs and mines; one of the worst assaults came on 8 July. However, by the middle week of July, the crew was buoyed not only by the knowledge that the campaign was nearing its end and they had again acquitted themselves admirably, but also by the knowledge HMAS *Hobart* would shortly assume *Perth*'s duties. They would indeed soon be on their way home. The young men, who had sailed from Australia confident and cocky, were changed by their war service. AB James Nelson believed he and his three closest shipmates were 'no longer the fun-loving four that arrived on station five months ago. We have aged and grown up prematurely into men'.[44] The stress had taken its toll. A number of sailors deserted ship in Alexandria and began to make their way south by any means they could. They had suffered enough of this war and hoped they would find a ship willing to take them back to Australia. Caught by authorities and returned to *Perth*, Bowyer-Smyth was under no doubt that they had 'deserted in the face of enemy fire', and Admiralty regulations called for the maximum punishment, death. He refused to administer such a penalty; he too had been subjected to the harrowing Mediterranean war experience and these young Australians deserved sympathetic consideration.

John Kirkmoe served with the 2/10th Battalion. On leave he was walking around Haifa with AIF mates when another soldier told him he had met his younger brother from *Perth*. John was delighted and approached any Aussie sailors he saw. Cap bands were no longer emblazoned with the ship's name as they had been in the first days of the war, but he finally found a *Perth* sailor who took him to the dockyard gates and went to collect Don. Donald Kirkmoe, a Stoker 3rd Class was likely the youngest member of the *Perth* crew when he had joined in May 1940. Enlisting at the age of 16, the former messenger boy from South Australia could not wait to join the war effort. The four Kirkmoe boys had grown up imbued with the military tradition and believed 'Gallipoli must be the most famous place in the world'.[45] Their father, Julius, was a Gallipoli veteran. He spoke little of the campaign or World War I, but Australian folklore had promoted Gallipoli to iconic status. Consequently war appeared like a big adventure where boys proved themselves men, and young Don had been captivated. Given his brothers were in the army, his choice of the navy was not so much due to a love of the ocean as to the fact that he could join at an earlier age. He was pleased to be drafted to *Perth* in time for the ship's deployment to the Mediterranean. The reality of war had blown away any visions of a glorious adventure.

When his brother John appeared, Don was granted leave and the brothers spent a 'wonderful day' together. There was something surreal in two Aussie teenagers from quiet, suburban Adelaide, meeting up across the world in such a foreign environment. John Kirkmoe was delighted for the opportunity, but while they talked he realised Don 'was visibly shaken by the actions that they had been through'. The brothers had their photograph taken together and Don's eyes appeared haunted. John was concerned by the eighteen year old's transformation and hoped that when *Perth* returned to Australian waters Don would be posted to a 'somewhat less stressful area'. When they shook hands and parted John, 'stood and watched him until he disappeared from my sight, and I had a strong premonition that I would never see him again'.[46]

Men waited impatiently for the time when their cruiser would cast off and start the trip home, then they heard that *Perth* would depart on 14 July. Words could not express the sense of relief felt, but for 120 of the crew the next news was depressing. They were to replace men on RAN destroyers serving in the Med; they would not return to Australia. Torpedoman Basil Hayler, 'did all I could to remain on *Perth* because she was a proud and happy ship', but instead he joined HMAS

Stuart then *Nizam*.[47] Recently promoted sailors were the most likely to be drafted, no sooner did they celebrate their promotion than they faced the knowledge of remaining part of the Mediterranean campaign. Some of the more desperate convinced another of the same rating and rank to exchange drafts, but the unofficial incentive was £50 and few sailors could afford such a princely sum. AB James Cooper was very relieved he was not included in the draft and would return home, but suffering from 'Chronic Bronchitis' and 'Anxiety' he struggled with his health. Cooper served in *Deloraine* and *Toowoomba* between periods of hospitalisation, until he was discharged 'Permanently Unfit for Naval Service (PUNS)' on 11 January 1944.

Norm King, now a Leading Stoker, was one of the *Autolycus* contingent. He had spent a great deal of time out of Australian waters since May 1939. He had grumbled about *Autolycus* accommodation and was unhappy about going to one of the 'Scrap Iron Flotilla' destroyers. His war service continued with a draft to *Nizam,* by which time he was an Acting Stoker PO. By the end of the war he had also served on *Quiberon, Arunta, Burdekin, Norman* and *Queenborough*. King was typical of so many of the permanent RAN lower deck, someone who complained about his officers, his ship, his conditions of service and his shipmates, but would have it no other way. He chose to remain in the RAN after the war and transferred to the Mechanician branch, the navy was all he had known and he would be lost without it. Unfortunately, his war service left its mark and he was troubled by anxiety. After a number of medical surveys citing 'nervous disorder' he transferred to the RAFR in 1956. But in July 1941, after a testing six months, he could be forgiven for grumbling about not going home. Shipmate PO Roy Norris wrote, 'I don't think I could stick it if I had to remain behind now'.[48] Stoker Vic Brand was drafted to *Waterhen*. If he felt disturbed he could not admit relief when *Waterhen* was sunk with no loss of crew on 30 June. Brand would return to Australia after all.

By the morning of 15 July *Perth* had returned to Alexandria and drafted crew members left the ship to take up other Mediterranean duties. News of more drafts arrived, 'making all hands quiver nervously'[49] and encouraged further rumours that *Perth* would now not return to Australia. When they had expected to be of high spirits, crew members were now plagued with rumours by day and air raids by night. Syd Triffitt was not going home, nor Gordon Steele. The Stoker classmates whose service cards could be so easily confused, found the tradition was to be continued and they were drafted to *Stuart*, but at least they were still alive. Harry Smith wasn't. Another twist for Triffitt came when *Stuart* returned to Australia and he was working in the engine room during the destroyer's six-month refit in Melbourne. An older dockyard fitter working alongside asked if he knew any *Perth* sailors. The man was 'Harry's father. Poor old chap ... he broke down and told us how his great loss broke his heart'.[50]

By choice, the navigator Lieut Gerard Talbot-Smith, a native of Surrey, England, was replaced by another RN officer, Lieut John Alexander Harper. Harper wanted to marry a girl named Irma and she was in Australia. The RN permitted the exchange, and Harper married his girl on 27 August in Melbourne. Probationary Sub Lieut John Martin, RANVR, joined. Born in Western Australia, Martin had been mobilised as a sailor at the beginning of September 1939. He was commissioned on 4 February 1941 and sent to the Mediterranean to join *Swan*. He too was glad to be returning to Australia.

—

On Thursday 17 July a cheer rippled through the ship. Men below decks scrambled topside to see what the excitement was about, then joined in the shouting as they saw the most wonderful sight, HMAS *Hobart* steaming up the channel. It felt even better when *Perth*'s Breda guns were removed and installed on *Hobart*.

The following morning *Perth* slipped out of Alexandria for the last time. Captain Bowyer-Smyth addressed the crew. Whilst it was still officially 'secret' information, the ship was indeed returning to Australia and the message from Admiral Cunningham was: 'I am very sorry to lose *Perth* from the Station. She has been with us during most stirring times and goes home with a proud record of good work, well done. I wish you a safe passage and a very happy homecoming'. The sentiment was well received and crew members hoped a sense of achievement would eventually replace the more nervous sense they felt now. With relief they watched each major landmark pass. They managed to traverse the Suez Canal, and the cruiser reached the Red Sea. Nonetheless, capricious weather still troubled the ship. Crossing the Arabian Sea was rough and the heat extreme. As boiler and engine rooms heated up to 130° Fahrenheit (54° Celsius), men went into convulsions for lack of salt and calcium, and eight stokers collapsed. Commander Robert 'Dolly' Gray had ordered them to take a spoonful of salt every half hour, but after what they had been through, young stokers believed they were invincible and that the order was not intended for them, until they suffered the effects of heat stroke. Gray could well be excused for being exhausted. It seemed an eternity since he had joined the cruiser. He would be awarded a DSO for, 'bravery and enterprise when engaged by superior forces', and for, 'cheerful resolution and his exceptional powers of leadership coupled with outstanding technical ability'.

On arriving in Aden on 24 July, the crew was surprised to see the heavy Kent class cruiser, HMAS *Australia*. Mooring astern the larger ship offered opportunity for welcome interaction of personnel. Prior to leaving Alexandria, crew members of *Waterhen* boarded *Perth* to hitch a ride home. One of these was Surgeon Lieut Samuel Stening. It had been a strange adventure for the paediatrician. Named after his maternal grandfather, Samuel Edward Lees, the second Lord Mayor of Sydney, he was one of four brothers, all medical practitioners by decision of their mother, Muriel Stening. Malcolm and George were gynaecologist/obstetricians. George had joined the army. Also serving in the army was Warwick, an orthopaedic surgeon, who in 1941, was Medical Officer to the 7th Division Engineers in the Middle East. Malcolm Stening had chosen the navy because he thought the army would require him to march a lot more and he did not fancy marching. He travelled to England for post-graduate study, then war broke out. Wearing his RANR uniform Malcolm reported to the Admiralty in London. Being totally unfamiliar with the RAN Reserve, Admiralty officials appointed him an RN Medical Officer. Soon afterwards HMAS *Australia* arrived in Liverpool for refuelling and stores; Malcolm went onboard and was swiftly reclaimed. He received news his older brother Samuel had also joined the Australian Navy.

Initially Sam Stening had been a Medical Officer attached to Naval Recruiting. The RAN became concerned with how many recruits were being declared 'unsuitable for naval service' due to colour blindness. They tested their Medical Officer and found that it was he who was colour blind. Samuel was quickly posted out of Naval Recruiting, to be Medical Officer in *Waterhen*. By the time *Australia* arrived at the port of Aden, *Waterhen* had sunk, and Malcolm was concerned for his brother's wellbeing. On the afternoon of 23 July 1941, *Perth* tied up astern of *Australia* in Aden, and Malcolm was informed an officer from *Perth* had arrived onboard on an important mission. It turned out to be Sam. The brothers were delighted to catch up before Sam returned to his new ship, *Perth,* having completed his mission to trade a quantity of 'liberated' Italian Chianti for beer.

On 25 July *Perth* was at sea and steamed out of the 'war zone', Don Kirkmoe wrote: 'Everyone is now happy but everyone thinks of our shipmates who are now lying at the bottom of the Mediterranean Sea'. Without further incident the crew and the cruiser continued on their journey south. Two days in Colombo did not seem to go by quickly enough, although the rain from tropical storms refreshed souls parched by the Middle East, and the non-blackout city with its bright lights, 'put everybody in the best of spirits'.[51]

The closer the cruiser got to Australia, the better the weather became. By August they were muttering about the cold, but with the radio shack now tuned to Australian radio stations, the sounds of Australian voices and news were joyous to the ear. The mood was lightened further by the unique brilliance of the Southern Cross. The sense of anticipation was intense and *Perth*'s sailors tried to keep occupied, preparing their kit for leave. Those onboard owning cameras, who plied their latest snaps for 3d each throughout the deployment, did a brisk trade. Those who could afford £10 had opportunity to purchase a watercolour of their ship from the talented artist who was also Captain of the Foretop, PO Ray Parkin. Captain Bowyer-Smyth again addressed his crew, acknowledging the remarkable feats of the previous half a year. He assured them he would do his utmost to retain the crew intact. It would be an empty promise, and some present were unsure they wished to remain if the ship was to be redeployed overseas. Nonetheless, they took it as it was intended, as a vote of confidence. In a most benevolent gesture, *Perth*'s Captain restored all members of the ship's company, regardless of misdemeanour to full leave privileges.[52] This was a far cry from Bowyer-Smyth's predecessor who had ensured an unprecedented number of punishments remained noted against members of *Perth*'s ship's company, when the ship had returned from the Caribbean.

—

AB Jim Nelson turned twenty on 6 August 1941, and he could think of no better present than being able to set foot on Australian soil again, which he did as the ship berthed in Fremantle. No one was on the dockyard to herald the ship's arrival, as no one was aware the crew and cruiser were due. Startled West Australian families rejoiced as officers and sailors simply arrived. Families on the East Coast were equally overjoyed to receive telephone calls and telegrams that their loved ones were on the way. *Perth* cast off 24 hours later; as unheralded as the ship's arrival had been, so too was the ship's departure. The Great Australian Bight lived up to its reputation as one of the roughest strips of water RAN ships commonly encountered. Crew members became ill, stopped eating and wondered if seasickness or excitement were the cause of churning stomachs.

About this time a signal appeared on the notice board. Volunteers were needed for 'dangerous and hazardous missions in small boats'. AB Jim Nelson figured he had seen some pretty hazardous missions on a large ship, so he volunteered for something smaller. Nelson was accepted into the elite Services Reconnaissance Division of the combat force of 'Z' Special Unit. He would participate in a number of covert operations to insert and retrieve allied personnel from Japanese-occupied territory. In 1943 he was involved in the *Krait* 'Z' raid on Singapore, codenamed 'Jaywick', as well as subsequent dangerous missions. Nelson left the RAN as a much decorated PO.[53]

As *Perth* steamed up the Australian East Coast, the Captain decided the ship looked rather battle scarred and should have a coat of paint. Sailors muttered something about 'bull shit', but set about painting the cruiser in record time. On 12 August *Perth* moored to No.1 buoy Farm Cove, Sydney Harbour, and 'Liberty Men Ashore' was piped, but then delayed. Families crammed on the wharf, craned to see the familiar face within the sea of uniforms manning guardrails, and wondered the cause of the delay. The Prime Minister, Sir Robert Menzies, had decided he would come onboard to welcome the crew home. He was also running about an hour late. When he finally arrived he launched into a lengthy speech. This was clearly a ridiculous and unpopular situation, and a chant rose from within the ship's company, 'What about liberty?' Realising the wisest course of action was to curtail his oration before he was shouted down or worse, Menzies acquiesced.

The cruiser was greatly in need of an extensive refit, as were the crew. *Perth* officers and sailors desperately needed to enjoy the creature comforts those left behind continued to take for granted. They needed the opportunity to return to familiar surroundings, to be able to walk as far as they cared in their own country. They needed time for personal affirmation, to try to make sense of the last half year: 'nearly everyone felt the effects of ragged nerves ... in fact I still marvel at being alive',[54] wrote George Vanselow. They needed to mourn shipmates and lost youth: 'I can still see the flash of the bomb and now the smell of hot oil fuel will always carry to me the memory of mutilated flesh and violent death', admitted PO Roy Norris. They wrestled creeping bitterness: 'The bungling of the powers that be ... what is the use of this useless slaughter'.[55] They believed they should be able to recover from the estimated 257 air attacks their ship and they had been subjected to, but recovery would not be easy, and, for some, recovery never eventuated.

SIX

*'In battleship grey with swirling black camouflage
stripes down her sides she was a thrilling sight.'*

Able Seaman Harold 'Tich' Hill

In various corners of Australia, *Perth* officers and ratings walked into their homes relieved and eager to return to the lives they had left the previous year, but this could not happen. They found children had grown, relatives had died and most of their peer group were absent. As the initial elation of being enveloped by their closest relatives diminished, a sense of unease seeped into their consciousness. Families struggled to catch up and to comprehend changes, that soon became apparent, but which they could never understand. Boys who had left Australia brimming with adolescent bravado had aged uncomfortably into wary men. The day-to-day concerns of families seemed infinitesimal compared to where they had been and would likely go again. One sailor wrote of his discomfort with his family, 'they seemed to have changed in some indefinable way. Later I came to realise that probably it was I who had changed'.[1]

With the battle honours of Atlantic convoys, as well as Crete, Greece, Malta, and the Battle of Matapan, *Perth*'s crew was treated favourably by the Australian media and their countrymen. Australians felt justifiably proud of these navy men. It was an appreciation expressed as the returned men walked the streets of Australian cities and towns. Civic receptions were conducted and there was a good deal of back-slapping and free beer. AB Allan Gee had been a naïve nineteen year old, when he left Australia in *Autolycus*. The world and the war had matured him rapidly. He was nonetheless, 'moved by the honour bestowed on me by my home town' when a capacity crowd filled the Town Hall in Beechworth, Victoria, for his civic welcome home. With the blare of 'patriotic airs' over the address system of the tannery from which Gee had escaped to enlist, the former employee was praised, presented with a gift and offered, 'the thanks of everyone for what he had already done in the defence of the country'.[2]

For some the acclaim was overwhelming, particularly as they felt less than grateful for their war experience. Joan Asplin hero-worshipped her big brother Doug, and was eager to listen to his war stories. However, she noticed a marked reluctance in him to discuss the previous months. The happy, energetic eighteen year old, who had joined the navy just two years before, was different. Doug seemed much older than twenty, 'he was a nervous wreck who would jump, startled at the sound of local sirens or whistles'.[3] It was invariably a relief to all concerned when sailors returned to their ships. Again part of their ship's crew, life was entirely structured through routine, no public face was required and no explanation needed, at least with 'old hands'. The situation in *Perth,* however, was different, as 40 per cent of the Mediterranean crew was replaced over the ensuing months. There were many new shipmates for AB Doug Asplin to get to know. Once a friendly bloke, Asplin now found it difficult to be as outgoing. War had become more than the big adventure imagined and yearned for; he had witnessed its reality. Messmates from the Mediterranean campaign preferred each other's company. They had been exposed to naval warfare and were bonded by shared emotions, emotions they would not discuss. It was easier to go ashore and drown out any nagging awareness in a pub. They had lost shipmates and this war was not done with them yet, for this reason alone it was better not to get to know these new messmates anyway.

Asplin observed the fresh young faces that swelled the ship's company and recognised himself, a year and a bit earlier, in men like

John Atkinson. Admittedly John had been born in Cairns, Queensland, but he too was an only son. John was as cheery and energetic as Doug had been. John too had left school before his father preferred, was good with his hands and had become a carpenter. Whereas Doug had built a yacht, John had built a house for his sister.[4]

Asplin also observed the enthusiasm he had once had in Frank Ritchie. They were the same age and the same rank but that was where the connection ended. AB Frank Ritchie had enlisted in April 1940, as an eighteen year old who passionately believed the navy would be more exciting than the army and air force. Frank had visions of great oceans and large warships, but instead was drafted to *Goolgwai,* a requisitioned trawler with a maximum speed of nine-and-a-half knots. This did not concern him unduly because he would still get to sea. His first months on the minesweeper were horrible, and he spent most of his time vomiting over the side or totally debilitated. The RAN noted on his service card, 'Unfit for service in small ships, owing to chronic seasickness', and drafted him to *Perth*. He was excited when he first boarded the cruiser. This was how he had imagined his life in the RAN, on a 'proper' warship which had already taken part in major sea battles. Ritchie believed by the end of the war he and *Perth* would return triumphant.

—

On 1 September Captain Sir Phillip Bowyer-Smyth relinquished command and returned to England with the words to his ship's company, 'I congratulate you heartily on your bearing under stress. Thank you for the faith I have had in you and still more for the trust I think you placed in me'.[5] He surprised many within *Perth*. The British baronet had not initially been a popular choice for a Commanding Officer of an Australian lower deck, but the manner with which he commanded, the dignity and courtesy with which he treated those onboard and his superior ship-handling skills had earned him their respect.

Navy men quickly became imbued with loyalty to their ship. Jimmy Millerick had been born in the tough mining town of Broken Hill and entered the RANR through Williamstown a month before his twenty-first birthday. He was sent to *Cerberus* to train as a Stoker, a little surprising considering he was a baker in civilian life. At least the hot working conditions were familiar. Millerick's father was a harsh taskmaster, particularly when it came to fitness. Days for young Jimmy started with a dawn run followed by a long surf swim. He encouraged his son to deliver milk in the evenings as a means of maintaining fitness. Jimmie Millerick became an excellent swimmer, so the navy had seemed a logical choice for war service and *Perth* was his first ship. He and the cruiser had survived the Med, but during the last torrid year he had called his ship many choice names, 'Chook', being the least offensive.[6] You could say what you liked about your own ship, and quite often did, but if anyone other than fellow crew was to say anything even slightly unflattering about one's ship, they were liable to have to physically defend themselves. Millerick was involved in a couple of scuffles defending the honour of his cruiser and wasn't unhappy to find his *Perth* draft extended to include the next war phase, whatever it may be.

Bob Noyce admitted he followed his brother Bill most of his life: into the world five years later; into Ithaca Creek State School, Brisbane; then into work on a dairy farm. Prior to the dairy farm Bill had worked in a bicycle shop. He loved bikes but couldn't afford to buy one himself, so Bill built himself one with wooden wheels. He and the bike went pretty well too, racing at the Hawthorne Velodrome and winning a trophy for the Brisbane to Southport, Southport to Brisbane race. Bill was a bit of a hero as far as Bob was concerned, and that was before Bill became a member of the 1939 *Perth* advance party and a Mediterranean veteran.

By October 1941 Bob had followed Bill into the RAN. The new Stoker caught up with his elder brother in Sydney. They were accompanied to the pub by a couple of Bill's *Perth* shipmates. Bob was enthusiastic with the prospect of a ship draft but it was unlikely he would be posted to *Perth*. The *Perth* men were subdued. Bill, now with the nickname of 'Rasus', apologised to his brother, he would not request a transfer so they could serve together. Bill tried to explain his loyalty to the cruiser, but it was a loyalty the uninitiated Bob could not yet comprehend. The Leading Torpedoman then took a lighter tack, explaining, 'I've got a really good job'; always a great movie fan, Bill Noyce supplemented his duties in *Perth*'s low power room, with those as the ship's projectionist.[7]

Not all shared the same conviction as Millerick and Noyce and were pleased to draft off, hoping to spend time in less demanding circumstances. Invariably men were torn by loyalties, between their ship and other concerns, and the Mediterranean campaign had reminded them how important their families were. Going to war was easier for single men than married.

Acting Chief ERA John 'Jack' James Madge had grown up in the rough and tumble of the Sydney working-class suburb of Balmain, for which he played reserve grade rugby league. He learnt quickly how to stand up for himself and defend what he believed in. Life took on a gentler tone when he married his childhood sweetheart, Florence, and their two children were born. Since joining the navy in 1933, Madge had been a model rating and, with superior reports, had been promoted rapidly. He was both respected and feared by his subordinates, a man hardened by life and naval service, except when it came to his family. In July 1941, as *Perth*'s Mediterranean service was ending, Madge received a moving letter from his daughter. In large, bold writing and childish spelling, Shirley wrote, 'Dear Daddy, Won't I be glad when you come home ... Someone said you would be home in Augst [sic]. But I hope you will be home next week'.[8] When he returned to the family home, three-year-old son John 'Warren', perched on top of a kitchen cupboard, made a grab for his father's cap in his excitement.

Jack's time with his family was going to be all too brief before *Perth* returned to sea. The Chief Artificer was troubled. Like most men of the sea Jack Madge was superstitious. As a lark he paid a fortune teller in Alexandria to look into his future. She muttered that he wouldn't reach 'old bones'. A cynical person could dismiss such a prediction, given that there was a war on, but Madge couldn't. When he returned to Sydney, the Chief ERA was offered a draft to the Sydney base *Penguin*, to train junior ratings. It was a vexed situation. It would be so easy to accept the shore draft and return home to his family most nights and weekends, but Madge believed, 'if I take the shore job and something happens to the ship, some will say I was a coward. If I stay with the ship and something happens to *Perth,* some will say I was a fool. I would rather be called a fool than a coward'.[9] For Madge, 'Wearing the green coat', the naval expression for being a coward, was as bad an insinuation as a career navy man could suffer, so the Chief ERA returned to his duties in *Perth*'s aft engine room.

As a peacetime recruiting inducement, the RAN had endeavoured to draft men to a ship bearing the name of their state or state capital. Every effort was made for the ship to visit its 'home' state as frequently as possible. In times of war this could not occur, but the RAN continued to consolidate the loyalty personnel had for their ship with loyalty to the state of their birth. For this reason during October and November 1941 a large number of West Australians joined *Perth*'s ship's company. For men from smaller capital cities like Perth, it was common for new recruits to have grown up together.

Charles 'Chas' Thomson, an apprentice coppersmith with the Midland Railway Company, was acquainted with Arthur Bancroft. Arthur was dating a girl named Mirla and they had gone to school in Subiaco with Nell, who Chas was rather 'keen on'.[10] Bancroft was an auburn-haired nineteen year old brimming with confidence. He was a prominent 'A' grade Australian Rules player and cricketer who worked for the Union Bank between sporting commitments.[11] Ord Seam Arthur Bancroft joined *Perth* in October, the same day as Ord Seam Norm Fuller from Geraldton, who nine days before, had celebrated his twenty-first birthday. Ord Seam Syd Harper, from Northam, and Ord Seam Fred Skeels, from Perth suburbs and both born in December 1922, also joined. Fred Skeels was the son of Horace and Dorothy. He had left school to work as a messenger boy for a motor parts company until he secured a clerical position with Wentworth Motors. With army cadet experience, Skeels applied to enlist in both the AIF and the RAN. The RAN called him up first.[12] The October WA draft also included Ord Seam Arthur Lund, who was quickly nicknamed 'Otto', and Ord Seam Harry Nagle, who because he was 6 foot 2 was nicknamed 'Lofty'. Nicknames were seldom original.

The Australian people were answering the call to arms. To most Australians, the United Kingdom was the mother country, and it went without saying any threat to the land of their ancestors was their responsibility. This sentiment was not universal. To some, the war was not yet 'real'. The war had been created by arrogant and recalcitrant European nations, whose leaders had learnt nothing from World War I. An AIF nationwide recruiting campaign in June had a target of 10,000, but they convinced only 7094 to sign on the dotted line. Not all families accepted the same destiny, and not all within a family felt compelled to serve.

Two Queensland families, who became inexorably intertwined with the fate of *Perth*, displayed such divergent views. The Turnbull family had emigrated from the north of England. It was not easy in an English working class town reliant on the ship-building industry; life would be better in Australia. All too soon Florence Turnbull was a widow, but she had gained strength through her children. Her eldest son, John James Samuel Turnbull, named in honour of his father and grandfather, joked he had salt water in his veins and enlisted in his adopted country's navy in 1934. He quickly adapted to life as a Stoker and saw war service in the Med in the Daring class destroyer *Waterhen*. Luck was on his side when he was drafted off the destroyer the month before it was sunk. Returned to Australia for promotion training for PO, it was the type of luck he hoped would continue through his next draft to the cruiser *Perth*. His brothers in Brisbane, 24-year-old Bill and 20-year-old Ken, were somewhat reluctant to enlist. This was the sort of tension that divided families.

In the Darling Downs town of Warwick, Queensland, Nora Toovey was proud of her mother's badge featuring two stars representing her AIF sons Syd and Peter, both serving in the Middle East. She was not overly anxious to see another star added for her son Ernie. Ernie was a very fit teenager, already regarded as a potential Queensland state cricketer. A quintessential, carefree eighteen year old, he did not embrace his mother's concern. Ernie had been allowed to join the militia but service in his home town did not satisfy his desire for 'active service'. Again he raised the subject, but with his father, not his mother. Syd Toovey senior was a veteran of the Merchant Marine and agreed Ernie could enlist in the RAN, less dangerous than the AIF, or so he hoped. Nora Toovey received her third star in January 1941 when Ernie commenced his RANR training.[13] In October 1941 he drafted to *Perth* and settled into the Ord Seam's mess, up forward. Ernie Toovey was one of many youthful faces to join the ship that month for whom the welcome quickly turned sour.

—

At around 0100 on 18 October those in *Perth* were woken by thick smoke and flames and hastily evacuated. The Boatswain's mate saved the life of the Navigator, Lieut John Harper, who was asleep in the Duty Officer's cabin in the bridge. Structural damage to the ship was minimal, but the fire caused considerable electrical damage and many a sailor returned to find his belongings destroyed or stolen. The completion of the refit was delayed another month. Senior RAN officers suspected a disgruntled sailor had started the fire to postpone the ship's departure.

A report to the War Cabinet by the Chief of Naval Staff, Admiral Sir Guy Royle, KCB, CMG RN, stated, 'whilst there was no direct evidence as to the cause of the fire, there had been a certain amount of slackness and laxity on board'.[14] Although only a skeleton crew had been left on the ship, the Acting Captain, Cmdr Reid, was made the scapegoat and, regardless of future glowing promotion recommendations, would find his RAN career prospects halted. In a later report CNS stated, 'the possibility of sabotage could not be ruled out'. *Perth* sailors, however, believed the blame lay with disenchanted civilian workers at Sydney's Garden Island and 'dockyard workers got the cold shoulder from that day'.[15]

On 24 October 1941, Captain Hector MacDonald Laws Waller, DSO, Bar, assumed command of *Perth*. Waller was born on 4 April 1900 in Benalla, Victoria. From the day he had entered the Royal Australian Naval College in 1914 at age thirteen, he shone amongst his contemporaries. During his final year he was Chief Cadet Officer and won the Kings Medal. In keeping with the period, many of his years as a junior officer were spent in England and on Royal Navy ships, but unlike some Australian naval officers he failed to develop a greater loyalty to the ways of the RN than to the RAN. Whilst in England he continued to excel, coming top in the RN's 'Dagger' signals course, and receiving the briefest taste of war on HMS *Agincourt* in 1918. When back in Australia he married Nancy on 7 April 1923. It became clear to his superiors Waller was a gifted officer, as he further distinguished himself in each posting. He was commanding the Australian destroyer *Stuart* when his country committed to war. By June the following year, he was promoted to Captain at age 40, and fast becoming a legend. By 1940 Waller was in charge of the 10th Destroyer Flotilla, and played an 'outstanding brilliant part in Mediterranean operations'.[16] His sailors gave him the endearing nickname of 'Hardover Hec' because of his ship-handling skill, tossing his destroyer around out of harm's way as if it were a toy. Navy hierarchy gave him a DSO followed by two 'Mentioned in Despatches'. The Battle of Matapan brought a Bar to the DSO. By the time the new Commanding Officer joined *Perth*, tales of his feats, true and exaggerated, filled the messdecks. Soon, those who served in *Perth* 'respected and worshipped' Waller, and 'all felt we were fortunate to sail with him'.[17]

Captain Hector Waller addressed *Perth* officers and men warmly for the first time. Waller valued his senior hands, knowing how important they were to the operation of a warship and was pleased to find some familiar faces. Chief ERA Cedric Mellish; POs Payne, Revie and Tyrrell; Ordnance Artificer II Marcus Goodwin and Chief Stoker Harry Thomas had been with Waller in *Stuart*, during the most demanding period of his professional life; the Battle of Matapan. Mellish was solid in build and professional capability. From the New South Wales New England town of Armidale, Mellish thrived under Waller's command. Joining *Stuart* one month before war was declared, his proficiency reports improved to 'Superior' for the first time since he had enlisted in 1934 and remained there. Promotions followed.

Waller, it seemed, had the capacity to make his subordinates believe in their own abilities and excel. Born in Perth, Thomas had been promoted to Chief Stoker before his thirty-fifth birthday and Waller ensured Thomas was mentioned in despatches for 'Bravery and enterprise' after *Stuart* participated in the Battle of Matapan. There could be few more dependable Chiefs to oversee Boiler 'A' in *Perth*.

It was also under the Waller tutelage that Ed Tyrrell was promoted to Leading Seaman, then Acting PO. The Dublin Irishman was just one month shy of two years in *Stuart* when it was decided he needed a break and should join *Perth* for a return to Australia.

Like Thomas and Tyrrell, PO George Revie also returned from the Mediterranean in *Perth,* then drafted to *Stuart.* Born in the outback Queensland town of Childers, Revie had been a wood trimmer prior to RAN enlistment in 1927. Another recent draft was the eighteen-year-old Sydneyite Ed Payne. With no trade in the Depression years, he realised how much the RAN offered. He would be fed, clothed, accommodated and encouraged to acquire skills to prosper within his country's navy. Within three years he felt secure enough to marry Jessie. Payne spent the first twelve months of the war in *Stuart* and the experienced gunnery specialist was now directing *Perth*'s port No.1, 4-inch gun crew.

Ordnance Artificer Marcus Goodwin was another to be promoted during his time on *Stuart*, to Ordnance Artificer II, the equivalent of PO. Born in Waratah, Tasmania, the former fitter and turner found his destroyer caught up in the Battle of Matapan. His 'Bravery and enterprise' during the battle resulted in Waller's recommendation that the 26 year old be awarded the DSM. In September the same year he arrived onboard *Perth* comforted by the fact that Waller would also command this warship.

Surgeon Lieut Sam Stening expected to be relieved when *Perth* returned to Sydney. Having been in the Mediterranean theatre since May 1940 and with *Waterhen* sunk from beneath him, he knew he needed a break. Permission for relief was 'delayed', then 'indefinite' and in *Perth* he remained as a Surgeon Lieutenant.[18] Others off *Waterhen* remained also, some thought 'forgotten'. There were simply not enough officers and sailors to replace these men who clearly needed respite.

The RAN faced a critical personnel shortage. The fleet was expanding faster than the navy could recruit and train. The operational effectiveness of the RAN and security of the Australian mainland was compromised by the myopic nature of previous RAN personnel policy. The fickleness of Australian Government defence spending, since the RAN had been inaugurated in 1911, had resulted in a reliance on Empire

Defence and a high degree of Royal Navy dependence. Whilst the RN Admirals who primarily made up the Commonwealth Naval Board did little to discourage this doctrine, Australian naval autonomy was impossible, given the Australian government's inherent resistance to peacetime defence spending.

There were advantages to coupling to RN might, but there were also disadvantages. British capital ship investments and the Singapore naval base became of greater priority than the recruitment and training of Australian naval volunteers. Throughout the RAN's history, between 25 and 33 per cent of the lower deck had been RN ratings on loan or transfer, who commonly filled the senior sailor billets. This provided instant lower-deck expertise for the fledgling RAN. The augmentation of such a policy was also based on the preference of RN officers who filled RAN command positions. RN sailors were seen as more malleable to naval discipline than Australian-born sailors, more accepting of the rigidly defined class division found in the RN between officer and sailor. This bias meant the retrenchment of junior Australian sailors was an easy option to meet budget deficits, and ensured an onerous career path for Australian-born sailors.

Such a personnel policy became strained, as the technical expertise required by ratings increased. With the advent of World War II, senior sailors from the RN were no longer available, and too few Australian members of the lower deck were qualified to fulfil training positions and sea drafts. The RAN struggled to change direction and expand.

Acting Leading Seaman 'Ben' Chaffey rejoined *Perth*. 'Ben' had been one of the youngsters deemed 'of no particular loss to the service' when the RAN was looking to make lower deck cuts during 1930. When he was allowed to re-enlist, Chaffey spent a brief period in *Perth* during 1940 before drafting to *Canberra*. With a draft back to *Perth* and rumours that the cruiser was bound for operational duty, he 'scrounged' a few days' leave. He was a man on a mission: on his previous leave to his native Tasmania, he spied a particular girl at Hobart's Sandy Bay swimming pool, and it was 'love at first sight'.[19] Dorothea was now an army nurse on night duty, and, given his short leave, 'it was now or never'. They married on 8 August 1941.

Another with an interrupted career was Fred Lasslett. A wireless telephonist in civvy street, Lasslett had been readily accepted into the Navy Reserve in 1937. He explained to authorities that, due to night shifts, he was unable to attend some RANR night musters. No one noted that detail and Fred discovered he was discharged from the Reserve due to, 'unsatisfactory attendance'. He re-applied to join the RANR, and it took him a year to convince the navy to accept him. On reporting to *Cerberus* he was, somewhat to his amusement, made Class Captain, 'because of his previous naval service'.[20] Taking advantage of his new, favourable situation, he transferred to the RAN and convinced authorities he should become a Wiremen. Wireman received trade training to undertake electrical maintenance. Lasslett became one of only thirteen Wiremen in the RAN during the war. Having the 'gift of the gab' would prove an asset in the vacillating wartime experience of Fred Lasslett.

Had Eric Justelius been permitted to serve out his twelve-year enlistment, he may well have become a valuable senior rating. Instead he was cut in 1929. In 1940 he returned to the sea as a member of the RAFR and was drafted to the minesweeper *Doomba*. Personnel shortages meant he returned to Flinders, for torpedo training, in preparation for a draft to *Perth*. Justelius was amazed at how much the training depot had altered and developed to an establishment: 'about 3 or 4 times as big'.[21] The 34 year old looked at the so very young faces around him. In 1925, the first time he arrived at Flinders, he too had been only seventeen, but the faces looked so much younger now. He wondered how capable all these young sailors would be, given it seemed 'they were rushed through' their training.

Queenslander George Tibbits was one who arrived at *Cerberus* for his wartime training in 1941. With an Indian chief tattooed on his right forearm and a dagger on his upper right arm, George was one of the more colourful recruits. His tattoos may have impressed some of his willingness to serve in the RAN, but they had nothing to do with a life on the sea; they had just been a painful childhood prank.[22] Another trainee at *Cerberus* who joined in the second half of 1941 was Frank Chattaway. Frank was 'a naïve country boy' from the New South Wales country town of Junee. Prior to RAN entry he had been a teacher at the Grong Grong School, not an ordinary occupation for someone enlisting as an Ordinary Seaman. But these were not ordinary times, and Frank had more motivation than most to take up arms. His brother Jim, a member of Australia's 2/13th, 'the Devil's own', had been killed near Tobruk. Unable to join the RAAF because of colour blindness and wanting to avoid trench warfare, the RAN it had to be. Frank couldn't swim so he hoped whatever ship he was sent to stayed afloat.[23] After challenging RAN training, Ord Seam Chattaway took his place as Loader, one of the sixteen-man, 2nd port-side 4-inch gun crew, in *Perth*.

—

There was a collective sigh of relief onboard the cruiser when they finally put to sea on 24 November, and the real hands-on training for new crew members commenced. Power trials and gunnery practice tested crew new and old. Drills acquainted crew with their duties and encouraged teamwork. Gun crews trained to perfect unison and speed. One drill after another, over and over again, boat crew drills, action stations and abandon ship drills.

Ord Seam Ernie Toovey found the first months challenging. There seemed a lot to learn in a short period of time. Some of his duties he was non-too keen on, like using chipping hammers to remove old paint from heavy cables, and using the red lead, light grey and dark grey paints which followed. His action station was in the 'Y' Turrett Cordite Magazine. Old hands muttered how unsafe the explosive cordite was, particularly in the hands of inexperienced ordinary seamen. If this was meant to put 'the wind up' the youngster, it succeeded. Being two decks below, though, seemed safe. He said it had never crossed his mind that he may have had to abandon ship, from two decks below.[24]

The cruiser and crew were engaged in anti-aircraft practice in Victoria's Port Phillip Bay when the shocking news was received that sister cruiser *Sydney* had been lost with all hands on 19 November.[25] Some 240 kilometres south-west of Carnarvon, Western Australia, the German raider, *Kormoran*, a converted cargo ship, had lured *Sydney* to within a mile and opened fire at point blank range. The Australian cruiser was last seen fully ablaze, disappearing over the horizon taking 645 souls with it. AB Eric Justelius was home on leave when *Sydney* vanished. His sister, Isabel, remembered how quiet her brother went as, 'he looked down the long list of names of missing crew and recognised the names of friends ... it affected him greatly'.[26] It was a sentiment which affected many in the navy, an unnerving mixture of relief for being spared mixed with a great sense of loss.

AB Bert Parkes had enlisted in the RAN at sixteen. He was an Ord Seam 2nd Class when he drafted to *Sydney*. He took pride in the bronze medallion he was presented with following the sinking of the Italian warship *Bartolomeo Colleoni* in the Mediterranean on 19 July 1940. He carried his old *Sydney* cap ribbon as a lucky talisman when he joined *Perth* in October 1941. A month was all it had taken, the difference between his being one of the names in the black-edged columns he now cast his eyes over. The faces evoked by the names would stay with him.

Harold 'Tich' Hill's name would have been on the *Sydney* list had his surname started with the letters A, B or C. That was how the RAN drafted sailors to cruisers when he was at *Cerberus*. Hill took himself off to drink glasses of '"Murphy's White Flash", in memory of Vic, Ernie, Jack and the rest of the "Old Boys" of recruit classes R1, R2 and R3'. He then packed his kit to join *Perth*, because his name commenced with the initial H. AB Alec 'Spud' Murphy mourned his best mate AB Eric Devereux. He couldn't rationalise how a warship could disappear without a trace, destroyed by what on paper was an inferior ship and crew.

Onboard *Perth* the new Captain attempted to raise spirits by advising his crew he would not take *Perth* within range of any suspect vessel. However, Waller too had a personal link with *Sydney*; his cousin, Richard Sievey, had been onboard. Richard's brother AB John Sievey was also on *Perth*. John's messmates gave the 20 year old some quiet space. The young AB felt partly responsible for the fate of his brother. He and Richard had enlisted as Ordinary Seamen in March 1941. Richard, a Sydney Law graduate, had just been admitted to the Bar, but spurned officer training in the hope that he and John, four years his junior, could serve together. Added incentive came when *Perth* command was assumed by Waller. The Sievey boys couldn't think of a better CO to entrust their lives to. To their disappointment Richard was drafted to *Sydney*. Richard had promised John he would put forth a strong case for his transfer and, given his vocational abilities, the younger brother figured the RAN would relent. For the Sievey family their sorrow would be compounded in the months ahead.

The RAN did not discourage family members serving together. Brothers AB Charles and Richard Ryan were part of the *Autolycus* contingent and remained in *Perth*. AB Frank McGovern had recently joined his brother, Vincent, one of the cruiser's ERAs. Also onboard were the Victorian Delbridge brothers Charles and Fred. Charles, born in Ballarat, was the younger, by two and a half years. Fred, born in Bendigo, was married to Hilda and had two children. There were also a number of cousins serving in the cruiser, including Telegraphist George and ERA John Mathew from Tasmania.

Grief was palpable within the Partington family home. Son Leslie had been a Bandsman in *Sydney*. The family had yet to come to grips with the loss of son and brother Arnold. Arnold, 'a very fine trumpeter'[27] and valuable member of the *Canberra* band, had died the year before of acute appendicitis. He lay in a grave in a Mauritius Military Cemetery. Now trombonist Leslie had disappeared. It seemed only yesterday that the Partington family band had delighted dance audiences with their talent and melodies and now only one RAN son remained. The 21-year-old Bandsman Perce Partington, a *Perth* commissioning crew member, was still a trombonist in the cruiser's band.

The sinking of *Sydney* stunned Australians. Only months before, the ship's crew had marched through the streets of the city after which their cruiser was named, cheered on by a large crowd. Resplendent in summer dress whites, justifiably proud of their distinguished service in the Mediterranean, *Sydney*'s officers and sailors were enveloped by a tangled mass of coloured streamers in Martin Place. Equally stunning was the fact that the crew and ship had not perished in seas of a far away European theatre of war, but just off the West Australian coast. Poems penned by stricken citizens were featured in the daily media. One in the *Sydney Morning Herald* was titled *To the Heroes of the Sydney*:

We do not know the story of your triumph.

They told us only, how you nobly fell with victory in your hearts.

There is none to tell, the sorrows of a battle fought at dusk,
    the tidings of a victory that was yours.

But this we know, to guard our shores, with colours high you fell.

Our flags are flying low and hearts are sad, though mingled with
    a glow of lasting pride,

that you belonged to us, and have upheld the cause for which
    you died.

God knows the answer. He watched silently the poignant, cruel
    struggle through the dark, and he will lead you through the
    seas beyond, as you embark.

Such an emotional outburst was more than the lament for a lost warship
and crew, it was a lament for a loss of innocence, the loss of a comfortable
place far removed from the horrors suffered by Europeans. The war was
at Australia's shores and no one could afford to be complacent any more.
The black month for the nation's navy continued, with the sinking of the
Grimsby class sloop *Parramatta* off Tobruk on 27 November. In eight
days 783 officers and sailors on two RAN ships had died.

—

On 5 December AB Harold 'Tich' Hill watched from the shore as *Perth*
moored in Sydney Harbour. He felt a shiver of excitement race up his
spine as he looked at the ship he would join that day, 'I was struck by
her magnificent appearance. She was long and lean and symmetrical. In
battleship grey with swirling black camouflage stripes down her sides
she was a thrilling sight ... With a feeling of awe I reported aboard'.[28]
AB Hill discovered his action station was in the gunnery plotting room;
he would be one of those responsible for controlling the 4-inch guns. He
felt dwarfed by the huge machine that was covered with gauges, dials
and switches that processed information. Hill had barely familiarised
himself with his duties, when bad news and more bad news staggered
Australians. The British 'Force Z', the nucleus of the Royal Navy's Far

Eastern fleet, was no more. Japanese aircraft had sunk the battleships *Repulse* and *Prince of Wales*.

The battleships, in company with four World War I vintage destroyers, had been commanded by Admiral Sir Tom Phillips. While Phillips was considered a gifted staff officer, he had 'no recent operational experience'.[29] On 8 December Force Z sailed to intercept forces invading Malaya. Even after the huge loss of ships and men in the Mediterranean, British naval commanders did not yet fully appreciate the power of aviation in the naval environment, and Phillips was one who believed air cover was unnecessary for battleships to dispense an inferior Japanese foe. The 840 RN officers and men in *Repulse* and *Prince of Wales* appeared to have lost their lives because of this adherence to traditional thinking.

Singapore, linchpin of British Eastern strategy and defence of Australia, was now virtually without RN protection. In December AB Hill was unaware of the wider ramifications of the sinking of these RN battleships, of the direct consequences it would have in less than four months, on his ship, his life and the lives of his shipmates. However, he was in no doubt how calamitous the Japanese attack on Pearl Harbour was.

Australians were journeying to work on a Monday morning when the news broke. Faces drained as eyes consumed the pages of special editions fresh off the presses. Japanese forces had savagely struck simultaneously at Malaya, the Philippines, Guam, Hong Kong, Midway and Singapore, and had sunk more than half the American Pacific Fleet at its moorings in Pearl Harbor. In a radio broadcast the Australian Prime Minister, John Curtin, declared: 'This is the gravest hour in our history'. No one could still harbour the belief that Australia was not under direct threat and the war effort did not involve them. On 11 December Curtin called for a complete revision of Australia's war effort and rapid expansion of Australian military forces. He ordered the return home of navy, army and air force contingents from the Middle East and urged Australians to embrace the seriousness of the situation and react positively with, 'your courage, your physical and mental ability, your inflexible determination', so that, 'we as a free people shall survive ... Australia is at stake'.

A total mobilisation of the Australian economy and society was needed. Demands never before imagined had to be met. By February the military call-up embraced youths aged eighteen and single men as old as sixty. With the new threat the militia was expanded. The Australian Army since 1939 had consisted of two distinctive parts. The AIF was the volunteer expeditionary force serving overseas. The militia was the conscript force retained for service within Australia. By the end of December, PO John Turnbull's brothers Ken and Bill were in the militia. The utilisation of all those in khaki would soon make any such distinction null and void.

Prime Minister Curtin's call to arms was a little muffled in the halls of Navy Office. It took eighteen months of war before the Naval Board agreed to 'permit entry of desirable naturalised British subjects'.[30] Non-white Caucasian volunteers continued to be excluded. There was still a reluctance to re-enlist sailors discharged during the pre-war years for disciplinary reasons, no matter how trivial. One plea for re-engagement came from a Seaman Gunner who had been discharged for playing 'crown and anchor', a gambling game. The shortage of recruiters and instructors continued to impact on the RAN's ability to accept recruits. An exasperated letter to the government from one aspiring recruit alleged how it was, 'almost impossible to join the navy in Australia', how, 'well educated boys' like himself, found it impossible to see an RAN Recruiter to begin the enlistment process.[31] In 1942 a secret RAN report admitted recruitment was impaired because 'facilities' could not train more sailors. Despite people shortages, state recruiting quotas Australia-wide remained in place, and RAN officers and ratings continued to be sent to British ships to assist the RN with their manpower shortfall.[32]

In a meeting with the Australian War Cabinet, the officer in charge of the nation's navy, Chief of Naval Staff Admiral Sir Guy Royle, RN, conceded that the Royal Navy should be advised that Australia could no longer supply navy personnel. The move could be justified by the fact that many of the, 'more than 2500 officers and men of the RAN serving overseas in the Royal Navy' were serving in ships in the Indian Ocean.[33] By October 1942 Naval Board conceded the situation was desperate, there was indeed a shortage of nearly 4000 men. As the personnel crisis worsened, certain standards needed to be relaxed.

One then given the opportunity to enter the RAN was Fred Hutton. At *Cerberus* recruit classmates were astounded to find this man of 43 with a deformed left hand included in their number, but they were duly impressed when they managed to persuade the reticent Victorian to speak not of his World War II experience, but his World War I experience. The former silversmith had joined the AIF at the age of eighteen in August 1916. He had hurried to join his countrymen, only to encounter the slaughter grounds of the Western Front. Wounded and hospitalised in France, he was then assigned to the 2nd Australian Light Trench Mortar Battery. In April 1918, Hutton was severely wounded and invalided to the United Kingdom. He returned home with medals and a permanent deformity. Hutton's sense of patriotism had remained intact and by 1942 the 5th Class Engine Room Artificer, assumed his duties in *Perth*'s 'A' boiler room.

With World War I still vividly clear in the hearts and minds of Australian parents, many struggled with the situation that their children too were caught up in the same horror. Of the Allies, per head of population, only New Zealand lost more uniform personnel in World War I than Australia. Men who volunteered for 'King and Country' and for 'the Motherland', who sought resolve in the belief that this 'war would end all wars', now watched their sons put their lives in jeopardy for the same sentiments. The war cry sounded the same as it had a quarter of a century earlier. It was harder to adhere to the same resolve when the war machine consumed your children. Griffith Roberts was a Welshman. He had fought in World War I and witnessed its dreadfulness. Post-war life in Great Britain did little to reduce the trauma, so in 1927 Roberts made the brave decision to load his family onboard *SS Beltana* bound for Australia. It was a new start, far away from Europe, an opportunity for his family to grow up with better prospects. Griffith Roberts had worked hard as a labourer, so his children could receive a better education than he had. Now the world was again at war, and he and wife Elsie could but watch while sons Leonard and Roy were captivated by the sense of duty, adventure and glory held by the uninitiated, and joined the new nation's navy. Seventeen-year-old Roy 'Robbie' was drafted to the cruiser *Perth*.

Charles Gray was another father who wondered and waited. Seventeen-year-old Peter couldn't wait until he was old enough to enlist, ever since he heard Prime Minister Menzies say it was his 'melancholy duty' to announce Australia was at war. The West Australian had grown up in a nation where the ANZACs were revered and Gallipoli committed to national folklore. As an adolescent male he noticed at local dances 'the fellows in uniforms got the girls to dance with them'. It all seemed pretty glamorous really, and his brother, John, was already in the RAN. Their father Charles, who had been gassed in World War I, spoke little of it and watched his boys leave for war. In December 1941 Peter, now known by shipmates as 'Digby', was in *Perth* and skilled at his duties in the shell-handling room, from where the cruiser's two 6-inch guns were hydraulically supplied with ammunition. 'Digby's' superior was PO George 'Slim' Hedrick, an ex-*Tingira* Boy Seaman, who now amused young sailors in his charge with his ritual of securing his tobacco and cigarette papers in condoms each time *Perth* went to action stations. Drill or no drill, Hedrick was ready for the 'real thing' and intended to have a dry smoke at the end of it all. A youngster like 'Digby' Gray was 'supremely confident' this worst-case scenario would never happen.[34]

—

Perth and *Canberra* were despatched to Fiji to escort troop transports to Brisbane. The convoy was the first of its kind. Known as the 'Pensacola Convoy' and 'Task Force South Pacific', the ships held United States servicemen and women, who had left San Francisco for the Philippines in November. With the attack on Pearl Harbor, the convoy was diverted. RAN ships with the New Zealand warship *Achilles* escorted the convoy to Brisbane, arriving on 13 December. Men of the 2nd Battalion, 131st Field Artillery, 36th Division (Texas National Guard), were among those in the convoy. Unforeseen events would result in members of

Perth's crew reuniting with the Texan unit, and an ageless bond forged through grim circumstances.

With the convoy safely harboured in Brisbane, Brisbane natives were given two hours' leave. For Ord Seam Ernie Toovey it meant time to visit his AIF brother Peter, who had been severely wounded and invalided. Charlie Wray and 'Chilla' Goodchap also managed to get ashore. Charlie, from Coorparoo, had left his job as a storeman and packer to qualify, after six months RAN training in Victoria, as a Wireman. Ord Seam Goodchap, from Kangaroo Point, had been a prominent member of the Brisbane Rowing Club. Onboard *Perth* they met other Queenslanders within the crew of 681, men from all over the state, from city and town, all anxious 'to do their bit for the war effort'. Billy Girvan had laboured in the sugar farms around Ayr. Travis Hosking was a mill hand in Kingaroy and had a brother in the navy. Lenny Broomfield hailed from Eumundi and decided not to follow his brother into the army. PO John Harvey worked as a shop assistant until he joined the RAN from Ipswich in 1935. AB Reg Farrington joked no one onboard could spell his birthplace, Toogoolawah. That was until Stoker 2nd Class Colin Williams, also from Toogoolawah, joined the cruiser.

Chief Jack Madge was sad; he looked like he was going to miss another family Christmas. He broke the news to his wife, Florence, on 21 December, 'I'm afraid it looks as though you'll have to play Father Xmas again this year'. 'I'd give a lot' he wrote, to see his son's face when he saw 'the bike and boat'.[35] The Chief ERA closed his letter, 'sending all my love to my darling wife and children, from your ever loving husband'.

Rapid changes to a ship's program were common, and this time it worked in the favour of the *Perth* crew. The ship was ordered to make fast to number one buoy within sight of the magnificent Sydney Harbour Bridge. With just a couple of days leave, only those with families in the greater metropolitan area could make it home. Navy families were used to opening their homes to extra bodies and Xmas 1941 was no exception, *Perth* shipmates were treated like relatives, often better. A popular greeting was 'Have a Jerry Christmas and a Jappy New Year'.

'War can be one of man's most exhilarating experiences, just as it can be terrifying and repugnant.'

[1]

USS Houston crew member

By 28 December 1941 the *Perth* was leaving Australia again, escorting a convoy carrying 4500 troops and 10,000 tons of equipment to reinforce Port Moresby. In Australia the New Year welcome was subdued, bunting and parties were out of place in a nation coming to grips with an enemy on the doorstep. The most optimistic believed the Allies would soon triumph over the 'powers of evil'. In *Perth* the New Year was barely observed as the cruiser steamed north. For the next month the ship was part of an ANZAC fleet busy with patrols, exercises, manoeuvres and escort duties.

Ordinary Signalman Bill 'Buzzer' Bee was getting used to his sea duties but was still nervous after taking his position on the bridge. Everything seemed to bristle with urgency and purpose. The twenty year old's first priority was to memorise the three colour combinations and three letter groups that were the day's secret challenge-and-reply signals for flag and flashing light. Since the loss of *Sydney*, the pause between a challenge signal and a warship opening fire was now seconds. Watches were four hours of vigilance, scanning the horizon

360 degrees around *Perth*. On the bridge also were the Gunnery Officer, Lieut Peter Handcox, and the Officer of the Watch who, like Bee, stood scanning the horizon with binoculars. Handcox was a career naval officer. From Ipswich, Queensland, he had been a thirteen-year-old Cadet Midshipman entry in 1927, who graduated from RANC winning the coveted King's Medal. Handcox had spent two periods attached to the RN and specialised in Gunnery. The OOW moved restlessly to the bridge coaming. The coaming, the ship's nerve centre, was festooned with buttons. Brass button alarms activated the action stations bells and the fighting light display on the mast. Others alerted torpedo staff, the telephones to the engine room and to the guns, and to those responsible for launching depth charges. Bridge personnel needed to commit the position of the alarms, telephones and voicepipes to memory so there would be no hesitation during blacked-out night duty. Other than the Captain, the port and starboard lookouts were the only two furnished with steel swivel chairs. All was silent as the watch proceeded, except for the occasional voice of the OOW as he called alteration of course as the zig-zag alarm clock rang; and the incessant ping of the ASDIC loudspeaker.

Below AB Bob Collins was an ASDIC operator listening intently to variations. After Japan had entered the war, there was heightened anxiety concerning submarines. Nervousness resulted in an incident where ASDIC personnel hit the full-scale alarm. As *Perth* prepared to launch depth charges, a whale was sighted. This caused some mirth at the ASDIC section's expense, but all onboard preferred false alarms to the alternative of a missed submarine within torpedo range.

Collins and *Perth* had a chequered history. The Sydneysider had entered as an Ord Seam 2nd Class and was one of the wide-eyed youngsters sent around the world on *Autolycus*. Whilst this had been an amazing experience, he was not pleased at the prospect of leaving Australian waters again and became one of the 'missing' when the ship cast off for the Med at the end of 1940. Ninety days' detention, and countless days of shame was hard, and he rejoined his ship to be involved in the Greek and Crete evacuations.

Collins was also responsible for the cruiser's mascot. As Collins and mate AB Ray Firmington had farewelled family in Sydney, Firmington's small daughter gave him a tiny white and grey kitten. Not wishing to disappoint the two year old, Collins returned to *Perth* with the cat. Fellow sailors quickly adopted the feline, Collins made it a small hammock, and Chief Cook Bland turned a blind eye to the liberation of some choice cuts of meat from the ship's galley. It was given the name Red Lead when the playful kitten upset a pot of red lead paint. The XO Cdr Reid disliked cats on board his Majesty's ships, so the sailors were careful to hide the kitten to avoid detection during rounds. As she grew, it became increasingly difficult to hide her in kitbags, lockers and behind steam pipes. Collins decided affirmative action was needed, and Red Lead was released on the bridge. With confidence she rubbed against the legs of the ship's Captain. Waller reached down, picked up the cat and scratched her ears. Cdr Reid was less than pleased but Red Lead was now formerly the ship's mascot.

The *Perth* bridge was open to all weather, and the only relief during a four-hour bridge watch came in the form of a cup of 'Kai'. For generations of RAN officers and sailors, the thick chocolate-based drink, thick enough to stand a spoon upright in, had been a warming brew to raise blood sugar levels. Kai was no less welcome in the 2nd engine room even if the warming aspect was not required.

Three very junior Stokers were among those who toiled away in the noisy hub of the ship. Bill Luck, Lloyd Bessell and Max Burk entered together at Hobart in February 1941. Bessell, born in St Mary's, was the eldest and the married one of the three, with two young children. Luck had been a member of the Launceston Fire Brigade and turned 22 just after he enlisted. Burk, also 22, was a Hobart lad, who had jammed as much into his days as he possibly could. Captain of the Excelsior Badminton Club, he was club champion three years in succession, and runner-up for the Tasmanian Badminton title. Burk also rowed, in champion maiden eights and champion junior fours and eights. The three Tasmanians were sent to *Cerberus* in May. The RAN needed stokers, so stokers they became. Physically the men were very different, but they were Tasmanians, and, having developed a friendship, they hoped to serve on the same cruiser, preferably *Hobart*. Stokers 2nd Class Bessell, Burk and Luck drafted to *Perth*, and were shown their duties by Acting Leading Stoker Cecil Doggett.

Doggett was another 22 year old, but he seemed older and went about his duties methodically. A man of scant conversation, Doggett was born in the city of Perth. Having been a member of the *Autolycus* commissioning crew and a veteran of the cruiser's Mediterranean campaign, he knew the ways of a stoker very well.

—

One of the most critical personnel shortages was in the category of wireless operators. Communication systems expanded rapidly during the early stages of World War II, and there was a high demand for individuals with morse code and telegraphy skills, like Cecil Gwatkin. Cecil William Delafield Gwatkin was born in Leith, Scotland, in 1920, and had spent the first five years of his life living in various parts of Wales and England. His parents, Alfred and Edith, migrated to Australia under the Soldier Settlement Scheme. They arrived full of optimism only to find the scheme had collapsed and they would receive no land. The following years were a struggle for the family, until Alfred, who was a nurseryman and horticulturist, found a position at a Sydney nursery. By the mid-thirties their fortunes improved and they were able to purchase their own home in Sydney. Sons Cecil and Ted were growing quickly and receiving a good education. Cecil, with the classic auburn-haired Gaelic colouring, excelled at the 'other football code', Aussie Rules. The family appreciated the lifestyle their new country offered and enjoyed many camping and fishing trips. Cecil became enamoured with the technologies of radio and studied to become a Wireless Operator in the Merchant Marine. He proved adept at morse and with a speed of more than 20 words a minute was quickly recruited by the RAN. Cecil perfected his skill at *Maitland*, the Naval Station at Shepherd's Hill in Newcastle, and on *Kybra* a requisitioned motor vessel used as an anti submarine and RDF training ship. By the time he joined *Perth* in the second half of 1941, he was engaged to another wireless operator, a member of the nascent Women's Royal Australian Naval Service (WRANS).

The Naval Board struggled with the concept of women in the ranks, as did the Minister for the Navy, William Morris Hughes. However, Cdr Newman, the Director of RAN Communications, pleaded with RAN hierarchy to enlist members of the Women's Emergency Signal Corps. WESC Director, Florence 'Mrs Mac' McKenzie, was an exceptional woman who had formed the WESC six months before the outbreak of war. She had designed a model device to demonstrate correct arm and hand morse transmission, and over the next year WESC members trained an estimated 3500 RAAF recruits in morse. By April 1941 WESC Signallers were members of the fledgling Women's Australian Auxiliary Air Force and, in August, the Australian Women's Army Service. 'Mrs Mac' found it more formidable 'to persuade the Naval Board to accept the girls'.[2] Cdr Newman continued to emphasise the shortage of 560 communicators in his department. A senior RAN spokesman told the press that one concern in accepting women volunteers was the need 'to adjust female talkativeness to the tradition of a silent service.'[3] Even more damming was the telegram sent by Minister Hughes, to the Prime Minister on 2 April 1941: 'In my opinion the employment of females in the Navy is undesirable'. But the RAN Communications Branch was desperate, so, begrudgingly, permission was given for fourteen members of the WESC to serve at the RAN Communication Station outside Canberra,[4] after Hughes stipulated, 'no publicity' be given to 'this break with tradition'. More women signallers were accepted surreptitiously to work outside Canberra and in Melbourne, but they remained classified as 'enrolled uniformed civilians'. Not until October 1942 were they officially enlisted in the WRANS.

The fickleness of RAN recruiting, whilst impacting most on the lower deck, had consequences for Australian-born midshipmen also. David Manning was one of seventeen thirteen-year-old Cadet Midshipmen who had arrived at the Royal Australian Naval College in 1937. Military service had been a constant in the Manning family; his father, William, as a member of the Australian 4th Light Horse, had taken part in the Battle of Beersheba and was wounded at Gallipoli.[5] On a visit to RANC the following year, William became engaged in an earnest discussion with a college Divisional Officer. The RANC staff member informed him there was 'no future for naval officers'.[6] A bleak picture was painted on both career and promotion prospects, and it was unlikely the junior Manning would get to sea. Early compulsory retirement was to be expected. The year was 1938, yet RAN authorities lacked vision and an appreciation of European friction, and Japanese expansionism, which would see Australia at war the following year.[7] Acting on the advice, William Manning withdrew his son from RANC and returned him to school. David Manning next approached the RAN Recruiting Office at age eighteen. The year was 1941 and this time the Victorian was offered a commission as a Sub-Lieutenant Coder. The land-based posting, at St Kilda Headquarters in Victoria, held no appeal and he entered as an Ordinary Seaman because of the likelihood of war service at sea. The RAN agreed, after stipulating he would join an Officer Training Course following three months at sea. It would be a course David would never undertake. After recruit training at *Cerberus,* Ord Seam Manning reported to *Perth.*

When Manning arrived at *Perth,* the supervising Chief PO remembered David from the RANC and, recalling the more rigid distinctions between upper and lower decks of previous years, addressed him not as Ord Seam Manning, but as 'Mr' Manning, in the manner a Chief would address a very junior officer, causing him some embarrassment. From January 1942 things became more awkward when Sub Lieuts Norm 'Knocker' White and Jack Lester posted in. The three men had been Cadet Midshipmen together in 1937. Manning and White were pitted against each other at the college in a boxing contest, and the then fourteen year olds, 'knocked the hell out of each other'. White was now Manning's superior officer, which added another challenging dimension to the junior Seaman's life.

—

Accommodation in the modified Leander class cruiser was clearly defined. Officers had small cabins in either aft or midships. The XO had a slightly larger and better fitted cabin. Officers' domestic work was carried out by Officer Stewards. Free time and meals were conducted in the wardroom. The Captain had a stateroom with bathroom aft, and a cabin and bathroom in the bridge structure, which he occupied in 1st degree readiness and certain 2nd degree readiness situations. The upper deck of the foc's'le held quarters for Chief POs, POs, Writers, Radio Technicians and tradesmen ranks generally. Seaman ratings messdecks were in the lower level of the foc's'le, the area of the ship located below the bridge on two decks towards the prow.

—

Perth spent January operating in the South West Pacific and Coral Sea. With such an influx of inexperienced ratings, Waller needed to depend on experienced career sailors to prepare the newest members of the ship's company for war. Never before in the RAN fleet were crews from such diversified backgrounds required to adopt common naval drill and professional expertise so quickly and cohesively. Waller was fortunate to have some of the best senior rates the RAN had in *Perth*. Men like Yeoman of Signals Neil Biddel; No.1 Fire and Repair Party linchpin Acting Stoker PO Al Blakey; Mechanician Spencer Blanch who divided his time between the forward engine room and being in charge of the aircraft catapult; Stoker PO Reg Frost who was normally found in the 'A' boiler room; and PO Geoff Balshaw who had left England on *Perth* in 1939 on loan from the RN to be in charge of the ASDIC until an Australian became qualified. Balshaw had started his navy career as an RN Boy Seaman but decided he liked *Perth* so much he would transfer to the RAN. Two others were Regulating PO Al Furey, who had been a member of the advance commissioning group and whose action station was the 4-inch magazine; and no one could miss the leader of *Perth's* No.2 Fire and Repair Party, Welshman Chief Stoker Gerwyn Llewellyn Evans.

Evans had enlisted in World War I and became a Chief Stoker in 1924. Evans was navy through and through and had served in most of the RAN fleet, including a couple of drafts on the old *Adelaide*, which was commonly spoken of by sailors as, 'the world's largest sea-going submarine', because it seemed *Adelaide* 'spent more time under water than above'. Evans's left forearm was emblazoned with the Welsh dragon; a 'Japanese lady' highlighted his right forearm; and birds and flowers covered his chest. Evans was one of the more colourful characters on *Perth* and for more reason than his tattoos.

—

Within the ocean of navy and white uniforms were six of a different hue. The RAAF had arrived onboard, along with a Walrus amphibious aircraft in November, in the form of Flying Officer Allen McDonough, Sergeant Harold Sparks, Corporals Ronald Bradshaw, Colin Nott and Phillip Will, and Aircraftsman Ernest Toe. Aircraft had proven valuable on cruisers and their operational success stretched resources of aircraft and personnel. The 9 Squadron (Fleet Co-operation) at the Richmond RAAF base had commenced with a skeleton staff. At the outbreak of war RAAF Seagull detachments had served in RAN ships: *Australia, Sydney, Hobart, Perth, Manoora, Westralia* and *Canberra*.[8] In December 1939 the squadron moved to RAAF Rathmines, north of Sydney. Training of crews and maintenance of aircraft often occurred at Rose Bay, Sydney Harbour, and the number of aircraft increased to 21 Seagulls. Within a short time many aircraft were destroyed, including *Perth*'s, or were put out of service, and only eight remained flying. Amphibians were borrowed from wherever they could be found, including the RN Walrus now fastened to *Perth*'s deck. Australian observers were initially trained by the RN. Telegraphist air gunners were trained at Sydney's Evans Head and Victoria's Point Cook before more training at Rathmines.

McDonough had joined the No.1 Flying Training School at Parafield, South Australia, as an Aircraftsman 2nd Class. His progression was rapid: first he was a Leading Aircraftsman undergoing Seaplane Training; within eight months of entry he was a Sergeant Airman Pilot; then he was discharged in February 1941 so he could be re-entered as a Pilot Officer, to join *Hobart,* then *Perth.*

Harold Sparks had not enjoyed being a salesman and desperately wanted to join his country's air force. He applied and was rejected for being medically unfit, for 'dental reasons', a legacy of a harsh childhood. This only increased his determination and he signed up at Melbourne

Technical College to do an 'Aero Engine Course'. For eighteen months he spent his days as a salesman to support his family, nights studying at Tech, and weekends and holidays at the local Aero Club. When he was re-interviewed for the RAAF he wore his suit and the recruiter noted: 'Tall, athletic build, very good appearance, particularly keen, bright, well spoken, very suitable type as airman'. It was August 1938 when a happy Sparks fulfilled his dream and put on his uniform for the first time. By 1941 he was a Sergeant Flight Fitter surrounded by sailors.

Unlike Sparks, Ron Bradshaw was a tall, gangly RAAF war entry. He had enjoyed his work as a Western Australian Railways mechanic. The RAAF trained him as a Fitter Armourer, and he spent time on *Hobart*. He could reflect on a diverse life, from trains to planes to ships, and had certainly found it interesting. He wondered what the next adventure would bring.

Colin Nott wrote on his 1940 enlistment form that he was 'keen' to join the RAAF 'to do his bit'. The blacksmith from Roma, Queensland, was a Private of the 61st Btn Queensland Cameron Highlanders, but the 61st didn't seem to be going anywhere soon enough and Nott wanted active service. The air force sent him to Laverton to train as an Aircraft Handler Technical (Fitter).

Phillip Will was another blacksmith, well at least he had been an apprentice for four and a half years and before that he had been a farmer. He was a quiet man who answered questions reluctantly. The South Australian would not have entered the armed forces if there had not been a war on.

The junior member of the RAAF men, and by far the shortest, was Aircraftsman Ernie Toe, a former Melbourne clerk/storekeeper. It was a profession he continued in the RAAF, his job being to ensure all parts necessary to keep the aircraft operational were there. He thought he entered the RAAF, but within months he was in a RAN cruiser on the high seas.

Ken Wallace from Sydney, on the other hand, had entered the RAN as a communicator and was then selected to be an Air Gunner. The first time he strapped himself into the Walrus to be catapulted off *Perth*'s deck, he was nervous. Adjusting his seat harness as tightly as he could,

Wallace looked to the Observer, Lieut David McWilliam for confidence, only to be told by McWilliam that it was the first time he too had been catapulted off a cruiser deck. Both men turned a little anxiously to the pilot Flying Officer Allen McDonough, and McWilliam said, 'Hope this is not your first catapult Mac'? The 26-year-old pilot nodded and McWilliam commented, 'Guess we'll all learn together'.[9]

The men braced themselves, as they hurtled along the 70-foot (21-metre) catapult platform in about two seconds. It was a dangerous procedure because the driving force was a charge of 5 kilograms of high explosive. If the catapult was not level, the results could be disastrous. If there was an upward tilt the aircraft would stall and crash; if there was a downward tilt the aircraft would be fired into the water. Wallace described it as like 'being in a car with a drunk who revs the engine to its peak and lets out the clutch. Very nasty'.[10] Should aircraft and crew survive the launch experience, they would return to as close to the ship's hull as possible and be hauled onboard by means of the crane and a good deal of sailor elbow grease. Those ordered to donate the elbow grease cursed the difficult and taxing chore. The cruiser itself was not well designed to house the crane and aircraft, and as *Perth* ploughed through an angry Bass Strait in February 1942 'clear lower deck' was piped to manhandle the heavy crane, which was 'listing the ship to a dangerous level'.[11]

—

When *Perth* pulled out of Sydney on 1 February 1942 for another trip down the Australian coastline, officers and sailors regarded the beauty of the rugged cliffs and long stretches of beach as their ship steamed toward Melbourne. None realised this would be the last time the cruiser would grace these waters. None, including the Captain, were privy to the political, diplomatic wranglings that enveloped the halls of the top Allied offices in several continents, or to the discord that would determine their fate.

The ship reached Melbourne on 4 February and all night leave was granted. *Perth* left Melbourne the following afternoon having taken on a new Executive Officer and ordered to proceed to Fremantle at speed.

Cdr William Harold Martin, RAN, had relieved the unpopular Cdr Reid. Reid's unhappy period on *Perth* was in part due to health problems and these continued to intrude on what he believed would be successful lifelong career. *Perth* was his last sea posting. After serving in shore establishments for the rest of the war, he was declared medically unfit, transferred to the emergency list, then the retired list in 1953. His promotion to the War Service rank of Commander was never confirmed. His replacement Cdr Martin, had also started out as a thirteen-year-old Cadet Midshipman RANC entry in 1917. Martin saw exchange service not only in the RN, but also with the South African Naval Forces. With the speciality of hydrography, most of his RAN sea time was spent in *Moresby*. The only other Australian ships Martin had served in were as a Sub Lieutenant in *Adelaide* in 1925, and three months as a Lieutenant in 1930 in *Canberra*. XO of *Perth* was going to be an amazing challenge.

It was fortunate that many of the senior sailors on the cruiser were familiar with the ship and the many comings and goings of junior crew, because the *Perth* wardroom suffered a huge posting upheaval. Wartime officer establishment for *Perth* was 43, only RN Lieut Cdrs Guy Clarke and John Johnson, Lieuts Cyril Palairet and Michael Highton, Warrant Engineer James Tuersley, Commissioned Gunners Hawkins and Ross, as well as RAN Engineer Cdr Robert 'Dolly' Gray remained from the first days of *Perth*. Sixteen of the 43 officers had joined the cruiser between October 1941 and February 1942. Of these, six officers arrived in February.

The *Perth* wardroom was a very unusual collection of officers. The youngest was Paymaster Midshipman Frank Murray Tranby-White, RAN. Born on his parents' country property near Winton, Queensland, it was a little strange that he should enter the navy in January 1940. So imbued was he with his outback heritage, he changed his name by deed poll a month later from White to include the name of his family property, Tranby. He joined *Perth* in November 1941 aged nineteen. Others hastily added in 1942 included Sub Lieut (Prob) Albert Leonard Ball, RANR. Ball had originally been mobilised for service as a sailor on small merchant vessels operating around the Australian coastline, known as Defensively Equipped Merchant Ships. Within a year he was selected for officer training. As a newly commissioned Sub Lieutenant, he went back to small ships until the urgent call to make up numbers on a cruiser, on 26 February 1942.

Paymaster Sub Lieut (Prob) Ray McCredie Barker was another who had joined as a nineteen-year-old sailor, as a Supply Assistant in 1939. He was promoted to Leading Supply Assistant before being sent back to *Cerberus* to undergoing officer training. Before joining *Perth* he had not been to sea. Another Paymaster was Sub Lieut Gavin Roy Campbell. Compared to Barker he had vast sea experience. Joining at eighteen from Portland, Victoria, Campbell, as a Paymaster Cadet, was posted to *Canberra* and *Hobart*. As a Midshipman he was returned to *Canberra*. A fortnight before his twenty-first birthday he joined *Perth*. This was a lot of sea duty compared to Engineer Lieut Francis Davidson Gillan, RANR(S). The 34-year-old engineer from Goondi, Queensland, donned a naval uniform for the first time in December 1941.

Another officer who joined in February 1942 was Lieut Cdr Llewellyn Leigh Watkins, RAN (Emergency List). Watkins was at the other end of the age spectrum to Barker. His date of birth was October 1899. His service card contained all manner of designation – RAN, RANR, Retired, Emergency List, Emergency Service. Watkins entered the RANC in 1912. As a Midshipman he was sent to England and saw war service during World War I on RN ships. Returning to Australia in 1921, Lieut Watkins served in HMAS *Sydney*. A year later, at just 23 years of age, he transferred to the 'Retired List'. A successful civilian career followed until January 1942, when he was hastily fitted for new uniforms and rushed to sea in *Perth*. It was truly a 'sea change'; Watkins had last set foot on a warship in 1921, the year Gavin Campbell was born.

—

Nations had watched as Japan launched a policy of expansionism in 1936. The previous year Japan had demanded equality in naval strength. When talks failed, the Japanese withdrew from the League of Nations and the Naval Treaty. The rest of the world took no action as the Japanese embarked on an accelerated warship manufacturing program. While British and American naval development between 1935 and 1938 was modest, by December 1941 the Japanese Navy had achieved 70 per cent of American naval strength. There were but diplomatic murmuring as Japan launched a brutal war of conquest against China. By 22 September 1941 Japanese forces occupied parts of Indo-China, and five days later signed the Tripartite Pact with Germany and Italy. British response was inaction.

As late as 1938 the British Government was assuring the Australian Government that, in the unlikely event Japan should move towards countries belonging to the British Commonwealth, seven capital ships would reinforce Singapore, even if the Empire was waging war against Germany. However, in the halls of the British Parliament few believed a Japanese attack would occur. In 1939 British Prime Minister Winston Churchill commented that the Japanese were 'a prudent people who would not embark upon such a mad enterprise'.[12] The British Admiralty was firm in their conviction to accept 'full responsibility of the defence of Australia, New Zealand or Singapore from Japanese attack'. Whether this was an oversight or deceit has been hotly debated. In the 1930s the British preferred not to admit that British naval supremacy had been lost, and the defence of Australia was never the main objective of imperial defence strategy. Australian authorities willingly subscribed to the strategic illusion that a navy in one hemisphere would and could protect interests in another. Whilst defence autonomy was beyond the nation's means, Australian politicians willingly coupled their country's security to a superior nation, ignoring the fact that the superior power was essentially interested in its own security. This delusion was still embraced many decades later.

The Australian Government allowed itself to be lulled into a false sense of security. This was compounded by British and Australian racial superiority beliefs, which led to a complete underestimation of the Japanese. By December 1941 Japanese forces occupied parts of Thailand, the Philippines, Hong Kong, Malaya, Borneo and Burma and had sunk not only HM *Prince of Wales* and *Repulse*, but a considerable portion of the United States Pacific fleet. Yet still Allied high command dithered. In January General Wavell was appointed Supreme

Commander in South West Pacific, and the joint American, British, Dutch and Australian Command (ABDA) was formed, to prevent the Japanese capturing the Dutch East Indies – at least that was the theory.

Wavell was contemptuous of the Japanese. He declared, 'the Jap has a very poor chance of successfully attacking Malaya, and I don't think myself, there is much prospect of his trying'. British General Robert Brooke-Popham, Commander in Chief of British Forces in the Far East, made the observation in December 1940 that the Japanese troop was a 'sub-human specimen', who would be unable to form 'an intelligent fighting force'. One of his battalion commanders even lamented that British soldiers should have to face such inferior opposition; another thought it a pity that British strength in Malay would mean the Japanese would never attack.[13] A senior Royal Air Force officer retorted, 'Jap planes are a joke. They're tied together with bits of string and bamboo, and not many of those'.[14]

The Japanese were not listening and attacked Malaya. On 23 January 1942 Japanese forces captured Rabaul and New Britain (Papua New Guinea). John Curtin, Australian Prime Minister since October, cabled Churchill: 'after all the assurances we have been given the evacuation of Singapore would be regarded ... as an inexcusable betrayal'. Five different national authorities controlled naval dispositions in different regions, and there was little liaison between them. Further divergence of views existed between those who controlled naval strategic dispositions from Washington and those in London, confusion reigned. Unbeknown to the British Admiralty, the Chiefs of Staff based in Washington DC, had on 29 January requested *Perth* be sent to the ABDA region to reinforce Allied forces. Yet British military command in Malaya had conceded the area was no longer defendable and with their forces in retreat from the mainland to Singapore Island, closed Singapore naval dockyard on 30 January.[15] Meanwhile *Perth* was on its way to Fremantle to escort a convoy to the ABDA region, a convoy which had nowhere to go.

—

The cruiser reached Fremantle the afternoon of 5 February 1942 and leave was granted. Next day *Perth* adopted a northerly course, for the

Dutch East Indies. The orders were countermanded and *Perth* returned to Fremantle. Lieut Albert Ball asked his Captain if he needed permission to get married. Rapid changes of orders and the rumours flying around meant Ball and his fiancée Beryl had decided 'better now than later'. Waller gave his blessing. New orders were received to rendezvous with a convoy that included a freighter and five empty tankers on their way to the port of Palembang, Sumatra, for oil. *Canberra* had been due to undertake the escort duty but developed mechanical trouble and could not sail. It was just another one of those quirks of fate.

Rather than stir any superstitions his crew harboured concerning Friday the thirteenth, Waller deferred Fremantle departure time to 0030 on the fourteenth. The convoy was reached the following day and *Adelaide* relieved. Intelligence filtered through. Dutch East Indies oil was no longer available so the convoy was ordered to return to Fremantle. Shortly after the convoy assumed a southerly course, the order was countermanded, and *Perth* ordered to 'about face' and continue a solitary course for Java. Sailors muttered it was a little like a slapstick movie, enough to make anyone giddy, and certainly didn't increase their confidence in those in command.

On 15 February Singapore capitulated. The 'impregnable fortress' the 'mighty island fortress', the 'Guardian of the East' had been a farce. Some 1789 Australian troops had been killed, a further 1300 wounded and another 15,395 Australians were now POWs. One Australian soldier's reaction was:

> A thousand planes at least
> It simply can't be taken,
> We'll stand a siege for years.
> We'll hold the place forever.
> And reduce the foe to tears.
> Our men are there in thousands.
> The defences are unique.
> But the Japs would not believe it
> And took it in a week.[16]

The news of the fall of Singapore was received at sea and broadcast throughout the ship. There were those onboard who believed *Perth* should never have been detached from the Australian fleet based in Brisbane and operating in the Coral Sea area.[17] It was difficult to avoid a sense of doom, and the question, 'Why then are we heading in that direction?'[18] It is a question that should have received urgent debate in the Australian War Cabinet. Churchill's Defence Committee decided against reinforcing the Dutch East Indies in preference to consolidating the British position in Burma. This decision either never made it to Australia or was lost in translation, because Australian troops returning from the Middle East were not rerouted to Burma or Australia, but to the Dutch East Indies, and *Perth* continued to sail north.

While 'Black Friday' had been avoided, the more superstitious in the cruiser were still unsettled. *Perth* left Fremantle with two navy chaplains onboard, and according to superstition this was never a good omen. James Keith Wilson Mathieson had spent his impressionable years watching his father serve customers in the family shop in Cobden, Victoria. Religion was also a big influence, and his paternal grandfather, after whom he was named, was a Methodist minister. Whether there was something in the name or not, he too became a Methodist minister. With the advent of war, 'Keith' Mathieson believed he could be of more use to his God and others, in the military. He could not have foreseen how great that need would be, or how important he would be in the grand scheme. The Reverend Mathieson was accepted an RAN Chaplain in 1941. On that day known as 'Black Friday', a day for witches, demons and mayhem, he boarded *Perth* for the journey north to transfer to his new ship *Hobart*.

Joining on Friday the thirteenth was bad enough, but being the second chaplain onboard really had old seafarers muttering. He needed patience in this new world of sea, ships and superstitions. There was time on the trip to Java to learn more from *Perth*'s 'real chaplain', who was an experienced and interesting man. The Reverend Ronald Sutton Bevington was as English as Mathieson was Australian. While Mathieson had followed his grandfather, the 30-year-old Church of England chaplain had followed his father into the ministry. The

Reverend Bevington Snr was currently tending the flock at St Saviour's in Capetown, South Africa. His son was *Perth*'s commissioning chaplain and had overseen funerals at sea and counselled men during the difficult days of the Med campaign. Yes, there was a lot Mathieson could learn.

At 0930 on 19 February the drone of heavy bombers drew the people of Darwin outside. As citizens craned their necks upwards, there was barely time to register the wings were adorned with an ominous red sun, before the aircraft released their deadly cargo. Masses of ships moored around Darwin were unprotected. The 81 Japanese aircraft that attacked Australia's northern capital in the first run were detected too late and they faced minimal resistance.[19] A second raid involving 54 Japanese bombers hit the city at around midday. In all 242 Japanese aircraft were involved in the audacious raid and 243 Australians were believed killed.[20] Destruction to the harbour, to shipping, to the cityscape and airfield was enormous. The extent of the damage and loss of life was initially censored from the southern media, in a bid to minimise panic within the Australian population. There would be a further 62 raids on Darwin, and others on the northern perimeter of Australia from Broome in Western Australia to Townsville in Queensland. Among those killed in this first attack on Darwin were three sailors in the minesweeper *Swan*; one in the boom working vessel HMAS *Kangaroo*; two sailors in the boom gate vessel HMAS *Kara Kara*, and Ord Seam Herb Shepherd died of wounds received onboard the auxiliary minesweeper *Gunbar*. Two dozen members of the RAN were wounded. Leading Seaman Johnny Salt, AB Sandy Purden and AB Ernie Hodgson were gunners in *Swan*. The three were ex-*Perth* sailors. Having survived the Mediterranean campaign, they were unconcerned about service out of the 'top end', but Purden and Salt were both killed when Japanese aircraft attacked the harbour. Hodgson was wounded. The irony was not lost on their families, or the families of Leading Cook Frank Emms and PO Frank Moore. These men were killed serving with 29 others in a single screw, a former Derwent River ferry and now a boom gate vessel, named HMAS *Kara Kara*, in a northern Australian port; navy men at sea were never really safe.

Perth shortly received another order from Navy HQ; the cruiser was to return to Fremantle. No sooner was this conveyed to the Captain and bridge duty personnel, but this order also was countermanded and *Perth* was finally left to journey north into a hopeless situation.

ABDA's commands came too little too late, and confusion reigned. On 20 February, General Wavell issued a 'no surrender of Java' order to Allied forces, yet four days earlier in a message to Churchill he divulged the hopelessness of the situation: 'Loss of Java, though a severe blow from every point of view, would not be fatal. Efforts should not therefore be made to reinforce Java'.[21] Then, the day after Wavell issued the 'no surrender of Java' order, he again cabled Churchill that defence was impossible, 'Java cannot now last long. Anything put into Java now can do little to prolong the struggle; it is more a question of what you will choose to save'.[22]

There was little liaison between land and sea commanders and the many levels of international command confused the situation further. The Combined Chiefs of Staff in faraway Washington DC, reiterated that Java should be held at all cost and there should be no withdrawal. Being subjected to an overwhelming Japanese attack, Wavell lacked their conviction. Rear Admiral Glassford, US Navy, who commanded the US Asiatic Fleet, ordered his auxiliary ships and tenders to Australia. Dutch Admiral Conrad Helfrich condemned any withdrawal proposals and demanded more naval forces. The man in charge of the British China Force, Commodore John Collins, seemed to agree with Helfrich and issued the final order for *Perth* to maintain course for Java, an order that appeared to contravene an earlier order from his British superiors. It is unclear who was responsible for the lapse of judgement, but it continued the tradition of sacrificing Australian defence personnel in ill-conceived strategic campaigns implemented by overseas authorities. The Australian cruiser was the last-minute pawn in a belated attempt to appease the Dutch. Those who dictated British Dutch East Indies strategy, due to arrogance or ignorance, or a combination of both, completely misjudged the capability of the Japanese and had forsaken *Perth* and crew to a deadly fate.

EIGHT

'Perth in anger was one of the finest sights.'[1]
USS Houston officer

The situation was chaotic when *Perth* entered the port of Tanjong Priok on the north-western end of the island of Java, shortly after daybreak on 24 February. The harbour was crowded with ships of all sizes, overflowing with passengers anxious to escape. Waller and Lieut John Harper went ashore to Navy Office to discuss the situation with Commodore Collins. The Australian Commodore was unavailable, believed to be elsewhere in Java. No other navy staff members could be found, so *Perth*'s CO and Navigator returned to their ship. Had there been any doubts about the seriousness of the situation, these were quickly dispelled when the harbour was attacked by Japanese aircraft that afternoon. Continued confusion within the highest offices of command rendered the situation facing the Australian cruiser and crew increasingly dangerous. On 25 February ABDA command, always fragile, quickly crumbled. General Wavell ceased being Supreme Commander and retreated to India.

The Australian River class sloop *Yarra* was a comforting sight in harbour,[2] and morale rose further at the sight of HMAS *Hobart* entering the harbour to commence refuelling. The elation was mutual; onboard *Hobart* Chief PO Robert Blain was delighted to see the familiar shape of the sister cruiser. His 'delight' was, however, 'mixed with fear.

Almost trapped ourselves, we hated to feel that another Aussie ship might be trapped too'.[3] The Australians were looking forward to social interaction with classmates and friends, even if it was hasty. Lieut Cdrs 'Polo' Owen and Watkins, a number of ratings, and the second chaplain, the Rev. Mathieson, prepared to transship to *Hobart*. However, the motorboat was half way between the cruisers when the shrill noise of the air-raid siren sounded.

Officer of the Watch, Lieut William Gay, recalled the boat. *Perth* guns were elevated to avoid the dockyard godowns (warehouses) and all turrets fired simultaneously, as Japanese aircraft screamed in on their attacking runs. The barrage forced the aircraft to break off and retreat, but not before the oil tanker refuelling *Hobart* caught fire, forcing the warship to withdraw hastily to a harbour anchorage. When the smoke dissipated it was found fabric had been torn from *Perth*'s plane, rendering it unserviceable. How unfortunate this was would be fully appreciated later, when air reconnaissance may have revealed the peril that lurked in adjacent waters.

Orders were received to leave port without further delay and rendezvous with the ABDA fleet in Surabaya, the main port at the eastern end of Java. *Hobart* was told to remain until fully fuelled. The men who had been due to transship could not, and, in another twist of fate, their futures were cemented to those of others in *Perth*.

ABDA Commander Admiral Helfrich, who had assumed command, was determined to save his beloved Dutch East Indies and signalled, 'Sacrifice is necessary for the defence of Java'.[4] On 25 February the destiny of Indies-based Australian warships and their crews hung in the balance. Allied Command and/or the Australian War Cabinet could still order their return to Australian waters, to protect the nation's vulnerable north. But no such order was given. They attempted to justify this action on the grounds that Japanese forces were better stopped in the East Indies, 'better there than Australia'. But land commanders such as Wavell had already deemed the situation indefensible – there was little resistance to the Japanese ashore. From 16 February, when Wavell had advised 'Efforts should not therefore be made to reinforce Java',[5] the security of the Dutch East Indies had been compromised;

any naval attempt to resist could do little more than 'demonstrate the gallantry of the defenders'.[6] During the evening of 25 February orders were changed twice. Finally ABDA ships congregated at Surabaya at midday on 26 February. Waller reported to Navy HQ for a conference with Admiral Karel Doorman and other ship Commanding Officers. It would be the first and the last such conference. The question of air cover was raised, and they were told the US aircraft transport ship *Langley* was on its way. Doorman, being the senior ranked officer, and with the blessing of Admiral Helfrich, assumed command of the ABDA Fleet. When Waller returned, it was clear to his own officers he was unhappy with the confused and hasty arrangements. How could this multi-national fleet with no previous operational service integrate successfully into a viable combat force?

—

Perth's crew had been closed up most of the night. The baptism of fire for the uninitiated onboard was exciting and scary at the same time. The ship's Acting Leading Telegraphist Air Gunner, Ken 'Tag' Wallace like so many of the younger men, had welcomed the opportunity to participate in the adventure of war. His eagerness was already quelled: 'I was disgusted with myself to think that one air raid had thoroughly frightened me and I was not the hero I had imagined myself to be. I was quite happy to go home to Australia now and live a nice peaceful existence.'[7]

Alan Geier was another first timer. The air raid at Tanjong Priok had certainly got the adrenalin soaring and now he was thoroughly tired. The brown-haired Wireman looked out at the assembled fleet and thought it pretty impressive. Five cruisers and nine destroyers under the flags of four nations, it was obvious something big was going to happen fairly soon. As he flexed stiff shoulders he reflected on the date, it was his birthday. No longer was he a teenager; today he was 20. He knew the family back in Albury, New South Wales, would be thinking of him and would be lucky enough to raise a beer or two in his honour. They could not have imagined how he was spending his twentieth birthday. To youngsters like Geier, the ABDA fleet looked impressive, the 8-inch cruisers HMS *Exeter* and USS *Houston*; the 6-inch cruiser *Perth*; two 5.9-inch Dutch cruisers HNM ships *De Ruyter* and *Java*; and nine destroyers, HM ships *Electra*, *Encounter* and *Jupiter*, US ships *John D. Edwards*, *John D. Ford*, *Alden* and *Paul Jones*, and HNM ships *Kortenaer* and *Witte de With*.

As big ships went USS *Houston* was 'one hell of a good looking ship'. The Japanese claimed to have sunk the heavy cruiser so many times during the previous months that the American ship assumed the nickname 'The Galloping Ghost of the Java Coast'. Six hundred feet (183 metres) long, with a displacement of over 10,000 tons, a top speed of 35 knots and 8-inch guns with a range of around 31,000 yards (28,300 metres), was enough to excite any 'old salt' within the *Perth* crew. For the Australians the story of *Houston*'s most recent foray was as exhilarating as it was sobering. On 4 February in the Flores Sea, north of Bali, *Houston* was attacked by Japanese dive bombers. A 500-pound bomb slammed into the searchlight platform on the main mast, through the radio shack, and blasted a 12-foot (3.7-metre) hole in the deck, just forward of the number three turret. Ammunition ignited, killing all hands in the turret and in the ammunition handling room below.[8] During the action 48 sailors were killed and many more injured. *Houston* retreated to the port of Tjilatjap to bury the dead. The loss of life shocked those onboard and those ashore, who stood with heads bowed as the slow procession of trucks loaded with caskets moved through the dusty streets towards the cemetery overlooking the Indian Ocean. The 'dull roll of muffled drums' brought an Australian airman out of his building:

A long funeral procession was passing … dozens of draped coffins, hundreds of American sailors. What tragedy was this? The wounded were disembarked later, a score of them with shockingly burnt faces and sightless eyes. It seemed almost ghoulish to inquire the details.[9]

Perth officers and sailors, who reflected on what they heard, would shortly have their futures inexorably interwoven with those who remained in *Houston*.

—

Admiral Helfrich dispatched the command 'to attack until you have demolished the Japanese force'.[10] Crews were closed up at action stations all night and well into the day as the fleet swept to the west and north-east. Intelligence reports were wrong, the enemy was not found and the naval force returned to Surabaya. Crews needed rest and ships needed fuel, but a reconnaissance aircraft sighted Japanese ships 190 miles (305 kilometres) north-east, and the ABDA fleet was instructed to proceed at speed to intercept.

Morale in *Perth* was good, sailors although tense believed the Allies would, 'engage the elusive enemy as quickly as possible and do maximum damage to any invasion force'.[11] Few onboard were privy to the concerns Waller carried about the readiness and cohesiveness of the ABDA fleet. The Mediterranean had given him battle experience lacking in the captains of other ABDA ships. Waller had learnt to gauge his enemy carefully, but now he needed to reassure his crew, 'We hope to meet the Japanese tonight and give them hell'. Cheers rang through the ship. AB Ernie Toovey on hearing the scuttlebutt about the opposing force figured, 'the job looked easy – only 30 transports escorted by two cruisers and four destroyers ... we would be home for breakfast'.[12]

Doorman's final plea for air cover went unfulfilled. Japanese bombers sank USS *Langley* on 27 February. Even had the aircraft not been destroyed, it is unlikely they would have arrived in time. Nothing was sighted that night, or the following morning. Closed up at action stations, ship crews sweated in the tropical heat, and exhaustion increased as temperatures exceeded 100° Fahrenheit (38° Celsius). In areas like the *Perth* magazine it 'was like an oven'.[13] Heat exhaustion was a common affliction for those in the cruiser's engine and boiler rooms, where temperatures of 140° Fahrenheit (60° Celsius) were recorded. During action stations, others closed up in the shell handling rooms, the transmitting station, and the aft steering position, a compartment beneath the quarterdeck, were also of particular concern to Surgeon Lieut Sam Stening: 'I place special stress on the appalling conditions in those places under action conditions in the tropics'. Of these days in February he wrote, 'conditions were at their worst.'[14]

The afternoon of 27 February dragged on until out of seemingly nowhere a stick of bombs fell dangerously close to HMS *Jupiter*. An eerie silence returned. ABDA officers and men wiped fogged up binocular lenses as sweat trickled down their faces, and scanned the horizon with increased urgency. Allied Intelligence was vague on specific details concerning the convoy, then they saw the enemy fleet for the first time and it quickly became clear that this was not the thinly protected transports expected, 'a veritable forest of masts filled the whole rim of the horizon as far as the eye could see'.[15] Furthermore, the Japanese command was fully aware of the disposition of the ABDA fleet. Japanese spotting aircraft had enabled their transports to be despatched prior to contact, and ensured the Allies would be the only ones surprised.

—

The Battle of Java Sea commenced at 1616 as a long-range gunnery duel, when the Japanese heavy cruisers *Nachi* and *Haguro* opened fire from a distance of 30,000 yards (27,400 metres). *Perth* crew knew this range far exceeded that of their own ship and felt thoroughly exposed as shells exploded closer and closer. For Sub Lieut Gavin Campbell it was 'seeing flashes on the horizon and then the dreadful wait for the shells to arrive. The screech and then the splash – not the great splashes one sees in pictures but small and brown and they straddled us'.[16] Doorman failed to close the range for nearly an hour, during which time the Japanese brought their twenty 8-inch guns to bear on the ABDA fleet, whilst being opposed by twelve. This exemplified the mismatched contest unfolding. After what seemed an eternity, HMS *Exeter* and USS *Houston* finally opened fire. Waller was unhappy. *Perth* was second last in line and exposed to salvos without the ability to return fire. Waller was immediately impressed by enemy long-range fire, which was 'extremely accurate' and 'found a long period of being "Aunt Sally" very trying, without being able to return the fire'.[17]

Fourteen Japanese destroyers joined the battle and released their torpedoes. Unbeknown to the Allies the Japanese arsenal included the Long Lance Torpedo, a torpedo much superior to their own. *Exeter* was hit by a 6-inch shell in the aft boiler room at 1714, and the cruiser's speed dropped dramatically.

Confusion dominated the Allied attack. Because the fleet had never operated together, signal communication was of even greater importance, but communication between the Allied ships was poor. The flagship's signalling apparatus was affected by the vibration of its own guns. With no universal language, orders from the flagship were sent via short-wave radio to *Houston,* and an interpreter on the US cruiser translated orders for relay by radio or light to British ships.[18] A *Houston* officer observed 'the British, on occasion, used their own flag signals, which no one else could read.'[19] ABDA HQ ordered codes and cyphers common only to the British be dispensed with and the seldom-used Anglo French Tactical Code utilised instead. *Perth* communicators did as they were instructed, but when it became clear the Dutch and Americans were no more familiar with this code, they went to standard naval cyphers.[20] The adage 'the blind leading the blind' took on an ominous meaning.

At one point *Houston* altered course suddenly to avoid hitting *Exeter*. Waller, believing he had missed a signal from the flagship, followed *Houston*. Waller ordered another high-speed course change to lay a protective smoke screen around *Exeter*. Ironically the Japanese regarded these rapid course changes as 'an ingenious tactical move to thwart the school of advancing torpedoes'.[21]

At 1715 the Dutch destroyer *Kortenaer* was hit by torpedo and 'exploded into a big fireball. The two masts flew skywards and the hull broke in two'.[22] Ord Seam David Manning was in the lookout position between the port and the starboard guns. He had a full view of the battle, of warships moving in and out of smoke, of guns flashing on the horizon and the horrifying sight of the two halves of *Kortenaer* with its crew disappearing downwards. Another destroyer was hit and began to sink. Most ships, except the 'lucky ship *Perth*', had already sustained damage.

Doorman ordered the Allied ships into 'line ahead' behind the flagship, but the 'line' was quickly becoming sparser. *Exeter* with a destroyer escort limped back towards port.

HMS *Electra* was the next ship to plunge to the depths of the Java Sea. Doorman ordered the four US destroyers to counter attack, then cancelled the order, then ordered them 'to cover his retirement'. The mixed messages confused and resulted in the US destroyers releasing their torpedoes. They rejoined the line without inflicting damage. Japanese floatplanes dropped flares illuminating the remaining ABDA ships. *Perth*'s 6-inch guns opened fire at 1933, the battle had been waging around them for three hours. The US destroyers, low on fuel and with no torpedoes, turned away towards Java. ABDA command had grossly underestimated the Japanese. The Allied fleet was outnumbered and outgunned; it lacked cohesion and proper command; and with no supporting air cover it was totally compromised. Yeoman Jack Willis had a bird's eye view of the Japanese fleet from his position on *Perth*: 'The Nipponese appeared to have a splendid organisation and aircraft and submarine operations in perfect co-ordination with their surface craft'.[23] Waller noted 'the enemy's disposition of his forces must have been ridiculously easy'.[24] He had been correct in his concerns regarding the ABDA Fleet. The Japanese had learnt their lessons from the RN well.[25]

At 2125 the destroyer HMS *Jupiter* exploded and was engulfed in flames. Ironically, it had hit a Dutch laid mine. *Encounter* picked up 113 *Kortenaer* survivors and left for Surabaya. Only the Dutch cruisers *De Ruyter* and *Java*, and *Houston* and *Perth* remained. An officer onboard *Houston* watched *Perth*:

... in admiration, the large, snow-white wave at her bow like a bone in her teeth. From the yardarms and the gaff there streamed three huge battle ensigns, proud and stiff with the speed of the ship. All her guns were firing rapidly. *Perth* in anger was one of the finest sights.[26]

Those in the Australian ship were no less impressed, particularly with the handling skills of their Captain. With rapid course changes he danced *Perth* through the deadly ballet. Officers and men below decks braced themselves against bulkheads and swore, as lockers and storage spaces opened and cleared themselves of their contents. "'Hardover Hec" is at it again' they muttered, and their curses were good natured ones.

At 2250 *De Ruyter* was hit by torpedo and caught fire. Subsequent explosions onboard sent shock waves severe enough to knock some *Perth* upper-deck personnel off their feet; others felt the heat blast. Terrifying pyrotechnics accompanied the flagship's total destruction. Pieces of wreckage fell on the Australian ship and as *Perth* 'scraped along *De Ruyter's* port side we could hear the screams of injured men and smell the unmistakable odour of burning flesh'.[27]

Perth bridge personnel had barely time to register how fortunate their ship was to avoid the detonation, when *Java* was torpedoed and sank rapidly. Of the 965 officers and sailors onboard *De Ruyter* and *Java,* 855 perished. Wireman Fred Lasslett noted, 'I'd never seen so many big tough men turning to religion and praying'.[28]

Only the Australian and American cruisers remained. Admiral Helfrich had ordered the attack to continue until the enemy was destroyed, no matter what the cost. The ABDA force had fought with conviction, but the cost had been huge and the enemy barely rebuked.[29] It was pointless to continue the useless sacrifice. Waller, as senior officer, assumed command, and without hesitation ordered a retreat to Tanjong Priok. From Headquarters Admiral Helfrich continued his opposition to the withdrawal. Waller had directly disobeyed his order and Helfrich believed those onboard *Perth* and *Houston* should have 'sold their lives at great cost to the enemy'.[30] In his official report, Cdr Henry E. Eccles, USN, of the destroyer USS *John D. Edwards*, wrote of the Battle of Java Sea:

A tragic commentary on the futility of attempting to oppose a powerful, determined, well-equipped and organised enemy by makeshift improvisation. It was evident that the Dutch had little tactical experience: their knowledge of Communications was rudimentary; and they went under the assumption that a hastily organised, uncoordinated force of ships, from three navies, could be assembled and taken into a major action.[31]

—

The remaining cruisers arrived in the port at 1430 the following day. Tanjong Priok was a mess. The stench of death hung heavy in the harbour air, as the cruisers carefully manoeuvred towards the wharf. Crews were met with the unnerving sight of sunken ship superstructures stark above the waterline, warehouses with shattered windows and buckled dockyard cranes – all testimony to the Allied defeat.

Perth and *Houston* were low on fuel and ammunition, but initial requests for fuel were denied by port authorities, who wished to safeguard the remaining 1000 tons of oil for Dutch warships. They could not be convinced that the Dutch East Indies Fleet would not be returning. After protest the Australians were allowed to take on 300 tons, little more than 50 per cent capacity. *Houston* was not permitted fuel, as port authorities argued the Americans had sufficient.[32]

Shore parties were dispatched in search of ammunition and supplies. Only some 4-inch ammunition was found, and this, plus assorted goods, were brought onboard. Along with tinned food, sailors availed themselves of cartons of cigarettes and bottles of whiskey. Almost as an afterthought, 24 copper and wood 'Pilgrim' rafts were dragged up gangways and stored on the quarterdeck. Sailors grumbled at the chore, they had no way of knowing how important these would soon become.

Everyone hurried to prepare *Perth* for sailing. The upper deck was littered with cordite boxes and shell cases. Below deck anything not secured had smashed to the deck, and the superstitious were muttering again. The portrait of the commissioning lady, Princess Marina, had twice fallen from the bulkhead in the starboard waist; there were still two navy chaplains onboard; and worst still, the ship's cat, Red Lead, had tried to escape. Twice the cat had scurried off the cruiser to the dockside, twice she was retrieved by sailors. Red Lead had never tried to escape before; this was indeed a bad omen. Then, as *Perth*'s lines were slipped at 1900, the ship crunched against the concrete wharf and smashed one of the starboard propellers.

Just prior to departure Waller asked Lieut Cdr 'Polo' Owen a question. Owen had been so far unable to join his ship *Hobart*. Waller and Owen had endured the Mediterranean campaign in *Stuart,* so the question was made in a familiar, humorous tone: 'Polo, we're sailing for Tjilatjap. Are you coming with us or going ashore to become a prisoner of the Japs?'[33] The question caused Owen to smile, then and later.

—

After carefully negotiating the minefield, the two cruisers again moved into the Java Sea. Only now did those onboard have time to reflect on the previous days, and on what may lie ahead. For many in *Perth* their battle initiation had raced past in a blur, fear dulled by activity. Now the adrenaline had subsided, weariness hung heavily in its place, that flat, thoroughly depleted feeling, but they were alive and their ship miraculously unscathed. Thoughts of the many seamen from several nations who had perished were hidden beneath swagger and jocular comments. AB 'Tich' Hill participated in discussion about the damage to enemy ships *Perth* had likely inflicted, but now 'in calmer retrospect I began to think of the Japanese sailors our shells had probably killed'.[34]

Their Captain was raised to even greater status as sailors shook their heads and discussed how Waller seemed to know exactly where each enemy salvo was destined to fall, swinging the cruiser on rapid course changes as if it was a destroyer. There was general agreement that the Battle of the Java Sea would have had a more successful outcome had Waller been in charge of the Allied fleet, at least as far as the his ship's company was concerned.

Before the battle, comments like: 'The Japs can't see in the dark' reflected generally held racial superiority beliefs. Whilst historians may find fault in Japanese naval operational effectiveness, this naval battle encouraged some reassessment of February 1942 perceptions. Yeoman Jack Willis wasn't the only man who admired the opposing naval forces, or who had been startled by the strength of their numbers. One *Houston* crew member described the situation in very blunt terms, likening the Allies to 'gnats'. Against the Japanese naval forces, it was a case of 'gnats on the back of an elephant.'[35]

Perth's crew was very fatigued; there had been little rest in four days. The Battle of the Java Sea, constant air alarms and enemy contacts, required great vigilance, plus physical and mental exertion. Battle stations had been manned for more than half of the period. Meals had been irregular, there had been no time to bathe or change clothes. Engineering staff were exhausted by the sustained effort, so too the gun crews and ammunition supply parties. The tropical conditions exacerbated time spent at 1st and 2nd stage readiness. Ord Seam Arthur Bancroft was getting used to being out in the elements, having been transferred from the 6-inch magazine lobby to the 4-inch gun deck. He did not realise at the time how fortunate this was, one of several lucky twists of fate that would bless Arthur Bancroft.

Still at 2nd degree readiness, men remained at their action stations, and heads slumped on chests. Waller told the ship's company early in his command that he did not intend to be caught 'napping', so they could expect to spend a great deal of time closed up. His men had no problem with this; it was a good idea to put one's trust in this CO. PO Steward Bill Davis, a small slight man, lay near the port-side 4-inch gun. Born in Bristol, England, Davis had enlisted in the RAN in 1927 as a 22-year-old Officer Steward. AB Keith Gosden wondered if he should leave his position in the 'Y' turret gun lobby. The steel room where he had spent much of the last five days was oppressively hot. Much of the time he was stripped down to underpants and boots. His duty was to load 6-inch ammunition into the shell rack on the automatic hoist, which moved noisily into the turret. Perspiration covered his body. He had been almost as hot on the beach at Glenelg, in his native Adelaide, but that had been a dry heat and the scenery much more pleasant. Oh, to be on that Aussie beach now.

Sub Lieut Gavin Campbell settled down at his 'readiness' position at the .5-inch machine gun station above the 'Y' 6-inch gun turret. He had been a last-minute replacement, joining the cruiser just seventeen days ago, and what a seventeen days it had been! It seemed this was the first opportunity he had to draw breath and think about what had taken place. As Captain's Secretary, much of the previous eighteeen hours were spent writing up Waller's Battle Report, so Campbell knew better than most his Captain's disenchantment on the conduct of the battle:

> Yes, that Battle Report, utter trauma. I had only a few hours to get it together from all heads of departments and then *DO* it. I held back the Commodore's driver so that he could take the finished report before the ship sailed, otherwise, as it happened, no one would have known what had occurred.[36]

Campbell stretched out his six-foot plus frame in his white officer issue overalls. His action station was a long way from the bridge and offered a perspective of the stern region (back end) of the cruiser. Campbell had turned 21 on the eve of the Battle of Java Sea, 'as *Yarra* was alongside I had the CO LCDR Bob Rankin to help "shove the boat out"'. Nonetheless Campbell could be forgiven for hoping his next birthday would be spent in more enjoyable circumstances. It wouldn't. The CO of *Yarra*, Lieut Cdr Bob Rankin, would be killed in enemy action just two days later.

Waller and Captain Albert Rooks, the Commanding Officer of *Houston*, had conferred on the only course of action – an escape to Australia, the best route appearing to be through Sunda Strait. Dutch reconnaissance assured Waller no enemy naval forces were within ten hours steaming time of Sunda Strait, and course was set for Toppers Island. An audible sigh of relief swept through *Perth* as their Captain announced they were returning home without further delay. Although there was a report of a large enemy convoy some 50 miles (80 kilometres) to the north-east, they were unlikely 'to meet enemy forces'.[37] Optimism rose, and the tension dissipated slightly. Sailors so wanted to believe this fight was over and they were truly on their way home. AB 'Tich' Hill looked out at the moonlit Java mainland and mused:

> On such a night, with romantic Bali just over the horizon, I should have been on a white cruise liner with a girl beside me. Instead I found myself on a lean grey cruiser built expressly for the purpose of killing, retreating from a lost battle.[38]

There was rarely any respite for the engineering section. Even during the time in Tanjong Priok, they had kept steam up, ready for a rapid departure. Acting Stoker PO Patrick 'Chopper' Sands was in 'A' boiler room supervising 20-year-old Stoker IIs like Les McMurdo from Sydney and Charlie Bennett. McMurdo was only 5 foot 2 but a willing worker. Bennett was less inclined and someone Sands needed to encourage more. By the time the young Victorian drafted to *Perth* in December, his reputation had preceded him. Clearly he never really wanted to join the navy, he enjoyed life just as it was, wheeling and dealing in civvy street, but the war left him no option. He did not settle well into hierarchical RAN life; he didn't like being told what to do every minute of the day. In May 1941, six months after he put on a navy uniform, he deserted his ship at the port of Cairns in far north Queensland. Authorities caught up with him in Mackay, and he was arrested and returned to Sydney to be tried. He spent 53 days locked up, then was sent to the tug *Heros*. Stokers were needed in *Perth* so he was drafted to the cruiser. He didn't settle well to *Perth* life either and was sentenced to five more days locked up in December. His service record was marked only 'Moderate' for 'Character' and 'Fair' for 'Efficiency', giving him the worst classification on the ship. Bennett wanted to be finished with the ship and this whole damn war.

Sands looked at the incredibly young-looking sailors. Surely he was never that young. He had been with *Perth* since commissioning and although only 31, the Mediterranean campaign meant he felt a lot older. He needed to get off this ship and knew other senior rates who felt the same way. Chief EA Reg Whiting shared his weariness, an almost desperate need for down time. Whiting had been another member of the commissioning crew and, when he had not been drafted off, he put in a request. He received no answer, so asked to see his Captain. Whiting knew he was tired and subsequently no longer his normal 'enthusiastic' self. In a letter to his wife Alice, he confided how it was a case of hoping:

> I can weather it all ... What hurts is having to go through it all
> again, especially when you know there are many who haven't
> had a go up to date ... When you get a chap being ashore for

four and a half years, and cannot move him something is wrong somewhere ... there are not many left on board now of the original ships company and I feel like a break, being not quite the man I used to be.[39]

Acting Stoker PO Frank Steele, stationed in the forward engine room, was Sands's equivalent. They were both Victorian, had joined the RAN within seven months of each other and were members of the *Autolycus* group. Both needed a break from the constant war tempo. Steele shouted orders. He was a solid, tough-looking man, but the young men he supervised quickly learnt his bark was worse than his bite. They nonetheless respected his rank and his experience.

Stoker IIs Henry 'Stuart' Absalom and David Crick would have liked to be on deck enjoying the vista 'Tich' Hill was admiring. Instead they were sweating profusely in the forward engine room. They had been in the same class at Flinders in June 1941 before being whisked off to *Perth* in October. Henry was a Victorian from Terang, from a large family of six boys and one girl. He was the youngest and the only one to join the navy. Eldest brother Arthur had become an army chaplain. Keith and Gordon had joined the army too, while Irvine was to spend a lively war in the RAAF, which would include being shot down a number of times.

Dave Crick was the fourth child and youngest son of Reginald and Annie Crick. He had grown up part of a close family and spent many a day rabbiting with country cousins. He had been a 'happy-go-lucky lad who enjoyed life to the full'. Dave was particularly close to his brother Perc. As young children they shared a double bed in the family kitchen. Dave followed Perc into the Austral Sheet Metal Works as a metal spinner and the two men purchased adjoining blocks of land in the Adelaide suburb of Sefton Park so they could build houses next to each other. Perc was married, with one child and another on the way and Dave, somewhat homesick, found himself writing in a letter to Perc: 'I bet you think you are just lovely when you go shopping down the street with your family'.[40] Thoughts of family were comforting as Dave Crick laboured in the heat and noise. He was engaged to Joyce and he was going to enjoy settling down and building that house, next to the house of his brother and best mate.

ERA IV Frank Trevor was also in this porthole-less space. He continued to speak with a distinctly non-Australian accent, a legacy of being from Axminster, England. Although he regarded himself as a South Australian, after his family immigrated to Murray Bridge, his English birthright caused him to leave his job as a fitter and turner and enlist immediately war was declared. On *Perth* since March 1940, Frank returned on leave a few months later to marry his sweetheart, Kathleen.

The Stokers messdeck was midships, between engine rooms and boilers, to avoid disturbing other ratings at change of watch. Despite their rough-and-ready reputation, the Stokers of *Perth* had the cleanest messdeck on the ship.[41] Their Head of Department 'Dolly' Gray was in the wardroom eating Cornish pasties with Engineer Lieut Frank Gillan. Gillan was receiving on-the-job training from Gray, and there was nothing the Engineer Cdr didn't know about *Perth*'s propulsion systems. They were two very different men: the senior, a career RAN veteran of the previous war and the junior, a former member of the Merchant Marine, now RAN Engineering Officer RANR(S), since just December.

Sam Stening was in the wardroom also, having just returned from seeing the XO. Martin had sprained an ankle but was nonetheless cheerful and confident. He reiterated to the junior ship's doctor, 'We've just had a signal from a Dutch recce that Sunda Strait is clear. We're going to Tjilatjap to fuel. We're all right now'.[42]

The blond, 31-year-old Stening was in his white overalls festooned with medical paraphernalia; scissors, syringes, hypodermic needles, bottles of morphia. Returning to the wardroom, he looked around at the emergency casualty station set up there. The portable operating table and the smaller table holding instruments had gone unused, he and his ten assistants had ridden out the previous day's battle without patients, and no one regretted this one bit. Taking confidence from his recent conversation with the XO and the broadcast made by *Perth*'s Captain, he told the medical staff they could relax and he was going to his cabin for his first sleep in some 30 hours.

Elsewhere others too were relaxing, pleased to be able to enjoy long overdue food and sleep. The Assistant Navigator, Lieut Lloyd Burgess, had been awake for 50 hours. Like Gillan he was RANR(S). There were others with RANR(S) after their officer rank and name: another Engineer, Lieut Bill Gidney, whose wife lived in Western Australia; Acting Sub-Lieut Tom Wolley, whose parents had a farming property near Warwick on the rich-soiled Queensland Darling Downs; and Temporary Lieut John Thode, whose family lived in Auckland, New Zealand. Thode's typically Kiwi diction added to the interesting blend of English and Australian accents in *Perth*'s wardroom.

Burgess was busy drawing the official plot of the Battle of Java Sea before taking up his four-hour stint as Officer of the Watch. He was a very weary man and happy to heave a depleted body into his bunk for what was expected to be an uneventful few hours.

—

At 2300 *Perth* was at the entrance of Sunda Strait. Signalman Bill 'Buzzer' Bee stood by the starboard 18-inch signal projector. There were two such projectors, one on either side of the flag deck. When not being used for signalling, the projectors doubled as searchlights, their carbon filament lamps producing powerful beams. Bee waited for the order to turn the light on. He had an unrestricted 180-degree view, visibility was good this night. The ack-ack gun mounted just below Bee's position was manned by Chief PTI Don Viney, the man who had calmly fed birds during a Mediterranean air raid. Telegraphist Bob Newton came out of the remote control office for some fresh air.

Yeoman Eric Lucius Meacher Piper was pacing back and forth urging Signal staff to be sharp-eyed. The former Victorian farmhand had joined the RAN during the Depression years and had taken to navy life and signals training with enthusiasm. He had been a member of the *Autolycus* group and a mainstay of *Perth*. Since the commissioning of *Perth,* he used his expertise to train the many new Signalmen drafted to the cruiser. He knew them all, their strengths and their weaknesses. He looked around at the young men on the flag deck: Ord Telegraphist Bill Newman, from Melbourne; Signalman Bill Brachter, from the Sydney suburb of Clovelly who had enlisted the month war was declared; Signalman Bob Dodwell, an ex-Brisbane Boys Grammar School student. Signalman Howard Sneyd from South Australia was standing there too, in his tin hat and Mae West (life jacket).[43] Although he had just turned nineteen, Sneyd was already a war casualty. Serving in *Yarra* he had been invalided back to Australia suffering malaria. After hospitalisation his service record was notated 'Unfit for further service in the tropics'. This clause was lost in the manpower shortage and he was in the tropics again.

There was little conversation on the bridge, the ship's Commanding Officer was asleep there. Before he lay down on the deck he told the Officer of the Watch, Lieut Bill 'Willy' Gay 'Kick me if anything breaks'.[44] Gay was tense, they just needed to get through the Strait, probably by dawn, then into the open waters of the Indian Ocean where *Perth* stood a better chance to outmanoeuvre and outrun the enemy. It was comforting to see *Houston* stationed in close order astern, approximately 2 cables (370 metres) distant.

His thoughts were abruptly interrupted. At 2306 a lookout sighted a dark shape, five degrees on the starboard bow, at a range of about 5000 yards (4500 metres). Waller was awake, hopeful it was an Allied corvette. He ordered, 'Make the Challenge'. The Chief Yeoman, Bert Hatwell, blinked the code letters on his Aldis lamp. The reply made no sense, 'Repeat the Challenge' ordered Waller. As Hatwell obeyed, the warship made smoke and moved away at high speed.

'Alarm Starboard' was the next order from *Perth's* Captain, and the cruiser's course was altered to allow for a full broadside of the forward guns. The Gunnery Officer, Lieut Peter Handcox, stood by the voice-pipe to the 6-inch director and called, 'Main Armaments ready, Sir'. Waller replied, 'Thank you, Guns'. The Torpedo Officer, Lieut Cdr Guy Clark, called, 'All tubes ready Sir'. Without looking at the RN exchange officer, Waller answered, 'Thanks Torps', then gave the order to open fire. *Perth's* forward 6-inch guns belched angry orange flame. Ever so briefly there was the thrill of the chase, until lookouts sighted more shapes. Dark silhouettes moved out from seemingly every piece of land cover and opened fire: 'There's another, and another ... Hell they're all round us', came the voice of the RAAF Pilot, Flying Officer Allen McDonough, on the darkened bridge. Waller was heard to say to the Navigator, 'Looks like a bit of a trap', and ordered independent control so each turret officer could choose his own targets.

Just after 2300 Signalman 'Buzzer' Bee became aware of increased activity on the bridge, as 'A' and 'B' turrets swung to starboard and the forward 6-inch guns commenced firing. Bee remembered that Yeoman of Signals Percy Stokan had told him, it was the shell you didn't hear which caused the worst damage. Stokan imbued a lot of confidence in the junior signal staff, but he seemed to thrive on activity and declared before they left Tanjong Priok, 'make no mistake about it we are not finished with those little yellow bastards yet'.[45] By 2315 *Perth* was engaged from all points of the compass, so too *Houston*. At 2326 the Australian ship was hit.

Shells whistled over Bee's head and one tore into the ship's port side, abreast of the forward funnel. The next one Bee didn't hear and he was thrown towards the 'B' turret. Regaining his senses he found Chief Don Viney lying in a pool of blood beside him. Bee's right leg had been struck by shrapnel: 'I got Don by the legs, because I couldn't stand. I was crawling ... I felt sick because I realised then that he had his arm blown off ... he was groaning, "OOOH Jesus, don't, don't, leave me alone"'.[46] Bee called for a stretcher and began to drag himself towards the signal distributing office. He pushed through bodies and parts of bodies that once were men he knew – Yeoman Eric Piper, Ordinary Telegraphist Bill Newman, Signalmen Bob Dodwell and Bill Brachter were dead, so too Signalman Howard Sneyd and the youngest member of the wardroom, Midshipman Frank Tranby-White. Signalman Tom Risley and another carried Viney to Sick Bay. On their return trip they were both killed. Telegraphist Bob Newton did not survive, his obituary in Brisbane's *Courier Mail* would read: 'only child of Mr and Mrs W.Newton, Beryl Crescent, Holland Park, enlisted in July 1940: well-known cricketer and swimmer'.

Sub Lieut Gavin Campbell was woken although not cheerful and grumbled to AB Doug Findlay how, 'The bastards never let you sleep'.[47] At the aft machine gun they could not see what was going on, but the

'Y' 6-inch turret below sounded and opened fire, sending a shock wave through Campbell's body. The 6-inch guns on the cruiser's stern were soon firing rapidly, and Campbell and Findlay were blinded by the flashes, making it difficult for them to find their own targets.

Below Campbell in 'Y' turret, Turret Captain PO Alf Coyne yelled at his crew, 'there are hundreds of the bastards'. Yeoman Jack Willis was woken by the roar of the 6-inch guns. Adjusting his clothing he ran to the signal distribution office. The battle momentum accelerated and soon, 'the din was terrifying and every now and again the ship lurched when hit by shell fire'. Willis decided he would go to the flag deck. As he approached the area there was an explosion, and his momentum was halted by a 'bespattered screaming lad', a sailor he could not instantly recognise, who had been struck by shrapnel. Willis entered what was once his pride of place, the flag deck. Stepping over bodies he realised most were dead – young signalmen he had mentored, now no more. He turned toward the bridge, 'Nip ships seemed to be everywhere', more and more silhouettes emerging from the cover of islands. The light show of battle filled the night sky and the black waters churned with the wakes of warships manoeuvring violently. Another communicator, Chief PO Telegraphist Harry Knight, despatched the signal that enemy contact had been made. No other wireless transmission would be sent from HMAS *Perth*.

Intelligence reports had been completely wrong, Sunda Strait was not clear. Indeed, it was jammed with ships, none friendly, and *Perth* and *Houston* had blundered into the massive armada. Just a few miles away in Bantam Bay, close to St Nicholas Point, large numbers of enemy transports were disembarking troops who would quickly overwhelm and occupy Java. The heavy cruisers *Mogami* and *Mikuma*, a seaplane carrier and tender, as well as torpedo boats, were part of the covering fleet.

More Japanese destroyers charged into the fray. The Australian 6-inch guns were depressed as low as they would go. Wireman Fred Lasslett was at the bottom of *Perth*'s bow, 'I could reach out and touch both sides of the hull',[48] to maintain the Sperry Gyro, a compass which indicated north based on the rotation of the earth around its axis. As the battle intensified he could see the cruiser's hull plates flex with each depth charge explosion.[49] He was 'greatly relieved' when ordered to the bridge plot room.

Supply Assistant Ron Clohessy was there in the steel room helping *Perth*'s School Teacher, Neville 'Tiger' Lyons. Lyons was an officer, currently ranked Probationary Schoolmaster. It was common practice to have a Schoolmaster, Instructor Officer, onboard to help sailors improve their education levels and qualify for advancement. It seemed a little superfluous in wartime, but Lyons doubled as a minister of religion of types, conducting Catholic church services. Perhaps this religious duty might count for something if the worst happened, but at present Lyons was fully concentrated on jotting down speed, engine revolutions, time, enemy positions and plotting his warship's zig-zag course.

By 2330 the 6-inch guns were running short of ammunition, *Perth* lookouts reported more and more targets, more and more torpedo tracks, until their calls meant nothing, it was merely academic. There was no escape. By 2340 ships from the Japanese 5th, 11th and 12th squadrons had joined the attack, and shortly after *Mykuma* and *Mogami* catapulted aircraft for gunnery observation and fired their torpedoes.

Onboard *Perth* the scene was 'mad bedlam with flashes of guns and a horrific din – it was like a bar-room brawl'.[50] Ord Seam Arthur Bancroft and Marcus Clark were manning one of the 4-inch guns. There were sixteen men in a 4-inch gun crew and Ord Seam Frank Chattaway was the loader on the Port 2 4-inch. The men worked at a frenetic pace, surrounded by noise and smoke. Each 60-pound 4-inch shell had to be carried from the Sickbay Flat where they were fused, along the exposed upper deck, then shell handling parties began to take casualties. Each time 'Tag' Wallace survived a trip and returned to collect another shell there were fewer and fewer men in front of him. As he ran again he looked up at his plane on the catapult and saw it was 'literally riddled with bullets'.

Soon the 4-inch ammunition supply was exhausted and gun crews resorted to firing star shells. Ord Seam David Manning was still in a lookout position and wasn't sure why, given there was nothing more that he could report that wasn't painfully obvious. He became fascinated by the searchlights. The Japanese ships took it in turns to bathe *Perth* in light, about twenty seconds at a time. Manning was witness to a kaleidoscope of colour. Red, blue and amber tracers poured from *Houston's* guns, and fires had broken out on the American warship.

At around 2340 Waller told Clarke, 'Get rid of those fish of yours Torps'. In the torpedo space Temporary Gunner Len Smith, AB Eric Justelius and AB Russell Goddard stood waiting. Sinister-looking torpedoes were before them, pins pulled out of the warheads, charges ready. The command came and the four starboard 'fish' leapt outward. The torpedo men moved to the port side, and released four more, willing the torpedoes straight into opposing ships.

At 2350 a shell crashed into the seamen's mess before the waterline. The darkened bridge was lit up by a powerful Japanese searchlight. Waller screamed at his gunners: 'For God's sake shoot that bloody light out'. It was an order repeated in a different language in rival warships, and AB David Coles, a former electrician from Sydney, was cut down at *Perth's* starboard searchlight. AB Ron Reynolds and AB Kevin McCormack, both 21-year-old West Australian 'hostilities only' sailors, died at the forward searchlight.

AB Leo Lohrisch had taken his share of ridicule given his German ancestry, even if his grandparents had settled in Queensland way back in 1870. Leo's dad had the proud German name of Otto Ferdinand Lohrisch. Perhaps because of this young Leo became pretty handy with his fists. He learnt the hard way, strapping on boxing gloves against his uncle but, 'every time he was knocked down he got up for more'.[51] He became a station hand, then surprised his relatives when he joined the RAN. Lohrisch was on the port-side searchlight, and this time he would not get back up again.

In 'Y' turret lobby Leading Seaman Keith Gosden was feeding shells into the hoist at a furious pace, then he realised there were no more and shouted to the Turret Captain PO Alf Coyne. On the bridge Handcox informed his Captain only 'A' turret had ammunition left, just five shells. In a final act of defiance Waller ordered another change of course and full steam ahead for Toppers Island in an attempt to force passage through the Strait. As his ship settled on the new course, there was a thud and the Australian ship rose out of the water when a torpedo hit midships on the starboard side. The Captain was standing by the voice-pipe, with an arm around the Pelorus,[52] when he said almost laconically, 'Oh well, that's buggered the whole show'[53] before he called 'Prepare to abandon ship'. It was 0005, the first day of March 1942.

NINE

'We fought like hell, but it was never going to be enough.'

Able Seaman Allan 'Elmo' Gee

The first torpedo hit below the waterline, between the forward engine and boiler rooms. The workshop flat above became eerie, the deck turned red hot before it melted and collapsed, taking Stoker PO Clarence Hill with it. Suffering the same fate was 21-year-old Stoker, Donald Burgess and Mechanician Spencer Blanch. Blacksmith Alf Saunders, who had felt so lucky to have suffered only superficial wounds when a bomb passed through the workshop during the air raid on *Perth* at the end of May 1941 killing others, was not lucky this time.

The torpedo released an inferno within the forward engine and boiler rooms from which only one man escaped. It wasn't Acting Leading Stoker Arnold Kirby, a former packer from Kew, Victoria; nor Stoker Thomas Watts from Wallaroo, South Australia, who 'sort of' celebrated his twentieth birthday during the Battle of Matapan. Had he worked in the stern part of the ship he may well have survived, given he was a 'keen lifesaver and rower'. Nor was it Leading Stoker Joseph Hartley. Hartley was the Aussie sailor who, in 1939, had delighted a capacity crowd by hitting a ball out of New York stadium.

Acting Stoker PO Frank Steele, with *Perth* since the cruiser was commissioned, was trapped in the cruiser's forward engine room. ERA IV Frank Trevor formerly from Axminster now Murray Bridge, South Australia, would remain there also, as would two 'ring-ins'. ERA IV Des Scally had been there to make up numbers. The grey-eyed fitter and turner from Sandgate, Queensland, had joined the RAN the month war was declared. His training had taken an unusual twist when he was sent to the RAAF Engineering School in Victoria, to undertake the Aero Fitting Course. He then spent time at RAAF Richmond feeling a little out of place in his square rig uniform. Only when he joined *Perth* did he truly feel in the navy. He was in *Perth* to support a RAAF group, but like Trevor, he died in the forward engine room supporting a navy group. Stoker II Stanley Thomas from Perth had hitched a ride in the warship of the same name to join *Hobart*. Had Thomas transshipped he would have returned to Australia.

Lieut (E) Arthur Harold Mears, who was born in Edinburgh, Scotland, and who entered the RAN as a Cadet Midshipman in 1932 to uphold the family tradition set by his father, Engineer Cdr A.C.W Mears, was another who perished there. With him went Lieut Bill Gidney, a civilian commissioned twelve months previously because of his engineering qualifications.

Leading Stoker Peter Allom, born in the Federal Malayan States, and a member of the *Autolycus* group, had been awarded a BEM for his heroics in Malta. Allom was Chief of Watch in the forward engine room, and was due to change watch when the torpedo hit. Like Allom ERA 'Chas' Thomson had also finished his watch and moved out of the engine room; Allom, however, hesitated. A couple of minutes were all it took – Thomson survived, and Peter Allom did not.

Supervising them all was Cdr 'Dolly' Gray, DSO. Approaching his fortieth birthday, his RAN career a distinguished one, he knew the cruiser better than anyone, better than he knew anyone or anything else – and so it would remain, the Engineering Department Head and the cruiser *Perth*, victims of a cruel conflict.

Acting Stoker PO Patrick 'Chopper' Sands was in 'A' boiler room. With him from beginning to end was Stoker PO Reg Frost. Stoker Des

East, a former boilermaker born in Albury New South Wales, was there. So too, Chief ERA Vincent Edwards another former boilermaker, who had joined the RAN in 1925, and *Perth* less than a month ago. Captain Waller had been pleased to see Chief Stoker Harry Thomas draft to the cruiser shortly after he assumed command. Thomas was a trustworthy and valuable senior rating and they had survived the Mediterranean campaign together on *Stuart*. Waller ensured the Chief Stoker was 'Mentioned in Despatches for Bravery and Enterprise in the Battle of Matapan'. Thomas did not survive the first torpedo, and his wife Rita would raise son Harry alone. Gwenda Brown and her 20-month-old son wouldn't see Mechanician Don Brown again. The troubled Stoker II Charlie Bennett was killed, as well as the enthusiastic Henry Absalom. Fellow Stoker II, Dave Crick, would never build that house next to his brother and best mate Perc. For the rest of his life Perc Crick would keep the homesick letter Dave wrote two weeks before he died.

Stoker II Les McMurdo died. With him was an ERA IV also at *Cerberus* the previous July. Classmates and instructors alike had treated Fred Hutton a little differently than other new recruits. Hutton was a bit of a legend and inspired those around him, because he had entered the AIF to fight the last war as an eighteen year old. Private Hutton had travelled around the world to disembark in Plymouth in November 1916. Whilst with the 2nd Australian Light Trench Mortar Battery in France in 1918, he had been shot and repatriated home with a partially paralysed left arm. The RAN did not see the permanent injury as an impediment to his enlistment, so Recruit Hutton had reported to *Perth* wearing the Victory Medal and British War Medal. His wife Phyllis would need to find comfort in these and the 1939–45 Star, Pacific Star and War Medals.

—

Leading Stoker John McQuade had been moving forwards in the ship when the force of the first torpedo tossed 'Macca' over and he lost consciousness. EA III Vic Duncan was ferrying 4-inch ammunition and was also thrown into the air. He tumbled unceremoniously and painfully back to the steel deck, concussed. Plumber Ernie Kynvin was blown across the upper deck. As he picked himself up a further explosion catapulted him off the cruiser.

Nineteen-year-old Ord Seam Arthur 'Otto' Lund, had just celebrated his first year of RAN service. The chaos and excitement of the Battle of Java Sea had exhilarated him, 'it had been marvellous'. He was so glad to be at sea in the action, which he was sure, 'could not have been better in Nelson's day!' This night's combat, 'with all its speed and brilliance was even better'.[1] Lund had been running with fixed 4-inch ammunition, from the locker to the breech of the gun. His heart was thumping; it was like being caught in a thrilling action movie, then 'kerummph!' the first torpedo. 'It sat me fair on my arse with the projey across my chest. I sat up looked about. Suddenly it all looked different. "Christ!" I said, "This is serious!" And I was scared stiff'.[2]

Shipwright Fred 'Chips' King was carrying a 4-inch shell when the blast blew him over the side. He hit the water still holding the heavy shell, and in a second decided it would be clever to let the shell go or he 'would touch bottom'. Bobbing to the surface he watched, all alone, as his warship continued under way.

—

When the first torpedo tore into *Perth*'s midsection, it obliterated Damage Control Headquarters and the men within. This was so vital to the life of the cruiser and lives of the crew. Damage Control was the nerve centre, the men who waited there the most skilled in directing and supervising immediate fire control and damage repair. It was difficult to envisage a more critical situation than that rendered by this torpedo. Men of enormous experience and value were lost, like Acting Warrant Mechanician Henry Hill, an Englishman who had adopted the RAN and *Perth*. During the Battle of Crete he had raced to the forward boiler room to assist evacuating the area, helped Stoker PO Bill Reece remove two scalded stokers, and set about turning off steam valves and isolating the boiler. At Crete the two senior rates returned to the black, steam-filled space to retrieve the body of Stoker Harry Smith, and suffered burns themselves. For this Hill was awarded a DSC for his, 'outstanding gallantry, fortitude and resolution and for coolness and determination in dealing with a difficult situation'. Bill Reece, a recruiting poster sailor and member of *Perth*'s forwarding commissioning party was awarded a Distinguished Service Medal, for 'outstanding gallantry, fortitude and resolution'. The first torpedo had killed Hill, but Reece, this time in the aft boiler room, was still alive, for the moment.

Also in Damage Control HQ was Harry Haylock. Haylock was a rare being in the RAN, a Commissioned Shipwright. A man of tremendous knowledge, Haylock was killed waiting to save his ship. Chief Stoker Lachlan MacQuarie, a member of the hand-picked advance party who had arrived in England before the commissioning group left Australian shores on *Autolycus* also died. There was nothing the 41 year old didn't know about damage control of Leander class cruisers. MacQuarie was navy through and through, having enlisted during the last war as a seventeen-year-old Stoker 3rd Class.

Leading Stoker Fred Olsen, a former fitter and turner and member of the *Autolycus* group, had also been in Damage Control HQ, as had Leading Cook (S) John Hill. It was not an obvious place for a cook, but it was his action station. Stoker 2nd Class Rodger Banks had been nervous to be in the company of such men as Haylock, Reece and MacQuarie. Banks had entered the navy three days after Christmas 1939 and trained to be a signaller. He never quite meshed with the visual signalling aspects of his category so retrained as a Stoker. The worst part of the re-rating was spending ten months at the Flinders Training establishment when busting to get into the game. He had been thoroughly pleased to draft to *Perth* in October. He had so much to learn from these men with whom he sat waiting. Banks managed leave at home in Mannum, South Australia, just before the *Perth*'s trip north to Java. His brother Leith, was away serving with the RAAF, but he spent time with his kid sister, Mary. They had a singalong around the piano and Rodger asked Mary to offer her rendition of the 'Maoris' Farewell'. Its lyrics included the words: 'now is the hour to say goodbye'.[3]

—

The cruiser slowed dramatically under the power of one engine room. Enemy ship searchlights lit up *Perth*'s decks as if it were daylight, adding to the incredible sense of exposure and vulnerability. AB Allan 'Elmo' Gee had been a helmsman since commissioning crew days. He had suffered the Mediterranean campaign, so though only 22 years of age, he was a battle-seasoned warrior. On this evening at his action station on the bridge, experience really stood for little. The noise was deafening as shrapnel strafed the upper deck and an atmosphere full of smoke made breathing difficult:

> We were in the thick of destroyers and cruisers firing at each other with machine guns at a frighteningly close range ... We fought like hell, but it was never going to be enough. We were relentlessly bombarded, and it was only a matter of time before we were history.[4]

A shell blew the Walrus off its catapult and the crane collapsed into the ship's waist, killing members of the commissioning crew AB Charles Essex and RN loan officer, Lieut Cyril Palairet. Ord Seam 'Otto' Lund was attempting to control his fear. The 4-inch ammunition was now gone and the aft guns had resorted to firing star shells and now practice projectiles. 'What do we use after those?' Lund's voice was higher and thinner than usual. The calmer voice of an older hand replied, 'Rat the bloody spud locker', and Lund almost smiled.

Sam Stening was woken from deep sleep. For an instant he wondered which hospital he was in. The unmistakable pounding of 6-inch guns ripped him into reality and, pulling on his white overalls, he ran to the wardroom. His assistants were assembled, looking apprehensive. The second Chaplain, the Reverend Mathieson, asked what he should do and Stening replied, to everyone really, 'We just wait'.[5] There was nothing else to do just then, but soon there was likely to be a lot to do. It started, as a trickle, then a flood of men with shocking wounds arrived. The slightly wounded were still out there fighting as best they could. Surgeon Lieut Cdr Eric Tymms and Sam Stening were soon overwhelmed, 'treating men with arms and legs blown away, riddled with shrapnel, burned beyond recognition'.[6] Sick Berth Attendants made rapid judgement calls: men who could be saved, others who just had to be left, 'consigned to the growing pile of bodies'. The Doctors operated on the most urgent. Whilst Stening was a wartime commissioned surgeon, Tymms had served with the RAN since 1935, but no peacetime medical service could prepare them for this.

—

On the bridge Captain Waller's attention was drawn to the unmistakable tracks of another torpedo. There was no time to avoid it, and the torpedo exploded into the cruiser abreast of the 'A' Turret. It was then Waller gave the order no Captain wished to give, 'Abandon Ship'. Chief Quartermaster PO Ray Parkin had been in the lower steering position when the first torpedo hit. He had been thrown violently away from the wheel and against the bulkhead. He had shaken himself, 'nothing broken', returned to the wheel and realised the gyro-compass was busted, meaning that it was no longer possible to control the ship. Above his Captain, realising this, made a voice-pipe to Parkin, 'Leave both engines half speed ahead – I don't want the Old Girl to take anyone with her'. Parkin replied with a crisp 'Aye, aye, sir!' and then asked if he should remain at his station. Waller's voice came back clearly, 'Get to buggery out of it!'[7]

Officer of the Watch, Lieut Bill 'Willy' Gay turned to look at his Captain and hesitated; Waller said, 'Get off the bridge, Gay'.[8] Gay went down the starboard ladder; Lieut Peter Handcox went down the port ladder and 'It was the last time'[9] Gay saw the Gunnery Officer, because another shell landed on the port side of the bridge. The Navigator, Lieut John Harper, had been moving slowly towards the port ladder while putting on his life jacket. When the shell struck the bridge, he was propelled overboard with an injured cheek and part of an ear missing. Like Handcox, others in the bridge area were not as fortunate. Chief Yeoman Bert Hatwell, who transmitted the signal of challenge and was a former Boy Seaman awarded an MBE in the 1942 New Year's Honours List, died. AB Norm Dixon, a 25 year old from Melbourne, was killed at the Rangefinder Trainer.

Ord Seam Bill Boreham had been just shy of his seventeenth birthday when he had enlisted in the RAN at the end of 1939. His father

Arthur was the postmaster of the tiny town of Piawaning, about 150 kilometres north east of Perth. His mother, Florence, had taken over the Post Office when Arthur died in 1940. She was well versed on the transmission and receipt of telegrams. The one she was not prepared for was the one addressed to her, explaining Bill had been killed in action when a shell hit his position on the lower bridge, four days shy of his nineteenth birthday.

Perth's Commanding Officer was last seen standing silently and alone at the front of the bridge. It appeared he had no intention of leaving his ship, then a shell shattered the bridge and the life of Captain Hector MacDonald Laws Waller.

—

Deafening noise corrupted the tranquil scene AB 'Tich' Hill had envisaged a couple of hours earlier. Hill was in the 4-inch gunnery control room and when the first torpedo struck, all the lights had gone out. He fumbled in the darkness for the emergency switch and was relieved when the space filled with light. The instruments were dead and the order came to evacuate. Hill hesitated, feeling a strange reluctance to leave. He was knocked over by the force of another torpedo, and on regaining his feet he hesitated no more.

Wireman Fred Lasslett was in the plot room with Schoolmaster 'Tiger' Lyons. They felt the warship jerk upwards. When the ship fell back, all the pigeon-holes emptied and Lasslett muttered, 'Now it's a bloody snowstorm'. He and EA IV Dave Griffiths shoved the papers roughly back into the pigeon holes. The second jolt meant the pigeon holes emptied again, Lasslett shrugged, retrieved a chocolate bar from his pocket and munched on it. Taking his lead, Supply Assistant Ron Clohesy opened a tin of biscuits and began to eat as if it was just a normal brew time. Yeoman Jack Willis fell overboard when the abandon ship order was piped. He surfaced, found himself alone and watched *Perth* move away:

For one awful moment as I lay in the water and watched the ship glide past, I thought that the order to abandon ship had been just a hallucination of my mind. I could hear no one near me in the water, and the ship still appeared to be proceeding in a normal manner. Had I just imagined the order or was it true? Surely, I thought, there should be some other unfortunate sailors in the water besides myself.[10]

Leading Telegraphist Air Gunner Ken 'Tag' Wallace had continued to ferry 4-inch shells along the murderous upper deck to gun crews as long as he could find shells. When he found only two of the sixteen-man starboard party still alive, he changed to the port side where the party was reduced to six but two turrets were still in action. Each time he had tried to leave the sick bay flat it was harder, because of the 'growing pile of bodies in the starboard waist'. When the cruiser altered course, 'the pile' would 'spread across the whole side of the deck and I was forced to climb over this mounting pile of dead'. Then he was thrown upwards, his steel helmet striking the deck above. Winded, he realised a torpedo had hit his ship, and he listened to the 'screams of men in the boiler room just below me, being scalded to death'.[11] Wallace was preparing to abandon ship when RAAF Sergeant Harold Sparks asked him to help free some men. He and Sparks moved to a hatchway where they could hear someone banging. The two members of the Walrus contingent used crowbars to dislodge the cover. Out came several men, 'with hair and clothing alight, they brushed straight past us and jumped into the sea'.[12] As another storm of machine-gun fire raked the deck. Wallace went overboard but Sparks, the man who had studied so hard to become a member of the RAAF, died on a RAN cruiser.

Eighteen-year-old Acting AB John Woods, in the No.2 Lookout position, was having the wildest ride of his life. All around him guns fired, *Perth*'s and so many enemy guns he gave up counting. He wasn't sure what had happened when the first torpedo hit, but he had it figured by the time the second one hit. He thought of his mother, Katherine, back in Sydney and what she had already gone through. Woods was a Legacy kid at three, one of so many children of men killed in the last war. Legacy struggled to help look after all the children, a little assistance here and there; the organisation had the best intentions and was overstretched already. It had been a struggle for his mum since his dad had died in 1925, after failing to recover fully from wounds suffered in France. Woods thought again of his Mum and two sisters and prayed, 'Look after the family, God, and try to look after me if you can'.[13] Woods heard the call to abandon ship but was surprised to find that he was in no rush. He cut free a float and sent it over the port side. An inner voice cautioned him against following the float, and he watched as it drifted astern and disappeared in the suction and wash, perhaps there was power in prayer after all. Another shell tore into his area and this time he jumped.

Woods's reluctance to move was not uncommon; men hesitated, through fear, confusion and through regret. This was more than a ship; this was their home and it was difficult to accept immediately that their home was about to disappear. Most of what they owned was here. 'Elmo' Gee went to retrieve the bugle he had been presented with as *Perth*'s commissioning bugler. He paused to remove the mouthpiece, then realised it was nonsensical and threw both away.[14] Ord Seam David Manning moved to the quarterdeck. He shook hands with Ord Seam Frank Chattaway and wished him luck. Manning took off his boots and placed them carefully as if they were ready for inspection.[15] Chattaway moved away and recalls: 'with a quick feel of my life jacket to make sure it was fully inflated and a short but fervent prayer, I jumped over the side'.[16]

Wireman Fred Lasslett and Supply Assistant Ron Clohesy had their mouths full of chocolate and biscuits when they heard the pipe to 'abandon ship'. They didn't hurry. They shook hands with Schoolmaster 'Tiger' Lyons and PO Telegraphist Tony Spriggins who appeared at the door of the plot room, then calmly moved out. Lasslett went off the cruiser from the region of the fo'c'sle and 'got quite a shock'. Normally the fo'c'sle was about 30 feet (9 metres) above the waterline, now with the ship listing it was just 6 feet (2 metres). Spriggins who had worked for the Post Office before he made the RAN his career from 1929, abandoned ship further forward and was dragged under. Lyons remembered the code books and retraced his steps. He was thrown violently to the deck when a shell hit the bridge. Smoke filled the space and he had to crawl on hands and knees through the flag deck. He felt a wet lump, turned his torch on, and wished he hadn't. Shattered bodies and blood were everywhere. He gagged and pushed himself overboard.

—

Unlike land-based forces there was no option to surrender. Warships and their crews could not negotiate the laying down of arms, the battle was over only when the ship was destroyed. A shell hit in the vicinity of 'A' and 'B' turret just as the crews were coming out to abandon ship, and they died. AB David Headford, who had been a pastry cook from Melbourne before entering the RAN, was a member of the 'A' turret group. It was likely cold comfort when his mother Isabel and wife Phyllis were informed that death was instant.

AB Doug Asplin was a member of the same turret crew. He had grown up on his grandfather's stories about glamorous sailing clippers racing to and from the East Indies. It was a different century, but Asplin died in those same East Indies. He had spoken of death to his teenage sister Joan, discussing gruesome stories of young Australians like him being killed in the trenches of World War I. At least in the navy, he argued, it would be a 'clean death'. As he came out of turret 'A' and the enemy shell hit, death was not 'clean'. Asplin never knew what hit him, but death on this warship in World War II was also, 'gruesome'. After the war friends from the Largs Bay Yacht Club sailed the yacht he had built as an eighteen year old but never had the chance to sail. They figured Doug would like that, and they won several championships in *Mercury*.[17] The other young carpenter with whom Asplin had found a common interest was Queenslander John Atkinson. Atkinson, who had built a house for his sister, died with his turret crew.

—

The ship's superstructure was being pounded with shells of various calibres. AB Arthur 'Blood' Bancroft was on the Port 1 4-inch gun. 'The [enemy] ships were so close that I could see the Japanese gunners behind their guns from the flashes from the star shells and guns firing'.[18]

Successive explosions twisted metal formwork, jamming hatches and trapping those below. Two fortunate sailors were Wireman Charlie Wray and Stoker 'Tiny' Savage. Both were in the No.3 diesel room. 'Tiny' was a canny rogue who had wondered how long his ship's luck would hold out. To increase his survival chances in the worst-case scenario, he asked a fellow Stoker to loosen the clips on the diesel room hatch. It was certainly not in keeping with protocol, but his mate did so and 'Tiny' continued his duty with more confidence. His precaution was justified when he and Wray scrambled up the ladder to abandon ship. From the diesel room they edged their way along the passage to the next hatch. This hatch was slightly jammed and they pushed hard until it finally gave way. By this time the ship was listing and Savage and Wray lunged to grab the ladder that led to the upper deck. If they missed they would tumble back to the depths of the ship. Metal and hands caught, then the list suddenly worsened and Wray struggled to retain his grip and heave himself up each run. It seemed to take forever. By the time the sailors reached the upper deck, they could walk down the side of their ship to the water.

The messmate who had loosened the clips for Savage and Wray never made it off the cruiser. Nor did the forward magazine party and 4-inch magazine party, because shell bursts jammed their hatches. Regulating PO Albert Furey was in the 4-inch magazine. Born in Barnsley, England, Furey had looked forward to the prospect of catching up with relatives when he sailed for the UK on *Ormonde*. He was nonetheless concerned when he said farewell to his wife Ruby in Sydney, because the war drums were beating again in Europe. As a young boy he remembered the sea of military uniforms of World War I, and of injured and broken men returning. It had been a sad time then for so many, and this time the sadness would envelope Ruby and their children, because Al Furey never escaped the 4-inch magazine.

At action stations it was commonly non-seaman personnel who ferried and loaded ammunition. Leading Steward Louis Smith from Carlton, Melbourne died in the 6-inch magazine, as did Steward Percy Stealey who was born in Grimsby, England, and whose mother still lived in Lansdowne Road, Cardiff. Ord Seam George Osgood was a strong, fit eighteen year old. He was a fine swimmer and excelled at water polo. Osgood was below decks when the abandon ship order was given. Struggling through the honeycombed compartments of a cruiser in death throes was difficult, but he made it topside. It was like he was a robot moving to his abandon ship station on the deck, as he had practiced so many times, his brain trying to comprehend this was not a drill, when a Japanese searchlight exposed a hatch cover. 'I could see men's hands thrust out and their faces: they were shouting, "Open the hatch!"' *Perth* was bows down and sinking. Gunfire peppered the deck. Osgood turned and yanked hard at the cover. It was about a foot (30 centimetres) open but buckled. Another sailor stopped and their combined strength could not clear the hatch. The task was beyond human capabilities, it would have taken oxy welding equipment to remove the distorted metal. Osgood could but move away and plunge into the water. It would be a story he would not tell for decades after the sinking, yet the thrusting hands and pleading faces would haunt him forever, and he would continue to ask himself, 'If only I had tried a little harder, a little longer'.[19]

—

It was mayhem, men fought the enemy no longer; they fought to survive. Leading Seaman Ben Chaffey tried to reach the bridge, but everything was a tangle of red-hot iron and steel. He needed to get out somewhere, get off somehow. PO Steward Bill Davis had left the Port 4-inch gun to go to sick bay to assist. The second torpedo hit and he was thrown onto wreckage that littered the deck. He realised his leg was broken, so he crawled to the side and fell overboard. He knew not who, but someone grabbed him and pulled him into a float.

AB Fred Skeels was a former messenger boy, one of the large draft of West Australian war enlistment sailors who arrived onboard the previous October. The nineteen year old was on the Starboard 1 4-inch when he was dispatched by his Gun Captain to investigate why the ammunition supply had been interrupted. Skeels was making his way along the deck when the second torpedo hit and he was thrown to the deck. Picking himself up he returned to S1 to find few there, the abandon ship order had been given. A cacophony of noise and light battered his senses. He scrambled to his abandon ship station on the quarterdeck and helped unlash pilgrim rafts. As he watched them disappear over the side, he realised he still wore his tin hat. Skeels hurled the hat over the side and then scolded himself, it might have hit some poor bastard in the water. Before he followed the hat, a thought popped into his mind: 'If only Mum and Dad could see me now'. Perplexed at why he should think 'such a thing at that time' he jumped.[20]

Sub Lieut Gavin Campbell did not hear the order to 'abandon ship' at his position at the aft machine gun. He was wearing his Mae West half inflated. As the second torpedo hit he was blown into the air, his shoes torn off his feet, and he plunged unconscious into the water. Had his life jacket not been partially inflated he would not have survived. He regained consciousness and knew his leg was badly broken.

One of the more unlikely heroes of the Battle of Matapan had been Canteen Manager 'Happy' Hawkins, BEM. Wounded, he was helped over the side by his son, Alfred Jnr. When the boy surfaced he found his father had not. The seventeen year old swam through debris, shouting and searching for the older Hawkins. Exhausted he dragged himself on to a float. Two bandsmen, Ron Sparks and George Vanselow, found the youth unconscious but still on the raft the following morning. 'Happy' Hawkins was nowhere to be seen.

—

The Allied cruisers were cornered prey, and the enemy closed in on the stricken, defenceless Australian ship. There was no mercy given. A direct hit on the 4-inch gun deck killed most still in the vicinity. These included AB Sid James, a 21 year old from Mile End, South Australia. Sid went by his second name, it didn't cause the comments his first name, Merle, did. PO Steward Walter Morris was a Steward not a Seaman, but his action station meant he was on the 4-inch gun deck. Also there was Acting Leading Seaman Eric Eckermann. Eckermann was of German descent, a Lutheran, university-educated 21 year old from Eudunda, South Australia. AB Dennis Kingston was one of the 'two years or duration of hostilities sailor', but in war it didn't matter how long you were enlisted for. He had scored 81.4 per cent in his gunnery exam, but neither did this help when vastly superior forces were destroying his ship. Peter Timmens was born not too far from Eckermann, in Kapunda, and the Ordinary Seaman died at his post on the Starboard I, 4-inch gun, not too far from his friend Ord Seam Peter Seppelt from Adelaide. Also at the Starboard I 4-inch was AB John MacMillan one of several *Perth* crew members born in Scotland.

Another Scot, AB Charlie Scullion, was killed at the Starboard II 4-inch. Alongside him perished: AB Robert Groves, who had married the previous November; nineteen-year-old Ord Seam John Witt from Sydney's Neutral Bay; nineteen-year-old AB David Haskins from Goulburn, New South Wales; and AB Les Walmsley from Brisbane.

Acting PO George Hatfield was one of the more experienced gunners on the cruiser and a member of the *Autolycus* commissioning party. He had been under immense pressure during the insane days of the Mediterranean campaign, but survived the 257 air attacks thrown at his ship by the Italians and Germans. He did not survive this Japanese attack. Enemy fire concentrated on *Perth*'s decks meant many were killed as they attempted to escape their sinking ship. Crew moved to their abandon ship stations only to find the majority of ship boats and rafts riddled with holes. No boats were successfully launched; survival of *Perth* crew largely depended on those two dozen 'Pilgrim' rafts loaded in Tanjong Priok as an afterthought.

The scene was one of bedlam, 'all you see is smoke, flashes and hear gunfire. When the smoke clears, there is nobody left'.[21] Sick Berth Attendant 2nd Class Les McMillan stopped to tend an injured sailor and was cut down. PO Walter Salmon moved rapidly to his position at No.1 cutter, shouting orders in preparation for the release of the boat. His voice was muffled by the noise of Japanese shells ripping into the superstructure of the cruiser. Another burst of gunfire and the 34-year-old PO fell to the deck mortally wounded. Lieut Michael Highton, was in charge of 'B' turret. After the order to abandon ship, Highton had seen his men out of the turret and, under heavy fire, organised the launching of rafts and carley floats. The cutter he was supervising as it was lowered took a direct hit and he was killed. He left a wife, Clothiede, and daughter in Brisbane.

Water was pouring in through huge, jagged holes in *Perth*'s hull. PO Horrie Abbott joined others at a boat station when he saw a sailor he knew well sitting hunched over. He called to him to join them. The man had his arms folded strangely, low around his body: 'Don't worry about me – I've had it. I'll go with the old girl'. Abbott was about to protest, when he saw the man was virtually cut in two, and was holding his body together. As Abbott and the others went over the side he remembered the dying sailor had six children.[22] Supply PO Eric Burton, who had been a member of the advance *Perth* party, was moving hurriedly to the side, when there was a flash and he plummeted forward. The back of his overalls was blasted away and there were severe wounds to his back. The human spirit was still strong, he heaved himself semi-upright and pushed over the side. The former school teacher managed to dog paddle to a boat only to find it badly holed. Burton could but cling to its side as it sank.

—

Ray Parkin made his way to sick bay to assist the medical parties. Sick bay had been hit and it was carnage: 'The deck was littered with bloody, dead men'. Many were dressed in white overalls that all-too-vividly accentuated the blood. The situation was hopeless with so many wounded. Stoker Horace Foster, who had been in 'A' ammunition lobby, was brought in badly burnt by acid. Foster was one of the smallest men onboard, and his diminutive height of 5 foot 2 made him look somehow even more pathetic. Parkin realised the young Stoker would not survive. Another burnt in the A lobby was Acting AB Darrell Manning from Western Australian, who died shortly after being brought in.

Parkin implored those who could to move topside, because the 'abandon ship' order had been given. Lieut Cdr Llewellyn Watkins was brought in injured. An officer of enormous experience he had been appointed an RAN Cadet Midshipman in 1912 and, as a junior officer, had served in World War I attached to RN ships in the Northern Hemisphere. Watkins was re-activated from the retired list to a temporary commission in January 1942 and rushed to *Perth*. He was given assistance to abandon ship and not seen thereafter. Chief PO Don Viney, who had enlisted as a *Tingira* Boy Seaman in 1920, could not be moved.

Several young sailors who were stretcher bearers stood to one side of the sick bay, their faces masked with the expression of the severely traumatised. The PO yelled at them to follow him. There was no response. Parkin grabbed one, shook him and propelled the youngster towards the starboard waist, shouting at the others to follow. The group threw rafts overboard, and the PO led the sailors into the murky waters of Sunda Strait. Another group ferried some of the injured on stretchers. The ship was listing badly and they strained to load shipmates on to *Perth*'s motorboat. The boat was holed, but it was believed the ballast tanks would keep it afloat. As the boat reached the water, it just kept going downwards.

Surgeon Lieut Sam Stening ensured all who could leave had, and realised he really should have gone himself. Stening struggled to the quarterdeck; it was empty of the living. The ship twitched violently: a third torpedo. He ran to the stern, blew up his Mae West and was about to vault over the rail when there was another violent movement. The ship rail reared up, smashed his nose and threw him on his back. Before he could think, a wave of water washed him overboard. Stening was now one of the wounded, suffering a fractured skull, broken nose and hurt knee. He was also unable to focus out of one eye. Thoroughly disoriented, he believed the ship was about to roll on him and became hysterical. Stening was fortunate he was noticed by the most seasoned of *Perth* sailors.

EA III Arthur Kiesey was struggling with his own burns but grabbed the doctor and hauled him onto a raft. Nothing was making sense to Stening, and he immediately jumped overboard. Few situations phased Kiesey. He was approaching his forty-eighth birthday and he had been with this navy since 1915, four years after the Royal Australian Navy came into being. He even changed his name from Kieswetter because it didn't sound Australian enough. On the third time he retrieved the confused doctor from the water, Kiesey delivered a well-directed punch to the jaw and the Surgeon Lieut went quiet.

AB 'Tich' Hill landed too close to the ship and the suction from *Perth* threatened to drag him under:

> I listened to the beat of the port propeller as it turned nearer and nearer. I feared that any moment I would be hit by the spinning blades, but miraculously I was thrust aside by the water. The propeller passed and the turbulence abated. I pulled myself back to the surface, choking and spluttering.[23]

Ord Seam David Manning helped a group throw carley floats over the side, climbed over the rails and started to walk down the port side. Realising his Mae West was not properly inflated, he was fumbling for the inlet valve when the fourth torpedo hit, and he plummeted into the water and rapidly tumbled down and down. Those he had helped with the rafts were killed. For an instant Manning thought he too would die as he struggled to stop his descent. When he finally broke the surface, his life jacket was gone and so was his ship. A non-swimmer, Manning thrashed about, unable to stop vomiting sea water and fuel oil, and then 'a couple of blokes hoisted' him onto the netting around the side of a carley float.[24]

AB Bob Collins gave his Mae West to Stoker Jeff Latch and went over the side hanging on to Red Lead the cat. Collins had brought the ship's mascot onboard and now he had her in his sights as he left. All he could find to hang onto in the water was half a carley float. Red Lead fell into the water and, despite desperate attempts from Collins to grab her again, the cat paddled away until her energy gave out.

The absolute randomness of the attack: being in the wrong place at the wrong time, in the forward engine and boiler rooms and not the aft; at the forward 6-inch guns; at a particular place on the 4-inch gun deck, was obvious. PO William Speers had been hastily drafted to *Perth* the previous month, and he died in the vicinity of Port 1 gun, so too did PO Ed Payne.

The RAN had quickly recruited Wireman Norm Patten because of his experience as an electrical mechanic. From Houghton, South Australia, he had not yet been twelve months in the navy when he struggled to abandon ship. He left the cruiser's switchboard but only made it as far as the Stokers messdeck. As one of the tallest men onboard, perhaps he was unable to squirm through wreckage like his smaller counterparts. Band members were sprinkled throughout the ship during action stations, it was luck really where you were and luck was fickle. Bandsman Harry Freestone, a musician born in London, but who now made his home with wife Jean in Sydney, died at his action station as a member of the Transmitting Station Crew. Life and death came down to quirks of fate, perhaps even a particular body shape.

Japanese gunners were firing into the water. For some men who jumped to escape, there was no escape. West Australian Sub Lieut Al Ball, who had joined the ship a fortnight earlier and requested permission from Waller to marry just before *Perth* sailed north, and young Billy Girvan, from Queensland sugarcane country, died under the brilliance of enemy searchlights and gunfire. When AB Frank McGovern abandoned *Perth*, he was too far aft and became caught in the stream from the cruiser's screws. He tumbled round and round as if he were in a giant washing machine. He thought he would die, but just as his lungs felt they would burst he was shot up to the surface like a cork. Later he discovered his elder brother Vincent did not survive the sinking. Yes, fate was unfathomable.

ERA Vic Duncan was concussed when the second torpedo struck. He fortunately regained consciousness in time to help Leading Wireman Al Parker and Acting PO Tommy Johnston to throw rafts overboard. John 'Macca' McQuade had also come out of his stunned stupor and staggered to the side of the ship. A young sailor stood gripping the rails. He stammered to McQuade that he couldn't swim. The Leading Stoker removed his life jacket and handed it to the junior sailor and they went over the side together. When 'Macca' surfaced after what seemed an eternity, he had swallowed a great deal of salt water. Concussion from exploding shells meant he 'spewed up all the salt water'.[25]

More explosions sent shock waves into the bodies of others in the water. At best it meant stomachs emptied into the ocean, at worst internal injuries rendered their condition hopeless. Signalman Jim Hiskens was one of few Signal Staff to escape the cruiser, but he was not safe in the water and died when hit by an underwater shock wave. AB Willoughby Stebbins Hamilton, who had travelled half way around the world to join *Perth* in November 1939, was killed. The concussion from an underwater explosion felt akin to being hit in the stomach with the back of a shovel.

Walter Douglass had joined the navy at 23, not so much to see the world as to make music. He had been promoted to Band Corporal in 1938 and left for the UK on *Autolycus*. He had celebrated being promoted to Bandmaster when *Perth* was in the Caribbean, and his twelve-year enlistment was up in a few months. He managed to leave the ship only to die in the water. Leading Steward Tom McKenzie, who had been injured when *Perth* was battered by wild Atlantic waters in 1939, did not survive these waters. PO Writer Frank Watson had been a 'news reporter' prior to enlistment. He was living the biggest story of his life, then his world exploded.

AB 'Elmo' Gee cut loose several floats with the help of AB 'Moggy' Catmull. As they leapt into the black void below, Catmull, one of the more recalcitrant members of the ship's company, in typical 'Moggy' style yelled, 'I'll see you in Young and Jacksons', a Melbourne hotel renowned for its female nude painting 'Chloe'.[26] Catmull did not reach one of the carley floats he had thrown overboard, instead he drowned. The first time Gee bobbed to the surface, he hit the bottom of his ship and descended again:

> For the first time in my life I thought I was going to die. It would have been so easy to succumb to the sensation of drowning ... I had this beautiful feeling of floating, and being incredibly light and happy. I had no pain and no fear ... I remember thinking how lovely it was.[27]

Gee then had a vision of his sister, Miriam, laughing at him, and he shot to a surface now devoid of his ship. *Perth*'s Master at Arms, Jan Creber, had recognised Catmull as an interesting challenge when they travelled to the UK on *Autolycus*. Creber was, in turn referred to by Cdr Charles Reid as a 'very big man with a light and sprightly step'.[28] It was Creber who pulled Allan Gee onto a small wooden table before the 42-year-old Creber, one of the most formidable and respected men onboard, weakened, released his grip and vanished.

—

Ernie Toovey had been at his action station well below the water line in the cordite handling room supplying to 'Y' gun house. Oil fuel seeped through the bulkheads making the deck slippery, which meant every time *Perth* did a rapid course change, Toovey lost his footing and slid one way and then the other. He felt like he was 'inside a circus ring with nowhere to go'.[29] The order to get off the ship was relayed by voice, but not until after a third torpedo buried itself into *Perth*'s hull under 'X' Turret, and it felt like, 'we were lifted in the air then slammed down as if by some giant hand'.

It seemed an eternity before the hatch was opened, enabling Toovey to scramble up ladders to the upper deck. He was sure there had not been so many ladders before; it seemed to take ages. Gun house doors were ajar, 6-inch guns were still smoking. The deck was bathed in light and heavy enemy gunfire. As shells screamed and crashed, and with the air thick with shrapnel, Toovey ran through, 'the biggest and deadliest fireworks display I had ever seen', and to his horror, 'I found it difficult to avoid stepping on obviously dead men'. Toovey stopped to help throw over a couple of wooden benches. A well-modulated voice cautioned him to watch for swimmers below. He turned to see *Perth*'s Executive Officer, Cdr Martin. Trying to harden himself to the moans of the wounded, Toovey removed his boots. *Perth* lifted again as the fourth torpedo exploded into the port side, and he was thrown against the gun house and felt a sharp pain in his right thigh. The cruiser was listing heavily to port; Toovey went into the water thinking about the

'Waterhole' in his home town of Warwick, Queensland. He hit part of the stern and felt a sharp pain in his right knee.[30]

—

Since leaving Tanjong Priok, Chief Stoker Reece had watched the fluctuations of the pressure gauges and discharge valves in boiler room II. *Perth*'s propulsion systems were capable of generating 72,000 horsepower. Prior to the first torpedo, the Captain had increased speed to 28 knots in an attempt to push through enemy shipping. Everything was working pretty hard. The ship rarely wound up to its maximum of 32.5 knots. Above deck crew were exposed to direct fire, but being down here carried its own brand of fear. Engineering staff were particularly vulnerable to torpedoes, closeted away 20 feet (5 metres) below the waterline, behind air locks and watertight hatches. It could feel safe but it could also felt like a steel coffin. Reece concentrated on the pumping pistons and whining turbines. Nearby were Engineer Lieut Frank Gillan and Warrant Engineer Jim Tuersley. Tuersley was all navy, a career RN engineer rating who had been loaned to the RAN and *Perth* on commissioning for a period of two years. He was still here in an atmosphere which stank of oil and hot steel; the smell was with you even when you finished watch, even after you showered; perhaps it got into your bloodstream; Tuersley would have it no other way. As the ship twitched, steam pipes vibrated and tiny pieces of asbestos packing flew like snow. There was a huge thump, which jerked men into the air and then dropped them to the steel plates, jarring joints and teeth. Water sprayed from a broken gauge and one of the fans above their heads stopped. The cruiser slowed dramatically, listed to starboard, levelled then rolled to port. Duty men in No.2 engine and boiler rooms knew what this meant. Any explosion strong enough to knock out their equivalent in the bow section would have brought fatalities. How many of their mates had been killed? Their ship could not survive now; how soon would it be before they were told to leave this metal place? What was going on above them? Would they live to see tomorrow? They waited to meet their destiny.

Stoker 'Bert' Mynard reflected too, on his brother Charles. Bert was one of six children born to Christopher and Elizabeth Mynard of Victoria, five boys and one girl with a large age difference. Charles Mynard had been killed at Gallipoli; Bert was born during the war his brother was killed in. It seemed that the same families fought the wars. Bert Mynard had been a fun-loving type who loved to play sport and go dancing. There had been no fun these last months and the days seemed so long.

There were others from Mynard's recruit class in *Perth*'s second engine room.[31] Fred Mason was another Victorian, with the unusual physical characteristic of having 'eye colour: left, brown, right green', at least according to his recruiting officer. Mason's uncle, Albert Reynolds, had been a Stoker in the RAN during World War I. To the impressionable Fred, his uncle's war stories sounded wonderful. That was the trouble with war stories, the bad bits were normally left out. So Fred decided to enlist in the World War II RAN as a Stoker. He had barely had time to adjust to wearing naval rig before Mason, Mynard and six other same class Stokers were drafted to *Perth* in January 1942. Mason was pleased, he considered destroyers 'kerosene tins', and wanted something more substantial between him and enemy fire. Mason considered his job 'cushy', he was required to check engine temperature gauges every half hour.[32] Fred Mason felt safe down in the depths of this ship. A rating's category was not a matter of choice during World War II, it depended on your name – that and a few 'washouts' from other rates. Bit annoying really, the belief that anyone could be a Stoker. It wasn't true. Mason was chuffed his name allowed him to be a Stoker, but some others weren't.

A classmate who did not share Mason's pleasure was Morton O'Loughlan. O'Loughlan had applied for a transfer within days of joining *Perth*. It wasn't so much a Stoker thing, he wanted out of the cruiser and the RAN. From the Victorian town of Yackandandah, the Stoker 2nd Class suffered badly from seasickness. It was agreed he could transfer to the army, but the paperwork was proceeding incredibly slowly.

After the second torpedo, communication with the rest of the ship was cut. Engine and boiler room personnel watched their seniors, waiting for the order to move to the ship's well-worn ladders and proceed up. Stoker Jim Millerick, known for his referring to *Perth* as 'Chook' and fighting anyone not from his ship who referred to the cruiser in the same terms, looked at the expressions of those around him, a mixture of apprehension and sadness more than fear. As the signal was given, another torpedo hit and the ship was listing at 45 degrees. They struggled through ship corridors rapidly filling with water. Pulling himself through the final hatch Millerick was blown off the deck as the fourth torpedo exploded into the port side.[33]

John 'Jack' Madge ensured engine room personnel left, but with his ship disintegrating around him he wondered if he had missed someone, hesitated and went back to check. It was a fatal decision for the Chief ERA who had refused a land posting because he did not wish to be called a coward should anything happen to *Perth*. Gillan, Tuersley and Reece were the last up the boiler room ladder. By this time the ship was listing heavily to one side, so the ladders were almost horizontal and their bodies fought to adjust. A Stoker lost his footing and fell. Gillan threw his arm out in time to grab the youngster and they started to climb again.

By the time they reached the entrance, floors had become walls and the steel door had become the roof. It took the combined strength of four to push it up and back. Heaving themselves through, the men were now faced with a well-like gap to the escape manhole. The young Stoker jumped first; 'his boots slipped as he was taking off and he fell screaming into the well', into the blackness. The three senior men shouted but there was no answer. Chief Reece said, 'Oh, God', and jumped.[34] Engineer Lieut Gillan watched Reece and Tuersley pull themselves through the manhole and disappear. He was gearing himself to follow when a spout of water roared through the manhole, *Perth* was turning over, and the lights went out. In that split second, he realised the ship was going in bow first and that displaced water would go back and up, at least that was the theory. Willing himself not to struggle, he rolled himself up in a ball and let the water carry him to wherever. Fortunately his Mae West was not fully inflated, otherwise he would have become stuck to whatever was then the ceiling. He shot backwards, upwards, turned over and over like a ball, bouncing off everything, over and over. He knew he was going in the right direction, and then his miner's hat battery cord became entangled with some part of the upside-down ship and he was jerked to a stop. It took a split second to break the cord and wriggle free, the current grabbed him and he was in a whirlpool – he thought he was going to drown. His senses were screaming and then all became peaceful and quiet; he was in a very serene place but he knew, 'If I don't struggle now I'll drown'.[35] Gillan clawed his way up and, breaking the surface, he swung round gulping air to see *Perth*'s propeller blades disappear beneath the surface. Chief Reece and Warrant Officer Tuersley had not come up.

—

At 0020 on Sunday 1 March, the fourth torpedo entered the port side. Like a gallant but punch-drunk fighter, the cruiser yet again struggled to right itself, but this was no longer possible. Five minutes later, some 4 miles (6 kilometres) north-east of St Nicholas Point, HMAS *Perth* slid in an almost graceful motion beneath the surface of Sunda Strait. Men in the water watched as the ship sank at the bows with the stern raised, a solitary figure could be seen near the propeller before he and the ship disappeared.

Signalman 'Buzzer' Bee watched from the water. Someone had applied a piece of signal halyard as a tourniquet to his leg, he never knew who it was, or if the crewmate survived, but the thoughtful action meant Bee would. The shrapnel that had sliced through his right calf and lodged in the bone was not now his major worry. Bee had groped and crawled towards the ship's rails and felt almost grateful that *Perth* was listing so heavily to port he could simply roll over the side. Revived by the water his immediate fear was that the cruiser would roll on him, so he struck out in a weird swim stroke hampered by one useless leg, then turned to see the ship glide quietly by him, 'bows down, the starboard screws clear of the water and still turning'.[36]

Ord Seam Frank Chattaway surfaced and couldn't see a thing. It wasn't pleasant in the dark waters, 'it was a queer and unforgettable experience', and in the pitch-blackness the weirdest thought came to him: perhaps he should 'get back on the ship'.[37] Chattaway clutched at floating cordite boxes, only to find they quickly sank; he floated there, 'in the darkness now and again hearing faraway cries but for the most part drifting in silence'. Everything Chattaway tried to grasp disappeared beneath his weight, and after 45 minutes he became a 'little concerned'. As he thrashed about, a voice asked if he was okay. His reply was a gurgled, 'Not too good', and hands grabbed him and pulled him onto the side of a float. The float was fully loaded, so Chattaway wound the side rope over his arm and felt safer.

Bandsman Perce Partington had lost his beloved trombone, and, as he trod water, his mind wandered to his mother in Tasmania. The war had already taken the lives of his brothers Arnold and Leslie, both RAN Bandsmen, surely this war could not claim the life of her last son.

Ord Seam 'Robbie' Roberts was overcome with sadness as he watched his ship descend, because it was also 'my home' and 'everything I owned' was in that home.[38] He could not see the expression on Ord Seam 'Digby' Gray's face, but doubtless it reflected his own. 'Digby' had had 'supreme confidence' in his 'beautiful ship'. Now as he drifted in the inky blackness of Sunda Strait, he desperately tried to recoup his confidence and struggled with the image of the 'beautiful ship' disappearing below him. The incredible activity of the previous hour and a half was replaced by nothingness, by feelings of utter abandonment and loneliness, as he wallowed in a black ocean. The mind struggled to comprehend the gravity of the circumstances, rational actions gave way to irrational thoughts, 'I must be the only one to survive', and 'it would be best not to bring notice to myself. I must stay quiet in case the Japs hear, yes, stay quiet until daybreak'.[39]

TEN

'They fought for King and Country and sleep in sailor's graves.'

ERA Vic Duncan

The attention of men struggling in Sunda Strait turned to *Houston*. The cruiser was clearly in its death throes, 'beaten down by weight of metal'.[1] The American warship was ablaze and taking a pounding; onboard it was dreadful. Captain Rooks gave the order to 'Abandon Ship' at 0025, just before he was killed by shrapnel. As the ship was still underway, the Executive Officer, Cdr Roberts, countermanded the order. By this time, however, Japanese destroyers were practically alongside, strafing the decks with machine-gun fire. Roberts ordered 'Abandon Ship' at 0033. ERA Vic Duncan watched from the water as the 'Galloping Ghost', 'well down but on an even keel, slightly down at the stern', vanished.[2] Signalman 'Buzzer' Bee, clinging tenaciously to a plank of wood, felt sadness as, 'The gallant *Houston* ... battered into submission, slid beneath the surface to rejoin *Perth* in one last rendezvous'.[3] It was 0045 and Japanese searchlights were extinguished, leaving an inky blackness. It had taken an estimated six torpedoes and countless shells to sink *Houston*.[4] Of the 1008 crew, 638 were lost in the battle; only 266 would return to the United States, after 104 would not survive being Japanese prisoners of war.

For *Perth* officers and sailors fighting to stay alive in Sunda Strait this 1 March, physical hardship took on new meaning as the minutes and hours ticked over, injuries and exposure would test even the strongest man. The mental and emotional ordeal was beyond comprehension; the men felt a huge sense of loss and a fear of the totally unknown. The lack of control for men used to lives governed by rules, regulations and orders from superiors, was totally unfamiliar. For men of this era, the sense of helplessness was devastating, not just because they were incapacitated, but because of their limited ability to help others. Wounded men cried out, then disappeared. AB Ron Williams had been one of the *Autolycus* group. He had survived the Med but this time the ship sank, he was injured and had no life jacket. Stoker II Don Leitch drowned when the bullet-riddled ship's cutter filled with water and sank. Shipmates wondered if he was wounded or if he just couldn't swim, but they were in no condition to help him, they were barely alive themselves.

In the distance there were light flashes and the dark, sinister shapes of enemy shipping. The disconcerting silence was all-enveloping, broken only by the occasional shout of a sailor searching for a mate. Stoker II Lloyd Bessell peered into the night and wondered about Max Burk and Bill Luck. They had enlisted together, travelled to *Cerberus* for training and had been in the part of the line told they would be Stokers. Luck had been a 22-year-old member of the Launceston Fire Brigade so that suited him down to the ground. Burk, also 22, from Hobart, was a champion sportsman and had no qualms with anything physical. Bessell, married with three children, didn't want the younger men to show him up, so they became a team and looked out for each other when all three drafted to *Perth* the previous October. Bessell wished he'd had time to ensure the younger men got off the ship. He eventually found Max Burk, but he never found the Launceston fireman.

The speed of the destruction of *Perth,* caused by four torpedoes in 20 minutes, had given crew in the bowels of the cruiser limited survival opportunities. Not only had there been jammed hatches and buckled bulkheads to negotiate, but the ocean had flooded in through the torpedo-torn hull with astonishing speed. AB Russell Goddard a former grocer's assistant from Sydney and AB Eric Justelius had ensured *Perth*'s torpedoes were released, but neither made it off the ship. Leading Wireman John Innes did not get away from the region of No.2 low power room. The former electrician had made his home in Sydney with wife Wilma, a nurse. Leading Stoker Allan Farley had been released from the RAN during the 1931 culling period, but convinced the navy to allow him to re-enlist in 1932, and had been delighted when chosen for the commissioning crew. He had been with the *Perth* for its life and remained near the Port Diesel.

It had taken a huge effort for Chief EA John Huggan to arrive topside. He had been one of the most experienced men on the cruiser, a member of the pre-commission group who had sailed to England in *Comorin*. He had pushed forward as the ship's bows began to burrow downwards and was not seen again. So too Leading Seaman Arthur 'Olga' Close, who, under the influence of too much cheap champagne in Papeete in March 1940, had misappropriated the icon belonging to the indigenous chief who foretold the sinking.

Ord Coder Geoffrey Ward from Warracknabeal, Victoria, had been in the main wireless transmitting office. Life for Ward prior to the latter part of 1941 had been as a bank clerk, and he had proved adept at the more technical application of figures and machines, becoming the only Coder in *Perth*. He had been with Telegraphist John Day and Ord Telegraphist Alf Degner, Aussie mates who would keep company in death. In the 2nd W/T office, Ord Telegraphist Neville Green, from Sydney, would have celebrated his twentieth birthday in three weeks. Telegraphist Cecil Gwatkin had the classic Gaelic colouring of someone born in Leith, Scotland had been engaged to Pat Abbott, a WRAN Wireless Operator. On duty in the RAN's main shore radio station, outside Canberra.[5] WRAN Pat Abbot would be one of the first to know *Perth* was missing, one of the first to worry about the fate of the man she loved. It would be nearly four years before her worst fears were officially confirmed, that Cecil Gwatkin had last been seen in the 3rd W/T office of his sinking ship. He had always wanted to be a Wireless Operator so was doing what he enjoyed most; he was just doing it in a very dangerous place. The Captain's cousin, AB John Sievey, did not escape. The Sievey family had lost two sons to this war in less than four months, one in *Sydney*, one in *Perth*, and they would be unable to bury either.

—

A thick film of oil floated in, enveloping everything in its wake. Men gagged as they inhaled and swallowed; breathing passages became blocked; eyes glued shut; for some, it proved too much. Engineer Lieut Frank Gillan was still coming to terms with his escape from an upside-down sinking cruiser as the oil invaded his eyes, mouth and ears. He found a plank. Another man grasped the end of the timber and Gillan paddled them to a raft. The voice of Cdr Martin asked if they would like to join this band of survivors. Gillan's companion agreed, but for some unknown reason Gillan declined and the raft moved off. The ship's XO and those with him were not seen again.

Having heaved himself onto another raft Lieut Cdr Polo Owen was trying to catch his breath when he sensed movement close by. Owen asked the man to identify himself. The answer was muffled, but he recognised the voice of Lieut David McWilliam, 'I don't think I'll live much longer, Polo'.[6] With the help of others, Owen lifted McWilliam into a raft. 'Ironic' was a word closely associated with McWilliam. He had been discharged from the RAN as a Cadet Midshipman due to 'Defective Eyesight', only to be mobilised in the RANR to undergo the Observer course. He had arrived onboard *Perth* to fly in the Walrus. In 1940 he had been awarded a Royal Humane Society Bronze Medal for the rescue of a drowning woman in Sydney Harbour, and now it was he being rescued.

Leading Seaman Keith Gosden was struggling to get his bearings; the previous hour was a blur. He remembered the sweltering heat of the 'Y' turret lobby. He remembered a gunner above yelling 'Abandon ship'; he remembered the rising water. Then he remembered how he had attempted to open the hatch, which led to the shell-room below and the five men there. The weight of water had made this impossible, and he had turned away and waded to the ladder that took him to the upper deck. A torpedo hit, he didn't know which one, but the jolt propelled him high, very high, into the air. As he plummeted down, he was tumbled overboard by a wave. His descent was rapid. Gosden pictured his mother reading the telegram reporting his death. Her face was oh so close and she was crying, then he shot to the surface. Now he felt a sort of guilty, giddy elation.

Gosden swam to a raft Lieut Cdr Clarke and RAAF Corporal Bradshaw had commandeered. They collected a sailor whose right leg had been blasted away, but he died shortly after.[7] Gosden was feeling relieved as he drifted on the raft, until someone grabbed his legs as they attempted to board. Gosden was shocked to see a Japanese soldier in full battle dress. He kicked to free his legs and saw more soldiers, calling out in a language he did not understand, but he knew they were close to drowning. In that split second he realised he did not care and pushed the soldiers away with his boots. Another sailor on the float was kicking too, shouting, 'You killed my mate, you bastards, you killed my mate'.[8]

Treading water and endeavouring to absorb where and who he was, another Perth sailor asked Yeoman Percy Stokan if he had a knife. When the Yeoman asked why, the sailor replied he wished to kill some 'Japs' in the water nearby.

A group of survivors spied a raft and, urging each other on, moved towards it. As they got closer they realised the raft had red hydro graphics on it; it was not from *Perth*. As they approached they saw members of the opposing force huddled onboard. The Australians were greater in numbers; they needed the raft and took it.

The Walrus Telegraphist Gunner Ken 'Tag' Wallace was disoriented. He had earlier succeeded in escaping 'the merciless hail of heavy machine-gun bullets' that fell on the men who were attempting to abandon ship'[9] from the guns of *Fubuki*, but when he surfaced, machine-gun fire peppered the water. His left arm was spurting blood and he was attempting to stem the bleeding, when he realised he was being dragged down by his own ship's suction. He danced along the hull and tumbled down, head over heels. After what seemed an eternity, he popped to the surface with men all around him, but they were all dead. Grabbing a large piece of timber, Wallace observed a sight that puzzled him: men, lots of men, with what looked like periscopes attached – strange, very strange. They came closer and he realised they were enemy soldiers in the water with their rifles slung on their backs. He hoped they wouldn't notice him. A small figure spotted him and, screaming in Japanese, clutched at the timber. Wallace was attempting to wrestle the wooden debris away, when the enemy raised a slender blade and thrust it at his throat. The knife passed through Wallace's mouth piercing his palate and penetrating his left nostril. 'This attack so incensed me that I kicked him viciously in the face and pushed him away unconscious'.[10]

Japanese destroyers switched to their navigation lights and moved through the men in the water. One ship Captain clearly regarded those in the water with respect, as he edged his ship very carefully and waited until clear before re-engaging the screws. Another ship was not so gentle in its effort to find Japanese survivors: 'one of them bore down on us, and we were actually fending it off … We looked up and could see these little figures in white uniforms waving torches around'.[11]

'Tag' Wallace refused to climb aboard an enemy destroyer and sailors threw objects at him, 'it was a great joke by the sounds of the laughter from the ship'.[12] Leading Seaman Harry Lambden from Lismore, New South Wales, started to board a destroyer but was pushed back into the water and died. So too, Painter IV Dick Stapleton. Another oil-blackened sailor was ordered to identify his group and shouted, 'We're Australians and we're fucking proud of it'.[13] But from the darkened bridge of the destroyer came the 'cool, sardonic voice speaking well-articulated English: "We bloody good boys now, eh, Aussie"'.[14] Then the waters were quiet again and each man was left to his own thoughts.

The less strong, the wounded, took their last breath as oil gurgled into their lungs. The euphoric sensation that came when near to drowning was seductive. Some thought of their families and survived. AB Bob Collins saw himself lying peacefully on the ocean floor until he thought, 'I can't die here. Poor old Mum would be devastated'.[15] Sub Lieut 'Knocker' White was brought out of his stupor by different motivation: 'if I drown now, I'll never have bacon and eggs again, so I'll go on swimming a little bit longer.'[16] 'Buzzer' Bee, with the tourniquet still attached to his wounded leg, wondered how much longer he could last, then he recognised the voice of Signalman Ken 'Slug' Elliott. Bee could just make out the boat crammed with men, then Elliott dragged the younger Communicator onboard the raft.

AB Ernie Toovey fought to disentangle himself from a net, and upon freeing himself found he had drifted off alone. Fighting fatigue and anxiety, he thought of his family and began talking aloud. He wondered what his father, who had served with the Light Horse in the previous war, thought about all this. His army brother Peter was likely still home in Warwick recovering from wounds. His brother Jim was likely pestering their parents, just as he had, to join the RAN, until they gave in and agreed he could enlist. Brother Syd would have recovered from injuries and likely be somewhere in a Middle Eastern desert, and here he was, 'nineteen years old and slowly floating round the unfriendly waters of the East Indies'. Toovey could now make out blackened swimmers going in all directions, and realised the treacherous nature of the cross current was sweeping many further out to sea: 'We will never know how many seemingly uninjured men were drowned at this point'.[17] Toovey promised himself out loud, he would stay alive for his family and to play test cricket for Queensland.

Everywhere *Perth* survivors tried to make the most of their predicament, because, as Wireman Fred Lasslett said in a classic understatement, 'things weren't too healthy in the water'. However, things were looking up for Ernie Toovey; he found sanctuary on a raft. The shrapnel wounds to his thigh made him grimace with pain but the combination of salt water and oil stopped the bleeding, and when he looked around, he was humbled: 'compared to others in the boat my injuries did not exist'.[18]

AB Bob Collins found pieces of timber to splint Sub Lieut Gavin Campbell's leg. Unknown to Campbell, he was inspiring others, as Toovey observed, 'One officer, a man over six feet in height, from Sydney, had a shocking compound fracture of his leg and he never complained'.[19] PO Bill Davis had fractured his left tibia and fibula. EA III Arthur Kiesey had extensive burns to the back and shoulders; Leading Seaman Ben Talbot had a smashed collarbone, broken ribs and other injuries; AB Gordon Webster carried a broken wrist; Stoker Jeff Latch, Assistant Cook Merv Scott, and Bandsman Perce Partington, had suffered internal injuries when the third torpedo exploded into the ship and they were in the water.

Clearly Claud Maslem was in a bad way. The 25-year-old Stoker from Quirindi, New South Wales, may have been the only man to escape the forward boiler room but he was shockingly wounded. Indeed, from what Toovey could observe, there seemed few on his raft or those adjacent who were not injured, yet few complained. Commissioned Gunner George Ross realised he had fractured a few ribs. Ross knew nothing could be done right then and there, so it was pointless to tell anyone else. Instead Ross leant over the side of his raft and told 'Tiger' Lyons clinging to the side, he would hold onto him so the Schoolmaster could sleep. AB Dick Ryan had suffered shrapnel wounds to his back and right leg, but the only concerned noises he made formed the question, had anyone seen his brother Charlie? The two were great mates, eighteen months apart in age, had enlisted eleven months apart and had been wide-eyed members of the *Autolycus* commissioning crew. He did not yet know that Charlie had been killed. Of course that was the difference, the men who clung precariously to rafts, debris and each other were still alive, the rest of *Perth*'s crew were already dead.

During this night and the many to follow, the Reverend Keith 'Bish' Mathieson could be forgiven for questioning his faith in a merciful God. All around he observed men, good men, suffering. He had seen them on the embattled decks, heard their cries as he abandoned ship and watched as more were swept out to sea by a merciless current. AB Verdun Blackwell, a 25-year-old former motor mechanic from Tasmania; AB Robert Williams, a 22-year-old labourer, from Lismore, New South Wales; AB George Lawson, a 21-year-old from Perth; Signalman Walter Hopton, a nineteen-year-old chemist's assistant from Sydney; and the 26-year-old Observer, Lieut David McWilliam, all died of their wounds in the night, and were gently rolled off rafts, as Mathieson led men in prayer and committed the bodies to the deep.

—

Land was tantalisingly close but rafts were being carried rapidly around St Nicholas Point and into the Strait. *Perth*'s red-bearded

Quartermaster, Leading Seaman Ben Chaffey, was a good long-distance swimmer and fancied his chances; Java looked only about 4 miles (6 kilometres) away. Chaffey would try for hours but the current kept pushing him back. Wireman Allan Geier, who had realised he was no longer a teenager on the eve of the Battle of Java Sea, struck out for Java, and after a Herculean effort pulled himself ashore. EA III Vic Duncan swam for the Java shore, and it was oh so near before the rip pulled him back. He set off again, and this time made land.

AB 'Tich' Hill, who had spent his childhood in Busselton, Western Australia, felt more comfortable by and near water than he ever did on land, so leaving his raft was worth the risk. Another sailor asked if he could join him. They swam slowly trying to conserve energy and avoid cramp. Short conversation between the two sailors was comforting, but after a time conversation ceased. In the darkness of night, Hill tried to find his companion but there was no answer, 'I realised that he must have drowned, or been taken by sharks'.[20] Alone, Hill continued on his way. 'Tag' Wallace was making good speed with a locker grating pushed out in front of him like a kick board. As he approached what he later realised was Bantam Bay, he observed soldiers with small hurricane lamps searching the beach. 'I heard screams and the flash of swords as some unfortunate wretches were despatched'. The Japanese were clearly not taking prisoners and Wallace swam silently back into the Strait.[21]

—

As the first shards of morning light broke the night sky, wreckage, rafts, flotsam and bodies, were scattered over the ocean as far as one could see, and everything was covered in a sticky mess of fuel oil. The carley raft was an oval-shaped copper tube divided into watertight compartments by internal bulkheads. The raft was covered with canvas and cork, the internal timber platform fixed by rope netting. Over the sides of the raft, more rope netting. A standard raft was intended to support twelve men inside and a further eight on the sides. On 1 March 1942, the rafts saved the lives of many who abandoned *Perth*, their human cargoes vastly larger than those recommended by manufacturers.

As survivors were swept along Sunda Strait, they squinted through eyes fused together with oil and fought their demons. The sun quickly heated the oil on their bodies until it sizzled and they slipped into the water and felt relief. They knew they shouldn't swallow, but throats were so parched and they were so thirsty, it was so easy to take that mouthful, or more, to simply stop, to relinquish their tenuous hold on life. A desperate need to stop the pain and fear clashed with the desperate urge that forced them on. Sick men began to rant, their delirium more upsetting to others than themselves. But even under these grave circumstances there was some humour. Someone was singing a bawdy dirge; AB 'Chesty' Bond kept morale up and men awake by telling endless dirty ditties. Engineer Lieut Frank Gillan was creating grander mirth. Gillan had always prided himself in being immaculately attired. On the morning of 1 March he was clad only in underpants, his entire body black from fuel oil, including his toupee. As he drifted past fellow survivors he raised the black and beaten hairpiece with the greeting 'Good morning, gentleman'.

In the clear and hot morning Toppers and Sangiang Islands appeared. Men could see the surf crashing onto white beaches. It looked an easy swim and many left rafts. Some succeeded, many more were unsuccessful. AB Wireman Charlie Wray looked longingly at the beach. Three times he tried, three times he was pushed back to the rafts. A sinking painting pontoon motivated Fred Skeels to risk everything, but the former messenger boy from the Perth suburb of Mt Lawley soon realised, 'he wasn't getting anywhere and was going to drown' if he did not manage to reach another raft. He had not seen his closest friend Ord Seam Bob Johnson who had been stationed in the forward magazine, in the water. AB John Woods's arms were sore from hanging onto the side of a raft. His eyes were on fire and when he looked to the sun, the burning and itching increased. Woods asked PO Plumber Ernie Kynvin if he would like to swim for it. The older man declined. The island beach was clearly in view, only 200 or so yards away (around 180 metres), it was worth a go. Woods pushed off and the current grabbed him in a vice-like grip, spun him around and pulled him under. The nineteen year old battled against its pull and spluttered back towards the raft. As

Woods's energy evaporated, Kynvin reached out, pulled Woods to the side and held him until his breathing came easier.

The Reverend Ronald Sutton Bevington decided to take on the current and the *Perth* Church of England chaplain was not sighted again. Supply Assistant Ron Clohesy who had calmly munched biscuits awaiting the order to abandon ship, was seen for the last time calmly swimming towards land. Dan Padfield left for the islands, but the 33-year-old sick Berth Attendant never made land. Twenty-year-old Stoker II John Roberts from Port Adelaide was seen in the water, but then he disappeared. The popular Yeoman of Signals, Percy Stokan, who had inspired many junior signal staff, asked 'Tiger' Lyons if he wanted to swim for Toppers Island. Lyons shook his head and apologised, he just didn't have the strength. Stokan left the raft, shouting he would have breakfast ready by the time Lyons arrived. The current swept the Yeoman back. Grasping the side of a raft, Stokan paused and struck out again. The current proved relentless and this time Stokan drowned.

Ord Seam Frank Chattaway was a non-swimmer, so he declined the invitation to accompany six others. He may have felt regret in the moments that followed as he clung to a raft, but later Chattaway would discover that none of the six survived. Ironically, Chattaway stayed alive in Sunda Strait because of his inability to swim.

In the light of the new morning, Ord Seam 'Tich' Hill acknowledged he was no closer to land. Panic coursed through his body as he searched the horizon and saw no one. Then he observed two life jackets quite close. Swimming in their direction, he thought how foolish his fellow seamen were to have removed their Mae Wests. Hill made a grasp for the jackets and realised they still held their occupants. The drowned sailors were hanging below the oily surface and it filled him with horror, 'they reminded me of dead flies caught on dirty fly-paper and ... unless a miracle happened, I also would end up like that'.[22] Hill managed to get within 50 yards (45 metres) of the beach, but the current dragged him away and returned him to deep waters. Frustrated he turned his back on the white sands and tall palms and gave himself up to the ocean. He grabbed a box but it offered little respite and his mind wandered back to the school scripture classes he had attended under sufferance.

'Apart from the vague desire to avoid going to hell', Hill couldn't take religion seriously. He recalled the Minister's words, 'no prayer ever went unanswered'. Now seemed as good a time as any to test the theory, 'Feeling spineless ... I whispered "God help me"'.[23]

Norm Fuller and George Ward began to swim. The Ord Seamen had joined the RAN in January 1941, had been drafted to *Perth* in October the same year and were now both trying to stay alive in dangerous waters. They were pushed back out to sea. After the second attempt they were nearing exhaustion. A lifeboat was visible and they knew they needed to reach it to survive.

Nearby, a large plank banging into his side roused the semi-conscious Hill. Heaving himself on to it, the Busselton boy fell into a fitful stupor. When Hill again raised his head he saw fellow West Australians, Norm Fuller and George Ward. The glint of an oar had caught their attention and all three pushed towards the lifeboat. Each stroke incredibly hard, they were running on empty and being driven on by sheer will. Finally hands grabbed the sailors and they were pulled into the boat. For Hill any judgement as to whether 'God' had anything to do with it needed further consideration. For Fuller there was the realisation that the eighteen-year-old Ward was nowhere to be seen.

—

The day was heating up. The islands were slipping away when Leading Seaman Keith Gosden slid off his raft. It was a tough decision but the options looked bleak: stay on the float and be taken by the current into open water or attempt to swim and be taken by the current into open water – he may as well die trying. Within 50 yards (45 metres) of the beach the rip clutched at his body and cast him back from where he had come. Fighting disappointment, Gosden began to swim again. His progress was abruptly halted by a body and he shuddered when he recognised Peter Nelson. Pushing the body away, Gosden realised Nelson was not dead, but dead asleep. He woke Nelson and complained about the snoring. The Ord Telegraphist indignantly claimed he didn't snore, 'You were snoring your head off,'[24] shouted Gosden. The current pulled them apart and Gosden made for the beach again. On the verge of admitting defeat, he caught a wave and was dumped unceremoniously into the shallows. As he stood, coral and rocks tore at his skin and Gosden felt blood run, but he was ashore and felt little pain.

ERA Chas Thomson was another who managed the long and difficult swim ashore. Thomson had felt such 'emptiness' when his 'home' and all his belongings disappeared, he needed to regain a sense of control, so started to swim. Alone he swam, on and on, for just shy of twelve hours, and the first person he met on the island was his best mate, ERA Ron 'Roy' Rees.[25]

Lieut Lloyd Burgess may not have had the makings of a 'modern Major General' but he epitomised a modern naval officer. Even as a student at Scotch College, he had been fascinated by boats and joined the Royal Brighton Yacht Club. His love of the sea had directed him to a career not with the nation's navy but as an officer in the Merchant Marine. The war had come and Burgess had transferred to the RANR(S). Now, however, his love of the sea had turned to full-blown terror, as whirlpools pivoted him around and dragged him under. Burgess knew that he had only energy for one more attempt to breach the current and suddenly he was tossed into still water. Branches of coral slashed his feet and hands as he struggled to stand. Vomiting copious amounts of oily, salty water he instinctively looked at his wristwatch, it was still working and read 7.35 a.m., the morning after the longest night of his life. Someone else was propelled towards the beach, and Leading Seaman Frank Nash crawled up the sand. The two watched another body tumble in on a wave and fall face first into the shallows. They staggered to the inert body, dragged the coughing Sick Berth Attendant Ernie Noble ashore, and the three men fell exhausted into the welcome embrace of land, sweet land.

—

PO Horrie Abbott and Leading Seaman Frank Johnson found a lifeboat and they began collecting survivors, many of whom, like the two *Perth* Yeomen, were close to death. Jack Willis and Neil Biddel were the best of friends and urged each other on. They were within 'spitting distance' of the island, they could feel the firm sand supporting their bodies as the palms waved above, then the current swirled them 'around and around and swept us down the strait towards the ocean at an alarming rate'.[26] Biddel was spent and started to drown. Willis shouted at his companion but knew the swim and eleven hours in the water had made their position hopeless. He saw a boat and shouted, at the boat, at the elements and at Biddel to swim, Biddel couldn't. Willis left, determined to bring the boat to the exhausted Tasmanian. Battling the current and fear that his 'fast ebbing strength would give out', he was finally pulled aboard. Willis pointed to Biddel and shut his eyes. They were safe.

Survivors would analyse the events that took place in Sunda Strait. They would try to rationalise how and why they caught that wave; how they were freed from the grip of the current at just the right time; how with just a couple of breaths left they were seen and pulled into a boat; but there was no logic to it. It could not be rationalised and it would never really make sense. The law of averages suggested Lieut Cdr Polo Owen and PO Ed Tyrrell would not survive, but neither admitted such poor evaluations. Clinging to a plank they were being swept down the Strait as if there was a motor attached. The islands had all but disappeared along with their last chance to make landfall. Owen was tired, how easy it would be to simply slip beneath the surface. As the water covered Owen's eyes, Tyrrell hit him in the head with the plank shouting 'For God's sake don't leave me'.[27] Pulling his body further over the slippery surface, Owen apologised. Minutes later it was Owen's turn to whack Tyrrell. With the sun directly overhead they saw a smudge, rubbed a little oil from their eyes and the smudge turned into a boat. Tyrrell still wore a lanyard with a whistle around his neck. He blew, and blew, and blew. If only he had more strength, more breath, more time. Then there were arms, hands grabbing him, grabbing Owen, and a booming voice shouting in his ear, 'stop blowing that floggin' flute. We 'eard yer the first floggin' time'.[28]

Others defied the law of averages and were pulled into the Abbott boat. The last was Sub Lieut 'Knocker' White. White had left a raft to swim to Sangiang. Mere feet from the island, a whirlpool tore him away. After a dozen hours in the water, White had lapsed into unconsciousness. Those in the Abbott boat only just saw him, then they thought he was just another water-logged corpse. They very nearly didn't check, but they did. There were now around 40 in the lifeboat, and they raised a mast and sail as they began to row back to Sangiang Island. Oars were double banked and the crew strained against the current, with Abbott throwing buckets of ocean water over oil-covered bodies to offer a little relief from the sun. Only one landing area could be found, a small beach between two cliffs. Surf was running, so Abbott unshipped the rudder and rigged an oar to act as a sweep. There was so little room for error before the boat would be recaptured by the rip. In the best tradition of Australian lifesaving, with Abbott standing at the rear of the craft screaming encouragement and 'every swear word in the Australian vocabulary',[29] they rode a wave into a foreign beach.

—

Prior to dawn, a group that included Commissioned Gunner Len Smith, Able Seamen Joe Deegan and Ernie Brown found a Japanese lifeboat. It was equipped with oars, sails and provisions. Rapidly shipmates were collected, and for a short time optimism reigned as they began to plot a course for Australia. Just after dawn a Japanese destroyer closed in. The Australians pretended not to notice and kept rowing. The voice that came from the warship asked them to 'Heave to'; the Australians kept rowing. The destroyer's forward 5-inch gun swung in their direction, and the Australians stopped rowing. A line was tied to the lifeboat and it was towed down the Strait to where more *Perth* crew clung to rafts and debris.

The destroyer remained stationary whilst the lifeboat ferried survivors to the side. Men were allowed to board after removing oil-soaked clothing. With around 190 survivors sprawled on the destroyer deck, the lifeboat continued its lifesaving mission. Ord Seam David Manning was relieved when he climbed into the boat. As the group approached the destroyer, Manning removed his clothes and threw them overboard, everything except his money belt. Suddenly an aircraft alert caused the destroyer to leave abruptly. Those left in the boat looked on in bewilderment. Not only were they not being rescued, but they now had no clothes to combat the elements, only Chaplain Keith

Mathieson had retained a shirt because he could not bring himself to disrobe completely.

More and more men struck out for the lifeboat until it was almost submerged under the weight of about 70 *Perth* and *Houston* survivors, but none could, or would, be refused.[30] The uninjured were urged to push towards land. With everyone covered in oil, rowing proved difficult, 'We finished with eight people pulling on the oars, and about sixteen trying to hold them down'.[31] It was exasperating, 'Despite all the hard work the overloaded boat did not appear to be moving'.[32] More than a dozen times they tried to beach the boat and failed. Tempers were beginning to fray. All day and through another harsh night they fought on, tired, thirsty and hungry. The boat's water tanks had been damaged by gunfire and the water was contaminated. They broke open the Japanese rations. The hard tack biscuits were branded 'Sunshine Biscuits, Ballarat'. Life was full of ironies. A rain shower saw them look to the skies with mouths open wide. A breeze arose, a small sail filled and the boat was finally moving. Cries were heard and AB 'Jumma' Brown dived overboard and returned with two very lucky *Houston* sailors. The boat tiller vanished and one was fashioned out of driftwood. Finally the bow of the lifeboat crunched into a coral reef and its occupants smiled and staggered ashore.

—

Allan Gee was blinded by fuel oil. He had clung to the side of a float for more than a day before he was taken onboard a Japanese destroyer. Relief was tempered when, 'the bastards threw some of the wounded back into the sea. I couldn't believe it. Imagine coming through that nightmare only to be tossed back into the sea'.[33] Wireman Fred Lasslett too felt fortunate but was also worried, 'What happened to those boys?' *Perth* survivors were now distributed over a couple of destroyers.

Having discarded all clothing, kerosene was used, somewhat unsuccessfully, to divest bodies of oil. Survivors were each handed a G-string, a flap of material, 30 by 8 inches (75 by 20 centimetres), which offered some modesty. Little did they know this would be standard dress for years to come. A little water and a hard sea biscuit were handed out, but conditions on the upper deck of a destroyer were exposed and cramped. It was probably better than floating about in Sunda Strait, although at least in the water they were 'free'.

Surgeon Lieut Sam Stening, wounded himself, tried to help the injured, assisted by PO SBA James 'Jock' Cunningham and SBA Andy Mitchell. Cunningham, a 35-year-old Scot, had realised his calling early in life and was a hospital wardsman before he enlisted in the RAN in 1927. Stoker Jeff Latch was choking on oil. With both his nose and throat full of the muck, they gave him artificial respiration to keep him breathing while they struggled to clear his airways. They were less successful with AB Henry Vivian. The 24 year old born in Pontypool, England, who had enlisted in 1938, had married in September 1941. It was believed he had spent around 36 hours in the water before he was found. A shattered chest, ruptured stomach, exhaustion and exposure, proved too much for his body to bear. Before Vivian died he asked Joe Deegan to ensure the crucifix Vivian wore would be returned to his mother. *Perth* men were touched when a Japanese seaman crafted a cross out of timber to be attached to Vivian's shroud, then shipmates gently pushed the body over the side and someone muttered a prayer.

They were desperately in need of water. PO Bill 'Bull' Milne was a large man with a barrel chest. He rose and walked towards the ship's quarterdeck. Two Japanese guards barred his way with rifles but 'Bull' was in no mood to be stopped and pushed against both until the guards fell backwards. A watching Officer stopped an angry reaction from the guards and allowed Milne to ask for water.

After two nights, survivors were taken to Bantam Bay. Entering the bay, the stark superstructures of four enemy ships lay in various stages of submersion. It raised the spirits to know two Allied crews and their cruisers were responsible. A definitive Battle of Java Sea report would never be produced, estimates on Japanese vessels sunk ranged from four to seven. The Japanese admitted to one minesweeper, one transport and several ships damaged. On the night of 28 February and into 1 March, 85 torpedoes and 2650 shells had been fired at *Perth* and *Houston*.[34] A combination of overzealous and inexperienced Japanese crews and an Australian Captain adept at manoeuvring his ship had resulted in Japanese self-inflicted damage. For those now known as Prisoners of War, it made no difference; they had been responsible for the damage directly or indirectly, and when one Japanese officer suggested their ships must have been battleships, 'that pleased us too'.[35] An added highlight was that a transport that had sunk had been carrying the Commander of the invading force, General Imamura and his HQ staff. The vision of the Japanese general suffering the indignity of being fished out of the sea covered in black fuel oil, 'made one feel better.'[36]

The next transfer was to the 7000-ton cargo ship *Somedong Maru*. In what was to become a much repeated process, POWs were counted, then the 'tenko' would be repeated, sometimes it took 'three or four attempts to get it right'. They were herded into the forward hold, anyone ignoring the order to hasten or 'speedo-speedo,' was bashed with a rifle butt. 'Our introduction to the hospitality of the Imperial Japanese Army,'[37] realised Ord. Seaman 'Buzzer' Bee.

Sam Stening, 'Jock' Cunningham, Andy Mitchell, and PO Telegraphist Don Fowler, received a little assistance with the arrival of a Japanese army surgeon and a small supply of surgical equipment and medical supplies. It was difficult not to feel frustrated because there was so little they could do for the badly injured, wounds festered in the heat and grime. Each day, living conditions, if that was what they could be called, deteriorated. Food consisted of a little boiled barley or a serving of watery fish and rice soup, and men were allowed a cup of water a day, which meant a constant craving for water. A little humour, as when Stoker 'Tiny' Savage picked up a tin and wandered around asking 'any donations for a destitute sailor', or an impromptu concert from someone who refused to allow the situation to quell the human spirit, and the pure tones of AB Ross Birbeck singing a well known melody, would briefly raise morale.

New prisoners always created interest and were eagerly questioned, as men endeavoured to find more pieces of the jigsaw puzzle that dominated their minds. Who was with them when they left the ship? Who did they see in the water? Who had they seen elsewhere? By the time they were in the second week of their captivity, the ship's cramped hold held around 290 American and British (including Australian) officers and sailors. Then they were ordered up and off the *Somedong Maru* into landing barges, by agitated soldiers screaming 'speedo-speedo' and 'bugero', and who needed scant excuse to bash. Once on the beach POWs observed more heavily armed soldiers. AB Allan Gee believed, 'we were going to be mowed down by machine gun fire … I don't mind telling you I was scared'.[38] A Japanese officer told them they should be ashamed for allowing themselves to be captured. The tension rose further before, amid more shouting and threats, the POWs were herded onto trucks, which took off inland at great speed. They breathed sighs of relief and thought 'things might improve', but 'things changed immediately for the worse'.[39]

—

Upon landing on a Java beach, those from the Deegan/Brown lifeboat dug a hole above the high-water mark and found water, brackish, but very welcome. They were about 70 in number until Stoker Claud Maslem died. Believed to be the only survivor of 'A' boiler room, the 25-year-old born in Quirindi, New South Wales, had been terribly injured. Stoker II Fred Mason, Writer Don 'Sandy' McNab and AB Alec 'Spud' Murphy dug a grave in the sand. The men had not previously met, although they all had surnames starting with 'M', and now with their hands they dug a hole for the limp, lifeless body of their shipmate and covered him with sand, an act which would bind them the rest of their lives. AB Ernie Toovey thought it comforting that Chaplain Mathieson was there, so the Stoker could receive a Christian burial, 'even if the grave was dug in the sand of a foreign land'.[40]

It was decided the wounded, who included Lieut Cdr Ralph Lowe, Sub Lieut Gavin Campbell and Able Seamen John Cochrane, Danny Maher and Gordon Webster, would remain. The rest of the party, including Lieut Gillan who had been blinded with fuel oil but could be assisted by Stoker PO Bill Hogman, would move in groups, 'naked and unadorned,'[41] into the interior, hopefully to return with transport and medical assistance. They were black, scruffy, tired, hungry and thirsty but reasonably confident of a better outcome.

A group of men including Ord Seamen David Manning and 'Chilla' Goodchap were moving through a village when a Javanese approached on a bicycle carrying a large pile of blue sarongs. Manning produced a soggy 10 shilling note and bartered for two, then three as Lieut Gordon Black arrived. When the three walked into the village of Labuan they met other survivors, all regal in blue sarongs.

The Javanese were difficult to read, sometimes courteous, sometimes uncooperative. No food or water was offered with exception of coconuts. The *Perth* group decided to make for Pandeglang, a town in the mountains, where it was hoped they could link up with the remnants of the Dutch Army. The journey, particularly without footwear, was laborious – fast-flowing streams, steep slopes, thick vegetation. On the third night the men were invited to sleep on a bamboo platform outside a house, a welcome relief from the side of the road. They were woken by a mob of hostile Javanese carrying torches, waving parangs (machetes) and demanding valuables. The trek to Pandeglang continued but David Manning noticed his *Perth* companions changed constantly as some dropped to the roadside and others caught up. The Javanese were increasingly hostile. On arriving in the town the Australians were surrounded by a large crowd and herded into the local jail. The following morning Manning was awoken by a Japanese soldier, 'screaming at me in a language that I didn't understand, and making his point with the point of his bayonet'.[42] Manning's first response to the sight of the soldier was: 'He's not yellow, he's brown'.

AB Ernie Toovey and several others had fallen off the pace and become separated from Manning's group. They lay down beside the road to sleep. Toovey struggled with 'utter frustration'. He was tired, hungry and thirsty, his wounded leg ached and his bare feet hurt. He was woken abruptly. 'Practically standing over us were the fiercest characters I have ever seen, carrying long parangs'.[43] Toovey and his companions were pushed and kicked, 'I don't think I had too many thoughts at this stage, being too damn scared to think'. Eventually they too were shoved towards the Pandeglang jail.

There were by now around 60 survivors from the two cruisers in Pandeglang, and the Australians were separated from the Americans.

The Japanese seemed unsure what to do with the dishevelled Australians and an officer asked in English, 'What do you want to do?' The voice of 'Chilla' Goodchap came from the back of the group, 'Tell him we want to go home'.[44] Tied together at the wrists with telephone wire, the *Perth* men were marched to the town square while the local population demonstrated open dislike for the Australians. Machine guns were trained on the group and Ord Seam Norm Fuller believed they would be shot; 'they frightened the hell out of us'.[45] From buildings fluttered a white flag with a red dot and the prisoners below finally realised whose flag this was, 'later it was nicknamed the "Fried Egg" or the "Flaming A"'.[46] They were loaded like cattle onto trucks and driven some 40 to 50 kilometres to Serang. The next chapter of their lives, one that would almost defy description, was about to begin.

—

Meanwhile, the wounded lay on the beach and wondered when help would arrive. After the first day Lowe had felt well enough to leave and promised to send assistance. Another day dawned hot and the sun burnt deeper into oil-coated skin. John Cochrane, a 23 year old from the Melbourne suburb of Toorak, succumbed to wounds and exposure. The three men who remained had eaten only a few sea biscuits and coconuts, and wounds were beginning to turn septic. Webster then moved off in the opposite direction to Lowe, promising to send assistance. The day dragged on, then another cold uncomfortable night and yet another dawn.

No help came and Campbell decided he and Maher would die if they too did not leave. A sympathetic local fashioned a rough crutch out of a tree, and somehow Campbell raised himself upright and, still in the rough splints AB Bob Collins had placed around his busted leg, he began to hop painfully towards Labuan. All day Campbell hopped, all day the crutch tore at his armpit until it bled. As they neared the village, Campbell rested while Maher set off to beg for food. Maher was a 28-year-old Sydneysider. He had blond hair, blue eyes and fair complexion, but even his parents would not have recognised him beneath the oil and burnt skin and would not have wished to see the cruel shoulder and arm wounds that rendered one of their son's arms useless. With his good hand he brought back a handful of rice to Campbell and villagers followed.

After a difference of opinion as to whether these uninvited guests should be killed or saved, the men were given some assistance for the night, but they were asked to leave the next morning and Campbell hobbled on, with the ever-attentive Maher at his side. Eventually they arrived in Labuan and received a little care. The following morning the Japanese arrived and the strange-looking pair was taken to the hospital at Pandeglang. As he placed proper splints on Campbell's leg, the doctor commented that not only had the bones begun to knit, but whoever had placed the rough wooden splints on his leg had also saved his life.

AB Bob 'Buddy' Collins had honed the splints out of waterlogged debris just hours after *Perth* disappeared beneath the wash and Campbell would not forget him. But then Collins was an unforgettable character. Known for introducing Red Lead, the cat, to *Perth* and getting into trouble and extricating himself with flair, Collins would continue to defy the odds. The adventures of AB Bob Collins would be worthy of a book in their own right, and, as Sub Lieut Gavin Campbell was trying to stay alive on a Java beach near Labuan, so too was AB Bob Collins.

—

The morning after his ship sank Collins looked to the shore, left the raft and started swimming. He was still swimming two days later. When he finally flopped onto a beach he figured he had swum about 12 miles (20 kilometres). There was quite a group on the beach, approximately sixteen *Perth* men including Leading Seaman George Bretherton, PO John Harvey, ERA IV Don Smith and AB Ernie Owen. Men felt a great sense of relief for being delivered from a sinking ship, and from an ocean reluctant to release them, then the Javanese arrived and it was no longer safe. They came at the sailors with long knives and parangs, slashing as survivors backed into each other and attempted to fend the blows. One young sailor rushed for the water, but was caught and decapitated.

PO John Harvey, from Ipswich, Queensland had enlisted in 1935, a red-haired, seventeen-year-old kid looking for excitement. In his wildest dreams he could never have envisaged this sort of excitement. They screamed at him in a language he did not understand but in a manner he did. Standing with as much authority his 5 foot 5 stature would permit, he watched as they edged closer. Harvey should not have been there. A year ago he had faced a medical discharge. He fought that, and over the next nine months of being in and out of hospitals and subjected to four medical surveys, he managed to convince the RAN he was too valuable to be discharged. He was drafted to *Perth* because the cruiser carried a medical officer. In the end it was not the respiratory problems that took his life, but the savage blows from a people he never considered his enemy until that day at the beginning of March 1942. Bretherton was the next to be brutally felled by a Javanese parang, and the *Perth* men ran. The Javanese had cleared their beach and did not chase. The survivors headed for Menes because the local postmaster had told them there were no Japanese in the village – but Collins was to discover the postmaster was a 'Lying swine'.[47]

—

On another beach survivors from the Abbott boat began to stir. Their bodies ached, from physical exertion, from stress, from sunburn, from exposure, and were still plastered with invasive, suffocating fuel oil. They peered back at the ocean; some shuddered and promised themselves they would never return to it. Surely they would not be expected to go straight back to sea when they were rescued and returned to Australia. The glamour of the uniform and the glorious adventure had been forever stained black and red; no, surely they would not be expected to fight again in this wretched war. Looking in the opposite direction, they saw huts. The huts were quickly explored and they fell hungrily on food.

Other survivors appeared from the beach, Chief PO Harry Knight, PO Ray Parkin, Lieut Lloyd Burgess, Leading Seaman Keith Gosden and the Walrus Leading Telegraphist Air Gunner, Ken 'Tag' Wallace. The priority was now food and water. Telegraphist Peter Nelson cooked their harvest, a mixture of rice, pumpkin, wild tomatoes, papaws, corn, oysters, coconut and milk – nothing ever tasted better. Nelson had been a pastry cook before he enlisted and had an ambition to open a roadhouse, but in New South Wales, not Java. They scrounged tools, a parang, a tomahawk, a few tools and assorted rags, which were quickly turned into clothing of sorts. They used a tin of kerosene to rid bodies of some of the oil, then they slept.

The next day they butchered a sheep, but as they watched the glorious stew cook, villagers returned. Brandishing parangs and shouting angrily, the Javanese advanced towards the Australians. In haste watches were stripped from wrists and offered in reparation. The hut owners grabbed the offerings but continued to threaten, then, like some bad but wonderful Hollywood Western, the cavalry appeared over the horizon in the form of another party of fourteen *Perth* survivors – filthy, unshaven, scantily clad, marvellous Aussies.

The new group had come from Toppers Island and their adventure was the stuff of legend.[48] Having managed to pull themselves onto the rocky landscape of Toppers, the group was assessing their options when they observed a group of swimmers struggling on the wrong side of the rip. They quickly rigged a line with a lifebuoy attached and the strongest swimmers, Sub Lieut Ray Barker and Sick Berth Attendant Roy Turner, pushed into the Strait to rescue twelve *Houston* survivors including Surgeon Cdr Epstein. The Australians then walked the foreshore and, finding an abundance of wreckage, decided they could build a raft. PO Alfie Coyne had retained his 'pusser's dirk' (knife) and this greatly assisted construction of a seaworthy craft. The Americans watched, told them they were 'plumb crazy' and declined the invitation to come along. The Americans were confident of a rescue by US forces. The US rescue never came, but the Japanese did.

There was such comfort in numbers. Now, in company with Topper's group, the large band of survivors found another lifeboat and decided to push off for Java; no one wished to stay until aggrieved villagers returned with reinforcements. It was good to have a sense of purpose, and they worked to ensure the seaworthiness of the boats and to fit them out as best they could with provisions. 'Tag' Wallace convinced a Sick Berth Attendant to sew his wound, then wished he hadn't. A rusty curved needle and fishing line was all that could be found to undertake the surgery, and anaesthetic was in the shape of a couple of hefty blokes holding him down.

On the morning of 4 March, the 63 *Perth* officers and men gathered on the beach. The first group, with PO Jan Tyrrell in charge, pushed their wooden boat into the shallows and set off for Java, from where they could travel overland to Tjilatjap. They watched and waited as a patrolling Japanese destroyer went past and hoped they could cross the water before the destroyer returned on its next surveillance run. However, halfway across the Strait the destroyer bore down on them, and officers and sailors in crisp, white uniforms scrutinised the wooden boat through binoculars. The destroyer slowed, orders were shouted and sailors ran to the single gun mounted on the bow. They quickly removed the canvas muzzle-cap and swung the gun in the direction of the lifeboat. The Australians broke stroke, held their breath and expected 'a shell any minute'.[49] For ten long minutes the Japanese watched; for ten long minutes the Australians hoped their darkened bodies, pieces of native clothing, woven grass hats and non-aggressive body language, meant they would see the light of another day. The destroyer picked up speed and turned away, leaving the motley bunch of 'Javanese fishermen' to row at great speed to the Java coast.

Once on land the men of this first lifeboat broke into two groups, eleven favoured moving south, and twelve, led by PO Jan Tyrrell and including 'Tag' Wallace, preferred to move north. They were ill equipped for the journey, north or south – no maps, no shoes, little clothing and very little food, and they continued under the mistaken belief that the locals would be friendly and that the Allies were continuing to contest enemy advances. They would soon discover that Dutch General Hein ter Poorten had surrendered his force of approximately 25,000 and the local militia of 40,000. Even sooner they discovered the locals were not friendly. The Japanese offered the Javanese money for each allied soldier or sailor head, and the group that moved south suffered a dreadful fate: they ended up with 'their heads displayed on poles'.[50]

The Wallace/Tyrrell group walked north[51] towards the mountains, but were constantly threatened by 'natives brandishing parangs'. A policeman on the bicycle stopped to inform them that the Japanese were advancing and were 'executing all prisoners'.[52] He had been ordered to arrest all white men but pedalled way. They could hear the ominous rumbling of tanks and armoured vehicles, so left the road and pushed further into the jungle. After a cold and miserable night, there seemed no other option but to curtail the mountainous trek. They were not suitably equipped to take on the terrain, wild animals and snakes and decided to return to the boat. Upon descending to the Java coast they discovered the boat was gone. Feeling despondent the band broke into the nearby Anger Lighthouse and found the Dutch garrison logbook. The Dutch had left just hours previously; had they gone to the lighthouse initially, they would have been evacuated with the Dutch. It seemed little had gone their way since midnight on the last night of February; 'Tag' Wallace admitted, 'I had never felt more depressed'.[53]

The second lifeboat group of 40 had left Sangiang, avoiding the patrolling destroyer, beached on the Java shore. Consensus was difficult to achieve; shock and privation nullified rank structure that had been previously unquestioned. Lieut Cdr 'Polo' Owen believed the rumour that ships and the Allies were at Labuan and that survivors should travel overland to join them. From Labuan they could then travel overland to Tjilatjap to link up with the major Dutch force. Lieut John Thode, a New Zealander by birth, and PO Ray Parkin, wanted to try for Australia. Heated discussion ensued, until a compromise was reached. Owen would lead an overland group of eighteen south towards Labuan. The steel lifeboat would take the remaining 22, including the wounded, down the coast until the group reunited north of the village.

During the overland journey eight *Perth* men split off, voluntarily, to venture inland or because they were unable to keep up with the pace of the others. Javanese had been watching the group and waiting for such divergence. The men were attacked. Leading Seaman Nick Carter, Stoker Bernie Ferguson, AB Ernie Owen and the surviving Ryan brother were slashed. They would eventually receive medical attention, but 23-year-old Owen from Melbourne would die.

When the 'Polo' Owen party, depleted from eighteen to ten, reunited with their boat party, Thode, Parkin and 'Knocker' White were even more adamant that they preferred to risk a sea voyage to being slaughtered by Javanese or Japanese. Heated debate ensued for more than an hour. Thode, Parkin and White chose seven of the fittest volunteers – CPO Harry Knight, POs 'Horrie' Abbott and Alfie Coyne, Yeoman Jack Willis, Leading Seaman Keith Gosden, Able Seamen Norm Griffiths and Harry Mee – and took to their boat, the boat they hoped would deliver them far away from this madness. Owen was left with 22 men[54] including the wounded. Having watched the boat disappear, the overland party walked to Labuan. They were not greeted warmly and the following day were told to leave. By 8 March their bid for freedom was over, and the group was imprisoned at Pandaglang jail.

—

In the north, the 'Tag' Wallace/Jan Tyrrell group of twelve had been regarding their depressed state of affairs, but on finding another boat their mood lifted. Gear and supplies were scrounged, anything that could form a mast and sails. It was 6 March when they again took to the sea, for Tjilatajap. Pulling into the Java Head Lighthouse they were welcomed by the keeper and his family. It was easy to stay, and they did not set off again until 13 March. Then a boatload of refugees sailing in the opposite direction offered the sobering news that Tjilatajap had fallen to the Japanese a week before. The Australian boat returned to the Java Head Lighthouse. However, the Japanese were advancing and the men did not wish the lighthouse family to be caught harbouring white men, so they set off again, this time for Australia. Enemy soldiers arrived at the Lighthouse within days. They found no white men but slaughtered the family.

The *Perth* sailors knew they were kidding themselves, Australia was too far; then the makeshift mast snapped. Over the next week the sailors dodged the Japanese along the Sumatra coast desperately, until there was no option but to put into Kota Argoen for water. Japanese soldiers were waiting, and Wallace and Tyrrell were beaten before the Australians were frog marched along the beach and ordered to kneel, as 'thousands of natives gathered to watch our execution'.[55] The men lowered their heads and waited, waited for the fate that had befallen other *Perth* survivors who emerged from the terrible waters and thought themselves saved. Keeping their eyes to the sand, they tried to console themselves with the knowledge they had evaded the enemy for almost six weeks, and waited to be decapitated.

ELEVEN

'Hell on Earth.'

Able Seaman Frank McGovern

Like the rush of the current in Sunda Strait, so too the repercussions of the sinking of *Perth* washed through Australia. In the halls of Parliament and the Navy Office, and in the bunkered War Cabinet, high-ranking officials nodded sombrely and wondered how to best utilise the remaining pieces of the machinery of war. Whilst this would commonly be the focus of historical interpretation, elsewhere the sinking was felt poignantly, and the ripples of grief blighted the lives of thousands. Some could cope, some could not and no two were the same, which made the course of grief an ultimately lonely journey.

The news of the sinking of *Perth* was slow to reach the Australian public. The last signal sent from the cruiser had been 28 February, but not until 14 March did the media broadcast the announcement. Whilst authorities needed to allow sufficient time for the warship to make radio contact and to advise next of kin, the media was under heavy censorship. Victories and good news ensured the nation's citizenry remained loyal to the war effort, or so it was believed. A few relatives were not advised before media announcements because sailor service cards were not up to date, and Navy Office personnel scrambled to clarify who was really in *Perth*. Given the recent sinking of *Sydney,* such a lack of preparation was hard to excuse. As telegrams arrived in most corners of Australia the official language failed to touch the right sympathetic chord: 'With deep regret I have to inform you your son ... is missing as a result of enemy action. Minister for the Navy and the Naval Board desire to express to you their sincere sympathy'. Although, how could any mass produced pro-forma adequately convey the tragedy and the indelible mark it would leave?

Too many families were already grieving. In Junee, New South Wales, Clara Chattaway was deeply disturbed by the news *Perth* was missing. Her 21-year-old son Frank was a member of the ship's company. This war had already taken one son. Private James Chattaway, a member of the 'Devil's Own', the 2/13th, had been killed near Tobruk in June 1941. Too many families had already lost fathers and husbands to the 'war to end all wars' or to its residual effect on body and soul; now another war would rout more generations.

Joan, AB Doug Asplin's sister, was called out of class by a teacher, a teacher whose son had died in *Sydney*. As gently as he could, this man who wore the mark of grief himself, told the teenager to go home because, 'your Mother needs you'.[1] Joseph Asplin had died in 1940 and his wife Florence and daughter struggled on as best they could. Now a telegram told them their only son and brother was 'missing'. They would need to wait until the end of the war before it was confirmed Doug had died as he evacuated *Perth*'s 'A' turret. This would be four long years away and too long for Florence, whose health deteriorated rapidly. Joan was prematurely left to navigate her impressionable years alone.

Joan Asplin was not acquainted with Beryl Millerick and that was unfortunate. Beryl was fourteen when informed her brother, Stoker Jimmy Millerick, was missing. With both parents dead, Jimmy was all she had. There was a nine-year age difference but, as far as Beryl was concerned, her brother was 'the ants pants!' She had no intention of accepting Jimmy was not coming home, and vowed she would 'drive the Red Cross and the navy crazy', until this was confirmed.[2]

In Queenstown, Tasmania, John 'Jock' Mathew was listening to his crystal radio when over its scratchy reception he heard that contact had been lost with his son's ship. Mary Hine was seventeen and going out with George the youngest of the three Mathew brothers. Walking down a road in Queenstown, she was passed by a deeply upset neighbour telling everyone within hearing distance, 'They've killed him, they've killed "Jock"'. Mary thought her boyfriend's father had been involved in an accident, but George would confide that his eldest brother, ERA IV John 'Jock' Mathew, was 'missing'. It re-enforced his determination to join his other brother, ERA Thomas Mathew, in the RAN.[3] Later the Mathew family would be elated to hear 'Jock' had escaped the sinking cruiser and was a POW. Then they would learn 'Jock' died in August 1944, of malnutrition and dysentery, whilst working on the infamous Burma–Thailand Railway.

When *Perth* put into Brisbane in late 1941, Bob Noyce joined his brother Bill and other *Perth* boys for a drink at the Globe Hotel. The sailors had spoken little of their Mediterranean campaign, but clearly it had left its stain for they seemed strangely older than their real ages, and shared a bond Bob could not fathom. Bob Noyce told his brother he was enlisting in the RAN, but Bill barely responded. While Bob had been under training the brothers caught up briefly to discuss serving together. Bill wished to remain in *Perth*. It was not being a Leading Torpedo Man so much, but Bill was also the cruiser's projectionist and loved movies. Bob was at *Cerberus* when told *Perth* was missing. There was no time or privacy to grieve, but anyway, Bill's tenacity would get him through. It was at his station in the Low Power Room that Bill Noyce had met his death and not in the additional role he enjoyed so much. For the duration of the war Bob Noyce served in corvettes. When in 1945 the youngest Noyce brother said he was enlisting in the RAN, Bob replied, 'I will kick your bloody arse if you do'. The Noyce family had already paid a high price.[4]

Unlike Tasmania's Mathew family, the McCarrey family of Western Australia didn't have a radio, and decided it was imperative to obtain one when they heard that English broadcasts contained news of POWs. The McCarreys were doubly concerned because they too had sons named Bill and Bob, and both were 'missing in action'. William, a member of the AIF, was believed to be a POW in the Middle East, and Robert McCarrey was an AB with *Perth*.[5] It was difficult dealing with the possible loss of a son, let alone the possible loss of 23-year-old twins. The lack of information, the not knowing, gnawed away at the family. Their father had fought at Gallipoli, he buried his feelings, he was used to doing that, but 'had few illusions as to Bob's chances'.[6] Relief came when a cable from Bill told of his escape. He was in Alexandria when informed Bob was missing. These were worrying times, yet he attempted to relay an optimistic tone in a cable to his family, 'twins often know about each other' and so he 'knew' Bob was alive. Bill McCarrey was proven correct.

On the other side of the nation, Minnie McGovern worried, she had two sons in *Perth*. Her boys had grown up in the Sydney suburb of Paddington and were used to looking out for one another. Frank had enlisted in the RANVR in 1939 at nineteen. He had drafted to *Perth* as an AB, pleased to be serving in the same cruiser as brother, Vince, an ERA with the cruiser since September 1939. Now all their mother could do was wait, wait for news and pray. Minnie McGovern 'nearly went crazy' waiting for that news.[7]

Some sceptics wondered if Bertha Banks was not already a 'little crazy'. She was ill at ease during the first week in March, she had a vision concerning her son; 'Rodger was in trouble, in murky water'. Husband Sydney and thirteen-year-old daughter Mary were concerned because Bertha Banks had previously had alarmingly accurate visions. The telegram arrived at their home in Mannum, South Australia, on Friday 13 March; Bertha didn't want to open it. The officious print read: 'Stoker II Rodger Sydney George Banks was missing', because his ship had sunk in murky waters. For the Banks family the final news was terrible, Rodger, stationed in *Perth*'s Damage Control Headquarters, had been killed by the first torpedo. Bertha Banks did not overcome her grief; she receded into a shell, spurned visitors, and died a heartbroken woman.[8]

John Kirkmoe would not have dismissed Bertha Banks' premonition. John had experienced one when he and brother Don met up in July 1941 in Haifa. The brothers spent an enjoyable day together but when they farewelled, John couldn't shake the belief he would not see Don alive again; nor did he. Stoker Don Kirkmoe was killed with Stoker II Rodger Banks in *Perth*'s Damage Control Headquarters.

Chief ERA Jack Madge, as a lark, had paid a fortune teller in Alexandria to look into his future. She had muttered, he wouldn't reach 'old bones'. When *Perth* had returned to Sydney the Chief ERA had been offered a shore job. He had discussed it with wife Florence, but confided in her he would feel a coward leaving the cruiser at such a time. Florence received the dreaded telegram on Friday 13 March. Shortly after this she received a letter from a man who knew Jack:

> If all men were of his calibre, the world would be a better place.
> In this your hour of trial … you must be very thankful to think
> that he was such a thorough gentleman. If Jack has crossed to
> the other side, it is better for him to go like we think, than suffer
> some lingering illness.[9]

The words were heartfelt, but Florence Madge preferred not to contemplate the idea that her husband had 'crossed to the other side' just yet. The Prime Minister, Mr Curtin, when announcing the loss of *Perth*, added: 'whilst there is no news of survivors', given 'the proximity of land to the last radioed contact, survivors may have made it ashore.' Florence needed to cling to this hope and maintain faith that Jack would return to her and her children; but he did not.

—

Families were asked to send a photograph of their *Perth* relative 'for identification purposes'. They received letters from the RAN Relief Fund Welfare Committee, extending sympathy and offering a little assistance. A Naval Chaplain, or a member of the committee, was available to visit. Undoubtedly the sentiment was appreciated, but the six-member committee consisted of Commodore G.C.Muirhead-Gold, his wife and the wives of four other very senior officers. *Perth* relatives would not initiate contact with such committee members because they represented a different world. It would have been easier had the committee included wives of non-commissioned personnel. Unofficial groups of navy wives did what they could, but few World War II navy families lived in 'married patches' (housing attached to navy bases).

Municipal Patriotic and War Fund organisations sent condolences to family members of 'those brave Australians who manned the "*Perth*"'. Such associations believed when a relative 'lost the keen poignancy of your sorrow, you, too, will come to a feeling of pride in your Sailor'.[10] As well intentioned as this was, the language was trite, particularly in March 1942. Before the 'keen poignancy' of sorrow, could be alleviated in the slightest, individuals needed to be allowed to grieve. Not only was this difficult in a society awkward with such emotion, but for *Perth* families, circumstances would not allow closure for four long years, until POWs were freed and interviewed and until all islands in the Sunda Strait region were searched.

For many the sinking of *Perth* was a tremendous shock because they were unaware the warship was even in a 'war zone'. Whilst the need for censorship and Government propaganda sayings, like 'Loose lips sink ships', were generally appreciated, it was difficult being 'family' when doubt and rumour were omnipresent. The Stening family struggled to separate fact from fiction. There was a rumour that the transport returning from the Middle East with Army Medical Officer Warwick Stening and his 7th Division Engineers had been sunk. Another rumour was that radio contact had been lost with *Australia* in which Surgeon Lieut Malcolm Stening was a Medical Officer. Now they were officially advised 'Surgeon Lieut Samuel Edward Lees Stening, was missing due to enemy action'.

The Government had misled the Australian people on the extent of damage and casualties inflicted on Darwin. The ideas of 'need to know', 'security requirements for the war effort' and 'civilian morale' promoted paranoia and confusion. Officialdom could not cope with the speed of war and had lost touch with what was 'real' to the Australian people. For many Australians it was no longer a case of 'no news is good news'.

For the Stening family there was relief concerning the safety of Warwick and Malcolm, but there was still no news concerning their brother, Samuel. Onboard *Australia* the Senior Chaplain suggested a requiem mass. Malcolm was troubled and approached Captain

Farncomb to contest the appropriateness of a requiem mass, given the fate of the *Perth* crew was unknown. Farncomb agreed, he was contending with his own memories of his former command, and a 'Special Service' was held instead.

When *Australia* berthed in Sydney there was another bizarre twist. A Sub Lieut Paymaster came onboard and after a couple of drinks in the wardroom announced he had first-hand information as to the fate of the *Perth* crew. Malcolm avidly listened to the visiting officer's exciting tale. The Sub Lieut told of being in the cruiser when the ship sank. He and five others had boarded a lifeboat and for days rowed in the direction of Australia. Sadly the other five died of thirst. As the spectre of death loomed he was rescued by an American submarine. Members of *Australia*'s wardroom, which included *Perth* relatives and friends, pressed the visiting officer for specific details. The Sub Lieut told Malcolm he had seen Sam abandon ship and reach the water safely, and Malcolm was relieved. However, the following day Captain Farncomb called *Australia*'s Medical Officer to his cabin. Investigation revealed that the visitor had never served in *Perth* and the story was pure fabrication. Farncomb promised the officer would face retribution. But the Paymaster Sub Lieut was a lawyer and his fellows in the Sydney legal profession ensured retribution was restricted to a RAN discharge on grounds of anxiety. He even went on to thrive in the NSW legal profession and became a Supreme Court Judge.[11]

Strangely, though, two groups of *Perth* survivors did set out in lifeboats for Australia and elude the Japanese for weeks. Furthermore, in 1944, after languishing on rafts for days, other *Perth* survivors were rescued by the very US submarines that sunk their Japanese transport.

—

The majority of *Perth* next of kin received their telegrams on Friday 13 March. The following day the front pages of newspapers were dominated by the loss of *Perth*. Brisbane's *Courier Mail* expressed alarm that the nation's navy had 'Suffered Heavily'. The paper listed the five ships – two cruisers, two sloops and a destroyer – lost since the start of hostilities. Given that the war in the Pacific had only commenced in December, this was of great concern. Australians were feeling vulnerable, scarce war resources should perhaps have been left protecting Australia's north. Less than a month before, Curtin had ordered: 'A complete mobilisation of all Australian resources, human, and material, to ensure the defence of Australia'; and his Government was of the opinion Australia could no longer look to the United Kingdom for defence: 'Australia looks to America, free of any pangs as to our traditional links or kinship with the United Kingdom'.[12] In *The Courier Mail,* a large public notice implored citizens to be more involved with the war effort: 'What are *you* doing for Australia in her darkest hour? Helping or Hindering?' The editorial took issue with citizens who preferred to indulge in the great Australian pastimes of football, horse racing and going to the pub: 'Brains and brawn are better than bets and booze'. Clearly these were disturbing times.

The sleepy Isabel Justelius who had opened the door to uniformed men demanding to see her brother Eric and deliver his call-up notice, read the paper on the second Saturday in March 1942. As she and her mother Jean cast their eyes over newsprint and the list of 682 names[13] of those missing in *Perth,* they really saw only one, AB Eric Justelius. Her family was typical of families throughout the nation struggling with reality, struggling with what was now their world.

In June 1941 Isabel had become engaged to Frank Tuckey. Frank had a way with words and she treasured his letters. Like so many men of his generation, Frank found himself in the unfamiliar surroundings of khaki uniforms and AIF training. He wrote to Jean, apologising for being unable to present himself in person to ask for Isabel's hand in marriage but he was confined to the AIF camp in Dubbo. He believed he and Isabel, 'with some luck from the Gods of war, will be very happy'. Isabel's brother AB Eric 'Boyce' Justelius had teased his sister that she 'just escaped being an old maid'.[14]

How life had changed! Isabel struggled to cope with devastating news. Her brother-in-law was seriously wounded in the Middle East. The man she wished to marry, Lance Corporal Frank Tuckey, was believed captured in Malaya and her brother Eric 'Boyce' was 'missing'. She attempted to console her mother, Eric was a 'powerful swimmer' and was therefore likely to have survived. Letters and cards of sympathy arrived, they and their envelopes eerily bordered in black. It made the situation all the more surreal. Nothing was known for certain of *Perth*'s crew, but the loss of *Sydney* with 'all hands' remained etched in the consciousness of Australians, and they were quick to assume the worst. Isabel's aunt wrote, 'How hard it is for the young ones, their life before them, their hopes and dreams crash about them'.[15] An acquaintance sent an extract from the poem 'The Children', with its grim words:

These were our children who died for our lands;
They were dear in our sight.
We have only the memory left of their home treasured sayings and laughter.
The price of our loss shall be paid too.
Our hands, not another's hereafter.
Neither the Alien nor Priest shall decide on it.
That is our right.
But who shall return us the children.[16]

Neil Justelius, stationed at a RAAF Base, wrote to his mother and sister, anxious not to raise their hopes but believing there was 'always a chance, so our "Boyce" may not be gone yet'. Neil articulated a sentiment commonly shared: 'This cursed war and everlasting bungling has caused such terrific desolation in so many homes'.[17]

On 14 March, from the large capital dailies to small district papers, the bleak print read the same, the only difference being the number of names featured. *The Courier Mail* printed 55 Queenslanders missing; *The Mercury* listed 37 Tasmanian names; whilst *The Camperdown Chronicle* mentioned just four. The smaller the newspaper, the larger the biographies of local officers and sailors presumed killed. For people who lived in the Shires of Hampden and Heytesbury, Victoria, *The Camperdown Chronicle* offered the latest local news. Between advertisements offering 'Fresh Fruit and Vegetables Delivered at Your Door' and 'Buy That Used Car or Utility Now, All Prices Below Cost' appeared the headline 'MISSING ON PERTH – Four District Lads';

Chaplain Keith Mathieson, Signalman Tom Goldsmith, Stoker Norm Toulmin and Bandsman George Vanselow. Tom Goldsmith was referred to as being of a 'reserved nature' and 'esteemed by all for his sincerity'. As patrol leader of Camperdown Scouts, he was 'extremely well liked by other lads'. He had enlisted the first week of the war, a month before his twenty-first birthday. One of five children, he had two brothers in the army. Stoker Toulmin had been given the first names of Norman Lindsay in honour of the Australian artist. With both his parents dead, life was hard and he needed to leave school to support himself. With Australia at war Norm had joined the AIF. It was not a happy alliance and he was out of the army six months later. Norm applied for the RAN and was accepted. Immediately he finished his training, Stoker 2nd class Toulmin was hurried to *Perth*. It had been 2 February 1942 when Toulmin joined the cruiser, twenty days later he turned 21, and a week after that he was fighting for his life.

Poetry loving George Vanselow was the youngest of three brothers and educated at Gnotuk School and Camperdown Higher Elementary. His plan to escape the stress of his job as an advertising manager by enlisting in the RAN to play music didn't work. Service in *Perth*, first in the Mediterranean, and then in Sunda Strait, made the stress of the civilian position pale by comparison.

—

At about the time his friends and family were intently reading this issue of *The Camperdown Chronicle*, Vanselow sat in a POW centre in Java. He scavenged a piece of paper and a small pencil and again sought refuge in his poetry. Eleven paragraphs later he had penned the poem 'The Battles of the Java Seas'. His words described the courage of his shipmates; portrayed the futility of a battle supposed to 'teach the "yellow" what "white" men are worth'; of the hope and the fear. With his small pencil George Vanselow scribbled:

The din and the turmoil, the blood and the slaughter.
The cries of the wounded, the shrieks from the water.
These live in the mind, we feel them yet.

A horror of War, we shall never forget.[18]

All around Vanselow were other *Perth* survivors. They had believed they were 'saved' when they escaped the treacherous waters; they had believed they would find sanctuary amongst the indigenous peoples of the islands, but instead they were menaced by angry, jeering, spitting, natives who then attacked with parangs and knives. They had believed they would find Allied resistance, but there was none. They wondered about life as Japanese prisoners of war and would then pray they could survive. Over the first days of March, *Perth* officers and sailors were brought to 'Hell on Earth',[19] to the Serang POW reception centre, about 40 miles (65 kilometres) inland from Bantam Bay. Some would be led to the jail, beneath gates bearing the inscription, 'Abandon hope all ye that enter here'. Twenty-six locked in a filthy, 8 x 6 feet (2.4 x 1.8 metre) cell, intended for no more than thirteen prisoners, with a wooden bucket as a latrine and no water to wash. Food consisted of one small rice ball a day and some water. There was no bedding, just bare concrete and the wounded were left unattended. After the first week, they contracted dysentery and were allowed to wash at the jail courtyard well.

The majority of POWs were herded into what was once the local cinema. An area that had entertained and delighted audiences was now a place of abject misery. On the stage no longer entertainers but Japanese soldiers and what AB 'Digby' Gray regarded as 'the biggest bloody machine guns I had seen'.[20] Occasionally the guards would fire into the ceiling to ease their boredom. The smallest hint of provocation resulted in a bashing with rifle butts. The main party of 270-odd *Perth* survivors, from the *Somedong Maru*, were landed at Merak, Java, to be taken to Serang. On the edge of the shore was the ferry waiting-shed, through which passengers for Sumatra had transited before the war. Inside the shed hung a colourful tourist poster depicting the NSW Blue Mountains; the starkly beautiful silhouettes of the 'Three Sisters' in the foreground above the caption, 'Come to sunny New South Wales'. For the bedraggled, suffering Australians it underlined the tenuous nature of their situation and how far away they felt from their cherished country.

The reuniting of shipmates at Serang offered a brief but joyous intermission before the formidable reality of life as Japanese POWs enveloped them. There was pleasure in a familiar face and voice, like that of AB Eric 'Chesty' Bond. 'Chesty' had enlisted in September 1939, determined 'to do his bit' in the war Australia had inherited from Europe. His early service had been on motor launches, minesweepers and tenders, until Bond misbehaved sufficiently to receive ten days' detention in December 1941. Authorities decided a larger ship would be more challenging for this larger-than-life rating with a less-than-satisfactory character report, so on 20 January 1942 'Chesty' had reported to *Perth*. Now, as he was shoved into the squalid intern centre, 'Chesty' quipped, 'What time do they show the Mickey Mouse?' For his retort Bond received a knock from a screaming guard. The atmosphere in the Serang cinema became tenser as 'arrogant little yellow guards whose fingers could be seen crooked around the triggers of machine guns',[21] did not share the Australian sense of humour or the elation of the reunion and were determined to enforce a no-talking rule.

The cinema was now so crowded that on the command 'All Men Sleep', men lay down, end to end, one man's feet under another's armpits, 'like rats in a cage'.[22] If one needed to turn, a whole row needed to turn. They lay uncomfortably on the hard tiles, sleep difficult to find under the blazing lights. The heat was stifling. At 0800 guards ensured all were woken and adopted a sitting, cross-legged position until 2200 when again they assumed a lying position at the next man's feet. One Japanese Officer, who AB Frank McGovern observed was a particularly 'sadistic swine', would pull his revolver from its holster and walk along the lines. If he found any POW with a leg outstretched, he would delight in using his handgun to strike the unfortunate culprit. For men like 'Buzzer' Bee with a large piece of shrapnel embedded in his calf, bending both legs was impossible, but the Officer did not discriminate between the wounded and non-wounded, he bashed them all.

Flying Officer 'Jock' McDonough tried hard to ignore his sore bottom, but the tiles were so hard, the discomfort dominated his mind so he pushed down on his hands with straight arms, elevating his backside off the floor. For the briefest time he felt relief:

The next thing I knew was that I was getting a belt in the shoulder with a Japanese rifle ... I was supposed to sit there and not move. They had rubber-soled shoes. Devil boots we called them. I didn't hear this other bloke coming up ... He kicked me around in the back, yabbering away like nothing on earth. He continued to kick me and I finished up black and blue and swollen and could hardly move my shoulders.[23]

War correspondent Rohan Rivett was brought to Serang as a POW. When a guard cleared a space for him by means of a rifle butt, he struggled to comprehend the condition of those around him:

'With few exceptions they were stark naked except for a small calico loincloth ... the *Perth* boys were covered with a thick coating of oil fuel ... [they] are grand with their six or seven wounded mates who have to be carried to and from the wretched latrine day and night'.[24]

Hygiene was non-existent. Cooking conditions were filthy, the galley was 'never cleaned and was traversed by a water channel used as a sewer'.[25] At 1300 POWs gagged on 'God awful'[26] foul, maggot-ridden rice and hot boiled water. The only other food, a 4-ounce (100-gram) loaf of bread at 1800, was only slightly easier to consume. The bread issue disappeared and the evening meal sometimes arrived, sometimes it did not. One evening each received a tiny piece of raw meat. Another evening it was two lumps of dough dipped in sugared water. Ord Seam Frank Chattaway likened them to, 'what one would get if lead and rubber were mixed together'.[27] Hunger monopolised their consciousness and conversation. Each man thought of his favourite food, menus were discussed. Chattaway decided, 'Never before have I seen a body of men so intensely interested in a common subject'.[28] Sanitary arrangements were appalling, consisting of a deep open cesspit about 6-foot (1.8-metres) square with crisscrossing wooden beams on which the POWs squatted, 'the stench of this pit was indescribable'.[29] Due to diet deficiencies, particularly salt, prisoners regularly blacked out, and more than one collapsed into the pit. When allowed, men took advantage of busted guttering and heavy rain showers to attempt to clean themselves, but without soap the invasive and debilitating oil remained. Later they were permitted to bathe in the polluted water of the nearby stream. To drink, it was necessary to boil the water from the well and POWs were limited to less than a small cup a day. Thirsty men needed to be physically restrained from drinking it unboiled; those who were not, contracted dysentery. Regardless, after the first two weeks dysentery became rife, the latrine hole overflowed and 'all you could see was maggots'.[30] Frank McGovern blacked out close to the cinema side door one evening only to awake with maggots on his scalp.

Surgeon Lieut Sam Stening cast his eyes over the human misery, over the 800 or so POWs in the cinema.[31] The largest group was from his ship. *Houston* crew were there also, and a number of Royal Navy, Royal Air Force and a few Dutch soldiers. Never could the 31-year-old doctor have envisaged such challenging conditions and a sense of his own uselessness. The lack of clothing worn by *Perth* men offered no protection from mosquitoes. The incidence of malaria rose dramatically, but there was very little quinine. At a daily muster Stening would 'treat' at least 100 men, except the word 'treat' seemed inappropriate. There was no sterilised water for washing wounds and few medical supplies. Four of the more serious cases were AB John Minnekin with a badly shattered ankle; Leading Seaman Nick Carter with 4-inch (10-centimetre) knife gashes beneath his right arm and on his back; PO Steward Bill Davis with a bad compound fracture of the leg; and Allan Geier, who had sort of celebrated his twentieth birthday on the eve of the Battle of Java Sea, with a severely lacerated leg. There was little that could be done to ease the discomfort of burns victims, the flesh just dropped from their bodies, leaving angry red welts. Stening operated only when absolutely necessary because anaesthetic was scarce and his surgical implements consisted of a 'pair of scissors and a pair of forceps, both rusty'.[32] As gangrene set in, the worst was feared for Davis's leg, 'there is nothing worse than rotting flesh – the stench was dreadful'.[33] Then the maggots found it and consumed the rotten flesh, and the leg was saved. It was not treatment Stening had been party to before, if 'treatment' was the appropriate word.

Signalman 'Buzzer' Bee continued to hobble around, a piece of shrapnel embedded in his calf until it became badly infected. Stening had him transferred to the jail where *Houston*'s doctors Surgeon Lieut Burroughs and Surgeon Cdr Epstein had set up a makeshift operating space. Bee was placed face down on a table and thought it nice that some burly looking Marines materialised and asked how he was. They then sat and leaned on him because there was no anaesthetic. 'When they started cutting my leg I could feel everything. I went out like a light ... they reckoned I was dead', and he was taken to the morgue. When Bee awoke he shouted for help. A *Perth* mate shouted back: 'You were supposed to be dead!' The Ord Signalman wasn't sure he was completely alive and confided he was 'feeling crook'. His mate kept making little rice cakes and goaded Bee constantly: 'Now, eat! Eat it!' pushing them in 'my bleedin' mouth'.[34]

In the squalid conditions dysentery and diarrhoea reached epidemic proportions, yet the only treatment available was a small amount of charcoal. Chief PO Cook Bob Bland appealed to the Japanese to be allowed to cook the rice ration. They grudgingly agreed and the rice was then 'not only palatable, but our health improved'.[35] Bland also gave 'invaluable assistance' to medical staff. Bland wasn't a flashy bloke, he was fairly introspective, in fact he was even referred to as 'boring', but in situations like this it was good to have men like Bob Bland at your back. He had been awarded a BEM (Mil) after the Med campaign and was an unlikely hero in the campaign to survive.

There was just so much anyone could do with so pathetically poor a food ration, and Bland and Stening were helpless in the fight to save the life of PO Cook Frank Cadge. Cadge was 41, born in Bury St Edmunds, England, and had given fifteen years of his life to the RAN. On 31 March he died from dysentery, and his shipmates buried him in the Serang European Cemetery.[36] Over the next weeks with so little food and water POWs rapidly lost weight and their health deteriorated to the point they could not stand without suffering a blackout. Then on 5 April their Medical Officer Sam Stening and four other *Perth* officers would be taken away. The officers were subjected to a vicious interrogation before being transported to Japan.

Fred Lasslett was a bit of a larrikin, and a bloke who really did not enjoy being restrained and ordered about. He had talked his way back into the Reserves in July 1940 and then the RAN in September after being discharged for lack of attendance. He had failed, however, to prevent his superiors docking his leave and making him pay for boisterous behaviour in December 1940, just a month after joining *Perth*. In the Serang cinema Lasslett decided the imprisonment and his captors were not to his liking and left. On Friday 18 March at 2015 when Lasslett made his way to the latrine, he waited until the guard marched to the other end of the alley way outside the theatre and climbed over the high stone wall fringed with spikes and broken glass. He jumped from roof to roof. A torrential downpour helped cover his leaps and bounds, until one roof gave way and he fell down onto some bicycle taxis: 'My heart was in my mouth and I expected detection any moment, but my luck still held'.[37] From yard to yard, he hid. Breaking open a set of gates, he was finally in the streets, deserted because of the heavy rain. Navigating by information he had extracted from a Dutch POW, he continued on his way. Lasslett walked on until almost dawn when he was stopped by a wide river and a wrecked bridge. Hunger and thirst became of paramount importance. He managed to knock down a coconut but was unable to break through the tough husk. Cautiously the Wireman approached a native working in a field with a parang, gestured to the blade and the coconut. The Javanese obliged but then disappeared. He returned with 30 others and the Australian sailor ran. In his weakened state his legs soon gave out and he took refuge in bushes: 'The suspense became unbearable and I wanted to scream out aloud ... I knew I was captured'.[38]

When the Javanese returned him to Serang, Lasslett attempted to befuddle Japanese authorities by saying he was not 'Fred' but his twin brother 'Jack'. The ruse appeared to be working until fellow Wireman, Charlie Wray, came into the area and unwittingly greeted him by name.[39] Wireman 'Fred' Lasslett was paraded before fellow POWs as the Commandant announced that his execution would be a warning to others who might attempt escape. Under armed escort the 23 year old was taken away and a solemn atmosphere spread throughout the cinema. Lasslett was bashed, taken to Japanese headquarters where a firing squad was assembled, and placed against a wall; 'I remember thinking what a beautiful day it was, pity about the firing squad'.[40]

His cheerful demeanour unsettled those who aimed guns at his chest. The superstitious Japanese could not decide if the Australian sailor was very brave or very stupid. Admiration of the former meant the prisoner needed to be kept alive for 24 hours to appease spirits and gods, so the squad was hastily disbanded and Lasslett thrown into a cell. During the next 24 hours, the headquarters' electrical power supply failed. Wireman Lasslett boasted loudly he could restore supply with little delay, while praying quietly it would be something simple enough for him to fix. Fortunately, it was. A grateful Commandant made him 'Serang Chief Electrician'. *Perth* shipmates wondered if the Australian colloquialism, 'You've got Buckley's chance' should be changed to, 'You've got Lasslett's chance!'

—

As the terrible Serang imprisonment ran into its sixth week, a Japanese officer speaking in perfect English addressed the POWs. He declared conditions were poor but as an 'invading force' they should expect 'a few hardships'.[41] *Perth* sailors wondered how they or their country could be accused of invading anyone. An issue of green trousers and shirts was handed out. No allowance was made for different shapes and sizes but compared to nothing this was luxury. On 15 April[42] the men were crammed into open trucks. Their depleted bodies were severely tested by the long, bumpy journey, although it was wonderful to be out in the open air, out in the countryside. AB Arthur 'Blood' Bancroft was captivated by the scenery, 'its beauty served as a tonic'.[43] They noticed a big change in the attitude of the Javanese standing on the roadside. Previously so hostile, they now threw fruit and biscuits into the trucks. The indigenous inhabitants had delighted in discarding the shackles of white colonialism, but quickly discovered there would be no racial equality granted by those who now inhabited their country; furthermore, their new masters were in no way benevolent.

As the exotic shades of a tropical sunset began to emerge, the trucks arrived at the gates of the huge Dutch colonial army garrison, 10th Military Barracks, Batavia, known commonly as 'The Bicycle Camp', because of the widespread use of bicycles by Dutch troops. After the horrors of Serang this camp was a pleasant surprise, 'as different as chalk and cheese' Fred Lasslett would happily jot in his diary. *Perth* survivors observed substantial brick-stucco buildings with tiled roofs. Here they found some 3500 British, Dutch and Australian military prisoners including members of the Australian 2/2nd Pioneers, 2/6th Engineers, 2/3rd and 2/4th Machine Gunners and 105 Transport.[44]

The condition of *Perth* personnel shocked POWs who gathered to greet them. Some sailors lay on stretchers, others thoroughly exhausted from the trip could not stand without assistance. Most wore little clothing and no footwear. It was incomprehensible these thin, dark bodies belonged to Australians. Corporal, J.R. Hocking, thought they 'looked a bit starved'. Private F. Clarkson concurred, 'they were not too good'. Other soldiers muttered, 'poor buggers'.[45] Someone pushed a cup of tea into the hand of Stoker II Fred Mason. It was in a jam tin, had no milk or sugar, but Mason later described it as 'the best cup of tea I had in my life'.[46] Sergeant Kevin Nolan of the 2/2 Pioneers realised for the first time how different it was for naval volunteers, 'when they lose a battle they also lose their personal gear'.[47] Nolan quickly spread the word and *Perth* survivors were overwhelmed by the generosity of their countrymen who broke open their military kits to offer what they could, 'I could never repay what they did for us',[48] AB Ernie Toovey would recall.

Two soldiers whose eyes searched the faces of these men from the sea were 24-year-old Private Bill Turnbull and his 20-year-old brother Ken, from the Brisbane suburb of West End. They cried out as they spied their brother John. The Turnbull family had migrated from the north of England for a better life in Australia. All too soon Florence Turnbull was a widow but she gained strength from her children. Eldest son, John James Samuel Turnbull, named in honour of his father and grandfather, had joked that he had salt water in his veins and enlisted in his adopted nation's navy in 1934. The Stoker PO was 29 when his cruiser sank. Bill and Ken were two of those hastily sent to the Dutch East Indies, in late January, to reinforce the 2/29 Btn. Like *Perth* it was too little too late. Members of the 2/29 Btn were involved in rigorous combat with the Japanese before being beaten back. 2/29 Btn survivors were astonished such green reinforcements were sent at all, 'some had barely touched a rifle', and were expected to face a seasoned and capable enemy: 'The Australian government should have been shot for sending them'.[49] The Turnbull boys had little military experience before they left Australia, and not long after arriving in Java they were surrendered. Theirs had been a very short war, or so they thought in April 1942. Bill and Ken were delighted that they had found John; he was emaciated, weak, blackened by oil and poorly clothed, but he was alive. The *Perth* PO was totally surprised, he had no idea his brothers had left Australia. Their mum would have received three telegrams telling her all her sons were 'missing'. The brothers were determined not to add to her grief, they would stick to each other like glue, they would survive whatever the Japanese threw at them, it would be 'one for all and all for one', the Turnbull boys would go home together or not at all.

—

For *Perth* survivors, who were now given to calling themselves the 'old dysenterians', this new camp was wonderful. The barracks were dry and roomy, each building had approximately 200 small cubicles. Cubicles were either 6 feet (1.8 metres) square and accommodated four POWs, or 10 feet (3 metres) square and accommodated five. Hammocks and bunks were fashioned from rice bags – luxury after the uncovered tiles at Serang. There were septic-style toilets. Electricity and water were freely available; a separate bathing area housed a huge concrete tank always full of hot water. Soap was provided, so finally the awful oil could be removed. The sick and injured quickly received medical attention. The first meal was plain unpolished rice. After a couple of spoonfuls a soldier was about to discard the remnants, 'when a long skinny bloke, ex-*Perth* said: "Don't you want that? Can I have it?" He then proceeded to devour it almost with relish. They were really hungry'.[50] Another soldier grunted, 'Struth, I haven't seen bloody Australians eat rice like this mob before.'[51] *Perth* crew ate voraciously; they gulped down cups of real tea, their first since the ship had sunk. Compared to Serang, food was abundant – rice, vegetables and a small amount of meat. A camp bakery enabled an issue of bread. Additional food was bravely smuggled in through the wire by Dutch women. Many were caught and punished severely by the Japanese, but they would return yet again to share what food they could.

The senior *Perth* officer was Lieut Cdr Ralph Lowe, and not knowing what lay ahead, he believed it best if survivors maintained cohesion. They needed little encouragement, they preferred it that way, they had little in common with 'Swotties' (soldiers). The cruiser crew monopolised Hut No.8. Fred Mason, David Manning, Lionel 'Doc' Neal and Hugh Pohl shared a cubicle. To acknowledge group solidarity the name *Capew Court* was placed outside, 'Capew' being an anagram of their home suburbs at 'C'amberwell (Melbourne), 'A'lbert 'P'ark (Melbourne), 'E'astwood (Sydney) and 'W'illiamstown (Melbourne).

After a few days the health of survivors began to improve and they joined work parties at the Tanjong Priok oil dumps and warehouses. With the promise of earning ten cents a day and the possibility of 'liberating' tinned food from warehouses, prospects looked good. Unlike soldiers, the sailors had no currency or additional gear with which to purchase or barter additional food or kit. Like so many Japanese promises, the money was not forthcoming, but for a while scrounging was profitable. They needed to wait until the guard nodded off in the heat of the day before a tin could be secreted beneath clothing. More brazen pilfering required one to keep watch while another misappropriated Japanese rations. They were always 'on the lookout for something to steal'.[52] One band smuggled some pure alcohol back to camp. Most of this precious spirit was delivered to medical staff, but some was turned into a very potent home brew. Before the father of all hangovers set in, several Australians needed to be restrained from giving guards a piece of their mind and a few other things.

POW work parties mixed engineering spare parts from box to box, so parts no longer resembled the box label. The effort to sabotage offered a small sense of empowerment. Opportunities to pilfer diminished when guard duties were handed to members of a Ghurka unit. *Perth* men needed to conjure up other means of supplementing their meagre belongings and this in part occurred thanks to the Americans.

Not long after the *Perth* POWs arrived, 534 Texans, members of the US 131st Field Artillery marched into camp. *Perth* had escorted their convoy to Brisbane in December 1941. The 131st had then left Queensland for Java with USS *Houston*, the cruiser with a Texan name, acting as escort.[53] On arriving at the Bicycle Camp, members of the unit shared their kit with *Houston* survivors and the bond between men of the two cruisers was extended to their US army brethren. *Houston* sailor, Jack Burge would recall: 'we Americans stayed pretty much to ourselves. Now some of us socialised with the Aussies, they were fine people ... good ol' boys, all of them'.[54]

This friendship did not prevent *Perth* survivors from profiteering off the cash-rich 131st soldiers. A camp canteen was permitted and commercial enterprises blossomed. Sailors being sailors quickly hatched all manner of schemes, mostly honest, some not entirely. To 'fight and flourish' was in keeping with their ship's motto. AB Arthur 'Blood' Bancroft admitted, 'Ali Baba and his Forty thieves were mere amateurs'[55] compared to his shipmates. They took full advantage of the hungry hordes and cooked imaginative delicacies out of rice or any other foodstuff they could beg, steal or borrow. Hut 8 became a marketplace with rickety stalls lit by pilfered candles to add a little atmosphere. Tins of milk and jam purchased from 'legitimate' sources could yield profits of 100 to 150 per cent. Eggs obtained for 20 cents were fried and served on fried bread, commonly known as 'two men on a raft', and yielded a large profit.[56] Sporadically there was a cigarette issue. The non-smokers became wealthier.

AB Isaac 'Izzy' Herman turned 21 in January. He was the only member of the *Perth* crew who had written 'Jewish' on his enlistment paper. AB Alec 'Spud' Murphy wasn't one to stereotype anyone on grounds of religion or race but he was amused as he watched 'Izzy' set himself up as a wheeler dealer. 'Izzy' convinced Murphy to sell his signature ring and entrust him with the cash. Murphy watched as the black-haired son of West Australians, Joseph and Gertrude Herman, purchased biscuits for one price and then sold them to Americans for twice the price. 'Once he had a balance we could eat the rest'.[57] *Perth* sailors heard that the Americans needed flints for their cigarette lighters so 'several lads sneaked out, cut up several lengths of fencing wire,' and cigarette lighter flints were now for sale.[58] Fortunately 'our Texan friends had a sense of humour' when they discovered the 'flints' did not work.[59] *Perth* crew were surprised how well off they felt as their reserves and possessions improved. Many now owned clothes, boots, eating utensils fashioned from scrounged metal objects, soap and a toothbrush. Life was pretty good.

Lectures and classes were organised, anyone who knew anything about something was cajoled into giving a talk. POW-manufactured chess sets and card packs were popular. As the men from the cruiser regained strength, they involved themselves in sports. Boxing was the preferred physical activity, not just as a sporting contest but as a means of releasing built-up tension. AB Ted 'Jesse' James became a bit of an Aussie hero when he out fought an American who was the Golden Gloves Asiatic Fleet Champion. A volleyball competition was organised and hugely popular, particularly the 'Aussies versus Yanks' games. The Americans won the final and the Australians, of course, maintained it was rigged. In May an old mule stable was transformed into a camp stage. Wireman Fred Lasslett, the 'Serang chief electrician', now became 'Illumination Director', and he wired the theatre with 33 lights and the stage with seven 40-watt bulbs. Audiences marveled at the quality of concerts, testimony to the abilities of the 60 players and the ingenuity of others who assembled backdrops and costumes out of seemingly nothing. The female impersonators were particularly popular and one of the best was a *Perth* sailor. With a dash of greasepaint, glitter and artificial breasts, ERA IV Lionel 'Poodles' Norley from Adelaide, 'looked remarkably like a woman'.[60]

Early in their Bicycle Camp incarceration, the men were introduced to Japanese discipline protocol. Prisoners were required to say 'Kiotski' (attention) and bow to express 'honour and respect' to their captors regardless of rank. Any perceived discourtesy or infraction met with a violent response. AB Bob 'Buddy' Collins seemed to attract more than his share of trouble, but then Collins had always prided himself in defying authority. One day he was so absorbed in a book, he failed to see a guard approach. The scream brought him back into reality. Collins rose slowly and failed to bow. The angry guard thrust at him with his rifle and bayonet. Collins had done a commando course and in a reflex action, 'relieved' the guard of his rifle. Collins was taken to the guardhouse and severely beaten; 'I came out of the guardhouse I could hardly see. My eyes were blown up and my lips split'.[61] But whilst the Japanese could hold the prisoners' bodies captive, they could not command their minds and hearts. They might bow but their thoughts and quiet mutterings belied their acquiescence. On 29 April POWs were assembled and ordered to face east. They were instructed to bow and send mental salutations to Japan's Emperor Hirohito on the occasion of his birthday. POWs agreed that if the mental salutations they endeavoured to conjure were indeed received, the Emperor would not live to see another birthday.

—

A new camp Commandant arrived and was immediately dissatisfied with discipline; 'the Japs decided we were too happy and started a blitz'.[62] Some activities were curtailed and POWs were subjected to increasingly cruel and physical treatment by the new Korean guards; 'brutality now became a way of life'.[63] The Japanese looked down on the Koreans so the Koreans needed to regain some self-respect by displaying their superiority to POWs:

> ... woe betide the man whose fingers weren't straight, feet at the correct angle, as he stood at attention, a few kicks in the shins, a couple of slaps in the face and a hit with a rifle ... some (POWs) were knocked unconscious.[64]

The Koreans were nicknamed 'Duckshooters' because they nursed their guns as if on a duck shoot. It was difficult not to retaliate against men over whom sailors had a height and reach advantage, but to react was fatal. POWs were subjected to interrogation. Western Australian sailors were taken, one at a time, to a room and questioned over the coastline of their home state. Many of the sailors were inexperienced young men, barely used to naval uniform before their ship had been sunk. The interrogation was harsh and their anxiety was compounded by the belief that the invasion of Australia was imminent. On 27 June POWs were informed they must sign an oath of allegiance to the Japanese Army. The senior Australian officer, Brigadier Blackburn, VC, refused on behalf of those interned. Not one POW broke ranks. Mass executions were threatened. When it appeared the Japanese would carry out their threat, Blackburn agreed POWs would sign. Three army officers and *Perth*'s Engineer Lieut Frank Gillan refused. The men were forced to kneel for a day in front of the guardhouse. As their bodies drooped in the fierce tropical heat they were beaten. Continuing to defy the directive the officers were thrown in cells. They signed only after receiving a direct order from Blackburn.

Within the privacy of their own quarters, *Perth* crew reflected on their messmates, on those who were seen during the sinking and days after and those who were not. Too many good men seemed to have just disappeared. Hopes remained high that stragglers would be brought into camp. As the days turned into weeks, then months, their faith faded but was never extinguished.

—

Lieuts John Thode and 'Knocker' White, CPO Harry Knight, POs 'Horrie' Abbott, Ray Parkin and Alfie Coyne, Yeoman Jack Willis, Leading Seaman Keith Gosden, and Able Seamen Norm Griffiths and Harry Mee had left the Java shore on a dismal morning in March. They had been full of optimism. They may have had a split sack as a makeshift sail, and provisions of a tin of biscuits, a few gallons of water, six tins of condensed milk and some green papaws and bananas, but they had survived hell so far and were doing something positive. The first stop was going to be Princes Island near Java, a row of about 35 miles (56 kilometres).

When the boat crunched into the rocky beach of their goal on 7 March, they could hardly believe their eyes, sixty boxes had washed ashore – Christmas! Better still, it was food glorious food! Using rocks to smash open the containers they found thousands of bank notes, Japanese occupation money. The remainder of boxes contained ammonia, 'bloody useless'. They slunk away dispirited and another box was spotted wedged in rocks. It contained manna from heaven, even better than food, it contained a full set of sails. This was most definitely a good omen. Collecting anything edible or drinkable they departed Princes Island on 9 March.

For the next week they tried very hard to follow their ambitious plan to sail the 1800 miles (2900 kilometres) to Australia, but the elements were against them. Every day was windless so they had to row. Every day they subjected their weary, all but starved, oil-covered bodies to the scorching sun. Sharks followed the boat, so cooling off in the water was not possible. At night the cool breeze renewed their enthusiasm, until the cold made their bodies shiver and ache. Rations consisted of a biscuit spread with condensed milk, one cup of brackish water and occasionally some coconut. Cloud cover complicated navigation and one night Thode lit a distress rocket to check the compass and the rocket shot into Gosden. The Leading Seaman screamed and leapt overboard. They struggled to retrieve Gosden who was badly burned about the midriff. It made reaching Tjilatjap even more important; there they would find allies and medical assistance.

On 16 March they turned into the outer harbour. On the distant shore was the unmistakable sight of enemy troops, hundreds of Japanese soldiers, and their spirits slumped. Thode swung the tiller and the men bent their backs and rowed away. On the other side of the harbour, a Dutch flag fluttered over a wharf. They had travelled 600 miles (1000 kilometres) from where their ship had sunk, but they needed food, they needed water, and they needed desperately to just stop, so the boat was brought alongside. The Australians climbed onto the wooden structure, the stronger helping others who had difficulty standing. They were amazed: food of all kinds littered the wharf and they immediately began to help themselves. There was a yell and two Dutch officers ran towards them, one carried a Tommy gun and the other a pistol. Thode introduced his party and explained they were making their way to Australia. The Dutch shook their heads and with weapons fixed retorted: 'Nippon is your friend'. Thode turned to his fellows and in a low voice asked if they wanted to surrender or 'take a crack' at the Dutch officers. They stood no hope against the spray of a Tommy gun, especially in their weakened state, so muttering 'You bastards – you yellow fifth-column bastards', they surrendered at gunpoint.[65]

They had travelled by boat for nine gruelling days since 7 March, only to find that the Dutch had capitulated on 8 March. Artist PO Ray Parkin souvenired their lifeboat's jibsail and over the next days, he drew *Perth*'s crest with the inscription 'TO THE MEMORY OF THE GALLANT SHIP HMAS PERTH' beneath. To it they each added a signature, determined that they and the sail would return home no matter how long it took.

After several months at Tjilatjap, all but Yeoman Jack Willis, who was ill, were moved to Bandung in central Java. Lieuts John Thode and 'Knocker' White remained in Java. The eight ratings were then reunited with other *Perth* survivors in a group known as 'Dunlop's Thousand' – 1000 POWs who were shunted to Thailand in January 1943, under the command of Lieut Colonel 'Weary' Dunlop – to toil on the terrible railway. To hide the sail from the Japanese, it went through many pairs of Australian hands and was brought home from Changi POW camp by a member of the AIF.[66] Those who signed it all tried to come home and very nearly did. However, PO 'Alfie' Coyne who had enlisted in the RAN as a boy seaman in 1926, been with *Perth* from commissioning day, and who was known affectionately by subordinates as 'The Black Prince', died in Thailand on 8 October 1943.

—

The other lifeboat carrying POs Tyrrell and Ernie Robinson, Corporal Ron Bradshaw (RAAF), Leading Seamen Stan Roberts and Ben Chaffey, Telegraphist Gunner, Ken 'Tag' Wallace, Stokers Clive 'Smiler' Henry,

Alan Axton and Dallas Pascoe, AB Eric Hurst and Ord Seam Max Jagger, had dodged the Japanese along the Sumatra coast until there was no option but to put into Kota Argoen for water. There Japanese soldiers had awaited them and frog marched the sailors to the beach, where they had been ordered to kneel, as 'thousands of natives gathered to watch our execution'.[67] It was 7 April and there was consolation knowing they had evaded the enemy for more than a month.

The *Perth* men had knelt and awaited the fall of blades. Nothing happened. There seemed to be confusion within the Japanese ranks and the locals were getting restless. After about twenty very long minutes the survivors were ordered off their knees and into a truck. When it was clear there was to be no execution, 'the natives set up such a screaming and shouting for our blood, that the sergeant ordered a volley of shots to be fired over their heads'.[68] The Australians would learn that the decision to take prisoners was very recent, others captured before them had indeed been taken to the beach and decapitated.

The lifeboat group were transported to a jail in Telok Betong.[69] For the next month conditions were poor and food scarce, and they were subjected to repeated interrogation by the Kempetai, the Japanese version of the German Gestapo. Details of Sydney Harbour were slowly extracted. The Kempetai were pleased to find the sailors gave the same details. The Kempetai were not to know that the sailors' version of Sydney Harbour surrounds, which were sent on to Japan, in no way resembled the real Sydney Harbour. When the twelve were moved to a larger POW camp at Palembang, they were already suffering from beri-beri. The new camp was 'luxury' compared to the jail, but the prisoners were required to work. Every day trains would arrive carrying thousands of 100-kilogram bags of rice, which the men had to offload. The work previously undertaken by 80 natives, now done by 30 POWs, 'was incredibly hard'.[70] And it got harder when the Japanese used POW labour to build an airfield and to work the wharves. By the middle of 1944 lack of food and medical supplies, compounded by hard manual labour, meant the POW death rate escalated, but the *Perth* blokes kept each other going. The twelve nearly made it through the nightmare, but on 16 August 1945 Leading Seaman Stanley 'Dool' Wills Roberts, from the pretty coastal Adelaide suburb of Semaphore, died, and then they were eleven. They would return after the war to place a tombstone on his grave, 'Peacefully Sleeping – Our Beloved "Dool", a Brave and Gallant Hero'.[71]

In early October *Perth* POWs at Bicycle Camp were informed they would be shipped to another camp, one 'which offered much better conditions'. It would not be the last time they would be subjected to this hollow promise. Speculation raged as to their destination, the most optimistic believed they would be exchanged for Japanese POWs, but then the most optimistic believed an Allied advance would see them freed by Christmas 1942. It was fortunate that none of the *Perth* survivors could know it would be several Christmases before some of them would be free, that three years of atrocious deprivation and inhumanity lay before them. Of the 681 crew of the cruiser *Perth*, 353 did not survive the sinking, of the 328 who did, only 214 would return to Australia.

'They were rotten with ulcers, malaria, and every other disease and the stench from their hut made one vomit.'

Ordinary Seaman Frank Chattaway

On 8 October 1942 a contingent of 1500 POWs, made up of members of the 2/2 Pioneer Battalion, the 2/3 Reserve Motor Transport unit, the 2/6 Field Company Engineers, RAAF personnel, 2nd Btn Dutch troops, and *Perth* and *Houston* survivors – under the charge of Australian Lt Colonels Jack M. Williams, and Chris M. Black – marched to Batavia's railway station and were pushed into carriages. Next stop was dockside Tanjong Priok.

Flying Officer 'Jock' McDonough was a member of the 211 RAN contingent, yet *Perth*'s pilot was frustrated by the Japanese, whom he regarded as 'dreadful organisers'.[1] Enemy orders to 'speedo-speedo' (hurry) were followed by complete inactivity. Efforts to 'tenko' (count) prisoners were repeated over and over as the guards seemed incapable of getting the same total twice. It was a constant case of hurry up and: 'All men back – all one big mistake'. Finally they were shoved into the holds of the derelict *Kinkon Maru* and again left to languish. 'We were terribly crowded, the heat was intense and the air foul',[2] wrote Ord

Seam Frank Chattaway. The *Kinkon Maru* groaned and shook through the three-day sea journey, it was 'a frightful nightmare'.[3]

Prayers were answered when the ship ground to a halt. Like so many cattle, the POWs were herded out by screaming guards. Eyes squinted against bright sunlight, bodies dipped to avoid rifle butts and Singapore Harbour lay before them. It was disconcerting to find the foreshores full of Japanese craft being loaded with looted personal possessions and supplies, and the white flag with the red circle fluttered everywhere. A *Perth* AB muttered the flag looked like a 'flaming arsehole'. As the trucks swept through Singapore streets, it was surprising to see little damage and how life appeared to be almost normal: Had there been no bombardment? Why was the 'island fortress' surrendered?

Changi POW camp, sprawled over 10 square miles (26 square kilometres) of the undulating, vivid green terrain of eastern Singapore, was formerly the Selerang British Army Camp. Substantial three-storey brick barracks were surrounded by coconut palms, trees and lawns. *Perth* survivors scrutinised Changi and realised how comfortable an existence these 50,000 or so Allied POWs had enjoyed. Never had they seen so many army blokes. Why had such a force capitulated so quickly? They would learn later that the Japanese had triumphed in a most non-militaristic manner. The 'impregnable fortress', the 'Guardian of the East', was conquered when the Japanese simply turned off the water. By cutting Singapore's water supply at Johor Bahru, the Japanese held not only the military but the civilian population captive.

For AB Arthur 'Blood' Bancroft, Changi was 'an eye opener'.[4] Compared to their last 'hell holes', Changi was 'a holiday camp,'[5] wrote AB 'Tich' Hill. Ord Sig 'Buzzer' Bee marvelled at the 'beaut views and great facilities' and 'how well fed and fit' the khaki-clad population appeared,[6] while Ord Seam David Manning considered: 'Changi was pretty easy' given that inmates 'seldom saw a Japanese'.[7] Essentials were in good supply and improved further with the arrival of a Swedish ship loaded with Red Cross parcels.

British military officers were unimpressed with this force they labelled the 'Java rabble'. Unlike those who had marched into Changi with their complete kits, the 'Java rabble', particularly those who had survived the sinking of their ships, were scruffy and dressed in a weird assortment of colours and types of clothing. The new arrivals hoped for Red Cross parcels, only to be told because they were a party 'in transit', they were not entitled to parcels. It was a harsh judgement, especially as those incarcerated in Changi had yet to suffer substantial deprivation. James Boyle a member of the Australian 4th Motor Transport Company thought: 'This ruling seemed rather severe on the fellows from Java,' they were 'given the rough end of the stick'.[8]

Further consideration was requested. Some *Perth* survivors finally received a couple of teaspoons of cocoa and sugar. The more fortunate received nine cigarettes, half a tin of milk, a tin of bully beef, a tin of stew, a quarter of a tin of beetroot and a small quantity of sugar, cocoa, biscuits and dried fruits.[9] It was a veritable feast, yet they knew to ration their precious bounty. The Americans were annoyed. *Houston* sailor Seldon Reese sort of understood why the British would not share with Americans, but he was puzzled, 'you would have thought they would have given more to the Australians, but they didn't.'[10] A request to British command for footwear for *Perth* crew was rejected.

The Japanese had despatched large groups of POWs to work camps, and the Williams Force's stay in this 'seventh heaven' was to be but a couple of days so they could journey north to join 'A' Force, commanded by Brigadier Arthur L. Varley. Questions as to why those already ensconced in Changi did not leave first went unanswered; they were 'bitterly disappointed' when they learnt their stay was to be so brief.[11] Many within the Williams *Perth* group needed medical confinement. A small number were admitted to hospital, but the Japanese assured POWs there would be ample medical facilities at the destination, that work would be light and food plentiful.

Sub Lieut Gavin Campbell searched for his brother in Changi, only to find he had already shipped north.[12] AB 'Tich' Hill tried to find his brother among members of the 2/4th Machine Gun Battalion. He was told Lance Corporal John Hill had been wounded, but had healed well and was away on a work party. 'Tich' was elated and disappointed all at once and left his brother a note. *Perth* survivors were delighted to be permitted to compile a letter card of 24 words for back home. Little did they realise it would be a year before the cards were delivered.

Attempts to keep *Perth* survivors together were rapidly being usurped as the Japanese shadow in Asia lengthened. Chief Cook Lou 'Maggie' Moore was retained in Changi's kitchen. Several *Perth* technicians were sent elsewhere, including the cruiser's Acting Warrant Electrician, Cecil Vowles, a 28 year old from Dandenong, Victoria, and Leading Wireman Fred Parker, a 25-year-old hostilities-only sailor and former electrical mechanic; and the 'Serang Chief Electrician', Wireman Fred Lasslett.

—

Fred Lasslett was hoping his luck would continue as they were bundled on to the *Tojuki Maru* on Monday 26 October to sail to Japan. By the time their transport arrived in the port of Moji on 8 November, after 'a nightmarish voyage', 27 of the 1200 POWs were dead.[13] For those still alive, the destination, Ohasi, Japan, was reached on 30 November. Half the POWs were ill, the weather was 'very cold and usually snowed at evening time'. More men died and Lasslett scribbled in his diary, 'it seems years since the *Perth* was sunk, instead of nine months'.[14]

All too soon William's Force was unceremoniously dumped into another 'hell ship'. *Perth* crew were disturbed by the dubious seaworthiness of the *Mae Baesi Maru*[15] and the fact that they were captive in a hold, 15 feet (4.5 metres) below the water line, with no lifebelts, and in a war. One seaman decided he'd really had his fill of Japanese ships: 'I have done more time in the Nip Navy than in our own'[16] and he preferred his own. This 'hell ship' so deserved its nickname. It was 14 October and 1799 POWs struggled with fetid air, little water, precious little food and no ablutions in the hold. Their tongues became swollen for lack of water, while their bodies streamed with perspiration in the extreme heat and humidity. The men were so jammed in they literally lay on one another, those with dysentery wedged in with those not yet afflicted. Rations consisted of tea and a meagre issue of rice and soya soup with something thought to be radish. By the time they arrived at their destination, fourteen were dead, scores more on the verge of death and half the force 'virtually incapacitated by dysentery'.[17]

The human cargo was transferred to the smaller *Yamagata Maru* at Rangoon before the journey finished at Moulmein, Burma. This was not the Far East trip anyone wished for. There was beauty in the glittering golden temples, but the charming words of Rudyard Kipling and joyous lyrics of 'On the Road to Mandalay' held no relevance on this grim adventure. After two days in Moulmein Gaol, the 599 officers and other ranks marched the 3 miles (5 kilometres) to the rail station. The date was now 26 October 1942, and POWs were heartened when Burmese risked being beaten by guards to push food into their hands.

Next stop was Thanbyuzayat, the northern base camp of the railway they were to build. The following morning came an address from the Commandant of No.3 POWs, 'A' Force, Lt Col Nagatomo.[18] The short, pompous, Japanese officer was immaculately turned out with a large Samurai sword on his left side. Launching into a long-winded speech, he informed POWs it was, 'thanks to the infinite goodness and mercy of the Japanese Emperor' that they had been spared death and granted the honour of building the railway that would link Burma and Thailand. According to Nagatomo, the men were:

a few remaining skeletons after the invasion of East Asia ...
pitiful victims. It is not your fault, but until your Government
wake up from dreams and discontinue their resistance all of you
will not be released.[19]

They must work 'cheerfully' in exchange for food. Anyone attempting to escape would face 'extreme punishment', because they were a, 'misled rabble of a defeated army'. *Perth* survivors decided he could not be referring to them because their Captain was a most capable and brave leader, and even though they had been sunk, it had taken overwhelming odds to do so and their cruiser had delivered several Japanese ships to the bottom with it. This knowledge meant they could forever hold their heads proudly.

Nagatomo agreed to the formation of two units. Williams Force would comprise of men of the 2/2 Pioneer Battalion, *Perth* survivors and odd personnel ex-Java – a total of 884 officers and other ranks. Black Force, with Lt Col Chris Black in charge, consisted of 593 Australian and 190 Americans, less 90 who would be assigned Base Camp duties. Each force was divided into battalions, and they would be divided into 'Kumis', each Kumi comprising of 50 POWs and a 'Han' containing two Kumis or 100 POWs. Commanders of each would be titled 'Kumicho' and 'Hancho', the former a non-commissioned officer or junior officer, the latter a more senior officer.

Camps would be known by their distance (kilo) from a town, which the men later referred to as Thanbyuzayat, to the Burma–Thailand border. 'A' Force dispositions were Green Force, No.3 Btn, commanded by Major Charles Green operating from 4-kilo, also known as Kendau. Anderson Force, No.2 Btn, under the command of Lt Col Charles Anderson, VC, operating from 18-kilo camp, also known as Alepauk. Ramsay Force, No.1 Btn, under the charge of Lt Col George Ramsay, would be positioned at 26-kilo, also known as Kun Knit Way. Williams Force would begin from 35-kilo, also known as Tanyin; Black Force would begin from 40-kilo, also known as Beke Taung. At least, that was the configuration set by the Japanese, practice would demand less rigidity. Within a month the water supply failed at 40-kilo camp, and Black Force moved back to 26-kilo camp where they linked with Ramsay Force. Over the ensuing months individual force compositions would blur as the faces of too many POWs vanished.

On 29 October, Williams Force were transported to 35-kilo camp. As they passed other Australian POWs they were asked to identify themselves, and when the answer 'sailors from *Perth*' was forthcoming, a soldier cried out: 'God help us, they have the navy also'.[20] Everything was strange to the eye as they perused what would be standard accommodation throughout Burma. Raised huts made from bamboo, with roofs and walls made of attap, a type of thatch manufactured from bamboo, leaves and bark. Narrow bamboo platforms running the length of each hut would suffice as beds. A separate kitchen contained six open fires. It was quiet and men felt reasonably good as they settled in and the cooks set to work. The tranquillity belied their predicament and the disease, starvation, brutality and impossible workload that awaited.

—

Having captured South East Asia, the Japanese needed an alternate troop and supply route to the hazardous sea lanes. To continue their dominance in the region and beyond, uninterrupted rail access as far as Singapore was crucial, but the railway line between Bangkok and Moulmein was incomplete. The British had surveyed the proposed railway in 1903. From the plains in the south, the countryside rose to mountains more than 5000 feet (1500 metres) high, scarred by deep ravines and rivers, which boiled and ran fast in the wet season. The humid dank jungle 'could rot a dead elephant down to tusks and bones in fourteen days'.[21] The railway needed to cover a distance of 263 miles (412 kilometres) through dense jungle and rocky terrain and would entail the building of roughly 700 bridges. The British had shelved the proposal because of the onerous nature of such an enterprise; it would take many years and likely cost lives. The Japanese had been preparing for this since 1934, and were determined to show that it would take only twelve months; the loss of life did not concern them because at their disposal were an estimated 30,000 British, 18,000 Dutch, 13,000 Australian and 650 American POWs, and 250,000 conscripted Asian labourers.

For *Perth* survivors in the Williams Force, the first day on the railway wasn't too bad. Embankments were to be constructed, but each man was required to dig only a cubic metre of earth. Tools were primitive; with a 'chunkel' (hoe) they removed the earth and shovelled it into wicker baskets, which were carried to the site of the railway line. They worked quickly, completing the excavation so they could return to camp by 1400. In their haste no allowance was made for the inadequate diet or Japanese cunning and expediency. The daily quota was raised to 1.2 cubic metres per man. Acres and acres of bamboo were cut and cleared, and days became longer. The 'yasume' (day off) was used to make and mend gear. Ingenuity was evident in what the men manufactured out of very little – nothing was wasted. Ord Seam David

Manning had arrived in Burma with a Ford hubcap that acted as both plate and drinking utensil and a piece of green billiard cloth baize used as a blanket. He had acquired 'a pair of rubber-soled, leather-tipped shoes', but the shoes were a little small so he cut the toes out and kept them for special occasions. Wooden 'cloppers', platforms over which pieces of old tyres were nailed, acted as the main footwear. G-strings remained standard clothing. They ventured into the jungle to find anything to supplement their meagre rations, watching what birds ate and harvesting the same. The fortunate would find a snake, a delicacy that tasted a little like chicken; commonly they would return with only edible grass; 'we ate anything that flew, moved or crawled',[22] anything stewed in a pot was a meal. There were limited trade opportunities with the indigenous population. Any prisoner found outside the camp was shot.

For Williams Force their first Christmas was their best as POWs. They were still reasonably well and found the resources to purchase a couple of pigs, which were boiled up with melons as a stew. AB Ernie Toovey thought 'our cooks did us proud', they were particularly adept at camouflaging rice in so many ways, 'it was a great day'.[23] There was even a musical concert provided by members of the 22nd Btn band, who somehow had retained many of their instruments. The lightness of mood quickly dissipated when Sergeant Ronnie O'Donnell was murdered by a guard nicknamed 'Peanut Tomoto'.[24]

POWs derived unflattering nicknames for many of their guards: 'Monster', 'Puss in Boots', 'The Maggot', 'Storm Trooper', 'Frankenstein', 'Tokyo Liar', 'Gold Tooth', 'Silver Tooth', 'Blubber Lips', 'The Grub' and 'The Prick'. 'Boofhead' was 'an aggressive Korean speedo merchant and a hulk of a man'.[25] 'Boy Bastard' was a vindictive little Korean who enjoyed firing shots over the heads of stragglers and shouting: 'You will never see your homes again. You will work for the Nipponese until you die'.[26] And there was 'Dillinger', a large, stocky evil-spirited Korean. 'Peanut Tomoto' was so named because 'we thought he had a brain the size of a pea and was totally nuts'.[27]

The Koreans were invariably taller and heavier than their Japanese counterparts, and more vicious towards prisoners. On Boxing Day

1942 Sergeant O'Donnell was taken into the jungle, beaten and shot. It was a grim warning to all, and the violence and brutality increased with the New Year. From the army belt of every guard hung a polished bayonet encased in a scabbard. It was common practice for bayonets to be unhooked, fixed to rifles and then used to stab the bare legs of POWs as enticement to hasten. Beatings and bashing were administered for any perceived misdemeanour or delay. The guttural exclamation 'Kora' meant: 'come here and be bashed' – one 'Kora' was a slapped face, two 'Koras' could mean a split scalp and three 'Koras' meant a stay in hospital. A POW's only defence was to have a wide-open stare to see the punches coming and attempt to roll with them. Unfortunately, a wide-open stare was a mark of disrespect.

—

Christmas 1942 was a better day for the much smaller group of *Perth* survivors, who had left the Bicycle Camp[28] with 1000 POWs on 11 October. They were still in Changi and their Christmas dinner was decidedly more nourishing, even including roast lamb. A 'superb concert' was staged the following evening. Ord Sig 'Buzzer' Bee believed the highlight was the female impersonator, who in real life was *Perth*'s AB John Woods, but then Bee admitted that he and the rest of the audience had been 'long deprived of the intimacy of the fair sex'.[29] 'Buzzer' was finally, feeling better than he had been since the ship went down.[30] The last piece of shrapnel was removed from his leg under anesthetic.

The small navy group also scored one against the 'Swotties' (soldiers). As POWs at Changi they were under the jurisdiction of Brigadier Frederick G. 'Black Jack' Galleghan, DSO, Commanding Officer of the AIF 2/30th. At this stage of the war, the Japanese allowed the British army to run Changi. The Brigadier was a stickler of polish and parades, and this was the reason that when the RAN contingent had appeared the army top brass had been decidedly less than impressed. Their military counterparts were fully clothed and kitted, particularly officers. *Perth* survivors remained very slightly blackened dressed in a strange mixture of clothing, some without footwear, and were clearly unwelcome. When it was conceded they should participate in an Armistice Day Parade, the motley crew was instructed to fall in at the back. The officer in charge of the *Perth* men was Commissioned Gunner George Ross, and this was unfortunate for the Army. Ross was old-school navy, not RAN but RN. A Scot by birth the 47-year-old Gunner with 25 years of service was a formidable man. Assuming his most redoubtable stance, Ross informed the parade commander that as the navy was the senior service, his squad would march from the front. Beside him stood Commissioned Gunner Frank Hawkins, also RN, nine years his junior but another navy gunnery man through and through. Hawkins was born in the English naval town of Portsmouth. He and Ross had been loaned to the Australian Navy when *Perth* was commissioned. Galleghan and his officers were not pleased, but the navy section of the 'Java rabble' marched from the front of the parade.

Following the parade Galleghan let it be known that he and his fellow officers had been insulted when given what he thought was the Japanese salute during the march past. Navy man Ross attempted to educate his army superiors. The palm facing inwards was the correct navy salute, adopted during the sailing ship era when sailors, climbing up and down sail rigging covered in tar, declined to show a dirty palm to officers. Ross closed with his own indignant comment to the Brigadier: 'I am sorry you should know the Japanese salute better than ours'.[31] *Perth* ratings were unimpressed with the ignorance and refused to salute Changi army officers thereafter.

—

Another transport arrived in Singapore laden with POWs. Within this group of men who filed down the gangway of the *USU Maru* with sunken eyes, gulping fresh air and stretching cramped limbs, were more *Perth* survivors. PO Ray Parkin and members of his lifeboat party had been captured at Tjilatjap and imprisoned at Bandung in central Java. They had then been sent to Makasura outside Batavia before leaving on 4 January 1943 for Singapore. Three of Parkin's lifeboat group, Lieuts John Thode and 'Knocker' White and Yeoman Jack Willis were detained in Java. The remaining seven – CPO Telegraphist Harry

Knight, POs Ray Parkin, Alf Coyne and Horrie Abbott, Leading Seaman Keith Gosden, and ABs Norm Griffiths and Harry Mee – had found themselves included in a sea of khaki called 'Dunlop's 1000'. Members of the Australian Machine Gun Btn, the 2/2nd Pioneers and 2/40th Btn, Army Engineers and RAAF personnel had adopted the name of the tall, gangly doctor in charge of an Australian hospital unit, Lt Col Edward 'Weary' Dunlop.

The *Perth* group was delighted to find the Ross/Hawkins *Perth* survivors in Changi. They knew little of who had survived the sinking. Learning that it was likely that 309 had survived was terrific. Of course, it would have been even better had that estimate been higher.[32]

The *Perth* survivors, like their Williams predecessors, were soon caught in a military dispute that would have dire consequences. Dunlop was immediately unimpressed with the military reception of staff officers, 'neatly dressed ... carrying canes, blowing out puffy moustaches and talking in an 'old chappy' way'.[33] In the officers mess Dunlop objected strongly to his men being criticised and referred to as the 'Java rabble'. He sprang to his feet and rattled off a list of battles – from the Middle East, to Greece, from the Atlantic to the Mediterranean to the Java Sea – that this 'rabble' had been involved in, as distinct from most of those present who were involved briefly in a failed Malayan campaign. Dunlop was 'cutting, sarcastic, angry'.[34] Lt Col 'Black Jack' Galleghan informed the lanky doctor that he too was unimpressed with the appearance of the troops, how they paraded poorly and failed to salute as often as they should. It did little to ease the 'tension between the 8th Division [AIF] and Dunlop Force'.[35]

As the Force prepared to leave Changi, their CO visited the British Q store, which the Japanese had left untouched and under British command. Dunlop was informed the store held an abundant supply of military kit. He requested boots, socks and hats. One hundred and seventy eight of his 878[36] men had no boots; he was given six pairs of size elevens. Many had no headgear; he was given twenty hats. Few had socks; he was given 150 pairs. Dunlop asked for some medical supplies, and Galleghan asked him to pay for them. Dunlop wrote official letters of complaint to the British Changi command. As far as he was concerned, Galleghan had failed as CO and 'had shamed' his men. Galleghan could have insisted Dunlop Force be better equipped, but instead 'had denied them decency and left them in rags'.[37] The ill feeling and lack of sympathy would have a direct bearing on the survival rate of Dunlop Force.

The seven lifeboat members were joined in 'Dunlop's 1000' by seven other ex-Java *Perth* survivors[38] – Telegraphist George MacDonald, Stoker Roy Dundon, Wiremen Allan Geier and Bryan McHugh, ABs Bob Costin, Bill Gilby, Isaac 'Izzy' Herman and Ord Seam Arthur 'Otto' Lund. Telegraphist George MacDonald was a 35 year old born in Wales, whose wife Marjorie and three children lived in South Australia. Wireman Allan Geier had sort of celebrated his twentieth birthday on the eve of the Battle of Java. Fellow Wireman Bryan McHugh, a 21 year old from Port Pirie, South Australia had been a telephone mechanic before he had been drafted into the wartime RAN. Stoker Roy Dundon was from an upper-middle-class Victorian family. Prior to the war he had been making a name for himself as a golfer and worked part time as an assistant greenkeeper for his father at the Peninsula Country Golf Club, Frankston. Dundon, who turned 21 the week Dunlop Force left Changi, had won many golf competitions including the 1939 Victorian 'B' grade championship. He was also a keen cricketer and had a brother in the RAN. The 26-year-old AB Bill Gilby was another 'hostilities only' sailor, married to Gwendoline who lived in Perth. AB Isaac 'Izzy' Herman, 22, was the only member of the *Perth* crew who wrote 'Jewish' on his enlistment paper. The black-haired son of West Australians, Joseph and Gertrude Herman, 'Izzy' had set himself up as a wheeler dealer in the Bicycle Camp helping to keep he and AB Alec 'Spud' Murphy alive. Ord Seam Arthur 'Otto' Lund had been exhilarated during the chaos and excitement of the Battle of Java Sea but terrified by the reality of war as his ship and crew were crushed by superior forces.

AB Bob Costin had been a member of the Reserves when war broke out and sent to guard the wireless station outside Canberra. Granted fourteen days leave, he had raced back to Brisbane to marry his childhood sweetheart, Maud. He made it through the ceremony before he was whisked off to join *Perth* on its way to Java. Before the cruiser left Australian waters he had received news his wife was undergoing emergency surgery for acute peritonitis. He never found out if she survived, 'I don't know if I am a widower or a husband',[39] the 22 year old confided to his companions.

In Changi PO Ray Parkin noted that the, 'Java rabble was 'like an irritating flea crawling over a large, well-fed body' that was the ensconced military. Parkin was concerned that the fifteen *Perth* survivors who left with 'Dunlop's 1,000' on 19 January to labour on the Thai end of the railway, had left as they arrived, 'dressed in rags'.[40] Parkin's concerns were justified; the lack of clothing alone left them at the mercy of the elements. Had the *Perth* sailors been given kit issue from Changi stores, it is likely eight out of the fifteen may not have died in Thailand. Parkin's best mate, fellow *Cerberus* Instructor, *Perth* commissioning crew member and lifeboat member, PO 'Alfie' Coyne died 8 October 1943. Ord Seam Arthur 'Otto' Lund died 24 July 1943; AB Isaac 'Izzy' Herman died 24 August 1943; AB Bill Gilby died 20 September 1943; Stoker Roy Dundon died 25 October 1943; Telegraphist George MacDonald died 9 December 1943; Wireman Allan Geier died 30 January 1944. AB Bob Costin died on 19 July 1943, his marriage unconsummated, never knowing that his wife survived surgery, that he was not a widower. Maud was now a widow.

—

The Ross/Hawkins *Perth* group moved out of Changi shortly after Parkin's group arrived. Some sailors remained in hospital. Stoker Syd Harper was diagnosed with retrobulbar neuritis, an eye disease caused by diet deficiencies, which destroyed the central vision nerve. He was nineteen and his life was irreparably damaged. Harper remained in the region of Changi for the remainder of the war. Bandsman Henry 'Ned' Kelly and AB George Morriss were also deemed unfit to travel with their shipmates on 9 January 1943, and this proved unfortunate when in 1945 they joined an ill-fated work force sent to Sandakan, Borneo.

The remainder of the Ross/Hawkins *Perth* group was now part of No.5 Branch, made up of around 2000 Australians, Americans and Dutch POWs. Taken by train into Malaya, they were then shoved into a rust bucket named *Moji Maru*. Like those before them, their time on the 'hell ship' defied description, they would arrive at their destination having 'eaten little, seen less, and expected nothing'.[41] Ord Seam 'Digby' Gray boarded with his sole possession, a water bottle. In the stifling atmosphere Telegraphist 'Buzzer' Bee let his eyes settle on his navy band of brothers. They were a diverse group in every way, hailing from each part of the United Kingdom and every Australian state. Crammed uncomfortably onboard the Japanese transport were Commissioned Gunners Ross and Hawkins from Scotland and England; another Scot, PO SBA 'Jock' Cunningham; Irishman, Stoker 'Tiny' Savage; and AB Bill Bevan from Cardiff, Wales. The Australian born were his best mate, Tasmanian Bandsman Ron Sparks; South Australian SBA Andy Mitchell; fellow West Australians ABs Fred Skeels, Alec 'Spud' Murphy, Les Bruse, Clarrie Glossop, Ord Seamen Wally Johnston, 'Digby' Gray and Alf 'Jim' Hewitt, and Steward Allen 'Des' Denic. AB Ed Burley from Sydney, although only 21, was a veteran of the *Perth* commissioning crew and the Med; another Sydneysider was AB Ted James. Steward Don McLean was from the tiny New South Wales town of Crookwell. The Victorians were fellow Communicator, big Pete Nelson, the larger-than-life AB 'Chesty' Bond, AB 'Ossie' Lomas, the 40-year-old AB Tom Mooney who had first entered the RAN as a boy seaman before the end of the last war, SBA Ernie Noble, Steward Roy Corcoran, Stokers Fred 'Popeye' Parke, Bert Simons and Jeff Latch, Stoker IIs George McCredie, and Norman Lindsay Toulmin – who was unaware he featured in his district's newspaper. Wireman Charlie Wray and Steward Robert Smith were the Queenslanders. Smith as a nineteen year old had marvelled that a former factory boy from Toowoomba, Queensland, could stand on the deck of *Autolycus* peering through the mists of Portsmouth, England, at Australia's newest cruiser, survive 257 air attacks in the Med, and circumnavigate the globe by the time he returned to his country at the beginning of 1941. Now he and the 31 other *Perth* survivors were with him on a voyage to somewhere, wondering what lay ahead, if they could stay together and when they would finally go home.

The rest in Changi had improved morale and there was good-natured banter between the Americans and Australian sailors. Members of US 131st Field Artillery kept trying to explain to these 'Ahhzies' that they preferred to be called 'Texan' than 'Yank'. AB 'Chesty' Bond was his boisterous self and kept smiles on faces with his constant flow of bawdy songs and 'ditties'. The deck of cards AB 'Spud' Murphy had manufactured proved very popular.

Around midday, when the transport was about a day from Rangoon, a pleased 'Buzzer' Bee was describing to Bandsman Ron Sparks how he had just traded a pair of boots too small for him, for a toothbrush, toothpaste and cigarettes, when they heard the unmistakable drone of aircraft. Through the open hatch they watched the low approach of Liberator bombers. The all-too-familiar sound and feel of shells bursting close by caused a sick feeling in the stomach; surely not again would they have a ship sunk from beneath them. Their immediate reaction was to get out of the hold.

'Buzzer' was half way up the ladder, when there was a loud 'swoosh' and he was covered by a sheet of salt water as the transport lifted and fell. Bee clambered topside: 'There were bodies and wreckage strewn all over the after deck'.[42] The ancient stern gun emplacement had blown up, killing its crew and anyone in the vicinity. The accompanying transport was sinking fast, the *Moji Maru* was listing to starboard and aircraft were approaching on another bombing run. Bee ran to the bridge. If he could get hold of the Aldis lamp he could signal the planes this ship carried POWs. As he entered the wheelhouse, the transport's captain whirled around and drew his pistol. Bee backed out so quickly he fell down the ladder to the deck below. It was perhaps a better option to retreat and live to see another day. AB 'Chesty' Bond and Stoker 'Tiny' Savage quickly took charge of the hoses and organised fire parties. *Perth*'s SBAs Andrew Mitchell and Ernie Noble tended the wounded including two of their own, while the *Moji Maru* limped into Moulmein, Burma. *Perth*'s Stoker II George McCredie, who had entered the RAN in June 1941 for 'three years or duration of war and six months after', died of shrapnel wounds aged 21. Steward Rob Smith's wondering was over; he died of blood loss and shock when he lost an arm – he was 23.

No.5 Branch with the now 29 *Perth* survivors[43] led by Commissioned Gunner Ross marched into 18-kilo camp. An American yelled out,

'Don't worry Aussie, Uncle Sam is on his way'. To which an Australian exclaimed: 'What! Have they got him too?'[44] It was a rare moment of mirth.

—

The Williams Force joined Anderson Force in January, swelling camp numbers to around 1700. POWs continued to build embankments until March 1943, then returned to 26-kilo camp to link with Ramsay Force. They would work together at 75 and 105-kilo camps and endure the same horrors: minimal rations, hard work, long hours, disease, minimal medical supplies and death. AB 'Tich' Hill quickly realised, the Japanese 'were determined to finish the railway on schedule regardless of the welfare or health of the prisoners'[45].

Perth Stoker Cecil Albert Harold Stokes, born in Jundah, Queensland, on 31 July 1923, died of 'chronic diarrhoea and malaria' in Thanbyuzayat, Burma on 1 March 1943, the anniversary of the sinking of his ship. Strangely, the same night an Allied Pathfinder aircraft dropped flares, which lit up the whole hospital camp where Stokes died. The commemoration of *Perth*'s sinking was a subdued affair, *Perth* survivors preferring to attend a church service on Sunday 7 March.

Day after day they faced exacting manual labour accompanied by the screams of dissatisfied Japanese engineers and guards. POWs dug cuttings and struggled with baskets of rock and dirt. The daily quota was increased to 1.7 cubic metres per man and the ground became rockier. Then it increased to 2 cubic metres per man per day, then 2.8 cubic metres. When heat, exhaustion and lack of water and food caused men to faint, the booted feet of guards crashed into their stricken bodies. AB Frank McGovern was with Williams Force working on an embankment under the blazing tropical sun. The army POW with him fell under the weight of the dirt-filled basket. He lay sobbing, declaring he could continue no longer. McGovern reacted the only way he could, 'get on your bloody feet, or that Jap guard will come up and belt the shit out of you';[46] the POW struggled to his feet and survived, at least, that day.

From the beginning of April, a 1500 strong Williams/Anderson group became No.1 Mobile Force and commenced to lay rails and ballast the track. Included were about 150 *Perth* crew. Stoker II Fred Mason laboured beside Stoker Jimmy Millerick, AB Ernie Toovey, Ord Seam 'Chilla' Goodchap, and in an effort to cheer his shipmates would say: 'Don't worry boys, it can't get any worse', but it did and Mason stopped using those words. Those on 'earthmoving' would clear the rubble and earth to expose the rocks. The 'hammer and tap' men, armed with an 8-pound (4-kilogram) hammer and a long chisel-headed drill, would pound away. After each swing of the hammer the drill would be turned again and again, chipping until each hole was a metre deep, a task which normally took five or so gruelling hours. The Japanese then used explosive to blast the rock, often detonating it so quickly POWs had insufficient time to take cover. Remaining POWs were the 'rock rollers', those who cleared away debris.

The main Mobile Work Force began unloading heavy teak sleepers from rail bogies. With the sleepers in position, spiking gangs would drill holes with tools resembling corkscrews and then attempt to drive rail spikes into the holes with poor quality hammers. As the effects of malnutrition and disease began to destroy bodies, men came and went, groups became jumbled and whilst each man struggled to stay with his mates, this was often not possible. According to AB Arthur 'Blood' Bancroft, during the next stage of the railway, 'our hitherto healthy body of men were soon reduced to mere shadows of their former selves'.[47] They arose in the dark, stumbled to the cookhouse fires and attempted to eat their mug of sugarless, unsalted, ground rice, known as 'pap'. As the first rays of dawn light streaked the sky, they were counted and marched to the cutting. Men's muscles appeared like taught strings, their rib cages protruded hard against sunburnt skin as their bodies began to lose any semblance of fat. All the time the jungle seemed to creep closer and *Perth* survivors yearned to see a horizon and sun rays shimmering on the surface of a blue ocean; this terrain was a most unnatural place for sailors.

Japanese engineers pursued the edict that the men work 'cheerfully', one even demanding POWs sing to show how much they were enjoying their imprisonment. He was delighted when the captives broke into the song 'Bless 'Em All', at least their version, with unprintable lyrics.

Not understanding English, the engineer remained blissfully ignorant. Nonetheless, POWs were then forbidden to sing or whistle as they worked.

—

The Japanese referred to themselves as 'The Sons of Heaven', but these were no sons of heaven. Guards armed with bamboo sticks paced up and down lines of emaciated and ill workers, screaming and lashing out at bodies. Officers, like *Perth*'s Lieut Lloyd Burgess and Sub Lieuts Ray Barker and Gavin Campbell, were bashed as they endeavoured to protect injured and sick men. If a POW did not stand and bow as a guard entered their hut, passed or addressed him, physical punishment was swift. POWs needed to accept their lack of status and appear acquiescent. Australians in particular appeared loathe to do so. This and their laconic sense of humour made them targets. Being so much taller than most of their guards, they would stand their ground and be punished for it. In May 1943, the very tall Sub Lieut Gavin Campbell was berated and slapped by a guard. Given the height difference, the guard realised the slap was ineffective. The small tormentor stood on a rail so he could deliver a better blow. As he swung Campbell swayed back just sufficiently for the fist to miss. Caught up in his own momentum, the guard overbalanced and fell flat on his back. Men in Campbell's Kumi 'watched in horror waiting for the repercussion,'[48] instead the guard collected himself and disappeared. Campbell had indeed been fortunate. Other national groups criticised the Australian stubbornness, but it was this very stubbornness that helped Australians survive, that, and, their sense of humour. They laughed at the most difficult situations and believed if you stopped laughing you died.

A common punishment required a POW to stand at attention for 24 hours in all weathers. In the early days, when camps held fitter men, a little subterfuge was possible. When guards changed shifts, another Australian POW of similar height to the man being punished, would take his place. All Australian POWs looked the same to the Japanese. Another punishment required a POW to stand in the sun holding a large rock at arm's length above his head. It was a lose–lose situation, because when endurance expired and the rock fell to the ground he was severely beaten. Men were also made to kneel down with bamboo sticks behind their knee joints, 'it was unbelievably painful and very cruel'.[49] Col Williams wrote in his diary, 'The sadism of the Japanese and Korean guards has to be seen to be believed'.[50] Williams and other Force Commanders were frequently targeted for punishment.

Wireman Allan Geier had badly lacerated his right leg escaping his ship. The leg was healing well until the guards spied it and kicked the injury at every opportunity. The leg deteriorated and camp doctors decided it needed to be amputated. Geier died during the operation.

AB Keith 'Freddie' Mills was a dark-haired Sydneysider, a 'hostilities only' sailor who had joined *Perth* in November 1941. Mills turned 21 on 11 April and was a member of the line party driving dog spikes into rail sleepers. Mills drove a spike in crookedly and the guard who observed the transgression told his officer, adding for effect that the Australian had hit him. Mills was savagely bashed. His Kumi officer, Lieut Burgess, managed to intervene, but for the remainder of the day each guard took it in turn to bash Mills as they passed. On the return to camp Mills and Burgess were escorted into the jungle fringe. Mills was beaten again and his jaw shattered. A shot was fired over Mills's head before Burgess was allowed to take him to hospital. Camp Doctor Rowley Richards quickly tended the sailor who was:

> a bloody mess. Purple bruising covered his cheeks, also beneath his tongue and on the floor of his mouth. He was having difficulty breathing normally and he couldn't talk or swallow.[51]

—

They hated the heat and the dust; then the wet descended and they hated that more. Monsoons broke in mid-April 1943. The rain on bodies wearing only G-strings stung like thousands of tiny needles. Rain of the type sailors had never witnessed sheeted down: 'the rain just never stopped and the nights were cold'.[52] Dirt turned into muddy quagmires, into which POWs sank to their knees: 'carrying heavy baskets with the mud running down one's back is no enviable experience'.[53] The humidity of the sodden jungle made it difficult to breathe. In lashing rain tools slipped, attracting the fury of guards. There was no reprieve back at camp, the incessant deluge blew sideways into huts and soaked through roofs; latrine pits overflowed and the foul mess washed through sleeping areas and kitchens. Clothes were forever wet, as were blankets for the fortunate who possessed such. The monsoonal deluge, which went on for months, dropping around 500 inches (12,700 millimetres) of rain, would have tested the strongest of men and these men were no longer strong. Within a month the POW force began to crack under the most impossible of regimes overseen by the most inhumane of captors.

On their arrival in Burma and Thailand, the Australians had quickly realised hygiene was critical to survival and adopted stringent regimes that focused attention on the four 'Fs' – food, flies, fingers and faeces – along with water. This was one reason Australians preferred the company of their own and were the 'most tribal' of all ethnic groups working on the railway. They would mix with the Yanks but spurned the less hygiene-conscious British. Occasionally, Australian doctor Captain Rowley Richards would be called on to visit British POW encampments: 'I was appalled by the condition of the British troops. They still failed to grasp the concepts of hygiene and sanitation'.[54] Another reason for their tribalism was because Australians believed their mates were pivotal to survival. AB Fred Skeels said:

No matter where you went no matter what happened to us, Australians stuck together more than other nationals who were around us. Of course the navy had strong common bonds.[55]

Signalman 'Buzzer' Bee firmly agreed, it 'gave one a strange feeling of strength and security to be among your old mates'.[56] Mates did everything they could to stay together and look out for one another and according to Rohan Rivett: 'The *Perth* boys were a happy bunch, who stuck together'.[57] Arthur 'Blood' Bancroft relied heavily on his closest mates, fellow ABs Mervil 'Merv' O'Donoughue, Edmund 'Marcus' Clark and Harry 'Lofty' Nagle, to help him, and they were equally dependent on him; if one or two were a bit crook one day, the others would work a bit harder.

Partly because of this, Australians established a reputation they would never live down. The Japanese preferred them on work parties, saying, 'One Aussie, fifteen Englishmen, four hundred Dutchmen'.[58] A British POW wrote: 'it was a punishing experience to find oneself working with an Australian'.[59] He considered Australians did not like being idle, but more would have survived had they worked less hard. Ord Seam 'Digby' Gray knew Aussies worked hard in the mornings but would 'cruise in the afternoon'.[60] AB Bob Collins believed the Japanese pushed 'the Navy guys harder than anyone, and it was the Navy blokes who did a great deal of the laying of the line'.[61] The bond between *Perth* survivors remained strong, no matter what their captors threw at them. Worse than earthworks was the construction of wooden bridges and culverts – hard, monotonous work, cutting and dragging timber, making scaffolding and pile driving. Occasionally the heavy work was undertaken by elephants, but there were few elephants and more POWs. The Japanese counted eight prisoners as equivalent to one elephant. POWs stood in water, covered with leeches, straining to drive heavy wooden piles into riverbeds, hauling on ropes, as guards screamed and hurled iron rail spikes at them. Ord Seam. 'Digby' Gray would never forget the physical pain involved with bridge building. At the time he tried not to scream out loud. Along the line battered, sick and wasted POWs clung desperately to life. As 1943 wore on they began to wonder not if there would be a tomorrow, but if there would be all of today.

As the Japanese realised the realities of carving a railway out of virgin jungle meant delays, they took out their frustration on those who toiled. As the scream 'speedo-speedo' became more and more prevalent from July, so too did the brutality and deprivation. Camp after camp was 'BA' (Bloody Awful); food rations were 'NBG' (No Bloody Good). In the main, food consisted of dollops of rice and minimal protein. If stew was forthcoming it was so watery it barely flavoured the rice. Ribs began to protrude from wasted bodies. The Mobile Force was moved to 60-kilo; the arduous task of shifting camp was exhausting enough, then they found the camp one of the 'filthiest places set aside for human accommodation'.[62] It was strewn with the bodies of dozens of Burmese who had died of the dreaded cholera. The men were allowed one day to clean up 'the putrid mess, then back to work on the line'.[63] Scurvy, pellagra, wet and dry beri-beri, two types of malaria, tropical ulcers, then cholera wreaked havoc on emaciated bodies. Camp Doctor Rowley Richards wrote:

> Even if the majority of our men escaped cholera, how, I questioned, could they survive the 'killer cycle' of malaria, dysentery and beri-beri on top of starvation, hard labour and acts of brutality, all the while watching comrades die around them?[64]

Perth men were beginning to spread far and wide throughout Burma. Some were at 60-kilo, other *Perth* men were sent to 80-kilo and another group was returned to 40-kilo to unload ballast. Ord Seam Frank Chattaway scribbled in his diary: 'we're very short handed. The work is exceedingly hard and daily tropical rains do not improve matters. The Japs are giving us a pretty rotten spin at present'.[65] The work party that returned to 40-kilo suffered greatly. When they were eventually reunited with the main Mobile Force, they would have already buried eight of their number, and their shipmates would be 'horrified' at their physical transformation; Chattaway believed they resembled 'a company of ghosts.'[66] The Japanese declared 'no work no food' and the death rate increased. In June 1943 three more *Perth* sailors succumbed to ill treatment and disease. AB Eric William Thompson survived the Med and the sinking of his cruiser but not the railway. He died on 8 June at 60-kilo. The official cause of death was written as malaria.

—

Perth's second Chaplain, Keith Mathieson, found himself at 40-kilo camp. He was commonly addressed as 'Bish' or 'Padre' and spent his days trying to comfort all. These were dark days, when he struggled to maintain his own faith, but he knew his religious beliefs were the essence of his being and important to those around him, in what surely must be their greatest time of need. Mathieson organised discussion and Bible study groups, tended the sick, conducted services and much more often than he wished, performed burials.

He acquired a notebook in Java to write the names of men he had watched die on rafts and the Javanese shore. Mathieson never expected that the notebook would soon overflow with names. On 23 June 1943 he carefully wrote: 'Kitcher D 20 years 40-kilo Dysentery'.[67] Acting AB David Kitcher had actually turned 21 two weeks previously. Born in the small town of Bungendore, New South Wales, just over the border from the national capital, the former stores clerk had enlisted in May 1941. Mathieson noted in tidy handwriting: 'A boy who would have gone a very long way, a thorough gentleman, most courteous and a good worker'. AB Eric William Thompson died 8 June of malaria at 60-kilo. Mathieson's entry on 29 June concerned the death of 39-year-old Shipwright III Ernest Frederick King. With his cruiser under heavy fire, King had been carrying a 4-inch shell when a blast blew him over the side. It would now be left to others to tell that story, and his chaplain wrote: 'very well thought of not only in ship's company but throughout the camp. Heart failure after septic throat'.

The 32-year-old AB John Hannaford from Port Adelaide, South Australia, died of 'Fever and Diarrhoea' at 40-kilo on 8 July. Ten days later at 55-kilo camp, the rangy, six-foot Sydneysider Assistant Cook Mervyn John Scott died from 'Dysentery'. According to Mathieson, Scott was a 'Nice lad'. On 30 July 1943 Melbourne-born 23-year-old Stoker John Arthur McDonald Woodhead died at 80-kilo of dysentery. Chief Stoker George Joseph Giles died from 'Debility and Dysentery' at 30-kilo camp, on 27 July, aged 41. As the news passed by word of mouth along the line, it jolted many within the *Perth* ranks. Giles had been an institution and thought to be tough as nails. His service record, which had commenced in February 1922, was crowded with the names of most of the ships ever to wear HMAS in front of their names. The men paused and considered: if the railway could kill Giles how would it not kill them?

—

One day AB 'Tich' Hill ventured to the stream that meandered close to his camp. It was a rare respite and he wanted to get away. He did not wish to be without his *Perth* mates, but a part of him desperately needed to be alone. He loved water and his pre-war free time had been spent fishing for garfish off the Busselton wharf. The Western Australian quietly studied the stream and was amazed to find garfish. He struggled to catch them with a fishing line made from string and a hook honed out of wire, but all he had for bait was rice, and the fish thought rice as unpalatable as he did. With his efforts frustrated, his attention was drawn to his own reflection and he shuddered at what he saw. His hair was unkempt, face unshaven and he was suffering the advanced stages of beri-beri. The man who looked back at him was grotesque. The bottom part of his body was bloated, while from the waist up he was skeletal. Hill wondered if the level of water in his body would continue to rise until he drowned in his own body fluid, something he had seen happen to others. Becoming angry he shouted aloud: 'Some day I'm going to catch a gardie, a Busselton gardie. Some day this crazy nightmare will be over and I'll be free. Somehow I'm going to stay alive till that day'[68].

When the main Mobile Force arrived at 80-kilo they were horrified to find a group of 200 sick POWs who had been brought from the Thai side and left to die, 'they were rotten with ulcers, malaria, and every other disease and the stench from their hut made one vomit'.[69] With their scant supplies they tried to help these men, but such visitations needed to be surreptitious because the Japanese wanted no attention given to the hapless POWs: 'all we could do was bury them',[70] wrote Frank Chattaway. The reality of the situation undercut the emotional and physical strength of the newly arrived prisoners, and some of their own died. No pause was given and the Mobile Force continued to slave away at 90-kilo then 100-kilo and then 105-kilo.

—

In the early period, the men were permitted one rest day in every ten, but after April 1943, rest days disappeared. Night work commenced, the sunset pallet of colour replaced by large oil-filled bamboo torches flooding the cuttings with light. They would hope a stop was called before midnight, and even then they needed to negotiate their way back to camp. Frank Chattaway extended one foot gingerly to the next railway sleeper and then the next. Some rubble came loose and he listened as it tumbled down the embankment to the river. He could not afford to lose his balance, to fall down the embankment meant certain death – if not immediately, later. Even if his mates realised he was missing, guards wouldn't permit a rescue. Deciding caution was the better part of survival Frank sank to his knees, and inched his way back to camp on all fours.

Japanese propaganda would have the world believe POWs were nurtured, fed well, provided with high-quality medical care and wages. They could purchase additional food and goods from well-stocked canteens. The reality was very different. POWs did what they could to trade for anything additional. Bandsman George Vanselow 'acquired' additional typing paper from his administrative position as a two-finger typist. This he traded to smokers who needed cigarette paper. Ord Seam David Manning decided if he was ever to become a POW again he would ensure he went, 'into camp with the complete works of Shakespeare – not because I am a lover of his work, but I would have a supply of cigarette paper that would keep me wealthy for years'.[71] Stoker II Fred Mason began to make dangerous trips outside the camps to trade goods with the Burmese on behalf of individuals not so willing to journey beyond the boundaries; his cut was 50 per cent of the proceeds. Fred wasn't sure if he was brave or stupid, only he was desperate to do 'anything for a bit of extra tucker'.[72] One trip out he took a gun belonging to a Dutch POW for trade. Mason told the owner he had no intention of returning with the weapon if there was no trade. He could have sold the gun for a tidy sum if it had come with a couple of bullets, but it didn't, so Fred lobbed the gun into the jungle so as not to be caught returning with it. Had it come with bullets, Mason figured he would have used it on a guard or two, bugger the consequences!

Perth crew struggled to survive again, over and over, day after day, each in their own way striving to find deep within themselves the determination, the belief that while you could not remove yourself from this hideous existence, you would not succumb to it. For some, their faith, be it religious or an unwavering faith that they would get back home, was enough. Charlie Wray was determined he would 'get home to see my mother', a sentiment shared by many. The three Turnbull brothers felt the same. Their mother, Florence, in Brisbane would be beside herself with worry. For some it was the ability to remove oneself mentally and emotionally from the dreadfulness, to withdraw within. AB 'Tich' Hill recalled trying to 'insulate myself against the ugliness ... To withdraw into a cocoon of indifference', but there were times when this was 'very difficult'.[73]

POWs were treated like beasts and acted like beasts. To watch men fight over a few grains of rice diminished something inside. AB Arthur Bancroft kept telling himself no matter what it took, he had 'no intention of dying' for the Japanese. It helped to try to focus on further than what you were doing, on further than what was happening to you, further than the railway. For any split second possible, it was good to marvel at the scenery, at the fabric of the jungle, some would call that 'day dreaming', others would call it 'surviving'.

LT Col. 'Weary' Dunlop described men like PO Ray Parkin as having 'both tough bodies and tough minds, and if in addition there was a vivid world of the intellect and the spirit, as in his case, the survival bit was strong.' Referring to PO 'Horrie' Abbott, Dunlop wrote: 'he was of immensely strong decent stuff. His buoyant, salty good-humoured morale was never crushed'.[74] Parkin took any opportunity to sketch animals, birds, vegetation. Paper and pencil were scarce, but there was always a stick and dirt. AB Frank Chattaway had been a teacher before war intervened. He enjoyed the challenge of maths and grammar, so he combined them in a mental game. Finding another POW interested in the test, one person would come up with a list of words and numbers. The other would then have to remember the numbers, words, and the sequence in which they were given. A harder test was remembering number and word combinations of previous days. Frank was determined to continue to challenge himself mentally; there was no sense in allowing your mind as well as your body to be lost in the morass.

Chattaway had teamed up with *Perth* SBA Freddie Wright, a Scottish-born Sick Berth Attendant who had studied dentistry prior to the war. As they slaved away, in whispers, they hatched a plan not to return to their previous occupations, they would set up a two-man bookie business and make themselves a tidy bundle. One needed to make plans for the future, any plans.

—

It worked wonders to receive any boost to morale. Letters were truly manna from heaven. 'Buzzer' Bee had the surprise of his life when he received several. Frank Chattaway received five at once. The letters were twelve to eighteen months old but that didn't matter. Unfortunately, as wonderful as it was to receive mail, it reminded POWs what they were missing. CPO John Rockey received a letter from wife Dolphine:

> Baby is coming on beautifully, eight months on the 22nd July darling and weighs 23 lbs. You wouldn't know him. He said 'dad' first beloved and says 'dee dee' for 'gee gee'. He is trying his utmost to talk dear, everybody loves him.[75]

For Ord Seam 'Digby' Gray the words were not as joyous, his father had died. Former West Australian schoolmates AB Fred Skeels and Ord Seam Wally Johnston returned to camp to discover that shipmates had remembered it was their twenty-first birthday and the cooks had conjured up a treat out of very little. The men were presented with a cake made from rice and compressed sugar. The top, decorated in rice flour, was adorned with two stick figures with halos, one labelled 'Wally', one labelled 'Fred' and in bold letters 'Happy 21st Birthday.' On this birthday cake, stick figures were most appropriate.

In late 1943 a small group of POWs began to stage shows at Camp Tamarkan and they proved very popular. The only problem, as far as Ord Seam 'Digby' Gray was concerned, was that 'the prime seats down front went to the Japs'. One of the performers was AB Les Luff. Les had been another member of *Perth*'s commissioning crew. In 1939, even Australians referred to the 'Mother Country, England' and Les Luff was more likely than any to use this saying, because he was born in England's Harrow Weald. He was a fairly quiet man, so his willingness to be involved in vaudeville came as a surprise to some of his shipmates, but then Tamarkan, Thailand, was a world away from Harrow Weald.

—

Even the strongest resolve failed when the body was assailed by the ravages of malnutrition and disease. As the physical shells of *Perth* survivors crumbled, they were taken to hospitals. *Perth* survivors tried hard not to fall behind, not to allow sickness to disable them so that they would be separated from their mates. They knew all too well that being sent to a hospital camp meant that they would die sooner. 'Hospital' was an inappropriate term on the railway. Hospital tents were defined by their wretchedness, by their stench, by the ubiquitous bugs, lice and flies, by their sense of doom and by their patients so emaciated it was a miracle to others they were still alive.

The health of AB 'Tich' Hill deteriorated dramatically and he 'lost all track of time'. He was separated from the Mobile Force and taken to the notorious 55-kilo hospital for the chronically sick, placed in a 'bed', 'past which the dead were carried each day'.[76] POW Doctor Rowley Richards wrote: 'The 55-kilo camp hospital was a soul-destroying sight ... It's hard to convey just how grim a prisoner of war hospital can be'.[77] It was here that Hill was told his brother, Johnny, had died in Singapore on 11 March 1943. Johnny's last words had been: 'say goodbye to the folks at home for me'. 'Tich' contracted cholera and was moved to the cholera camp. Cholera, sudden and dreadful, brought dizziness, nausea, painful convulsions and violent vomiting and diarrhoea followed by delirium, and men were reduced to bones and death. The disease could attack the fittest POWs in the morning and they could be dead by evening. A cholera victim and his effects were cremated quickly, and his ashes placed in a bottle for burial.

'Tich' Hill was lapsing in and out of consciousness, but when he came too he would be gently cared for by a *Perth* survivor he had not previously met. This man, 'Johnno', was good looking and athletic with dark, wavy hair and appeared in good health. Volunteering to look after those in a cholera hut took courage. 'Tich' asked: 'What sort of galah are you ... sticking your neck out by volunteering to look after cholera patients'.[78] His carer shrugged: 'What the hell? The bugs are everywhere. It's impossible to dodge them. I might just as well be here as anywhere else'.[79] The sailor grinned and gave Hill some boiled water. 'Tich' lapsed again into unconsciousness. Next time he came too Johnno wasn't there, he had succumbed to the disease. Leading Signalman Jack 'Johnno' Jackson, born in Melbourne during World War I, had enlisted in the RAN the week his nation entered World War II. He had married Jean in 1941, was sunk off Java in 1942 and died a long way from home in 1943.

More *Perth* men died and, as the news filtered down or up the railway, it was increasingly difficult to find reasons why some were still here and others not. Doctor Rowley Richards believed: 'Australians had mates to care for them when they were ill or simply when they were down'. In Thailand Chief Telegraphist Harry Knight slipped out into the night and negotiated the 3 miles (5 kilometres) to Hintock Road hospital camp to visit Ord Seam 'Otto' Lund. He found the 20 year old depressed and very ill. Lund told the Chief he was going to die and wanted him to have his duck eggs, a very precious commodity. Knight refused and spent time telling Lund how helpful he was to other POWs and that he should eat the eggs and get out of the hospital. '"Otto" seemed to buck up somewhat ... A day or two later Otto died'.[80]

PO Ray Parkin was saddened by the news. He liked Lund. Parkin recalled Lund had made him smile when they talked earnestly: 'true to youth: he could scoff and disbelieve the things he had not experienced, yet he hoped that they were in his future'.[81] Now there would be no future for 'Otto'. At the end the lad must have wondered what it was all about, Parkin decided: 'The thirteen-stone (83-kilogram) boy, who galloped the rugby line, died a shrunken skeleton of five stone (32 kilograms)'.[82]

AB Ernie Toovey was admitted to hospital after continual bouts of malaria, dengue fever and dysentery. He began to think he would 'give up', it seemed so much easier 'not wanting to live'. His mate Ord Seam 'Chilla' Goodchap materialised beside his bed and, 'gave me a serve ...

calling me a 'Catholic Bludger etc'. Toovey recovered and returned to the line, 'We live and learn first we have to keep living'.[83]

AB 'Elmo' Gee visited AB 'Seamus' O'Brien in hospital. O'Brien was another true navy character, who delighted other POWs by singing sea shanties. He knew them all, Gee figured, every shanty ever written. Seamus told Elmo he was going to die that night. O'Brien was a Catholic so Gee offered to find someone who could take his confession. O'Brien said he preferred Elmo stay and talk about 'all the happy times we had in the Navy, and the fun we had in Jamaica, and tonight I will die peacefully'.[84] Seamus died, and after burying him Elmo cried his eyes out: 'I will never forget that very cheerful, wonderful man'.[85] Gee had been raised in a strict Salvation Army household but his religious beliefs crumbled with the lives of shipmates. He would ask: 'God where are you now? How can I believe in you when you let this horror go on, day after day?'

They tried to persuade AB Geoffrey George Willis to live, but his diseased body gave up on 15 September. Ord Seam David Manning did everything he could to encourage his mate AB Bob Trimble to eat. Trimble was a mere shadow of the robust nineteen year old who enlisted. Manning knew the importance of the advice offered by POW Doctor Lt Col Coates, 'your ticket home is in the bottom of your dixie', (utensil used for rations) and urged Trimble to eat more rice. Trimble couldn't and died.[86]

*'A shining example of a good fellow, only a kid but
remarkable in spirit and everything else.'*

Chaplain Keith Mathieson

Families struggled with the lack of information; Red Cross officials
received little assistance from the Japanese. A broadcast made by
captured war correspondent Rohan Rivett in Java made headlines in
the Australian press. Rivett announced there were: '300 odd survivors
from the Australian cruiser *Perth*'.[1] In the early press report only the
names of Ord Seam David Manning and Chaplain Keith Mathieson were
mentioned. In a later report 30 *Perth* survivors were named, including
PO Bill Hogman and Yeoman Jack Willis. The Department of Navy
cautioned against too much credence being given to this 'unconfirmed
report'.

With the war going badly, Australians were under siege and the
general mood did little to discourage fearing the worst. The parents
of Flying Officer 'Jock' McDonough agreed to a memorial service in
Adelaide for their 'dearly departed son' to give them 'closure'. It didn't
feel right and didn't give them 'closure'. Like all *Perth* families they
wondered if not knowing was worse than knowing? The next official
letter did nothing to alleviate the foreboding:

I have been directed by the Minister to advise you that no definite information is at present available in regard to the whereabouts or circumstances of your son ... and to convey to you the sincere sympathy of the Minister and the Naval Board in your natural anxiety in the absence of news concerning him.

The power of that single page was great, for some it meant hope, for others it meant misery. Relatives struggled with ceremonies like the one conducted at Perth Town Hall on 5 August 1942. The West Australian Lieut-Governor, Sir James Mitchell, in the presence of the Premier, Mr Willcock, unveiled a plaque in honour of 'HMAS *Perth* and its ship's company', with the wording, 'in memory of their valorous deeds'. Newspaper prose continued:

There are no waters deep enough to take
Your memory from us; in our very heart
You live enshrined, and soon the dawn shall break
From night's dark arms, keen edged with victory's dart.
We mourn your loss and yet how glorious they
Who died as heroes die with face to foe,
Whose valour stirs a nation's soul today,
And whose bereaved are proud amidst their woe!
Brave ship that sailed the blue Tyrrhenian Sea,
Aegean Isles, and fought on Eastern shore,
Where'er our flag flies that has set men free,
Your name shall ring with praise for evermore.[2]

One wished to deny reality, but each well-intended verse or memorial asserted a realness the heart and mind were not ready to accept. It seemed to presume the crew was no more, gone forever like the crew of *Sydney*.

Else Willis received letters from all over Australia when her husband Jack was mentioned in the Rivett broadcast. Else had joined the Australian Women's Army Service as a signals operator, believing it was the closest she could get to information. After more than a year, heavily censored letter cards began to filter through. To the Sydney McGovern home arrived the words: 'Dear Mum and Dad. Am in the best of health. Hope you are well. Don't worry. Pray and Trust in God. Love to you all Frank'. Dorothea Chaffey was also delighted to receive from husband 'Ben':

> My Darling, I am a Japanese Prisoner of War and still in one piece and in good health. Hope you are O.K. so keep your chin up and keep smiling. I will always be right side up so don't worry.[3]

From Moulmein in May 1944 came a card from AB 'Robbie' Roberts: 'My health is good, I am working for pay'. Another from Roberts was intended to give hope to other *Perth* families: 'I am with friends, Syd Matson, J.Jewell and M.Kersting'. From George Vanselow, who spent much of the first year hospitalised, came the note: 'My health is excellent … the Japanese treat us well'. Another: 'We prisoners are permitted to write home by the generous government of Nippon … My health is excellent. My daily work is easy'.

Corporal Ron Bradshaw, Flying Officer McDonough and Leading Aircraftsman Ernie Toe, were the only survivors of the group of six RAAF men on *Perth*. Early in captivity Bradshaw sent a cryptic card: 'Dear Mum, I am quite well and fit, regards to all, Love to Sue, Mat and Rita'. Violet Bradshaw puzzled over the words; there were no relatives by those names. She ran the names together and it sounded like the word Sumatra, so Violet referred the intelligence to the Department of Navy. It wasn't the only subterfuge Ron Bradshaw was involved in. He convinced the Japanese he could fix an intermittent fault with their radio. The fault took just five minutes to repair, but the radio was being 'fixed' for three days.

Messages from Australian families were broadcast by the Department of Information and Broadcasting via 'All India Radio', but they were unaware *Perth* survivors did not have access to radio. Relatives were oblivious that parcels of clothing, food, books and gifts never made it past the Japanese, that such personal material was enjoyed only by the enemy. It was fortunate they were also ignorant of the conditions under which their men really slaved – and died. For now their ignorance was a comfort and they continued to write letters and imagine happy endings.

For families like the Ryans, this was but a short reprieve from devastating news. Philip and Rose Ryan were proud of their sons. Their boys, 21 months apart in age, had grown up good mates. Richard emulated the older Charles, so it came as no surprise when he followed him into the RAN as an Ordinary Seaman. The Sydney brothers asked to serve together and were pleased when sent on the grand adventure to the United Kingdom to collect the new cruiser. They had supported each other through the traumatic war in the Mediterranean and the Battle of the Java Sea. Their father Philip had died in 1941, and in 1945 their mother Rose would be officially informed that son Charles had died with his ship in Sunda Strait in 1942.

Like the brother he emulated, Dick Ryan had been struck by enemy fire on the night of 28 February, but unlike Charles he made it into the water and was dragged into a lifeboat. His party had managed to beach their boat on Java and, breaking into small groups, they had ventured into the hinterland hoping to find Javanese assistance. With wounds to his back and right leg, Ryan made easy prey and had been set upon and knifed by the unfriendly locals. Richard Ryan believed himself fortunate to escape, then to survive the terrible Serang imprisonment, and recover from his many wounds sufficiently so he could travel to Thailand with shipmates. But, under the atrocious conditions of the railway, his once robust body struggled to overcome all it had suffered. Mentally too it was a battle; there had been no time to grieve and he badly missed his best mate and brother. His body and mind succumbed on 7 October 1943, the cruellest month on the railway. It was fortunate that Rose Ryan never learnt of Richard's suffering. Nonetheless, her life was shattered.

—

In the 55-kilo hospital Electrical Artificer III Arthur Kieswetter moved from one POW to another, gently mopping foreheads. He would linger and try to persuade each to sip the boiled water he held to their lips as their bodies convulsed. If the POW was conscious the ERA would make conversation, egg them on, try to convince them to keep living. There seemed so many in the hospital, none the big strapping lads they once were.

Kieswetter's burnt back had healed reasonably well. It hurt like hell, he had known it would from the moment he first felt the heat and blood as he was blown off his ship. That seemed a lifetime ago. He was the oldest man in *Perth* with the original service number of 5460, so subsequently copped the nickname 'Grandad' from some of the cocky youngsters onboard. Maybe he had been foolish to re-enter the navy in 1940, but there was a war on and the RAN was so critically short of experienced enlisted men. He had struggled with the changes, with the electrical gear in this modern cruiser, after all, his first ship had been the ancient cruiser *Encounter* when Australia was in the last war. He had been sent to England to bring out the flagship *Australia* in 1918. Beautiful ship that, a 22,000-ton Indefatigable class battlecruiser. It had cost a bundle to build, was commissioned in December 1921 and then scuttled off Sydney Heads in April 1924, victim of the naval reduction policy of the day. Sailors who served in *Australia* mourned that day, such a waste. Kieswetter kept trying to prove himself year after year and this came with the territory of being of German ancestry. Perhaps he should change his name but he could do nothing about the classic Aryan colouring.

The *Perth* ERA gently goaded another POW to drink the tepid water, just a kid, and here he was facing his fiftieth birthday. He moved to another limp body and realised the POW was dead. Men could not survive on 'will to live' alone, bodies needed adequate sustenance and medicine as well. Physically starved and with their minds in turmoil, death seemed inevitable, and those 'who thought about it, usually found it'.[4] Too many dead, too many of his young shipmates brought to his care died.

Ord Tel Pete Nelson had been one of the fittest and happiest in the ship's company, but his body could not withstand the advanced stages of beri-beri, and it surrendered on 19 July 1943. Signalman Alfred

Angus Davies died of dysentery on 5 August. He was from Launceston, Tasmania, and was 21. AB Jesse Leonard Garrett, born in London the last year of the nineteenth century was another who died of dysentery, on 17 August 'after a brave struggle.'[5]

The list went on and on. Dysentery caused the death of AB William Joseph Lowis also. From Melbourne he had enlisted in December 1940 and just turned 20 when he died on 26 August. AB Henry Charles Partridge remained 'cheerful' to the end, when he died on 29 August of pellagra and chronic diarrhoea at 55-kilo. Partridge left a wife, Ruth, and baby back in Sydney. AB Lionel 'Doc' Neal was still only 20 when he succumbed to the wretched malaria on 10 September 1943, here at 55-kilo hospital. Neal was one of four *Perth* sailors who had hung the sign 'Capew Court', an anagram of their suburbs, outside their Bicycle Camp cubicle. Beside Neal's name Chaplain Keith Mathieson wrote: 'extremely popular'. Another Victorian, Ord Seam John Cameron Hodge, was 21 when he died eight days before Neal. Leading Seaman Frank Nash was another who had travelled to the UK in *Autolycus*. He had been subjected to 257 air raids in the Med and the Battles of the Java Sea and Sunda Strait. He died on 19 September 1943 at 55-kilo of 'Nutritional Oedema, Malaria and Diarrhoea.' 'The Bish' wrote in his book beside Nash's name, 'friendly lad and well liked'.

Kieswetter was upset when PO Geoff Balshaw died. Balshaw had been part of *Perth* from day one, on loan from the RN to be in charge of the ASDIC until an Australian could qualify. Balshaw had started his RN navy career as a Boy Seaman but decided he loved *Perth* and transferred to the RAN so he could remain onboard. Balshaw had not figured on becoming a prisoner of war, and after successive attacks of bacillary dysentery died on 27 August at 55-kilo.

Kieswetter wondered if there could be anywhere on this earth as bad as 55-kilo hospital. All around him dysentery patients passed slime and blood 30 or 40 times a day, dying from the inside out. Men with ulcerated legs screamed as the ulcers were gouged. As the physical self was assailed by the ravages of malnutrition, diet deficiencies undermined the ability of men to ward off infection; small cuts and bumps, even mosquito bites, rapidly turned into tropical ulcers. In a matter of days these could become a hole in the leg the depth and size of a saucer; a moist, yellow, stinking sore, which would continue to expand and destroy flesh until it was the size of a dinner plate, eating tendons and exposing bone. It was a hideous business digging away the dead flesh, often with no anesthetic to dull the pain, just 'holders', four other POWs leaning on the victim. If this 'treatment' did not 'cure' the patient, the leg was amputated with a carpenter's saw that the camp doctors had 'borrowed' from the Japanese.

The doctors told AB Ernie Toovey his leg needed to be removed. He was also suffering from dengue fever. The pain and suffering he could endure, but 'the futility of it all' was getting him down. The doctors needed to make rapid decisions. AB Bob McCarrey lost a couple of toes but figured he was fortunate. The doctor told Toovey he could 'go home with one leg' or be left in a grave 'with two'.[6] He swore and told them they were not taking his leg because he was going to play cricket for Queensland and for that he needed two legs.

It was not that Toovey didn't respect the doctors – they were heroes who truly faced horror every day. Doctors like Rowley Richards, 'Weary' Dunlop, Syd Krantz, Norman Eadie and Albert Coates. So too the medical orderlies, like *Perth*'s own SBAs Cunningham, Mitchell and Noble, who risked their lives daily to treat the hundreds of gravely ill men as best they could with a few improvised implements and fewer medical supplies. Dr Albert Coates suffered badly from amoebic dysentery and scrub typhus himself, and his weight dropped from 168 pounds (76 kilograms) to 98 pounds (44 kilograms). When he was too ill and weak to stand, orderlies carried him on a stretcher so he could continue to treat patients. However, Toovey still didn't want the camp doctors to take his leg.

Perth Stoker PO John 'Macca' McQuade was a Williams Force Orderly Sergeant. The job was a difficult one that involved deciding which men were fit enough to join work parties of four, six, twelve or twenty. Trying to protect sick men, McQuade was beaten regularly:

Their favourite trick with me was bashing me on the kneecaps.
Once I was bashed until I sank to the ground bleeding.
I couldn't walk for three days.[7]

In March 1944 Lt Col Williams appointed McQuade Regimental Sergeant Major of the battalion. Williams believed special qualities were needed to be a POW camp RSM, and: 'I felt he had the required ability to handle men under difficult conditions'.[8] The decision to appoint an Australian Petty Officer RSM was not well received. With assumed superiority the British looked down on officers and non-commissioned officers of other nationalities, and here was an Australian sailor appointed RSM of nearly 900 primarily army personnel. There was mixed support from Australians too. The force included two Australian Army Warrant Officers. Williams stuck by his conviction that McQuade:

> ... was a natural leader of men. His tact and sympathy in dealing with sick and tired men perfect and upon those who attempted to question or evade his authority he exercised the full power of his strong personality.[9]

By exercising the 'full power of his strong personality' and occasionally strength of a more physical kind, the *Perth* PO prevailed over those unhappy with the appointment.

McQuade's status rose following one particular incident, the story of which was passed in very hushed tones down the railway. Someone had built a radio out of scrap and ingeniously hidden in it the bamboo leg of an amputee. The Japanese suspected that there was a radio in camp and sprung frenzied searches. Very early one morning an inebriated guard appeared and after a lot of screaming and bashing seemed close to discovering the hiding place. McQuade decided there was no choice but 'to skittle' the guard:

> The big problem was how to dispose of his body. The
> ramifications of being caught with a dead Jap guard in our

midst didn't bear thinking about. We put him in the one place we knew he would never be found, down the camp latrine.[10]

The Japanese searched extensively for their missing comrade but they didn't look in the camp latrine.

—

Japanese high command decided that the railway would be completed by October 1943. Engineers and guards were utterly ruthless in ensuring this happened. Sick and injured POWs were pulled from beds and made to work. They changed camps constantly and this in itself was exhausting. The Mobile Force moved to 95-kilo, then, after a meal stop at 105-kilo, to 108-kilo. They were joined by remnants of Ramsay, Black and Green Forces and told they would lay the railway to 150-kilo, where they would meet POWs approaching from Thailand. They were to work 24 hours on and 24 hours off, commonly 10 kilometres from their camp, but this was extended to 36- to 48-hour stints. The longest stint worked by *Perth* men was 72 hours out of camp. Meals arrived and they would stop briefly to eat a handful of cold, rain-soaked rice stew. On 17 September they moved to 116-kilo, 'the worst camp yet occupied' by POWs.[11] Cholera-stricken victims were removed and left in the open so the putrid camp could hold the 'working party'. The pace of line-laying was frightening. By 13 October, men died along the track and 'stragglers who fell out were shot'.[12]

POWs dubbed the deepest cutting, 20 kilometres north-west of Nam Tok, 'Hellfire Pass', because of the night colours as they worked by candlelight. From high on the embankment they imagined it resembled 'the jaws of hell'. Working below certainly felt like hell. Japanese guards battered to death 68 POWs in 'Hellfire Pass'.[13]

Finally the railway was finished at about 3 kilometres south of Three Pagoda Pass, at Konkuita, on 17 October 1943. These prisoners of the Japanese had laid about 415 kilometres of track, at a rate of 890 metres a day.[14] The Japanese were celebrating, and AB Fred Skeels observed that 'they even smiled'.[15] The healthiest looking POWs were dressed in nice clothes, and they laid the last rail as a propaganda film crew recorded the momentous occasion, while a Japanese military band played. When the cameras stopped rolling, the Japanese took the clothes back. Two Japanese Commanders, the 9th from Kanchanaburi and the 5th from Thanbyuzayat, were filmed hammering in special spikes. Allied prisoners sniggered when the officers initially missed the spikes. A small staff railcar carrying high-ranking Japanese rolled over the last joints, as prisoners, encouraged by unfilmed, rifle-thrusting guards, cheered and waved. There were some additional rations that day and POWs took small comfort in the knowledge they had done their utmost to sabotage the railway. At any opportunity they drove spikes in at an angle, particularly on bends with steep drops, so the weight of a locomotive might separate the rails. When not closely observed they would tip rubbish rather than solid fill into an embankment. When guards were less vigilant, the occasional balsa log was used as a bridge support rather than a teak one, and Australian POWs specialised in filing a bolt between the nut and head and screwing in the ends. But uppermost in their minds when they looked at this completed railway was just how many of their mates had died building the bloody thing.

The following day they met up with men who had slaved from the Thai side at 153-kilo. For men of the Mobile Force, there was little cause for celebration. Out of the 1500 men, only 500 remained; the others either buried or too ill to work. Of these 500, few were fit enough to work. Lt Col Williams noted in his diary that when his Force had been formed 53 weeks ago they had numbered 884. His force now numbered 296, of whom only 100 were not in hospital.[16] Eventually it would be discovered that 12,399 Allied POWs died, including 2815 Australians.[17]

—

For *Perth* survivors, October 1943 saw the completion of the railway but it was also their worst month – nine shipmates died. The service documents of *Perth* sailors were officially marked 'death by natural causes', but there was nothing 'natural' about starvation and mental and physical abuse. AB Ed Burley from Sydney, although only 21, was a veteran of the *Perth* commissioning crew and the Med, and he died at 105-kilo of dysentery on 1 October. ERA IV John 'Jock' Mathew died on 2 October. AB 'Dick' Ryan died at 55-kilo on 7 October. William John Bevan, an AB small in stature, born in the heart of rugby country, Cardiff, Wales, had lived in Perth and died 8 October after amputation due to tropical ulcers, at 100-kilo, Burma. PO George Phillip Henry Harris, born on the Isle of Wight, England, who had also lived in Perth and been whisked to the cruiser bearing the same name in January 1942, died of dysentery at 55-kilo on 15 October 1943. AB Ronald Arthur Nicholls, a Victorian, died on 17 October from chronic diarrhoea and pellagra at 105-kilo, four days before his twenty-sixth birthday. Stoker Christopher Ryder Anderson, born in Tynemouth, England, was a former truck driver from Kalgoorlie, Western Australia, and had married less than a year before his ship was sunk. Anderson died of amoebic dysentery at 105-kilo on 29 October. In Thailand two of the PO Ray Parkin group died: PO 'Alfie' Coyne on 8 October and Stoker Roy Dundon on 25 October.

So many were dying the Reverend Mathieson was having trouble keeping up. It seemed he had been writing in his book of death with ever-increasing frequency since June. As he wrote beside the names of so many there seemed no reason why some should die and others did not. Men of strong religious faith died, young men as well as older men, city boys, country boys, men fitter than others perished while some of the frailest survived.

After the name of Ord Seam Paul Sebastian Doneley, a nineteen year old who succumbed to beri-beri and malaria on 3 October 1943, Mathieson wrote: 'A shining example of a good fellow, only a kid but remarkable in spirit and everything else'. Mathieson was a Methodist, the 'kid' from Toowoomba, Queensland, was a Roman Catholic, but it didn't matter, not in the jungles of Burma and Thailand. Nor did age, Chief Shipwright John Hickey, although an oldish man, 'did as much work as any man'. Hickey was 43.

'The Bish' marvelled at Alf Brown, an Englishman, who had joined the RAN to play music after serving with the British army during World War I. While gravely ill the Bandsman had remained 'cheerful (and) uncomplaining'.

Stoker Petty Officer John William Bowers from Sydney had enlisted in 1934 when he was nineteen and died at 105-kilo on 13 November aged 28.

Leading Seaman Cyril Benjamin Talbot born in Portsmouth in 1909, had returned there in 1939, tasked to bring Australia's newest cruiser home. It was estimated that 95 per cent of Allied POWs on the railway contracted malaria and Talbot died of it on 20 December. Waiting at home in Geelong were wife Shirley and two children.

AB Athol Gibbs was born on 4 June 1922 in Mordialloc, Victoria. He had left his job as a sheet metal worker to enlist in April 1940. Gibbs never backed away from a fight, which meant he spent time in navy detention in 1940. He had retained the fighting spirit until he died on 6 December, and the man who was his Chaplain wrote of how Gibbs 'very badly wanted to live'.

So many were dying, coffins were no longer available and men were wrapped in rice bags and hastily buried. There seemed no time to grieve, or perhaps there were no tears left to shed. Sometimes there were 'hardly enough fit men available to carry the body'.[18] Death certificates listed numerous diseases as cause of death, but doctors were not permitted to cite malnutrition, lest it reflect poorly on the Japanese. Nor were they allowed to cite suicide. When a *Perth* sailor committed suicide, the resident army padre refused to administer religious rites. *Perth* survivors gathered and gave their shipmate a naval funeral.

Few men attended more burials than AB 'Elmo' Gee. Prior to 1942 music had been a joy for Gee and he delighted in being one of *Perth*'s commissioning buglers. Life was now a struggle. His eyesight was severely damaged by retrobulbar neuritis, leaving him with only eight per cent vision. He made himself the camp's barber, touch and feel sufficient for such a duty; he worked when he could; and he played his bugle, but not in joyful tones now. It was a far distant memory, playing a specially presented bugle on the quarterdeck of a new RAN cruiser on a misty day off Portsmouth as a Princess drifted by in a cloud of perfume. Playing these days was restricted to the haunting melancholy lament 'The Last Post' over POW graves. Gee would play that perhaps 1500 times – one day he played it 33 times. POWs would shudder when they heard Gee's bugle. In the early months they would ask who had died, stand still and remove their hats as bodies 'so pitifully thin that they scarcely altered the surface plane of their wrapping rags'[19] were carried to the cemetery; then they stopped asking, and prayed Gee would never play the bugle specifically for them. Too many good men had died, deaths preventable but for the cruelty of their jailers. Gee believed:

> The ones who died looked like sticks, wide eyed staring heads
> on emaciated limbs. The awful part was that I knew I looked
> just the same.[20]

AB 'Digby' Gray voiced the anger and frustration felt: 'it was a worthless waste of life, and talented, wonderful people'. Parkin spoke for all remaining *Perth* survivors: 'You grieved for these men as if they were brothers'.[21] Those who remained turned their backs on the railway and wondered what other horrors their captors had waiting for them.

—

POWs were classified into three groups, 'the fit', 'the light sick' and the 'heavy sick'. A large hospital camp was built near Nakom Paton, 5 kilometres from Bangkok and it was to here the disabled and 'heavy sick' POWs were sent in April 1944, around 11,000 men, of whom 26 were from *Perth*. The 'fit' prisoners were sent to 105-kilo camp to continue railway maintenance while the remainder were moved to Tamarkan, Thailand, close to the town of Kanchanaburi (shortened to Kanburi by prisoners), 12 kilometres from Bangkok. The trip was gruelling and took six days.

On arrival Allan Gee was met by PO 'Slim' Hedrick whose group arrived earlier. Although Hedrick was 'rotten with dysentery and fever' he put an arm around Gee to support him and with a large smile said: 'I've got your wardrobe here, your urn for boiling water and a bamboo container for washing'.[22] The *Perth* PO had fashioned a new pair of pants for Gee out of a piece of canvas and the best news he kept to last, 'I've got you an egg!'[23] To survive on the railway you needed strength, endurance, luck, but most of all you needed a mate, and the

Perth survivors truly supported each other. When Gee 'pretty much went to pieces', it was Hedrick who 'talked me out of flipping my lid completely'.[24] To Gee: 'Slim was my mate. I owed him my life.'[25] Arthur 'Blood' Bancroft relied on his closest mates, fellow ABs Mervil 'Merv' O'Donoughue, Edmund 'Marcus' Clark and Harry 'Lofty' Nagle to help him, and they were equally dependent on him; if one or two were a bit crook one day the others would work a bit harder. The months and months of hard, unrelenting manual labour and poor diet had well and truly taken their toll on the four West Australians. They had enlisted only because there was a war on, and had chosen the navy to fight at sea. They had joined as fit, strong men with visions of glory and bright futures.

Over the months that followed *Perth* survivors spread throughout Asia. Some were separated from shipmates because of ill health. AB 'Tich' Hill marvelled at his recovery from cholera. As some strength returned he walked on wobbly legs away from the hospital hoping never to return. A POW passed, did a double take and said, 'You bugger, you're dead'. 'No, mate'. 'Tich' replied, 'I always look like this',[26] and 'Tich' could smile he had cheated death.

Flying Officer 'Jock' McDonough volunteered to help Col Albert Coates in the cholera tent. The pilot contracted the disease. His fever raged for days and he was given up for dead, but like 'Tich' Hill, McDonough refused to die. On recovery he marched with a group to a staging camp on the French Indo-China (renamed Cambodia) border.

In Burma Wireman Charlie Wray contracted amoebic dysentery. He woke up 'three months' later to discover, 'all my mates had left'. Hill, Wray, Bandsmen 'Tubby' Grant and Perce Partington, ABs Joe Deegan, Harry Mee and Arthur Bancroft, Signalman 'Buzzer' Bee and PO McQuade found themselves with members of the 70-odd *Perth* group sent to Tamarkan, Thailand, a camp they quickly dubbed 'the land of milk and honey' and 'the Garden of Eden'. The camp and the food were much better. There was a river nearby suitable for bathing. Mango and tamarind trees provided wonderful nourishment, a little further away banana and coconut trees. There were green vegetables and a canteen, which, at a price, supplied fruit, eggs and actual coffee. Books were found and some sacrificed to provide cigarette paper for 'Zigzags,' very rough cigarettes. AB Ernie Toovey wondered if those made from pages of a Bible offered 'Holy Smoke'.[27] The *Perth* survivors commandeered hut No.4 as their own.

For most the Tamarkan stay lasted five months. The improved nourishment enhanced body and spirit, and the Australians conducted a Melbourne Cup on the first Tuesday of November, much to the amusement of non-nationals. Crudely fashioned horses were made out of bamboo and these were dragged between legs like hobbyhorses. A course of 70 yards was swept of debris. The 'jockeys' for this cup had to be of uniform height of 5 foot 9, and preferably with two good legs. Names of the 'nags' were those of previous Melbourne Cup winners. Bookies did a roaring trade, although all bets were not in monetary form. There were even 'gaily-frocked damsels' strolling around the enclosure, until one took fright when a Japanese guard made a shy advance and the 'damsel' rapidly transformed back into a POW. Special police were sworn in lest the crowd became too boisterous, and medicos were on hand to ensure the jockeys survived the 70-yard sprint. As far as anyone can remember, 'The Trump' won from 'Wotan' and 'Phar Lap'.

—

Allied aircraft arrived in the skies above with increasing frequency. For POWs the bombers were both thrilling and terrifying. Clearly it meant Allied resurgence, but it added to their sense of vulnerability. The Japanese deliberately placed POW camps near the railway and bridges. Whilst no POW or hospital signs were permitted, the Japanese believed Allied intelligence was aware the camps held Allied POWs and would be thus disinclined to attack from the air. The POWs hoped Allied intelligence was this well informed. They also realised how important a target the railway they had built was. POWs died and many more were injured by Allied bombing, including Brigadier Varley.

'Tich' Hill was for once relieved to be sent out on a work party so he could quickly locate a rocky outcrop a short distance from camp, which he prayed would 'afford protection from American bombs and cannon fire'.[28] As the air vibrated yet again, POWs ran for cover and waited for the release of the deadly cargo, which they prayed would find the true targets. 'Tich' had no time to reach his rocky outcrop and threw himself into a slit trench with a shipmate. His companion cursed the winged warriors. He shouted aloud how he wished the air force had been around when *Perth* needed assistance. He continued to shout at the heavens as bombs rained down, 'after hanging on for years in these bloody prison camps, it would be just my luck to get knocked off by our own planes ... I'd be the maddest angel in heaven.'[29] 'Tich' and his companion survived this day, and Hill went to visit his rocky outcrop. A bomb had shattered the rocks and a huge felled tree lay where he had planned to take cover. A cold shiver coursed through his body: 'I stood staring for a long moment, then turned and walked unsteadily back to camp'.[30]

Not all were as fortunate. Acting Leading Stoker Ron 'Blue' Grieve from Roma, Queensland, ran for cover during an air raid and was killed by erratic Japanese gunfire. On 13 December AB Ken 'Mo' Ikin a 22-year-old Tasmanian was killed at Tamarkan, by 'friendly fire'. It angered *Perth* sailors close by: 'The plane had #29 on a checkerboard tail design, and he was so low faces could be clearly seen'.[31] Sixteen POWs were killed in the region of Thanbyuzayat Hospital and a further 44 injured. No Japanese were killed or injured during that raid. One unofficial report suggested that approximately 800 Allied POWs were killed by friendly fire in Burma and Thailand. For those who remained, 'the bombing raids made us nervous wrecks'.[32]

—

Christmas 1943 arrived, although it didn't feel much like Christmas as the men continued to try to survive their captors and dug foxholes in hillsides in an attempt to survive their allies. They wondered about the fate of the optimists in their midst who had believed this war would be over by Christmas 1942. A little seasonal joy was felt when mail was distributed. Ord Seam Frank Chattaway was trying to cheer himself up by thinking how much money he had saved on gifts since 1942, when his name was called and he gathered five letters. They were around eighteen months old but that didn't matter and he wrote in his diary:

'my delight can hardly be described'.[33] What mattered was that by the end of 1944, 42 *Perth* ratings lay buried along the track their shipmates called 'The Death Railway'. For those who remained it had been the longest year of their lives.

For AB Harold Wilkinson, from Western Australia, the first day of a new year was also the last and he died of malaria and dysentery at Tamarkan. So too for AB Mervil Francis O'Donoughue, the lanky 6 foot 2 West Australian who had been an integral part of a group of four *Perth* survivors. Arthur Bancroft and fellow ABs Edmund 'Marcus' Clark and Harry 'Lofty' Nagle were shaken and wondered what more they could have done for 'Merv'. On the second day of the new year, Stoker Malcolm Donald Black of Williamstown, Victoria, died of cerebral malaria. AB Hugh George Pohl a 23 year old from Melbourne died of pneumonia at Kanburi, on 15 January. He had been a member of the Batavia 'Capew Court' four; now only David Manning and Fred Mason remained.

POWs continue to shuttle back and forth, one group tasked with fixing damage caused by Allied bombs. The group sent to 105-kilo returned to the Tamarkan–Kanburi area where they cut firewood for the trains, 1 cubic metre a day per man, cut and stacked.

More of their shipmates died. They tried to convince themselves they were by now hardened to death, but they weren't. The truth was one was never prepared to lose a shipmate, and it was a constant reminder of how tenuous their own grasp on life was. At Tamarkan 22-year-old Leading Seaman William Ross Cowdroy, born in Kilcoy, Queensland, died on 2 February, following amputation due to tropical ulcers. AB Christopher Charles O'Neale from the New South Wales country town of Dubbo, died on 21 February of dysentery and bronchial pneumonia at Kanburi. Stoker II Jack Sidney Marshall from Waratah, Tasmania, died from cerebral malaria on 11 March at 105-kilo. AB Norman Walter Proctor, a carpenter from Springwood, New South Wales, died the next day of pellagra and dysentery. *Perth* survivors weren't sure their mates found eternal peace, but at least they had found peace from this place; they 'mourned for our dead mates' and knew 'we would never feel the same again'.[34]

Towards the end of February, the trickle of POWs coming in from the jungle to Tamarkan became a flood of thousands, and the Japanese announced that prisoners would be selected for transit to Japan. Those 'chosen' POWs would leave Thailand for a new life in Japan where 'food would be good, facilities would be better and the work light'. The announcement sounded all too familiar, so POWs expected the food would be scarce, the facilities would be terrible and the work awful. There was really little choice involved, they were lined up and those who looked the most alive were taken. A philosophical approach was needed, *Perth* survivors shrugged their shoulders, they were 'off again on our working tour of the east', besides, what could be worse than the jungle humidity and monsoonal rain? The 'chosen ones', were the 'fittest', even if most were fairly skeletal and quite a few looked pretty unwell. Anyone with a beard, bad scars or damaged legs was eliminated. AB Ernie Toovey was pleased he couldn't be selected. He preferred to stay with what he knew, as bad as it was. Others disagreed, they did not wish to 'rot in the jungle'.[35] For Signalman 'Buzzer' Bee, the decision was easy he preferred to take his chances with mates Ron Bradshaw, Stokers Bert Simons, Norm Toulmin and 'Tiny' Savage and AB 'Chesty' Bond. He twisted his leg inward to hide his scar.

Ord Seam David Manning was almost enjoying life in Kanburi. There were a lot of Dutch and English prisoners, and he liked the varied company and making new friends. A group of Dutch officers surprised him with a twenty-first birthday cake. His work group cut bamboo and he made himself 'camp librarian'. Manning had been given some clerical work in the orderly office when he came upon the list of 'the chosen ones'. Scanning the list he faltered on his own number. The *Perth* Ord Seam erased himself from the list: 'I had already been on three Japanese troop transport ships, and I had no ambition to be in any more'.[36] The party left without him. When Kanburi was deemed an Officers only camp in January 1945 he was moved on. With none of his mates nearby, he attached himself to members of the 2/2nd Pioneers. Unfortunately, the group were supposed to be diesel mechanics: 'I couldn't tell the difference between a petrol engine and a diesel engine', but Manning passed himself off as a diesel mechanic and joined them when they went to work at 450-kilo south of Bangkok.

By March the Japan parties were finalised and the 750 POWs divided into kumis of 150. They were issued boots and additional clothing – clearly G-strings had been deemed inappropriate should POWs be observed by the Japanese public, the decision could have nothing to do with their welfare in the Japanese winter. Indeed it was thought that because there was 'no issue of warm clothing, it seemed that destination Japan was a myth'.[37] Fabric on skin felt alien but comforting, boots would take a little more time to get reacquainted with. When the departure day for the first 450 men of 35, 36 and 37 kumis arrived, there were the 'usual farewells and wisecracks such as "See you in Sydney"',[38] flimsy attempts to disguise the sadness of those who stayed and 'wondered what was ahead'[39] for their mates.

AB Frank Chattaway thought seriously about 'borrowing' another POW's number so he and his best mate SBA Freddie Wright would both leave in the first Japan party. However, it could mean the wrong information being given to Red Cross officials and relatives back home, so Frank sadly bid his farewells to Freddie. Those leaving shared the same sense of trepidation. 'Buzzer' Bee felt 'a strange all-pervading and sombre feeling mixed with optimism'.[40] He wondered if he would ever be reunited with the *Perth* survivors left in Thailand. Yet again the vagaries of luck and fortune would blight some within the Japan parties and favour others.

—

Those who remained spread far and wide. Ten *Perth* survivors were sent on a road-building party near the Malay border and the 'conditions and death rate was far worse than anything experienced in 1943'.[41] Seventy *Perth* sailors were sent with a large party to a camp in southern Thailand. ABs 'Tich' Hill, Ernie Toovey and Les Luff, were part of a large work party sent to Chungkai a short distance away to clear bamboo. Lieut Cdr Ralph Lowe found himself senior officer and quickly appointed Neil 'Stumpy' Biddel in charge of the camp kitchen. Biddel had been one of *Perth*'s Signals Yeomen but he quickly got on with the job: the camp kitchen was re-named 'galley'; rations became 'scran'; prisoners had to line up on port and starboard sides to be served; back up for leftovers became 'gash'; and he didn't concern himself if the 'army bods' didn't understand. It was believed to be a total misconception by other POWs that *Perth* and *Houston* sailors increased in weight, while their non-navy counterparts did not. Some POWs were loaded into steel carriages and sent by train to Ratchaburi, Thailand. Others were sent further. AB Ernie Toovey's group was halted by a bombed-out bridge. Punts took the group over the swollen river and then they undertook a five-day march to an unfinished camp called Phetchburi, 'somewhere in the south-east part of Thailand', to build an airfield and work in a limestone quarry carved into Kaschu Mountain.[42] They were back to using chunkels and shovels. Like those around him, Toovey wondered when it would ever end. If he could slip away at the end of a day, he would summon strength to climb to the top of an earth mound in the failing light and sit looking out beyond the camp boundaries letting his mind wander, back to his native Queensland, back to life as it was before 1942, and: 'For this hour or so I felt I was a free man'.[43] He would also curse, 'Another bloody cricket season missed'. At least he still had both legs and believed it was no longer 'if' he got home but 'when'.

—

The transit plans for the Japan parties were completely confused by the Allied advance. It was April Fool's Day when the largest Japan contingent, made up entirely of Australians and Americans, including ERA Vic Duncan, AB Frank McGovern and Signalman 'Buzzer' Bee, boarded a train at Kanburi for the next leg of their journey. The enclosed box cars and flat tops crowded with POWs rattled and banged along the rails. Those onboard nervously hoped each section of this railway had not been sabotaged or would not be bombed this day.

Next stop Bangkok, but the stop was short and provided little relief from the cramped, sweltering carriages. Their new clothes were already sopping wet and pungent with sweat, and the trip continued, another 550 kilometres, more days and nights, towards Saigon.

They detrained at Phnom Penh and marched through the city. It was surprisingly invigorating, perhaps due to the French-influenced architecture. They next boarded a steamer for a trip down the Mekong River. The steamer only managed around seven knots and the water was a muddy brown, but for *Perth* survivors it felt good to again have a deck beneath the feet. The trip had taken six days by the time they arrived in Saigon. Saigon was bustling and their mouths opened in wonderment as they marched into their next staging camp. Electric lights, waterproof huts, music, tables and chairs. The camp was occupied by British POWs who gaped at these emaciated men. Food was abundant, 'life in Saigon was marvellous' and the prisoners from the railway gained weight rapidly.

The ensconced British military, initially sympathetic, quickly wished the Australians gone. It seemed that they pinched or 'liberated' anything, the British viewed them as 'raw, uncouth, undisciplined, a pack of thieves and brigands'.[44]

The Australians believed they had received the rough end of the POW experience and the Pommies were 'smug, humourless, lazy and unclean'.[45] The 'chosen ones' hoped they too could remain in Saigon until the Allies won the war. Increased Allied submarine activity led to further delays, two abortive convoy attempts and the very familiar shout: 'All men back, one big mistake.' Three hundred POWs were ordered to prepare to leave. Another group split meant their Yank buddies were to stay in French Indo-China. This was unsettling; the *Houston* and *Perth* survivors had been through so much together and staunch friendships had developed. It was the third week of June when they retraced their last journey as far as Phnom Penh, where they climbed aboard the all-too-familiar freight cars, this time bound for Singapore.

Another Japan party was sent directly to Singapore by train. Ord Seam Frank Chattaway was a member of the group and was pleased to be finally leaving the jungle behind. He wondered where his best mate SBA 'Shiner' Webb and other members of the first Japan party were. As the trains journeyed further and further south there were mixed emotions. AB Fred Skeels, a member of the Java 5A Force, noticed space in carriages that had previously offered no room to move. Now only the ghostly images of so many men remained. Skeels made up his mind early in the railway 'he was not going to die'.[46] The West Australian wasn't one who could appreciate the beauty of the jungle; he was just very determined and turned off the horror as best he could. Skeels had missed only five days work through sickness with a bout of dengue fever and felt strangely proud of that. But luck did play a large part of it; being at a particular place at a particular time on 28 February and 1 March: or in the water when another torpedo hit or Japanese gunfire peppered the water. As the train moved away from Burma and Thailand, a lot of good men were not there.

PO Cook Frederick Donald Clark was the last *Perth* man to die. He was 49, a native of Aberdeen, Scotland, a veteran of the last war, someone else loaned from the RN until he had wanted to call Australia home. It was 23 April 1945 when Clark died at Nakom Paton. *Perth* survivors sent to labour on the railway had numbered 272, and 57 ratings were left in graves in Burma and Thailand.

—

On 1 July the Parkin Japan party arrived in Singapore and were marched to the dock. Before them lay their transport for Japan. The *Byoki Maru* looked little more than a rusty hull, barely able to leave Singapore harbour let alone undertake a long journey. Parkin considered the vessel 'virtually a derelict' and wondered which harbour this wreck had been dredged up from. The name was apt, *Byoki* meant 'sick' in Japanese. The ship had no bridge, no hatch covers and the centre portion was a mass of twisted steel.

Their confidence was further depleted by the behaviour of the Japanese. The guards seemed particularly nervous and twitchy and endeavoured to cover this with much screaming, kicking and bashing. Unbeknown to the POWs the war was going badly for their enemy, and US submarines were playing havoc with Japanese shipping. POWs were each instructed to carry lumps of rubber 18 inches (45 centimetres) square and 7 inches (18 centimetres) thick on board. The comics in the group suggested this was to keep the 'boat afloat'. The Japanese insisted they were life preservers, but when one was knocked into the sea it disappeared rapidly and POWs knew this was just another way for the Japanese to get rubber home. Another squalid, fetid hold; perhaps they should have been used to it by now, but they never would.

Chief Telegraphist Harry Knight considered himself lucky to have survived the Burma–Thai railway, particularly given the fact that he had built and used a radio. Only those who absolutely needed to know this did, loose lips would have seen him executed and further reprisals taken. Thinking about it, 'I could well have done without the whole POW experience, particularly the period on the Thailand–Burma railway'.[47] He was still with his mates PO Ray Parkin and PO 'Horrie' Abbott, although they had buried PO 'Alfie' Coyne. Now he was one of this Japan force of 2250, which included the 1000 Australians leaving on the *Byoki Maru* destined undoubtedly for another hell hole.

As usual they languished for days in harbour. Each man was allowed only an 18-inch (45-centimetre) wide space with no room to stretch out, their knees in the back of the man in front. Conditions were akin to the slave ships of past centuries, but of course they were the slaves of this century. Their rations consisted of rice pap with rotten fish and maggots. The hold was alive with lice, which bit like crazy and made sleep impossible. The ship hugged the coast of Borneo, then moved to Manila Bay and there they were left, for two, or was it three days; in the heat, in the filth. A convoy of fourteen ships was formed and they ventured to sea again; at least now the air circulated a little. The many POWs who had dysentery attracted flies, and the Japanese instructed each POW to catch 100 flies. These were counted before the paltry rations were distributed.

In the China Sea the convoy came under attack and the oil tanker immediately behind the *Byoki Maru* exploded. They sat waiting for the thud and explosion, sat there trying to convince themselves they really cared that life was more important than a rapid release from the misery of the hold. Five ships went to the bottom and another three were damaged. The remnants of the convoy continued on and hit a typhoon. Knight mused that it was Friday 13th. Parkin decided it was one of the 'most hair-raising experiences' of his life. The ship rolled so violently the *Perth* Quartermaster was lifted to his feet from a prone position.

It rolled so far that POWs sitting in the hold saw the ocean. The ship creaked until the welds on the girders parted with loud cracks and the transport began to leak. Knight still found it possible to be impressed by seamanship: 'The Japanese captain was a marvellous seaman and did an excellent job of keeping her bow into the wind'. Surprisingly the ship made Formosa and then Okinawa, but more POWs died in the hold. Remaining POWs were instructed to tie iron ballast around the ankles of their dead comrades and tip them over the side, but this stopped when the Japanese became concerned the ship was losing too much ballast. Seventy days after the Singapore departure, the *Byoki Maru* landed its human cargo at the port of Moji.

—

It was 4 July when the Duncan, McGovern, 'Buzzer' Bee party of *Perth* survivors finally alighted from the train at Singapore and they thought of their American mates celebrating back in Saigon. Hopes were high for a return to Selerang Barracks, but the group kept marching until the River Valley Camp. It was close to Keppel Harbour and around 2000 POWs were encamped. In the interim they were to build a dry dock. Barges transported them to Jeep Island where they would live while building the dock. It was an awful place. It never failed to surprise how life could still get worse. The next five weeks were very grim with little food and too much disease, each morning fewer and fewer men well enough to work. Ord Seam Frank Chattaway was beaten severely when he was found picking grass to include with his evening rice.

The *Perth* survivors survived yet again and returned to River Valley Road Camp, where they were told that they really were going to Japan: 'We knew that the (the Allies) were bombing and sinking almost every Japanese ship ... we figured our chances of getting to Japan were pretty darn small' recalled 'Buzzer' Bee.[48] News had made it back that two *Perth* men had not survived another trip to sea. Chief ERA Cedric Bell Mellish was born in Armidale, New South Wales in 1912. A fitter and turner, he had joined the RAN in 1934 as a way out of the Depression, and perished on 24 June 1944 en route to Japan when his transport the *Eiko Maru* was sunk by a Royal Navy submarine. With him was Stoker

Bernard David Bowie Ferguson. Ferguson was from Hobart, a former student of St Virgil's College who had become a motor mechanic before he had enlisted in the RAN at the beginning of 1939. Ferguson and Mellish lost contact with shipmates because they had been admitted to hospital. Ferguson had been severely knifed by the Javanese. There was small consolation in the fact that the two *Perth* men died together.

Staying with another *Perth* man was important, and eventually the story of another two crew members would be told. AB George Bradshaw Morriss and Bandsman Henry Alfred Kelly had lost contact with other *Perth* survivors when they were retained in Changi also for medical attention. The pair could not have been more different, but their experience in *Perth* was indelibly imprinted in their minds and they stuck together.

Morriss was a tall Victorian, who believed he had been toughened by his early childhood. His mother Myrtle had given him the middle name of Bradshaw after his father who had refused to marry her. She chose to accept society's scorn and refused to give her son up for adoption. Myrtle had died of typhoid fever when George was six and he moved in with his grandparents. Morriss loved anything to do with the ocean and competed in long-distance swimming events in the waters off his hometown of Frankston. In 1939 he won the Frankston Standard Cup, a mile race.[49] He needed to leave school as soon as he could and worked as a paperboy and as a house painter until he was old enough to join the navy.[50] This he did on his seventeenth birthday, and by November 1940 he was a member of the ship's company *Perth*. In 1942 after he watched his ship sink beneath the darkened waters of Sunda Strait, the abilities he had honed in the ocean off Frankston helped him survive the long swim to shore.

Henry Kelly was a three badge Bandsman, a career navy man, born in England and a musician before he had enlisted in 1929. He was a Roman Catholic whereas Morriss wrote 'Church of England' on his entry form. Kelly was married with children. In true RAN tradition he had been given the nickname 'Ned'. Like the bushranger, Henry 'Ned' Kelly had experienced a few lucky escapes, none more so than surviving the sinking of his last ship – because he could not swim.

They made a very odd couple, the near 6-foot, Aussie-born 20 year old, and the English-born 38 year old who was more than half a foot shorter. Their differences were less important than the fact that they were both *Perth* survivors, pushed onto a Japanese transport with 2434 non-*Perth* survivors. By April 1944 the two RAN men were part of a workforce in Sandakan on the east coast of Borneo. As the Allies gained the upper hand in the Pacific, Japanese maritime supply lines were disrupted. With the POW-built airfield all but destroyed by Allied air raids, provisions to Borneo ceased and the POWs became expendable. They were ill and starving and in January 1945 the Japanese began marching them to Ranau in the interior of Borneo, 250 kilometres away through mountainous country. Those too ill to march were left to die. Henry Kelly, the musician, died of malaria on 20 January 1945, aged 40, eight days before the first group of 455 POWs marched out of camp.

One quarter of their number died en route. Weakened by torture, overwork and malnutrition, one by one they fell, those who did not die immediately were bayoneted or shot. Only six prisoners, all Australians, managed to slip into the jungle and were cared for by villagers until the end of the war.

At Sandakan a further 536 prisoners were ordered to undertake the same journey in May. Some 291 prisoners too ill to move were left to die. AB George Morriss, the champion swimmer from Frankston, was gravely ill with malaria on the day of the departure. He died before he reached the gates of the POW compound and was hastily buried with two others in a slit trench; he was 22 years of age.[51] Of those in this second 'Sandakan Death March', 140 reached Ranau. They were herded into an air raid shelter and shot.

—

The next group of Allied POWs lined up to board the transports *Kachidoki Maru* and *Rakuyo Maru*. Tenko after tenko, it seemed guards should have become more adept at counting POWs given the months and months of practice. PO John Turnbull and his younger brothers Bill and Ken were still together, always ensuring they were in the same kumi. In Batavia they had vowed it was: 'One for all, all for one'. They marvelled how they had beaten huge odds, all three had beaten the railway, cheated death, and there was no way were they going to be separated now. If they were going to be slave labourers in Japan they would at least do it as brothers.

As they trudged up the gangway each was given the square of crude rubber weighing about 80 pounds (36 kilograms). Most of the British were pushed into the *Kachidoki Maru*. The remaining Brits and the Australians boarded the *Rakuyo Maru,* but the Japanese had miscalculated. After much swearing, shouting and shoving, men in the *Rakuyo Maru* had standing-room only and the Australian line was halted, Kumi 40 would be left behind. *Perth* survivors were turned away, separated from 46 others and this was unsettling. AB Frank 'Mac' McGovern and his mate AB John 'Jerry' Parks managed to stay together. ABs Harry 'Lofty' Nagle and Arthur 'Blood' Bancroft were also determined because they had been separated from their other railway mate AB 'Marcus' Clark at Tamarkan. Bancroft had entrusted his diary to Clark with the instruction that if Clark was off to Japan too he should bury the diary rather than risk detection. AB Fred Skeels could but watch as his mate AB Wally Johnston disappeared onto the *Rakuyo Maru.*

They languished first in Keppel Harbour until 5 September, then again off Manila, and the heat became unbearable. After prolonged begging, a number of fortunate POWs in the *Rakuyo Maru* were permitted to sleep on deck. The convoy of twelve increased to twenty and included six escorts and two oil tankers.

EA Vic Duncan was a PO equivalent but was assigned the rank of Chief PO with Kumi 37 in Thailand. Born in Dundee, Scotland, he had migrated to Australia and joined the RAN at 22 in 1937. Described as 'an intelligent and fair man who quickly won the respect and admiration of the army men under his supervision',[52] onboard *Rakuyo Maru* Duncan assumed greater responsibility. He advised on abandon ship procedure, while others within the 45-man *Perth* group noted anything that would float. Some life jackets were found, and Duncan led officers to the 60 lashed wooden life rafts and instructed on how the rafts should be launched. Duncan also devised a method of lowering the hatch boards into the hold to enable POWs a quick escape. Army POWs were advised by their navy brethren of abandon ship procedure: of the need not to panic; to tie hat to head; to remove footwear; not to abandon ship over an area hit by torpedo so as to avoid being sucked in; not to leave until the transport was actually sinking; and to keep rafts together.

At 0200 on 12 September POWs were jerked from restless sleep by the sound of depth charges and then a destroyer blew up. There was a lull, disquieting in itself but soldiers watched *Perth* sailors calmly playing cards, so perhaps it wasn't as bad as they imagined. At around 0500 'all hell broke loose' when one of the oil tankers violently disintegrated. The other oil tanker was hit and *Perth* sailors knew this was not good, their own transport would now be silhouetted against a flaming tanker. POWs below heard anxious shouts as those above sighted torpedo tracks running towards the *Rakuyo Maru*. There was a sickening thud, the force of the explosion lifted the ship up and metal fragments rained down on prisoners. Another torpedo exploded into the engine room and the transport stopped dead.

As the second torpedo ripped into the hull, torrents of ocean water rushed across the deck and Ord Seam Syd Matsen grabbed at anything and everything as he tumbled along. Matsen's progress was halted when he was jammed against superstructure. Duncan's abandon ship regime was quickly put to the test. POWs struggled up as water cascaded into the hold. The Japanese crew commandeered the lifeboats and left, so POWs cut loose the rafts and prepared to follow them over the side. While *Perth* sailors prepared to jump into the oily ocean they perhaps found some black humour in their predicament.

Frank McGovern and 'Jerry' Parks judged that the ship was on an even keel, perhaps the lumps of rubber were proving useful after all. They made for the galley, it was partly flooded but they collected some burnt rice, a keg of 'mizu' paste and two small kegs of water. They shot up to the bridge to look for navigation gear and grabbed a couple of charts. Next they struggled to release a snagged lifeboat. A Japanese comfort woman appeared. McGovern indicated to her she should get into the lifeboat and the sailors fastened a rope around her waist and lowered her into the boat. By the time the two ABs left the ship, the boat they had struggled so hard to free was overfull with 100 POWs and one comfort woman so they were left to cling to the side. Still the *Rakuyo Maru* did not sink, and some POWs decided to return for further salvage. Parks asked McGovern if he wanted to accompany him back to the transport. 'Mac' declined and 'Jerry' took off; it was the last McGovern saw of his mate.

A lifeboat full of Japanese approached McGovern's party and Frank gestured to the comfort woman, 'they were none too gracious about her, we wanted her out of our boat'. As the reluctant transfer took place, the Japanese spied one of the kegs of water and demanded its transfer also. The second keg was hastily pushed behind legs.

Late in the afternoon Japanese frigates drifted through the human debris, collecting Japanese survivors but bludgeoning any POWs who attempted to board – clearly POWs were to be left to the elements. As the enemy warships prepared to speed away, a Japanese officer shouted 'Goodbye'; *Perth* men made crude gestures in reply. At least the abandoned lifeboats were welcome relief from the waters for more POWs. There were now eleven lifeboats including a leaky one. But even with 40 in each, too many survivors perched precariously on rafts or were in the oily water. It was decided to tie lifeboats together in groups to improve chances of visibility and rescue, but as the swell picked up several decided it was safer to cast off.

PO 'Bull' Milne was at the helm of a boat with other *Perth* blokes, ABs Danny Maher and AB Frank Ritchie. Ritchie had enlisted in 1940 and been posted to small ships. He had spent most of the time incapacitated or vomiting over the side. The RAN declared him, 'Unfit for service in small ships, owing to chronic seasickness' and drafted him to *Perth*, three and a half months before the cruiser sank. The 23 year old, like McGovern, was a Sydneysider, and as the lifeboats bobbed together, Ritchie asked 'Mac' if he would like to join them. McGovern was in the process of moving when two soldiers beat him to it. Clearly there were now enough bodies in the Ritchie lifeboat and McGovern resumed his position while giving Ritchie a wave.

Ritchie's lifeboat moved off with seven others, including one carrying Brigadier Varley, in the direction of the Philippines. In Varley's boat was Acting Leading Signalman Frank Dandridge Johnson, another 23 year old from Sydney. The Duncan–McGovern boat adopted a westerly course towards the China coastline. Their predicament was bleak, but there was a wonderful sense of freedom. For the first time in years they were their own masters. By dusk the eight Varley boats had disappeared beyond the horizon. The three Duncan boats were rationing men to a couple of dog biscuits and two egg cups of water per day per man.

On the morning of the third day, across the quiet stillness of a vast ocean from the direction taken by the Varley boats came the unmistakable sound of naval gun fire. Dr Rowley Richards was in Vic Duncan's boat and immediately noticed fear in men's eyes: 'all of a sudden, we were entering dark times again: more of our mates were presumably dead and we would probably be next'.[53] Three Japanese warships appeared from the direction of the gunfire and steamed towards them, 'a calm fatalism came into play. We simply accepted our time had come'.[54] *Perth* sailors ERA III Vic Duncan, PO Butcher Alf Thomas, Acting PO Tommy Johnston, ABs Frank McGovern, Hugh Campbell and Pat Major and Ord Seam Syd Matsen, shook hands, sat and waited. As a frigate approached the first boat, they could almost see the faces of the Japanese gun crews, again, just like on 28 February 1942. The *Perth* sailors lowered their eyes and waited yet again for the Japanese to open fire.

FOURTEEN

*'Some incidents I can never forget, as they are
indelibly imprinted in my mind.'*

AB Ernie Toovey

No gunfire came, and AB Frank McGovern lifted his eyes to see POWs scrambling up the sides of the frigate. With mixed emotions he joined them, regretting that the wonderful sense of freedom had been all too brief. They transferred to a Japanese tanker, then a whaling mother ship. Frank was going to need two hands to count how many times he should have died. Only eight out of 45 *Perth* sailors appeared to have survived this latest sinking. ERA Vic Duncan was there and PO Alf Thomas, both members of *Perth*'s commissioning crew, also Acting PO Tommy Johnston. AB Hugh Campbell from the fruit-growing town of Stanthorpe, Queensland. Campbell and 22-year-old Victorian, Pat Major, had been in the same 1941 recruit class and they were still together. AB Keith 'Freddie' Mills was slumped near McGovern. Ord Seam Syd Matsen was the youngest, the West Australian was still only 21.

The day after the *Rakuyo Maru* sank, the sun rose on a scene of desolation. POWs who had not been fortunate enough to cling to a boat or raft, floated in a field of debris, clinging to anything that floated. By the end of the day, there were fewer heads bobbing in the swell. Most who had escaped with army water bottles had found that the corks were not impervious to sea water and threw the bottles away in disgust. Stoker II Alec Petherbridge, a 21 year old from Melbourne was a good swimmer so he busied himself gathering ropes, timber and rafts and lashing them together. He handed his life jacket to a shipmate who couldn't swim.[1]

AB Arthur 'Blood' Bancroft and his mate AB 'Lofty' Nagle had abandoned ship together, each wore a life jacket and Bancroft held on tightly to his bottle of water. Over the ensuing hours the effects of fuel oil, sun and dehydration took effect. A thick oil scum enveloped all before it; and rafts became too slippery to hold. Men gagged; their tongues began to swell from lack of fresh water and their lips crusted with salt. PO John Turnbull was seen in the water, he was alone, there was no sign of brothers Bill and Ken; shortly after, he disappeared.[2] The vigorous Stoker II, Alex Petherbridge, overestimated his energy and having secured the safety of others could not save himself. Many could no longer avoid the temptation of the ocean; just a mouthful, just a few mouthfuls, and they became crazy and died. Sharks were active and men vanished.

On the morning of the third day, Bancroft and Nagle realised they needed to get out of the water and away from 'the raving lunatics' who drank the ocean. With three railway mates they collected five rafts and tried to stack them so they could escape the oily mess. The rafts were so slippery they could but tie the rafts together. Nagle swallowed a mouthful of ocean and begged Bancroft for his fresh water. 'Lofty' uncorked the bottle, lifted it to his mouth and the bottle slipped through his oily fingers. He was remorseful and restless. Bancroft tried to settle Nagle on a raft, but for whatever reason 'Lofty' said 'Sorry, Mate' and pushed away. Arthur struggled to accept that there was no more he could do. His group dragged a drowning POW out of the water and began paddling in the direction of China.

By the fourth day, survivors on rafts were in a pitiful situation, black with oil fuel, sunburnt, blistered and lapsing in and out of consciousness. The sun was a curse, but when night came the cold made them wish for the sun. The submarine USS *Pampanito* surfaced with the intention of picking up Japanese survivors for interrogation. The US sailors saw dark men floating on rafts, the sub crew broke out small arms. As they drifted closer their Captain shouted, 'find one who speaks English'. A head on the raft raised and the voice travelled across the water: 'you dumb bastards we all speak English'.[3] The Americans were startled, tough submariners deeply upset by the emaciated, half-dead POWs. More crew scrambled up from quarters, dived overboard and swam to the men in the sea, handling them as gently as they could. Urgent radio messages were transmitted to other submarines. US Submarines *Sealion*, *Barb* and *Queenfish* arrived and found more POWs.

Arthur Bancroft heard diesel engines. Darkness was settling in, but as he peered through eyes now reduced to slits, he thought a submarine was there. It kept stopping and starting so it must be collecting survivors. Balancing precariously on the rafts, he and his four companions waved and shouted. The submarine moved away. 'I don't think they saw us ... our hearts sank very low as we heard the engines fading in the distance'.[4] It was so hard not to give up, a man must have the right to say 'enough is enough', and Bancroft had faced more than enough.

On the fifth night they caught rainwater in hats. Another day and the sea rose, they lashed themselves to the rafts as waves grew larger and larger. They were now surfing huge seas and being thrashed as waves broke over them. They crested another wave and thought they saw another submarine, another wave and it was a submarine, another wave and the sub was pushing through rough seas away from them. The men turned away again in 'much disappointment'.[5] Mid-afternoon and Bancroft's rafts were still surfing, another wave crested and a submarine was there and motoring directly towards them, 'the sea was tossing her about like a cork'.[6] A line was cast and the AB managed to fasten it securely. Bancroft made quite a first impression on his rescuers. Members of the *Queenfish* retrieval party needed to swim to many, because the POWs were too weak to grab lines:

Then all of a sudden, here came Arthur Bancroft ... Here I am reaching down to get him ... he somehow managed to stand up on this pitching raft and saluted me in that British-Australian way ... saying, '*HMAS Perth*, what ship sailor?' When he got on deck, he almost bounded around ... and said 'I knew you bloody Yanks would rescue me'.[7]

Bancroft was amazed at his treatment: 'until we left the submarine nine days later, their kindness, sympathy, and consideration left us with a debt we can never repay'.[8] The sub crew, who looked so large and rugged, eased him below and placed him on a bunk. He protested, he was covered in oil and they were putting him on white sheets. He was ignored, but his body and hair carefully scrubbed. Medical personnel were uncertain of treatment and radioed for instructions, the condition of POWs was critical they suffered from 'acute exhaustion, exposure, shock, starvation, dehydration and skin sores. About 70 per cent had drunk seawater, urine or blood'.[9]

Food and drink of all varieties were offered but few could digest and retain nutrients. The four submarines collected 159 survivors, seven of whom died. Stoker Lloyd 'Darby' Munro was dragged onboard *Barb*; ABs John Houghton and Bob Collins were saved by *Sealion*. Collins also marvelled at his treatment:

> I will never forget the compassion, generosity and selflessness ... especially that tall red-haired character, 'Doc' Williams, and another sailor in the after torpedo room, James E.Carr. Fine chap. He took a religious medal from around his neck and gave it to me. His mother had given it to him before he sailed. He said, 'You need this more than I do'.[10]

Collins forever kept that medallion. When it was realised Collins was a sailor from the cruiser *Perth,* American seamen asked of *Houston* crew and were shocked and saddened by the story told.

The valuable cargo was raced to Saipan in the Carolina Islands and admitted to the US 148th General Hospital. Hospital staff had also never experienced such debilitated bodies and radioed the US mainland for advice. A duty Doctor wrote on Bancroft's medical report, 'Put to bed and made comfortable, pending orders ... slept well'. The Australian

POW had, 'an acute ulcer of the lower left leg, cause undetermined'. Regardless of these maladies it was notated on Bancroft's chart: 'Patient had no complaints'. The *Perth* AB was still coming to grips with his situation, he was safe having miraculously survived and certainly had no complaints. Bancroft even saw humour in the form he was asked to sign. Two of the more amusing questions were did he have 'money and valuables' to deposit and was he 'under the influence of alcoholic beverage or habit forming drugs'. Arthur could scarcely remember having any proper money, or drugs, or alcohol, but figured he could quite possibly kill for a cold Aussie beer. The officious language of documents continued to raise a smile: 'Patient states he was in good health until he was exposed to the salt water for six days, patient states that he in excellent shape now'.[11]

The four survivors arrived in Australia on 18 October, and while further medical treatment was administered the sailors were debriefed by military intelligence officers. The four could offer little information on those who may have died after the *Rakuyo Maru* sank, but they offered too many names of those who did not escape *Perth* or being a prisoner of the Japanese. An attempt was made to keep their Australian arrival subdued, not only for their own benefit but for the thousands and thousands of Australians with POW relatives. News of their experiences was withheld from the public until 17 November 1944, when the Acting Prime Minister, Mr Forde, read a statement in Parliament. He described to a stunned House the conditions under which it was now known Australian POWs were condemned. He explained how 92 Australian and 60 British POWs were rescued by US submarines; how a shipload of POWs was left to die in the water. The following day newspapers were dominated by indignant and aggrieved headlines: 'Japanese left prisoners to drown'.[12] By now Australians knew there was nothing decent or fair in war, but this was more than indecent and unfair; this was inexcusably callous.

The four *Perth* survivors were unaware of how many of their shipmates had perished in the vast ocean. Of the 1318 POWs onboard *Rakuyo Maru,* only 295 survived, of the 717 Australians, 543 died. Of the 46 *Perth* survivors who boarded the *Rakuyo Maru* 34 died,[13] four were now safe in Allied hands and the fate of the remaining eight was again in the hands of the Japanese. Bancroft, Collins, Houghton and Munro realised how fortunate they had been – the odds against surviving the first sinking high, the second, incalculable. It was something they would simply have to accept rather than attempt to rationalise. They had lost so many shipmates during their period of captivity, they had watched others disappear in Asian waters, they could picture more still incarcerated. It was an enormous burden of knowledge.

The *Perth* sailors were sent to hospital and Orwell Convalescence Home in St Kilda, Melbourne. Doctors were challenged in the treatment of bodies that had suffered so much. Bancroft's medical examination revealed, 'malaria, ulcers over much of body, liver tenderness, swollen liver, beri-beri, acute ulcer left lower leg and malnutrition'. RANR Surgeon Cdr Gavin Cameron wrote: 'undernourished but in moderate satisfactory physical condition ... somewhat tremulous ... recommend further mental and physical exams and expeditious dispatch of the rating to his home as first step towards rehabilitation'.[14]

Collins and Houghton requested immediate RAN discharge; Bancroft and Munro agreed to remain in the navy. Granted leave, the men were warned by superiors not to discuss the POW experience and told to avoid contact with *Perth* families. But their first allegiance was to their shipmates and the bond they had shared in life and death. As soon as he appeared in the newspapers, Bancroft received some 300 letters from all over Australia. It was heart-wrenching, families so desperate to learn if their loved one was still alive: 'I felt I owed it to them to tell them'. Bancroft and Munro visited homes and offered information. To some families they could offer hope; to others it was only sadness. Bancroft took his mother with him when he knew the information he needed to give was bad. One such visit was to Gwen Gilby. She quickly conveyed her delight at just receiving a postcard from husband Bill. Bancroft struggled to convince her, the card was many months old because the AB had died in Thailand on 20 September 1943.

Bancroft wasted no time in asking Mirla to marry him, and they exchanged vows on 10 March 1945. The couple were on their honeymoon when the RAN instructed Bancroft to return to be presented to the visiting Duke and Duchess of Gloucester. The AB refused because the invitation did not include his bride, and there was no way he was going to be separated from Mirla again. His superiors reconsidered and both were introduced to royalty. The navy was unsure what duties should be prescribed an ex-POW, so Bancroft was returned to *Cerberus* for general duties. He was handed a shovel and detailed to a work party assigned to ballast the *Cerberus* railway. Bancroft told the PO in charge 'What he could do with his bloody shovel'.[15] As the PO prepared to 'run him in' (place on disciplinary charge) an officer familiar with the AB's history ensured no further action was taken, and Arthur was returned to Orwell Convalescence Home. Deciding that he was as uncomfortable with the RAN as the RAN was with him, Bancroft applied for a discharge. He and Mirla left to live in Western Australia and Arthur returned to his pre-war employment with the Union Bank of Australia, later the Australian and New Zealand Bank (ANZ). After 40 years he retired in 1980 as Assistant State Manager. Arthur and Mirla had three children.[16] In 2008 they moved to a unit from which Arthur could watch AFL games on Subiaco Oval, surrounded by grandchildren and great grandchildren.

Lloyd 'Darby' Munro had started his RAN career as a seventeen-year-old Stoker III in 1941. In four years he had spent only a few months in a warship so decided to discover what life in the navy was really like. He returned to sea duty and eventually retired in 1966 as a PO Mechanician. There was one glitch during the second part of his RAN career, when his ship HMAS *Warrnambool* was sweeping for mines and fouled one on 13 September 1947. It blew up and *Warrnambool* sank. Munro simply said, 'I was only in the water for a little while'.[17]

Armed with information concerning the deaths of *Perth* crew gleaned from the four *Rakuyo Maru* survivors, RAN authorities began the difficult task of advising next of kin. Beatrice Bowers knew as she opened the door of her Sydney home what the news would be. Those who stood on her doorstep wore the sombre expressions of harbingers of death. Standing there in uniform, they clearly would have preferred to be anywhere else, but spoke as kindly as they could. Stoker PO Bill Bowers had helped others as he abandoned the cruiser and worked on the railway. Beatrice had continued to send letters and photos of the children, because Bill was confirmed a POW in September 1943. Now she was told he had died in November 1943. For two years she had been writing loving, supportive letters to a husband who was already dead.

The deaths of so many *Perth* survivors following the sinking of the *Rakuyo Maru* was particularly poignant given how much they had endured. Lloyd Bessell had enlisted with Bill Luck and Max Burk from Tasmania. The navy needed stokers when they had arrived at *Cerberus* at the beginning of May, so Stoker IIs they became. They were fine with that, particularly the Launceston fireman Burk. Bessell was the older man of the threesome so had needed to work just that much harder than the 'boys'. The Launceston fireman never made it off the cruiser; Lloyd Bessell, the father of two, didn't survive the *Rakuyo Maru*; only Stoker II Max Burk would return to Tasmania. On 29 September 1944 Florence Turnbull received three letters notifying her that her sons John, Bill and Ken were believed to have 'perished' when the *Rakuyo Maru* sank. Their medals were posted to her in January 1952; pieces of metal and coloured ribbon did little to fill the bottomless black void of grief.

—

ERA Vic Duncan, PO Alf Thomas, Acting PO Tommy Johnston, ABs Hugh Campbell, Pat Major, 'Freddie' Mills, Frank McGovern and Ord Seam Syd Matsen plucked from the ocean by the Japanese warship... finally arrived at the Port of Moji on 28 September 1944 and transferred to Camp 11D. By 2 October there were 191 POWs in camp. They marched each day to the Shibura Engineering Works. The first snow fell on 11 November bringing with it terrible cold. Their clothes consisted of a hessian suit, cloth cap with their number and any footwear they could find, even the wooden clogs they had worn in the jungle. If they were slow to fall in for daily parade, two guards would take it in turns to beat them. One needed to remain standing as long as possible because to fall meant you were at the mercy of their boots. By March they were being bombed by warriors from their own side.

In December the remaining Japan party POWs loaded onto the *Awa Maru*. News reached them that the previous party had sunk. They were supposed to have been on that transport, part of that group. AB Frank Chattaway was delighted to rejoin mates Freddie Wright and Ernie Toe in Singapore, only to be separated again when the POW line was severed just as he was to move onboard the *Rakuyo Maru.* Now he confided in his diary 'Heard that Shiner's (Wright's) crowd were sunk off Sumatra. God I hope not',[18] and was left to ponder the fickleness of fate. Nonetheless there was no option but to obey those with the guns. It was ten days before what promised to be a bleak Christmas when they descended into the hold of a 'hell ship'.[19] Clearly there was grossly insufficient space for 400 POWs, but this did not deter the Japanese from shoving more bodies down the ladder. The transport began to move and they were pleased. Within a short time the anchor cable rattled and clanged and engines stopped. The POWs were left in the stifling hold in the harbour for ten long days. 'Conditions in hold horrific', scribbled Chattaway. On the eleventh day the transport got underway. They sat uncomfortably jammed in next to each other and wondered if they had not just missed their last Christmas.

The voyage to Japan took fifteen days but, 'we had made it and defied the odds, thank the Lord'.[20] With their tropical tans and light clothing they filed down the gangway into a foreign land covered in snow. One minute they had been gasping for air in the stifling heat of the transport hold, now their breath smoked in front of faces and exposed features turned blue.

They were marched to mining camps in the Fukuoka district of the south island of Kyushu and: 'Ordered to strip off upper clothing and made to partake in physical exercise.' They were hosed with cold salt water, and sprayed with disinfectant. Few of the Australians had seen snow before and this was the coldest Japanese winter in 70 years. Their hair was cut to the scalp and many became ill with respiratory complaints, 'everyone suffering from the cold'.[21] Sick parade men were beaten and told they were not sick. AB 'Chilla' Goodchap was 'punched, kicked, hit with a stick and spat at, sometimes for one and a half hours.'[22] AB Alec 'Spud' Murphy's group were punished by being made to stand at attention so long that, 'the men each had a pillar of snow on their heads'.[23] Many were admitted to hospital with pneumonia. Requests for medical supplies were met with the comment: 'dying is very good ... all Australian soldiers will die very soon.'[24]

In camps no whistling, singing or smiling was allowed, folding arms was interpreted as a demonstration of arrogance. At one camp the Commandant was a man with an expressionless face. The Australians named him 'Rigor Mortis', though not to his face. The schedule of life quickly established itself. POWs rose at 4.30 a.m. They were then required to fling the windows open to the icy air and rub themselves with towels. This Japanese custom was supposed to invigorate the body. A small breakfast was followed by roll call, then a march to docks, mines or factories for a twelve-hour day. If any POW did not show complete subservience they were punished.

The wise cracks from AB Eric 'Chesty' Bond had lightened the mood during the long days of captivity. His attempts at humour did not have the same effect on the Japanese. He had come in for extra attention during his days on the railway, and in Japan was made to stand outside for hours, even when he wore a heavy hat of snow.

Acting Leading Seaman Allan Ross Lloyd Hawke from Mt Barker, South Australia, died of pneumonia on 18 January. According to the Adelaide *Advertiser*, Hawke was the 'eldest son ... formerly employed in the office of the Adelaide Steamship Co., Ltd ... He was a keen swimmer, played football and cricket for Prince Alfred College and the Prospect North Methodist Club, and represented the latter at tennis'.[25] The gregarious AB 'Chesty' Bond 'one of our toughest and the least likely to succumb'[26] died of pneumonia on 22 January 1945. The following month AB Hugh Campbell, one of the eight retrieved from the ocean by a Japanese warship after the *Rakuyo Maru* sank, died on 20 February. The 23 year old was beaten and, as further punishment, icy water was thrown over him, and he was made to work in the wet clothes. His tall body, gaunt from lack of protein, stooped from hard physical labour, and scarred from cruel beatings could not endure further. His death would be recorded as 'causes unknown', but the causes were many and avoidable but for a more benevolent gaoler. Campbell would eventually lie next to shipmates in the US Air Force Mausoleum, Yokohama, Honshu, Japan. It was such a long way away from Stanthorpe, Queensland.

Perth survivors were assigned to the mines – grim, terrible work, with men working in shifts all day and night. They spent their days breathing in metal dust, drilling, shovelling and pulling heavy ore-filled trolleys. Deep in shafts beneath the sea, it was dank and cold; occasionally a shaft would spring a leak and men would slave away standing in freezing water; rock falls were common. Guards were soldiers classified no longer fit for combat, a considerable fall in status, so they were particularly resentful and dangerous.

Perth's Acting Warrant Electrician Cecil Vowles knew the winters all too well and felt sorry for the new arrivals, Vowles had been in Japan since late 1942. He enjoyed re-acquainting himself with *Perth* survivors but felt helpless in their daily battle to survive: 'Normal hours of work were 6 a.m. to 6 p.m. but often extended to 9 p.m.' Because of his technical expertise, Vowles was moved from one Japanese camp to another and at each he would complain about POW conditions. He complained to the camp interpreter in one POW camp, but the camp interpreter was, 'one of the worst. He used to let out a growl, run up to a prisoner and beat him about the head until he fell down and then he would kick him while on the ground'. At most camps: 'There were beatings, every time a new guard came for a week, beatings were very bad', and Vowles had experienced this first hand. He had watched as Australians lost 5 or 6 kilograms a month and had complained about the non-issue of Red Cross parcels and medicine. Vowles was beaten. The Warrant Electrician observed a store of shoes yet POWs wore straw shoes consisting of a little bit of rope bound together with a couple of clasps to hold them on the feet. Vowles requested shoes and he was beaten. The memory of one particular beating stayed with him because it was administered by a particularly vicious guard nicknamed 'The Yankee Clipper'. The Clipper was so effective because he was big and heavy. Vowles had once been a solid man but he was no longer.[27]

Food became increasingly scarce in Japan, and POWs were the lowest on the food chain. Men began to lose further weight and condition. The same stubbornness that had got them through the railway still burnt, but 'men always hungry' wrote Chattaway, the meagre meal of rice and hot seaweed soup sprinkled with a sliver or two of whale meat insufficient for hard manual labour in the cold. POWs too ill or injured to work were given even less to eat. Spring in the land of the cherry blossom brought relief from the cold but not the hunger. Rice and vegetables were cut from the diet and their staple diet changed to coarse barley. They scrounged for food anywhere they could and would eat just about anything. POWs smuggled stalactites from the mines back to camp and rejoiced in the salty taste; they also resorted to eating fertiliser.

On 9 March American 325 B29s firebombed Tokyo. A huge terrifying inferno, with temperatures as high as 1800°Fahrenheit, evaporated whole city blocks and an area of some 16 square miles. An estimated 100,000 Japanese were killed.[28] ABs Frank McGovern and Keith Mills and ERA III Vic Duncan, survivors of the *Rakuyo Maru*, were fortunate to escape the destruction of their camp. McGovern saw a huge ball of fire roaring up the street. The timber houses were exploding, consuming inhabitants, 'the fire bombs coming down and exploding, spewed liquid fire as they hit, it was Dante's inferno'. Women with children strapped to their backs were jumping into the water, but 'the shallow water was boiling hot and the people were being cooked alive'. McGovern was running for his own life but he saw the hatred in the eyes of civilians and knew he 'could hardly blame them'. Bombing raids intensified.

PO Richard Nicholas McConnell had been born on 13 October 1905 in Mt Morgan, Queensland, and had been a farm hand before he took to the sea in 1925. He was one of the Parkin group that arrived in Japan in January 1945. All his family was told was that Dick McConnell was 'Presumed Dead' in Japan as of 30 March 1945, just another casualty of the Allied push to peace. On 24/25 May, the biggest single bombing mission on Japan to date, 558 planes ensured that much of what remained of Tokyo was destroyed. POWs slaved in unmarked camps, they slaved in the industrial and mining areas that were targeted, and hundreds died. By June the B29s were dropping bombs at the rate of 40,000 tons a month.

On 13 July the men again heard the unmistakable approach of bombers and bomb loads being released, 'it was like a roaring express train'.[29] Keith 'Freddie' Mills asked McGovern if they should go to the air-raid shelter. It was already too late. McGovern was blown into the air. It was as if he was in slow motion. He landed in water, his mind working overtime; 'Have I been blown out into the harbour?' McGovern struggled to get his head out of the water but debris lay above. It was in fact the roof, and water had rushed into the bomb crater that was once a POW camp. He tried to push but an excruciating pain shot down his back and he couldn't move his legs. Another POW heard Frank's shouts and pulled him out. Encased in mud, McGovern realised his spine was fractured. He lay helpless out in the open with other injured POWs. In great pain he suffered the longest night of his life, everything was eerily quiet and he wondered if he would see the dawn. As the sun rose he turned to the POW lying to his right, the man was dead, he turned to the POW on his left, the man was dead; he was still alive.

Vic Duncan had gone to the toilet. As he emerged everything was blown to smithereens. Duncan searched through the rubble for *Perth* men, he found his best mate with his face gone. Acting Petty Officer Thomas Charles Johnston from, Subiaco, Perth, was a former farm labourer who had enlisted in the RAN in 1938. Able Seaman Patrick Walker Major a 23 year old from Melbourne, who had enlisted in the RAN in August 1941, died with him. Major had considered himself lucky to be one of the few saved from the *Rakuyo Maru*, but he was killed by 'friendly fire'.

Life had certainly not turned out as Keith Mills had imagined. Life had been fun in Sydney in 1940. He had met this girl named Nan. They were both very young, but she thought him so handsome in his navy uniform. Keith had taken her to the 'pictures' before *Perth* left Sydney. Nan would have liked to get to know Keith better 'but the war took care of that'. She was at work when she heard *Perth* was sunk, 'that terrible day'.[30] She assumed he went down with his cruiser, but he didn't. AB Mills became a POW. His captors were cruel and in Burma he was beaten until his jaw shattered. Wonderful POW doctors wired the jaw and it healed. After eighteen months on the railway, Mills found himself sent to Japan as slave labour. All this and he was still only 22. His transport was sunk by an Allied submarine, but he was one of the dozen of 46 *Perth* crew who had survived and been allowed to board a Japanese warship with seven other *Perth* survivors. Like his mates, Mills knew his family was worried and he so much wanted to go home. On 13 July 1945 Keith 'Freddie' Wallace Everardt Mills was killed by Allied bombs.

When he finally reached hospital, McGovern received no medical attention for ten days for two broken vertebrae. He asked for something for the pain and was told there was nothing available. In his ward were two POWs suffering shrapnel wounds, each had a leg amputated. On the tenth day one of the two was returned to the operating theatre. He did not come out alive. The next day the second amputee was taken into the operating room. He did not come out alive. Both POWs had had their femoral artery cut and the blood drained from their bodies because the Japanese were short of blood transfusions for their own. Frank McGovern decided he must be next. Finding he could move a little, he knew he needed to. Gritting his teeth McGovern convinced guards he was walking wounded. Then the call came for all walking wounded to move outside the building. They found a Japanese army officer 'all spick and span', with a squad of soldiers. The wounded POWs were pushed to the back of the building and ordered to stand in a line. The officer drew a line in the dirt with his sword; the soldiers raised their guns. McGovern turned to the POW beside him and said: 'This doesn't look too bloody good mate'. Strangely it was all posturing and the POWs were taken to another camp and another factory. AB Frank McGovern was beginning to believe he had used up his nine lives.

—

On the clear morning of 6 August 1945 a single B29 named *Enola Gay* piloted by Colonel Paul Tibbets flew over Hiroshima and at 0815 a single atomic bomb code-named 'Little Boy' was released.[31] It destroyed most of the city and killed around 110,000 Japanese. US President Harry Truman called on Japan to surrender; there was no reply. On 9 August another single B29 dropped an atomic bomb code-named 'Fat Boy' over Nagasaki. Over 40,000 Japanese died and a POW camp in the Fukuoka district was destroyed along with the men within. PO Ray Parkin, the artist, studied the sky regularly, it seemed the only 'free' space he could regard. He studied the sky on 6 August and observed a giant swirling mushroom of smoke the likes of which he had never seen before. POWs in another camp turned to Nagasaki on 9 August and asked each other 'Look! Is that cloud or smoke?'[32]

POWs were herded into air-raid shelters, told the Emperor was about to address the Japanese people and unworthy prisoners were not to hear the address. They guessed something of significance was happening and hoped their prayers were finally being answered. One camp Commandant announced that peace negotiations were taking place, but POWs should realise, 'Nippon was still strong'. No one was about to argue with him, or believe him either. Vic Duncan turned to Frank McGovern: 'Mac, I think the bloody war is over'.[33] After so many years it was so hard to believe and celebrations remained very subdued.

The following day, another air raid, and they painted 'POW' on the roof of their building in very large letters. It was nerve-wracking. They had been told early in their Japanese imprisonment: 'In the event of an Allied invasion we were to be herded into an air-raid shelter, one end blocked and petrol thrown in the other end and ignited.'[34] The next day they received the long-awaited signal when a British fighter flew a victory roll over their building.

—

In another part of Japan on 15 August 1945 *Perth* survivors merged from mine shafts after another gruelling shift to be met by cries that the war was over. They wondered if they had not heard it all before, wished for it with the essence of their minds and bodies, and now it was too good to be true. They hesitantly moved to the guardhouse ready to salute, be searched and counted but guards did not appear. There was no screaming, no bashing, the quiet was unnerving. An announcement was made there would be no work tomorrow. The Japanese distributed a Red Cross parcel to each man. For the years of their long imprisonment they had been lucky if they had seen two Red Cross parcels shared between five or more POWs. Ord Seam Frank Chattaway wrote in his diary on 18 August 1945: 'The DAY has arrived – were notified by Camp Commandant the order has been given to stop the fight. Thank God

Thank God Thank God.' They were in a kind of limbo, not confident enough to really believe they were free; they were still in the land of the enemy. They took rifles and pistols from the guardhouse and felt a little safer. Australian soldier Bill Haskell was impressed when:

> A couple of chaps off HMAS *Perth* who knew about making sails made three flags, a Union Jack and an Australian flag and the Stars and Strips, and we ripped down the fried egg ... and hauled up our own flags ... we were no longer under the fried egg.[35]

Allied aircraft dropped leaflets that read 'take heart, we are coming'. With Allied bombs still fresh in their minds, it was also a case of 'take cover, here they come'. Large, white markers were placed on the ground. As the days went by and the Japanese remained absent, spirits rose, they sang and whistled as much as they wished, grins became fixed, there was a good deal of back-slapping, and sure enough from the heavens aircraft dropped gaily coloured parachutes with 44-gallon drums attached. McGovern ran outside with other POWs and the man standing next to him was hit by a food parcel. Frank retired to the building until this bombing run was finished: 'I had been through a lot, I decided I did not wish to be taken out of this world by a bloody food parcel'.[36]

POWs couldn't believe their eyes, after years of deprivation and starvation, beer, steaks, dairy products, tins of fruit. Often the impact would shatter the container and contents would tattoo the ground with a weird mixture. For men reduced to eating fertiliser, this was of no concern. They stuffed any and all into their mouths, be it pea soup or chocolate. They opted not to soak the dehydrated food first, they ate it dry and their stomachs rebelled. Thousands of cigarettes were dropped and the clean, unadulterated smoke left them light headed, boarding on comatose. 'God how good it is', wrote Ord Seam Frank Chattaway. They waited impatiently, they wanted out of this awful place and to be in the custody of Allied military, lots of Allied military, then perhaps they would feel safe again. 'I just wanted to get out of the place', confided

Chattaway to his diary.[37] Interred still in this camp something might go wrong, perhaps the Japanese would return. Irrational thoughts came after too many years of captivity.

—

On 14 September 1945 *Perth* survivors boarded another train, but this time they were delighted to do so. They peered out of windows at Nagasaki, 'a ruined city ... mile after mile, completely devastated – laid flat'.[38] They were greeted by Allied nurses and doctors and 'the tears flowed freely', remembered Chattaway. Donuts, ice-cream, coffee and chocolate were relished. They travelled to the harbour; Allied warships as far as the eye could see, incredible, modern warships the likes of which the men of *Perth* had never seen. Some navy survivors boarded converted aircraft carrier USS *Chinnago* and they were finally 'wallowing in freedom'. PO Ray Parkin, Chief Harry Knight, PO 'Horrie' Abbott and AB Les Golding were taken onboard USS *Consolation*. Medical and dental checks, interviews, photographs and service details taken and they wrote letters home, letters that would arrive in days and not years. It seemed like a dream, a wonderful dream. There was such tender kindness and what seemed like pure opulence. POWs stripped, were deloused and luxuriated in hot showers with 'real' soap, 'pink soap which smelt beautiful' until skin shrivelled. Clothes issued included underwear, socks, white T-shirts, jeans, all new, clean and not threadbare – and boots, it was 'bloody marvellous'. Disconcerting was the gentleness and reverent voices. For years the only interaction with non-POW personnel involved nerve-wracking screaming and bashing. Now those in uniforms treated them like newborns.

The McGovern and Duncan group was taken to Tokyo Bay and the appropriately named aircraft carrier, USS *Benevolence*. Crew 'could not do enough for us, they were absolutely wonderful Yanks ... unforgettable'.[39] The next day Duncan, McGovern, PO Alf Thomas, Ord Seam Syd Matsen were transferred to the flight deck of escort destroyer HMS *Speaker*. It was so good to be on a British warship again. The ship set sail with 660 Australian ex-POWs through lines of Allied ships which included the USS *Missouri*, on which the surrender document had been signed, and HMAS ships *Hobart*, *Shropshire* and *Pirie*.

The importance of the day was not lost on officers. Men of several nations assembled on decks, raising their caps and offering deafening cheers to those finally able to go home. A sailor in *Pirie* watched shipmates standing next to the limp Australian flag hold it taut, others rigged *Pirie's* ship's bell to the 4-inch barrel. Sailors jostled for the best viewing position to catch sight of the assembled POWs, their motley collection of donated khaki, brown and blue rig obvious within the sea of white uniforms of the carrier's crew. *Pirie* sailor Geoff Davis, described how: 'the most whole-hearted clamour of cheering I have ever heard' began. With 'great gusto' he joined shipmates singing *Waltzing Matilda*, 'the chorus of which echoed far across the bay' for 'these men who had sacrificed and suffered so much'. Davis believed he could observe in the way the POWs stood, 'the spirit which three long years of captivity and oppression could never quench', and 'there was a lump in the throat of every man onboard, and tears rose in the eyes of many veterans who had seen and scorned the terrors of war'.[40] Onboard *Speaker* McGovern went to the bridge and requested the signal 'Greetings from men of HMAS *Perth*' be flashed.

Some were flown to Manila on 20 September and met more *Perth* survivors. McGovern and Matsen decided to attend a Danny Kaye movie one evening. It had been raining and the area was very muddy. Frank McGovern 'didn't want to spoil my nice navy shoes', so he walked barefoot. Passing Americans thought it strange behaviour and asked what he was doing. When Frank said he didn't wish to mess up his new shoes the Americans thought the behaviour 'rather strange ... I guess to others we were'.[41]

McGovern was one of a *Perth* group who secured air passage to Australia. After a 24-hour stopover in Darwin, they flew to Sydney where 'a beautiful Spring morning (17 September 1945) saw us over Sydney Harbour, with the water sparkling in the sunshine'. Families waited at the RAN Balmoral Depot. McGovern was escorted to a room to have an 'emotional meeting 'with mother and father', before being driven home to greet extended family – words no longer came.

Parkin's group boarded HMS *Speaker* for the trip south. Chattaway's group were at the reception centre when the call 'Any navy blokes?' came. They put up their hands and much to their surprise and pleasure, were enveloped by RAN personnel and taken onto HMAS *Quiberon* for the trip home. It was too good to be true, Chattaway wrote in his diary: 'Having great time'. The warship reached Australia at 1000 on 9 October 1945, and in bold strong print on the diary that was his only surviving constant companion Chattaway printed 'FINIS'. Frank Chattaway decided not to become a bookie after all and returned to teaching. He married Nell on 12 January 1946 and they had two daughters and a son. Frank retired in March 1982 as Headmaster of Goulburn High School, New South Wales.

As the war had neared an end, *Perth* survivors had been scattered far and wide, in Java, Sumatra, Burma, Thailand, Indo-China, Singapore, Manchuria and Japan. Ten were found in Java: Lieut John Thode, Chief PO Writer John Rockey, Mechanician Tom Pollard, Yeoman Jack Willis, PO Steward Bill Davis, Bandsman John Coxhead, Stoker II Peter Cargill, SBA Roy Turner, AB Les Bruse, and writer Don McNab. Others had remained in Palembang, Sumatra: Stoker PO Ernest Robinson, Leading Seaman 'Ben' Chaffey, AB Hilston Boland, Ord Seam Max Jagger, Stokers Clive Henry and Dallas Pascoe and Stoker II Alan Axton.

Rehabilitated to Singapore, Don McNab wrote a letter home, a letter he had seriously wondered he would ever write: 'Dear Mother and family, it seems so strange to be able to just sit here and write you this ... Do not worry about me I am quite fit and well'. He struggled to fathom what he had survived, and now the thought of returning to a normal life was wonderful, scary, bewildering, all at once. His family, particularly sister Margaret, had refused to give up hope. Margaret McNab worked for the Post Master General's Department and using her knowledge and access to Australia's communication hub, had sent letter after letter in the hope her younger brother would receive them. Margaret McNab and her mother listened intently to radio reports on POWs found. At 11.15 a.m. on 13 September, Don's official number was read out, Margaret and her mother did 'a wild dance around the dining room table. 'Yippee! Yippee! what a wonderful day'. Excitedly she wrote to Don:

> Only a few more hours now and we will meet again after 3yrs
> and 8 months ...We will talk till our tongues get tired ...You
> will want a good rest when you come home dear, and your own
> friends and relations around you and good nourishing food once
> again and then after a little while we hope you will be your old
> self once again and the memory of all you have been through
> will gradually pass away.[42]

Only when her brother asked the question was he told that his father had died in 1943. His sister attempted to soften the news by telling Don that she had read the first lettercard from Don, saying he made it off the cruiser and was a POW, to their ill father. That short note had caused visible relief on the face of Arthur McNab and he died hours later. Margaret and her mother hoped Don would return to his 'old self', but he wouldn't, none of the *Perth* survivors could.

The cruiser's poet, Bandsman George Vanselow, missed the company of other *Perth* men; he seemed to spend each chapter of his incarceration with soldiers. He remained in hospital in Batavia until December 1943. When he was discharged he was sent by sea to the River Valley Road POW camp in Singapore. The River Valley Camp was notorious for the mosquitoes that bred in the turgid stream, which trickled through the camp. He was sent to Sumatra and a railway construction and maintenance camp. The gentle man who wrote poetry was subjected to a 'very severe bashing with rifle butts, also a severe kicking'.[43] Another time a guard struck him repeatedly with a sharp spade, severely lacerating the Bandsman's right foot. He was readmitted to hospital. Fortunately, the war finished before Vanselow could be bashed again. His advice to youth anxious to join a war, 'first think of the consequences!'[44]

—

In Sumatra the Walrus Telegraphist Gunner Ken 'Tag' Wallace helped build an airfield and worked the wharves with a group of POWs, as starved of news from the outside world as they were of food. In October they awoke to bombs striking the oil refineries. As the Japanese anticipated an Allied landing, they became ever more dangerous. By this stage Wallace and his group were eating dog food, 'camp inmates were in such dreadful condition, that we were literally walking skeletons.'[45] Wallace had beri-beri so badly that he was left in the hut euphemistically called a 'hospital', and like lying on that Sumatra beach in 1942, the Walrus gunner believed this was how he would die. POW bodies were kept in the 'hospital' until the smell was unbearable, so deceased rations could still be collected and spread amongst the living.

On 20 August Wallace suffered a heart attack and heard the doctor say there was no hope. Within a week canisters of supplies were dropped from a huge Flying Fortress. Wallace was given some of the Vitamin B powder and then food and he stirred. One morning Japanese soldiers splashed petrol around the huts and prepared to light and destroy the human testimony to their guilt. A violent fight broke out between POWs and the Japanese. All Wallace could do was lie, listen and pray the good guys won; they did. The Allies arrived and were so horrified by the condition of the POWs they immediately shot five guards.

On 16 September Wallace and other *Perth* survivors in Sumatra were flown to Singapore. The island was transformed, full of Allied personnel and Red Cross representatives. They were invited to help themselves to cigarettes and chocolate, they grabbed as much as they could, stuffing their mouths and shirts full, then furtively looked over their shoulders 'to see who would take' it away.[46]

More *Perth* survivors arrived, most with that hollowed out physical look but at least now their eyes shone and smiles rarely left their faces. Five meals a day, medical and dental care began to see their bodies blossom and resemble, at least in physical form, the men they had once been.

—

In Kaschu Mountain Camp in south-east Thailand ABs Les Luff and 'Tich' Hill stood on parade waiting for the next work detail. It was going to be just another day of difficult physical labour. Indecision on the part of the Japanese was obvious, and when the POWs were dismissed, someone asked what the date was. 'August 16th' came the reply. A murmur rippled through the ranks, but to avoid further disappointment they did not want to believe the war could actually be over. Just in case, Les Luff gathered scraps of material and began sewing a white ensign. On 18 August the announcement came and *Perth* survivors hoisted Les Luff's naval ensign: 'The sight of that patchwork Ensign overhead, floating free for the first time in nearly four years, was a very moving sight.'[47] The men who saluted the strange-looking flag were a cadaverous, near-naked crew but never was there a prouder, more grateful band.

At Phetburi and Rathburi Thailand *Perth* survivors were busy building airfields. Japanese guards went a little crazier than normal when they received news their nation had surrendered. It was a dangerous time as, 'Japs were rushing about, cocking rifles and screaming', so Ord Seam David Manning and others took refuge under a truck. The following morning a single English paratrooper arrived and he was all it took for guards and POWs to realise that the horrible nightmare was ending.

A USAF *Dakota* was the first aircraft to land and it took out American POWs. The Americans continued to take planeloads of other nation's POWs until the RAF took over. Rescuers marvelled that these men were still alive. A RAF airman remembered loading POWs into his plane and being deeply moved by their condition and how 'they clutched pieces of rag, old tin, their only possessions and I could not get them to give them up, even though they didn't need them any more, so onto the plane they went, it was so sad'.[48]

RAN men were the first Australian POWs flown to Rangoon. Unfortunately once in Rangoon: 'We sailors were alone and unwanted because Burma was under British Army control and 'a group of Australian ex-prisoners of war was a real embarrassment'.[49] Although they received great care, they waited and waited for someone to take responsibility for them. After ten days an RAAF Wing Commander arrived. His name was Vic Richardson, former captain of the Australian cricket team.[50] *Perth* sailors considered Richardson 'a larrikin', so they enjoyed his company over the ensuing days until he too wearied of the 'buck passing' and put the 80 sailors on *Highland Brigade,* much to the chagrin of the army. *Perth* survivors thought they were going home, but when the ship reached Singapore the Australian Army offloaded them and boarded soldiers instead. Again RAN men who had endured more were accorded less.

Anchored in Singapore Harbour was a lone RAN ship, HMAS *Hawkesbury. Perth* survivors commandeered a boat and visited; they were treated like heroes. Ex-*Perth* crew member Basil Hayler was now a member of *Hawkesbury*'s crew and was upset by 'the pitiful sight' of these men. *Hawkesbury*'s captain applied to take them back to Australia, but the red tape was insurmountable, so still the navy POWs waited. 'Tich' Hill stole away from carers to visit the cemetery. He searched amongst the many simple white crosses, until he found the one he was looking for, the one marked Lance Corporal Johnny Hill: 'That simple little cross, bearing his name and rank, was the only indication that warm, vibrant, fun-loving Johnny had ever existed'.[51]

It wasn't until 15 October that 'Tich' Hill and most of his shipmates were allowed to board *Moreton Bay* for the journey home. More were loaded onto *Highland Chief.* The *Moreton Bay* prior to the war had been owned by the Shaw, Saville and Albion line, translated irreverently by *Perth* survivors as 'Slow, Starvation and Agony'.[52] Each day they were fed boiled mutton and potatoes and the ship was slow, but no ship would be fast enough for this journey. As they departed Singapore *Hawkesbury* flew a massive Australian flag and the tunes 'Homeward Bound' and 'Waltzing Matilda' blasted from its loud-speaker system.

Perth survivors were happiest on the top deck. They gloried in the Southern Cross, the stars appeared particularly brilliant, their light showing the way home. Sleep deserted them but this was of no consequence and they waited for the colours of dawn to reveal the Australian coastline. It was more beautiful than they remembered and released powerful emotions in men who believed they had no more tears. HMS *Speaker* approached Sydney Heads at 0900 on 15 October. A huge flotilla of ships and boats lined the waterways, their horns releasing a cacophony of sound. As the ship reached its mooring nothing could drown out the screaming and cheering crowds who lined the docks and every harbour vantage point. Whichever the ship, whatever the port, the reception was the same, brass bands played and thousands of people, holding signs aloft, screamed and waved.

Telegrams arrived throughout Australia. Fingers trembled with a mixture of excitement and trepidation as they struggled with the envelopes. Sheila Parkes was so anxious she tore the telegram in half. Dorothea Chaffey received a telegram saying her husband 'Ben' was arriving that day by air, and a car would be sent to take her to Balmoral Naval Depot. So little warning, she could hardly contain her anticipation. Else Willis was taken to Balmoral to be reunited with husband Jack. Yeoman Jack Willis had been a robust fellow when she had waved goodbye in 1942: 'Sitting over in the far corner of the room there was a tiny little man, all bones holding up his shirt. I wouldn't look at him, I thought I might stare at him and it would be terribly rude, but I did take a second look at him and I did not recognise my own husband'.

Away from the celebrations, other next of kin continued to wait, to wait for word, to wait for telegrams or visits from the men in uniform who brought news they did not wish to hear. They could not join the dancing crowds of Australians who jammed the streets. They simply retired quietly to their homes. Yes, it was good the terrible war was over, but their loved ones were not coming back or were still 'missing, believed dead'.

Isabel Justelius could remember opening the door to uniformed men with a navy call-up notice for brother, Eric, in the wee hours after war was declared. In 1945 another telegram had arrived. 'I will never forget all the telegrams, the navy seemed only ever to use telegram boys to convey all those very formal and impersonal pieces of news that started with "the navy regrets"'.[53] This telegram informed Isabel that AB Eric 'Boyce' Justelius had died with his ship. An army sergeant arrived at her home. Stan Arneil of the 2/30th Btn AIF carried with him a bundle of letters her fiancé Lance Corporal Frank Tuckey had penned to her during his years as a POW. They were love letters, each in Frank's careful writing, none able to be posted. The ex-POW could do little but hand her the letters and leave, he had carried out his promise to his dying mate. Isabel had not married Frank before he went overseas because she was working to support herself and her mother, and women lost permanent Government employment when they married. Frank did not come back and Isabel never did marry.

Relatives like Jane McCall continued to pray and hope, living with uncertainty was cruel. The Dutch East Indies encompassed a huge area, of approximately 736,000 square miles, of around 3000 islands, perhaps survivors of *Perth* would still be found. The RAN dispatched HMAS *Macquarie* to scour the Sunda Strait region between 20 July and 20 August 1946.[54] A special interrogation team, including an interpreter and *Perth* survivor Lieut Bill Gay, was part of landing parties who searched extensively. In late 1945 the Australian Naval Board considered 'all likely areas had been searched', but decided to wait until after Christmas before sending a last communication to families. They decided letters should 'make it definite that there is no hope that any of the personnel are still alive'.[55] The last official RAN letter was not sent until mid 1946. It put an end to all the hope and offered little closure even if it was meant to: 'The search has been completed and I regret to inform you the result has furnished no information which could give any hope that there are more survivors'.[56]

—

Only 214 out of a crew of 681 were still alive. For women like Jane McCall, the vigil was over; her son, whom she had proudly named William Thomas Pulditch McCall, was 'officially dead'. It was hard not to be bitter, to be pleased when the sons, husbands and fathers of others arrived home safely if you were not as fortunate. On the bad days you hoped no one would visit, it was too hard to keep the public face. For navy families of men who went down with their ships, there were no graves to visit for quiet reflection.

In Victoria's Williamstown cemetery stands the Watson family plaque. Like all such tablets there is a story etched in metal and stone.

The first name is that of 'Veritas Ray Watson', born January 1909, died February 1918, and there is the sadness of parents burying a nine year old. The second name is that of Peter Storey Watson, born September 1917 during World War I, and who died on 1 March 1942 in another world war. Again the intense sadness of another son lost. Peter is not buried there, for he lies with his warship and many *Perth* shipmates, at the bottom of Sunda Strait; but in spirit Peter was reunited with his brother. The name of their mother, Rose, was etched below, just four year later, the same year she received that final RAN letter informing her there were no 'more survivors'. No longer could Rose Watson hope to see Peter alive. She died, her name united with those of two sons in metal and stone in a graveyard close to the sea.

Hospital ships brought home many too ill to travel earlier. Stoker Peter Cargill was suffering from pulmonary tuberculosis. Helen Cargill barely recognised her son. Peter was taken directly to hospital in Sydney, granted a disability pension and for the 25 year old, it would be a very uncertain future. Stoker Rhonsley Ernest Jetson from Scottsdale, Tasmania, was discharged to Rockingham Convalescent Home, in Kew, Victoria. His eyes were in a bad way and the RAN decided to send him to hospital in London.

Steward Allen Denic had been a tall, fit, nineteen year old when he entered the RAN. He was a mere shell of his former self when he returned to Western Australia. He spent a lot of the next two years in and out of hospital and was discharged medically unfit due to 'Anxiety'. Life was a struggle for Denic and the RAN stopped keeping records on him after he was again in hospital in 1957.

Neil Biddell was promoted to Chief of Signals. He was mentioned in despatches, 'For gallantry and resolution whilst serving in HMAS *Perth*'. He also received a pension of 15 shillings per fortnight. By 1954 the pension needed to be increased 60 per cent due to his poor health and recurring bronchitis, which made employment difficult.

AB Gerald Ellen had been a strapping timberyard employee in Launceston, Tasmania. He had begged his parents to allow him to enlist in the RAN at the age of seventeen in March 1941 so he could 'do his bit for the war effort'. He had been drafted to *Perth* by December 1941.

Ellen was still only 21 when he returned to Australia on the hospital ship *Karoo* suffering from 'severe retrobulbar neuritis'. He was sent to a convalescence home to study braille. Given a pension of £5 ($10) per fortnight, he was returned to his parents home in Launceston and they did what they could for their only son who now had very limited prospects.

For some families POW homecomings were bittersweet. Adelaide Delbridge was there to greet son Charlie, yet elder son Fred never made it off *Perth*. Fred was the married one with two children. In his quiet moments Charlie struggled to reason why; but thought he could help with the responsibility of raising Fred's children. He was not given such opportunity, because Fred's wife Hilda became distant and lost touch with the rest of the Delbridge family; it was too painful because it made no sense to her either.

The McGovern family needed to come to terms with the fact that Frank had returned but Vincent had stayed with his cruiser. The Partingtons lost two navy sons but Perc had survived being a member of the *Perth* crew.[57] There would always be some awkwardness, some unsettling disquiet.

'Tag' Ken Wallace felt that, 'Going back to my mother's house seemed like a dream. I think we were all in a state of euphoria'.[58] Wallace left the navy immediately and married within ten days of his return, but the honeymoon was short before his new wife, Linda, who was a WAAAF radar operator, returned to duty. Resplendent in new civilian clothes, Ken went to see her train off and soldiers boarding the same train made 'nasty remarks about guys who had avoided war service'.[59]

The adjustments were hard. Relatives were shocked at how thin and emaciated survivors looked. David Manning 'thought I looked pretty good', but his family were clearly of another opinion. There were difficulties in adapting to normal food, in having a proper breakfast, in using a knife and fork and not fingers, wearing trousers that needed to be zipped. Furniture went unused because it was more familiar to sit on the floor, beds were too soft and it was better to sleep on the floor.

After six weeks' leave, a group of ex-POWs reported to Port Melbourne for the next phase of their rehabilitation. As they attempted to gain admission, officious RAN and Naval Police personnel chastised them for inappropriate uniform. Ord Seam David Manning informed front gate officials his correct uniform was in his ship. A Chief roared, 'What ship, sailor?' Manning answered '*Perth* Chief' and continued on his way: 'It was a very satisfying end to an uncomfortable situation'.[60]

Grong Grong, a mansion in Toorak, Melbourne, was transformed into a rehabilitation centre. It was the intention of the two-week course to ease these ex-POWs back into 'real' society, to attempt to re-civilise them. Years of observing cruelty and deprivation had stripped them bare; the 'flight or fight' rawness that had kept them alive was not acceptable in normal society. The world had sped up and left them behind; Australia had changed much in the years of their absence. The men were given lectures on politics, entertainment, sports and cultural changes. The ex-POWs were treated cautiously by authorities. Fred Mason was amused when the RAN insisted he have a chaperone when he went out on his first post-war date, so when Fred squired a female acquaintance to a movie, his sister went too.

Grong Grong was well intended, but lectures were not compulsory, and it was easy to disappear 'to the pub and get pissed'. They were haunted men. They realised they were the fortunate ones but invariably did not feel fortunate. They struggled to reconcile why they survived and others did not. Their families had altered, relatives had died, children had grown; there seemed to be so many people around them, everything bustled, everything seemed to close in.

The 'Serang Chief Electrician', Wireman Fred Lasslett, had spent most of his POW time in Japan and all of his POW time writing a diary of letters to his sweetheart Nola. He had used cigarette paper and a tiny lead pencil. So many days, so many letters like the one on 2 June 1944, which included: 'Every night I look at your photo, say a short prayer and then dream of the happy times we had together ... I often think of the glorious times we will have'.[61] He had hoped the war would run out before his pencil but it didn't. Lasslett returned on *Speaker* and simply knocked on the door of his Melbourne home. 'Mum burst into tears and so did I'. [62] He found Nola had married.

Smells, sounds would jar and stir emotions. ERA Bill Barnes kept reminding himself he was fortunate because it all seemed so overwhelming. It took weeks before he worked up the courage to leave his home to travel to the city by tram. Everything was so loud, so fast, battering his senses, making it hard to breathe. Barnes was sitting uneasily when the conductor put out his hand for the fare. The ex-*Perth* POW asked how much the fare was and the conductor tersely replied 'Where have you been? Living in a cave?' Barnes left the train and returned home.[63]

Frank McGovern boarded an evening tram to travel to see future wife Merle. He was in uniform and there was only an older man in his compartment. A fuse blew with a load bang; 'My reaction was swift – I dived under the opposite seat'. Embarrassed, McGovern picked up his cap and sat down again. The older passenger who had not moved said kindly, 'Son you'll have to get used to it – and have some treatment'.[64] Frank left the RAN and returned to employment at Head Office of the Sydney Water Board. He found the nine-to-five office routine 'very difficult', but with marriage to Merle in 1947, 'buying a house and starting a family there were new responsibilities'; there was little alternative to safe and solid employment.[65]

—

'Anxiety' and 'Depression', were the most commonly cited aliments on *Perth* service records. These were also the least understood, and elicited the least sympathetic attention from medical authorities and the Australian public. *Perth* survivors were expected to 'get on with their lives', to not complain, to 'move on' as if nothing had happened. They struggled with relationships but also with the concept of being on their own. True, they were invariably surrounded by family, but it had been male comradeship that had kept them alive. They didn't have to explain their emotions or their nightmares with these men, it went without saying. *Perth* and *Perth* ex-POW Associations were established and became dominant forces in their lives. Alcohol was used to excess by some to ease the pain and dim the senses. Some lived dangerously.

Leading Stoker Cecil Doggett had survived when so many fellow stokers did not. It was difficult to settle back into his skin when he returned to Perth. He crashed his motorbike in 1948 and died in Royal Perth Hospital. Roy Roberts remembered a doctor on the railway saying: 'being youth, you will be able to forget it all', but the doctor was wrong. Four years had been ripped away, the opportunity to be young and carefree, to enjoy the wonderful period of discovery and excitement which came with the first job, first car, or first date were gone.

Older men struggled also. Electrical Artificer III Arthur Kieswetter having recovered from burns had spent his POW time tending the sick. He had suffered a horrible time in 55-kilo hospital, so many men had died dreadfully. He returned to Australia and tried to start afresh, even changed his name by deed poll to the less German sounding Kiesey. Now 52, it was impossible to return to his former life, it felt like an alien culture. He felt uncomfortable with his family and friends, the faces of the fallen continued to crowd his mind. He was awarded the Distinguished Service Medal, but it did nothing to improve his spirit. He deserted the society he felt had deserted him and became a recluse beachcomber on Rottnest Island, off the West Australian coast. Kiesey died in 1958.

Perth's pilot 'Jock' McDonough had been with a POW group near the Indo-China border, when he was told by a Japanese guard that POWs were going to be pushed into the jungle and shot to conceal evidence of maltreatment. The atomic bombs meant the war ended too suddenly for the order to be carried out. The group made their own way to Bangkok and killed several former guards they encountered.[66] McDonough, the only catapult pilot to survive the war, was not repatriated until December 1945 and was much debilitated. In keeping with advice not to engage in discussion on the POW experience, his 'father, mother and two brothers never once talked to him about his ordeals and yet they freely discussed the lesser experiences of his two brothers who never left Australia'.[67] Jock found this 'offensive'. McDonough married Gretta and had two sons, both of whom joined the RAN. He became an entreprencur, and as a hobby built and raced speedboats, proving he still had the need for speed and living precariously. *Perth*'s pilot died in 2005, shortly after celebrating his ninetieth birthday.

As he prepared to return to Australia, *Perth*'s poet, George Vanselow considered his future. He summed up the aspirations of most: 'what I hope for when I return, 1. A *permanent* job; 2. A quiet life; 3. Start my new life without girlfriend trouble and that sort of foolishness'.[68] Vanselow returned to his pre-war job in advertising, married Joan, and had four children. Like so many of his peers he suffered from anxiety. During the final years of his life Vanselow was diagnosed with mesothelioma, a disease that would blight generations of RAN personnel. But he continued to beat the odds and died in January 1997 aged 83.

'Elmo' Gee returned suffering the symptoms of 'war neurosis' or PTSD as it would be soon known: 'acute anxiety, temper, tantrums, nightmares, sleep disorders and panic attacks' plus the loss of 92 per cent of his sight.[69] Allan married his sweetheart Kath in September 1946, enjoyed a farming life, had a son and twin daughters and did the very best he could, but it was so hard; hard also for his wife and children.

Families of *Perth* survivors observed them as unpredictable, moody, sometimes morose, men who found it difficult to be in large groups. Bob Collins remembered feelings of claustrophobia. Curious family members would either find themselves shut out or given expansive renditions of the POW experience. If started, 'conversations had to go from beginning to end'.[70] *Perth* survivors felt frustrated their family could not appreciate how all-pervading their POW experience was, how for years they had lived on the edge, even when sick, at any time POWs 'could get a clip around the ear' or a bashing.[71] For wives and children understanding and appreciation was particularly difficult: 'Growing up with a man who had lost his eyesight and was severely traumatised as a result of his experiences as a POW wasn't always easy',[72] remembered Margaret Gee about a father deeply loved but not understood until maturity.

'Tich' Hill kept the promise he had made to himself in the oppressive jungles of Burma, to return to the Busselton wharf to fish for 'gardies'. He fished for hours without success. Only after other fishermen left for home and the moon reflected strongly from the heavens did he unroll the ground sheet on the roughly hewn jetty planks. Lying in the complete silence he watched the moon's rays bounce off the ocean, and looked towards the horizon. It was half past midnight on 1 March 1946 – this hour four years ago had changed his life when the *Perth* sunk. There was moisture on his face this evening; possibly it was salty ocean spray, likely it was not. Hill knew he needed to purge his memory of 'the ghosts of hundreds of my shipmates who were killed ... to erase the sounds of men struggling in the dark waters,' and memories of following days, months and years. He knew it would take time, lots of time. Too many of the following months were spent in hospital and the convalescent home. Rehabilitation training meant Hill qualified as a carpenter and joiner and he married Florrie in 1955. They decided to live in Busselton, not too far from the wharf and the elusive garfish, and they had three daughters.

David Manning found 'it difficult to settle' when he attempted to assimilate back into society. He returned to the insurance industry, but found 'working in an office too restrictive ... I couldn't equate with people'.[73] He worked in fire and general insurance until he retired in 1979. David married Audrey and they had three children. In March 2008 they had been married 58 years and were the proud grandparents of five granddaughters.

Bob McCarrey returned to his occupation as a painter with the West Australian Railway, but 'his balance was affected' by the toes he lost on another railway, 'making it hard for him to work on scaffolds'.[74] He managed to get a job on the wharves because his father was a wharfie. Fred Skeels knew how lucky he was, out of the six other members of his Recruit Class drafted to *Perth*, only one other, AB Leon Williams, returned home with him. He married his childhood sweetheart Bonnie and 'her love, understanding and support was the anchor which prevented' Fred 'from drifting – like many others unfortunately did'.[75] Fred Skeels took advantage of the Commonwealth Reconstruction Training Scheme to advance his education and enter the Commonwealth Public Service. In 2004 Fred and Bonnie had three children and ten grandchildren. Bonnie died in 2005.

Ernie Toovey nearly got charged with a disciplinary infringement minutes after he arrived back in Australia, when at Balmoral Naval Depot he took offence at how, 'a young naval officer spoke to me as if I had been "adrift" for years'.[76] Fortunately, before the situation escalated an older member of the RAN intervened. Ernie who had fought so hard in the jungle to keep both legs so he could play Sheffield Shield test cricket for Queensland, did just that. He also played baseball and was selected for the Australian team. When the Australian team toured, he withdrew. Toovey never left Australian shores again: 'it took me three and a half years to get back last time, I am not going to risk it again.'[77] When his Test cricket playing days were over, he was named a Queensland cricket selector, a role he undertook for a record 28 years. A stalwart member of the Returned Services League, Toovey was awarded an MBE for his contribution to the Queensland community. Ernie believed MBE in his case meant 'Made Bloody Eighty', and in his case that was truly death defying. He was also inducted into the 'Baseball Hall of Fame' and awarded an Order of Australia medal. Ernie Toovey married Jean in 1948 but when she entered a nursing home, all the life went out of him.

Wireman Charlie Wray tried unsuccessfully to get into the private electrical world. He returned to Gordon and Gotch, but some years later joined the ANZ bank working in the security area and retired after 20 years. He married Sylvia in 1948, they had three children and in 2004 were the proud grandparents of six. Charlie realised how 'lucky' he was to have survived. He also knew he would never 'forgive or forget' the Japanese.

Jimmy Millerick was a different person. He was still very caring towards his teenage sister, but his manner had changed towards others. Beryl found him 'very serious' and he would not speak of his time as a POW. He opened a bakery but it didn't succeed so he studied refrigeration and air-conditioning at night school. Millerick remained loyal to his peers and for 35 years was President of the Victorian Branch of the *Perth* POW Association, devoting much of his life to the care of their families.

Noel Laugher couldn't settle either and his health continued to restrict employment. He stayed in touch with mate George Tibbits. Tibbits headed away from cities and settled with wife Janice in the small, inland Queensland town of Biloela, where they had five children. He worked for the Public Works Department because it meant he would not be 'closed into an office'. Laugher and Tibbits enlisted in Brisbane and Noel's official number was B2913 and George's official number was B2931. The two died in 1997 within hours of each other.

Fred Mason went back to cyclone fencing. He found the noise and confinement of the factory hard, so he became a bricklayer. He worked for nearly 40 years, never constrained by just four walls. Fred Mason married Mavis in 1949 and in 2005 was surrounded by four children, twelve grandchildren and two great grandchildren. At 83 that 'never say never' gleam was still present in the comment: 'My ambition is to be shot by a jealous husband when I am 95'.[78]

Finding the civilian world too difficult, many attempted to rejoin the RAN but were found medically unfit. Ordnance Artificer Marcus Goodwin was awarded a DSM for his 'Bravery and Enterprise' during the Battle of Matapan and was one of the few to continue a distinguished career. Goodwin returned to sea service and was promoted to Chief. The retiring age was waived and he left the RAN in 1965 at age 50. Ill health then dominated his life and he died in 1976 aged 61.

'Ben' Chaffey realised he really was a navy man and stayed in the RAN. He rose to Chief PO in 1949 but was forced to retire due to ill health in 1957. 'Chas' Thomson married that girl Nell he was 'keen on' and remained in the navy. The RAN drafted him to the cruiser *Australia* in 1948 for a challenging tour of duty to Japan. The Chief ERA was not certain how comfortable he would be when confronted by his former enemy. He discovered he felt 'nothing for them at all'. Returning to Australia, he decided his priorities had altered and he no longer wished to be separated from family. Thomson retired in 1951. He joined the Commonwealth Public Service, where he remained until 1978. Charles Bosisto Thomson died in November 1996, just 27 days before his and Nell's golden wedding anniversary. In 1998 Nell attended the ANZAC day service at Hellfire Pass. Although the three-hour walk along the line was 'rocky, rough and humid' her determination kept her going.[79] Nell felt closer to 'Chas' that April day.

Illness and its repercussions caused great concern, and proud men were reduced to begging. Stoker Clive Henry was 23 when he returned and married Maureen in 1946. He spent much of the ensuing years in and out of hospital. By 1953 he, Maureen and daughters, four-year-old Irene and one-year-old Robyn, were struggling to stay afloat financially. A full-time job was difficult and his small war pension not sufficient to keep them above the poverty line. He applied to the POW Trust Fund in 1953 for assistance when he was again in Heidelberg Repatriation Hospital in Melbourne. His doctor listed a page of ailments. Others swore statements of how hard Henry tried to work and that the debts of £2000 ($4000, primarily his house mortgage), were not due to 'gambling or drinking'. Authorities granted the sum of £60 ($120) and the Henry family sank further into poverty.[80]

Chief Petty Officer Cook Bob Bland was awarded a BEM (Mil) and two 'Mentioned in Despatches'. He elected to remain in the RAN, it was all he had known since he was seventeen, but the RAN discharged him as medically unfit and he found his decorations meant 'squat' in post-war Australia. The dysentery that had afflicted him as a POW barred him from working as a cook, the craft he so enjoyed. He worked briefly as a storeman and then as a gatekeeper, but recurring illness restricted his employment.[81] Bob Bland did not aspire to greatness, he wanted a simple and quiet life for his wife and sons Stanley and Robert. By 1962 Bob Bland was struggling, physically, emotionally and financially. He suffered from 'anxiety', a condition he didn't understand, something a bloke should be able to overcome he thought. *Perth* POW reunions became very important if for no other reason but he would cook for his mates. They did not care, he couldn't infect them with anything they did not have already. Bob Bland died on 19 April 1989.

Another highly decorated *Perth* sailor was ERA Vic Duncan. He endeavoured to return to the occupation of fitter and turner, but a fractured wrist suffered between the 1942–45 years made this difficult. As Duncan endeavoured to requalify as a teacher the debts grew. In 1953 he asked for a grant to enable him to continue training whilst supporting wife, Elizabeth, six-year-old daughter Leonora and four-year-old son Roderick. Whilst some committee members believed Duncan 'sounds a first class man', the final judgement was that Duncan was, 'no different than any man retraining with a young family'.[82] But Duncan was 'different', as were those who sailed into the cruel conflict in *Perth*.

The crew of the cruiser *Perth* sailed off to war as strong and optimistic young men who gave little serious thought to their own mortality. They saw duty, adventure and the opportunity to be part of an ANZAC tradition, which they were indoctrinated to believe turned their country into a nation and boys into men. They are now few in number. A little bent and frail with age, they shuffle to lay a wreath in remembrance of the night their ship died. They stand in silence with ghosts and are comfortable to do so because the world may have moved on but part of them remained in 1942. A little hard of hearing, they shake their heads in annoyance when their mind cannot recall a face, name or incident with instant clarity. But their eyes remain bright with the wonderment that only those who survived great adversity can have, and the knowledge they have lived good and full lives for shipmates less fortunate. It is easy to envy them this, not the horror they saw, but that they cheated death and because of this have truly appreciated life.

ENDNOTES

One

1. Good Conduct Badges *resembled* the stripes of Army non-commissioned office stripes and were worn on the upper left arm of the sailor's uniform. Towards the end of the war the durations were altered to three, eight and twelve years.

2. It was also known as the 'Pea Doo Medal', Pea Doo being a soup; the name was applied to the LSGCM to suggest if one stayed alive long enough they would get the medal.

3. National Archives, Canberra, A5954/1 39/4, 'Sheddon Papers', Letter, 25 February 1931.

4. *Adelaide* was not de-commissioned. With the start of the war the ship received another crew.

5. Gee, Margaret. *A Long Way from Silver Creek*, Sydney, 2000, p.114.

6. *Argus*, 13 April 1938.

7. *Argus*, 30 April 1938.

8. *Argus*, 22 April 1938.

9. Hayler, Basil. Unpublished Autobiography, Private Family Papers, p.3.

10. *Ibid.*, p.4.

11. Gee, M, p.119.

12. King, Norm, MSS1502, Papers, Australian War Memorial, Canberra.

13. A uniform change, to standard RAN, was incorporated in 1960, perhaps in part, because the massed RAN bands at the 1956 Melbourne Olympic Games were announced as the 'Australian Army Band'.

14. Partington, Margaret. Correspondence, 9 July 2005.

15. Also known as 'Tubes' Grant.

16. The other RAN officers were Commander David Hughes Harries; Lieut Cdr Harley Chamberlain Wright; Lieut Arthur Stanley Storey; Lieut (E) Leonard Norman Dine.

17. *Naval Historical Review,* Volume 25, No.1–March 2004, Sydney, 'The Commissioning of HMAS *Perth*, 1939'.

18. Hayler, B, p.5.

19. Gee, Margaret. p.125.

Two

1. Roberts, R, *Age Shall Not Weary Them*, Patersons, Perth, 1942, p.34.

2. *Ibid.*, p.35.

3. Bracht, William H. PO, MSS1576, Manuscript, Australian War Memorial, Canberra.

4. PR901/161, *Perth War Diary*, Australian War Memorial, Canberra.

5. PR90/161, Baker, Keith, Diary, Australian War Memorial, Canberra. Also interview May 2006.

6. Grazebrook, A.W. 'First To A Flag: The Life of Rear Admiral H.B. Farncomb', in Frame, T.R, Goldrick, J.V.P and Jones, P.D. (eds). *Reflections on the Royal Australian Navy*, NSW, 1991, p.193.

7. King, Norm. Manuscript.

8. *Ibid.*

9. Cook, Capt. W, LVO, RAN. 'HMAS *Perth* 1939 Part 2 Outbreak of War', in *Naval Historical Review* June 2004, p.3.

10. Roberts, R, p.43.
11. MP981/1, 452/201/714, 'Incident on 4 August 1939', National Archives, Melbourne.
12. Gee, Margaret, p.131.
13. *Perth War Diary*, When purchased by the AWM, former *Perth I* officers, Farncomb and Bracegirdle, read the diary and chose to preface it with the following: 'This Leading Signalman whilst having access to more information than most of the ship's company has, however, neither the knowledge nor the ability to interpret the events which he has attempted to describe'.
14. Roberts, R, p.64.
15. *Ibid.*, p.60.
16. King, N, Manuscript.
17. Cook, W, p.4.
18. Hayler, Basil, p.5.
19. Roberts, R, p.10.
20. Justelius, Isabel. Interview, 17 June 2004.
21. PO 'Horrie' Abbott was Director Captain in communication by telephone with the 4-inch guns transmitting. Other members of the team were AB Ken Lynas, Director Layer and AB 'Tich' Drew, Rangetaker.
22. Hayler, Basil.
23. Allan 'Elmo' Gee, in Gee, M, p.128.
24. Whiting, Brendan. *Ship of Courage: The Epic Story of HMAS* Perth *and Her Crew*, Allen & Unwin, NSW, 1994.p. xv.
25. Bracht, W, Manuscript.
26. *Ibid.*
27. Gee, Margaret, p.137.
28. Cook, W, p.4.

Three

1. National Archives, Canberra, A5954/69, 'Review of RAN War Effort and Activities to 20 October 1943'.
2. Steele, Gordon. Interview, 23 August 2006.
3. 'Reflections of a Lower Deck Man', Navy History Directorate, Canberra, author unknown.
4. Promoted Lieutenant Commander 16 December 1942; Commander 30 June 1947.
5. The Australian Naval Aviation Museum, *Flying Stations: A Story of Australian Naval Aviation*, Allen & Unwin, 1998, p.21.
6. Murphy, Alec. Interview, 25 August 2005.
7. Norris, Roy. *A Cook's Tour: HMAS Perth's* Mediterranean War 1941, Naval Historical Society of Australia, New South Wales, 2005, p.9.
8. Vanselow, George. Private Family Papers, Letter, 16 June 1941
9. Bill Bracht returned to Australia. He demobilized in 1947 at age 30 as a three badge Petty Officer Gunnery Instructor. Under the Commonwealth Rehabilitation Training Scheme he became an Accountant.
10. Kirkmoe, D. Diary, Entry 23 December 1940, Kirkmoe Private Family Papers.
11. Nelson James K. The Mediterranean Diary–*The HMAS Perth in the Mediterranean Sea,* 24th December 1940 to 12 August 1941, self published, 2002, p. viii.
12. Payne, Alan. *HMAS Perth–The Story of the 6 inch Cruiser, 1936–1942*, Naval Historical Society, Garden Island, NSW, 1978, p.25.
13. Whiting, B, p.27.
14. Nelson J, p. viii.
15. Norris, R, p.21.
16. *Ibid.*, p.22.
17. *Ibid.*
18. Nelson, J, p.5.
19. *Ibid.*, p.6.

Four

1. Kirkmoe, D, Diary, Kirkmoe Private Family Papers.
2. Cooper, J, Papers.
3. Norris, R, p.26.
4. Kirkmoe, D, Diary.
5. Adam, 'Snowy', in Jones, T.M. and Idriess, Ion., *The Silent Service*, Sydney, 1952, p.107.
6. *Ibid.*, p.110.
7. Norris, R, p.28.
8. Hayler, B, p.8.
9. Norris, R, p.35.
10. *Ibid.*, p.30.
11. Nelson, J, p15.
12. Reid, Tony. Letter, 13 March 2008.
13. Nelson, J, p24.
14. Steele, Gordon, Stoker. Diary, Steele Private Family Papers.
15. Norris, R, p.46.
16. Kirkmoe, D, Diary.
17. Nelson, J, p.30.
18. *Ibid.*, p.31.
19. Norris, R, p.51.
20. Unknown diarist, RAN History Directorate, Defence Canberra.
21. Steele, Gordon, Interview, 7 October 2006.
22. Nelson, J, p.43.
23. *Ibid.*
24. Norris, R, p.63.
25. Nelson, J, p.43.
26. *Ibid.*
27. Norris, R, p.65.

Five

1. Nelson, J, p.47.
2. Kirkmoe, D, Diary.
3. Norris, R, p.69.
4. Cooper, J, Papers.
5. Hayler, B, Manuscript, p.10.
6. Nelson, J, p.49.
7. Jones, T.M. and Idriess, I, p.110.
8. *Ibid.*, 'Jack' is short for 'Jack Tar' the traditional name for a sailor.
9. Norris, R, p.72.
10. The second ANZAC corps was defeated in less than two weeks, an estimated 2,065 troops were taken prisoner.
11. Jones, T.M. and Idriess, I, p.110.
12. Vanselow, G. Letter, 21 June 1941, Vanselow Family Private Papers.
13. *Ibid.*
14. Beaumont survived the war. He was promoted to Chief on 1 April 1947 and then Wireless Instructor in 1948. Few of his students learned of his exploits over the 'Med'. He left the RAN in 1950.
15. Payne, A, p.48.
16. *Ibid.*, p.49.
17. Norris, R, p.72.
18. Steele, Gordon, Interview, 7 October 2006.
19. Whiting, B, p.12.
20. *Ibid.*
21. Nation, Andrew, Stoker, PRO0186, Papers, Australian War Memorial, Canberra.
22. Bracegirdle, Warwick. Short biography on Bowyer-Smyth, Reid Private Family Papers.
23. Nelson, J, p.62.
24. Winton, John LCDR. (ed) *The War at Sea 1939–45*, London, 1967, p.117.
25. Nelson, J, p.68.
26. *The Herald*, in Nelson, J, p.66.
27. *Ibid.*
28. An estimated 3,109 Australians were taken prisoner with the loss of Crete.
29. *Ibid.*
30. Nelson, J, p.60.
31. Hayler, B, p.10.
32. Whiting, B, p.11.
33. Nelson, J, p.71.

34. Norris, R. This rendition of events from, *A Cook's Tour*, p.88.

35. Triffitt, Sydney, Letter, 14 October 2006.

36. She was awarded a pension of £3/5/- per fortnight.

37. King, N, Papers.

38. Norris, R, p.88.

39. Triffitt, Sydney, Letter, 14 October 2006.

40. Nelson, J, pp.71–72.

41. Payne, A, p.56.

42. Whiting, B, p.18.

43. Payne, A, p.59.

44. Nelson, J, p.75.

45. Kirkmoe, John. Interview, 3 July 2007.

46. Kirkmoe, John, Letter, 14 June 2004. John Kirkmoe's war history included being a 'Rat of Tobruk', service in Milne Bay, Buna and Sanananda. Julius Kirkmoe was accepted for service by the Army in WWII, although his age resulted in his being designated 'not for overseas service', Sgt Kirkmoe was pleased to serve.

47. Basil Hayler returned to Australia in August 1943. He helped commission *Hawkesbury*, and when promoted to PO in April 1947 became Coxswain. On leaving *Hawkesbury* Basil served for six months on L.S.T. 3035; was then drafted to Ships in Reserve (HMAS Burdekin) at Geelong as Coxswain for 18mths. Prior to paying off in October 1951 he trained national servicemen at Flinders. As a civilian he opened a small electrical business and he and wife Pauline started a nursery, specialising in lilies. They had two daughters, Julie and Dianne.

48. Norris, R, p.103.

49. *Ibid*., p.105.

50. Triffitt, Sydney, Letter 14 October 2006. Gordon drafted to *Vendetta*. On his return to Australia he served on *Mildura* and was promoted to Leading Stoker in 1944 and demobilized in 1946. He married Nell, a member of the WRANS, and they had six children. Syd was also promoted to Leading Stoker in 1944, served on *Gascoyne*, at *Melville, Huon, Larus,* and also demobilized in 1946.

51. Kirkmoe, Don, Diary.

52. Sailors who were absent without leave were commonly restricted to 2nd class leave privileges.

53. Jim Nelson married Jean and had three children. In 2006 they celebrated their 65th wedding anniversary. Jim Nelson died in 2007.

54. Vansleow, G, Vanselow Private Family Papers.

55. Norris, R, p.116.

Six

1. Hill, Harold 'Tich' Hill, Able Seaman. *Wind Tracks on the Water*, self published, WA, 1992, p.55.

2. Gee, M, p.146.

3. Charles, Joan (Asplin), Correspondence, 1 July 2004.

4. Cooney, Judy. Correspondence, 1 June 2004 and 3 July 2004.

5. Reid, Charles. Address to HMAS PERTH Association, Reid Private Family Papers.

6. Nordish, Beryl. Interview, 19 August 2004; Millerick Family Papers.

7. Noyce, Bob. Interview, 9 September 2004; Letter, 23 September 2004; Mellish Private Family Papers.

8. Madge Private Family Papers.

9. Madge, Warren. Interview, 16 August 2004 and 26 August 2004.

10. Thomson, Nell. Interview, 2 May 2004 and 2 July 2004; Correspondence, 30 May 2004.

11. Bancroft, Arthur. Interview, 2 May 2004; Correspondence, 15 May 2004 and 27 June 2004.

12. Skeels, Fred. Interview, 2 May 2004; Correspondence, 4 July 2004.

13. Toovey, Ernie. Interviews, 19 August 2004 and 11 September 2004.

14. National Archives, Canberra, A5954 (A5954/69) 518/16–Navy–'Fire on HMAS Perth, 22/10/41–4/12/41'

15. Toovey, Ernie. 'For the Duration', unpublished manuscript, Toovey Private Family Papers, p.4.

16. Citation for DSO

17. Toovey, Ernie. p.4

18. Stening, Warwick. Interview, 19 August 2004.

19. Chaffey, Dorothea. Interview, 17 August 2004.

20. Lasslett, Fred. Interviews, 9 August 2004 and 25 August 2006.

21. Justelius, Eric. Letter, Justelius Private Family Papers.

22. Tibbets, Janice. Interview, 17 August 2004.

23. Chattaway, Frank. Interview, 29 June 2005.

24. Toovey, Ernie. 'For the Duration', p.4.

25. The loss of *Sydney* was not made public until 1 December.

26. Justelius, Isabel. Interview, 17 June 2004.

27. Partington, Margaret. Correspondence, 9 July 2005.

28. Hill, Harold, *Wind Tracks,* pp. 61–62.

29. Grove, Eric. J. 'A Service Vindicated, 1939–1946' in Hill, J.R.(ed) *The Oxford Illustrated History of the Royal Navy'*, Oxford, New York, 1995, p. 362.

30. National Archives, Canberra, A461/9 N337/1/5 ATT, 'Recruits for the RAN'.

31. *Ibid.*

32. National Archives, Canberra, A5954/69 303/4, 'Review of RAN War Effort and Activities to October 1942'.

33. National Archives, Canberra, A2684/3, 1074, 'Provision of RAN Personnel for the Royal Navy'.

34. Gray, Peter, Imperial War Museum tapes; copied by AWM; Correspondence, 26 June 2004.

35. Madge Private Family Papers.

Seven

1. Winslow, W. G. (Captain, USN). *The Ghost That Died at Sunda Strait*, Naval Institute Press, Annapolis, 1984, p. xix.

2. Spurling, Kathryn. 'The Women's Royal Australian Naval Service (WRANS): A Study in Discrimination', MA thesis, UNSW@ADFA, 1988.

3. *Sunday Sun*, 30 March 1941.

4. The station established in April 1941 would be commissioned on 1 July 1943, as HMAS *Harman*.

5. Lynes, Ted. *One Sailor's War,* Manning, David, Ord Seam story, Goodenia Rise, Ballarat, 1999, p.3.

6. Manning, David, Interview, 29 June 2005.

7. In 1940 only 20 Cadet Midshipmen were undergoing training at the RANC; in 1941, 15 and in 1942, 16.

8. *Flying Stations: A Story of Australian Naval Aviation*, p.22.

9. Wallace, Sydney. Leading Seaman Telegraphist Air Gunner. *Sunda Strait: The Last Day of Summer*, Drawquick, Sydney, 2007, p.4.

10. *Ibid.*

11. Toovey, E, p.5.

12. McIntyre, W.D. *The Rise and Fall of the Singapore Naval Base, 1919–1942,* MacMillan, London, 1979, pp.161 and 171.

13. Dower, John. *War Without Mercy: Race and Power in the Pacific War*, Faber & Faber, London, 1986, p.99.

14. Attiwill, Ken. *The Rising Sunset*, Hale, London, 1957, p.15.

15. Gill, Hermon G. *Australians in the War, 1939–1945, Series 2, Navy*, Vol 1, Australian War Memorial, Canberra, 1957, p.553.

16. MSS1530. Hatton, Alex. Manuscript, Australian War Memorial, Canberra.
17. Gee, M, p.209. This opinion of *Perth* survivor, Captain 'Knocker' White, (Rtd).
18. Toovey, E, p.5.
19. This number is quoted in Gill, H., but elsewhere it is 70.
20. This is another disputed statistic. Gill, H, gives the number as 250 people killed.
21. Gill, H, p.600.
22. Thomas, David. S. *Battle of the Java Sea*, Deutsch, London, 1968, p.149. See also Gill, H., p.600.

Eight

1. Thomas, D, p.190.
2. Parry, A.F., *HMAS Yarra,*Naval Historical Society, 1980, history of *Yarra*, mentions this bombing incident and *Hobart* but it is not mentioned that *Perth* is in harbour. A degree of animosity developed between survivors of *Yarra* and *Perth*, and the Battle of Java Sea commemorations would be observed separately. *Yarra* was sunk at 0615 on 4 March, when it was intercepted by a Japanese armada south of Java. There were thirteen survivors from a crew of 138.
3. Jones, T.M. and Idriess, I, p.231.
4. Gill, H, p.602.
5. *Ibid.*
6. Thomas, D, p.18.
7. Wallace, K, p.8.
8. Winston, W.G. *The Ghost That Died At Sunda Straits*, Naval Institute Press, Annapolis, 1984, p.93.
9. Attiwell, K, p.21.
10. *Ibid.*, p.159.
11. Bee, W.A. *All Men Back All One Big Mistake*, Hesperian, WA, 1998, p.13.
12. Toovey, E, p.6.
13. *Ibid.*
14. AWM54, 505/10/10 Part 1, 'Movements Actions and Subsequent Loss of HMAS *Perth*, Report on Health of Ship's Company of H.M.A.S. *PERTH* Prior to and After Sinking', Australian War Memorial.
15. Wallace, K, p.17.
16. Campbell, G. Email, 29 November 2007.
17. MP1185/8, 1932/2/220, 'Loss of HMAS *Perth*', National Archives, Melbourne.
18. Winston, W.G, p.113.
19. *Ibid.*
20. Bee, W.A, p.9.
21. Thomas, D, p.189.
22. Wallace, K, p.17.
23. Willis, Jack R.E. MSS 1106, Manuscript, Australian War Memorial, Canberra.
24. Payne, A, p.83.
25. It was commonplace for Japanese Midshipmen to be trained by the Royal Navy.
26. Thomas, D, p.190.
27. Wallace, K, p.19.
28. Lasslett, Fred. *War Diaries*, Brolga, Victoria, 2006, p.9.
29. The Japanese reported their fleet fired 35 torpedoes and 2,650 shells during The Battle of Java Sea. Gill, Hermon G. *Australians in the War, 1939–1945, Series 2, Navy*, Vol 1, Australian War Memorial, Canberra, 1957, p.624.
30. Gill, H, p.621.
31. Winston, W.G, p.125.
32. *Ibid.*, p.93.
33. McKie, Ronald. *Proud Echo*, Angus and Robertson, Sydney, 1953, p.8
34. Hill, H, p.69.
35. Charles, Robert H. *Last Man Out,* Eakin Press, Texas, 1988, p.1.
36. Campbell, Gavin. Email 29 November 2007.
37. Hill, H, p.69.
38. *Ibid.*, p.67.

39. Whiting, B, p.64.

40. Crick, Trevor. Letter, 13 June 2004.

41. Vanselow George, Vanselow Family Papers.

42. McKie, R, *Proud Echo*, p.15.

43. The popular name given to the standard life jacket, so named after the well-endowed Hollywood actress of the same name.

44. Payne, A, p.88.

45. Bee, W, p.19.

46. Adam-Smith, Patsy. *Prisoners of War: From Gallipoli to Korea*, Penguin, 1992, p.274.

47. McKie, R, *Proud Echo,* p.37.

48. Lasslett, Fred. Interview, 28 November 2007.

49. Lasslett, F, *War Diaries,* p.12.

50. Parkin, Ray. Interview, 2 July 2004.

51. Lohrisch, Bruce, Letter, 22 June 2004.

52. The navigational gyro-repeat on the side of the compass platform.

53. Gee, M, p.208. Quote offered by Capt. 'Knocker'

Nine

1. Parkin, Ray. *Out of the Smoke*, Hogarth Press, London, 1960, p.255.

2. *Ibid.*

3. Gowling, Mary. Letter, 14 June 2004.

4. Gee, M, p.158.

5. McKie, R, p.41.

6. Wallace, K, p.24.

7. Composite of Parkin, R. Interview, 2 July 2004, and Parkin, R. *Out of the Smoke*, pp. 254–257.

8. Payne, A, p.92.

9. *Ibid.*

10. Willis, J, Manuscript.

11. Wallace, K, p.24.

12. *Ibid.*, p.25.

13. Woods, John. Interview, 26 July 2004.

14. Gee, M, p.159.

15. Manning, David, Interview, 29 June 2005.

16. Chattaway, Frank. 'HMAS Perth, The Gallant Ship, Fight and Flourish', unpublished account of Ord Seam Frank Chattaway', Private Chattaway papers, and interview, 29 June 2005.

17. Charles, Joan. Letter, 1 July 2004.

18. Bancroft, Arthur. Interview, 2 May 2004.

19. Willis, J, p.5. Willis only refers to him as George O but investigation of service cards reveals this would have been Ord Seam George Frederick Earle Osgood, born Paddington, Sydney on 20 June 1923. His category was altered to Butcher.

20. Skeels, Fred. Letter, 16 February 2008.

21. Parkin, R, Interview, 2 July 2004.

22. Parkin, R, p.258.

23. Hill, H, p.74

24. Lynes, T, p.18.

25. Whiting, B, p.109.

26. Gee, M, p.160.

27. *Ibid.*

28. Reid, Charles. Address to HMAS *Perth* Association. Reid Private Family Papers.

29. Toovey, E, p.12.

30. Toovey, Ernie, Interview, 19 August 2004.

31. Donald Kilby; Joseph Lanagan; Vernon 'Bonza' Martin; Frederick Mason; Herbert Mynard; Morton O'Loughlan; Charles 'Alec' Petherbridge; Keith Viccars.

32. Mason, Fred. Interview, 25 August 2004.

33. Millerick Private Family Papers.

34. McKie, R, p.61.

35. *Ibid.*, p. 63.

36. Bee, W, p.22.

37. Chattaway, F. Interview, 29 June 2005.

38. Roberts, R. Interview, 2 May 2004.

39. Bee, W, p.22.

Ten

1. Parkin, Ray, p.264.
2. Payne, A, p.93.
3. Bee, W, p.22.
4. Page, T. p.219.
5. Would be commissioned in July 1943 as HMAS *Harman*.
6. McKie, R, p.59.
7. *Ibid*, p.57.
8. McKie, R, p.58.
9. Wallace, K, p.27.
10. *Ibid*., p.28.
11. Lynes, T, p.19.
12. Wallace, K, p.28.
13. Gee, M, p.215.
14. *Ibid*.
15. Gee, M, p.215.
16. *Ibid*., p.210.
17. Toovey, E, p.15.
18. *Ibid*., p.17.
19. Toovey, E, p.17.
20. Parkin, R, p.258.
21. Wallace, K, p.29. In Gee, M, p.161; Allan Gee quoted as saying 'the Japs were on the beach bayoneting the survivors as they came ashore'.
22. Hill, H, p.75.
23. *Ibid*., p.76.
24. McKie, R, p.78.
25. Thomson, Nell. Interview, 2 July 2004.
26. Willis, J, Manuscript.
27. McKie, R, p.76.
28. *Ibid*., p.77. Abbott, Johnson boat held among others, Leading Seamen Ben Chaffey, Stan Roberts; Stoker Jimmie Millerick; Ord Telegraphist Peter Nelson; and Able Seamen 'Tich' Hill, Harry Mee and the remaining Ryan brother, Richard; Ord Seam Norm Fuller.
29. Willis, J, Manuscript (MSS1106)
30. These included Lieut Cmdr Ralph Lowe, Lieuts Gillan and Black; Flying Officer Jock McDonough; Sub Lieut Gavin Campbell; Chaplain Keith Mathieson; Commissioned Gunner George Ross; POs Bill Hogman and Ernie Ratliff; Leading Stoker John McQuade; Canteen Assistant Arthur Hawkins; Able Seamen 'Jumma' Brown, Wally Jackson, Les Golding, Noel Laugher, Danny Maher, Gordon Webster and Ernie Toovey; Ordinary Seamen David Manning, 'Chilla' Goodchap.
31. Manning, D, in Lynes, T, p.21.
32. Toovey, E, p.17.
33. Gee, M, p.164.
34. Gill, H, p. 624.
35. Bee, W, p.28.
36. *Ibid*.
37. *Ibid*.
38. Gee, M, p.163.
39. *Ibid*.
40. Toovey, E, p.18.
41. *Ibid*., p.22.
42. Manning, D, in Lynes, pp.25–26
43. Toovey, E, p.21.
44. *Ibid*., p.22.
45. Fuller, N, Interview, 10 January 2007.
46. Toovey, E, p.22.
47. Gee, M, p. 215.
48. Lieut Thode, Sub Lieuts Ray Barker, Bill Roberts, John Martin; Warrant Officer Claude Woodley; PO Alfie Coyne: Leading Wireman Al Parker; Sick Berth Attendants Fred Wright and Roy Turner; Cook Tom Larkin; ERA IV Don Smith; Telegraphist Carlos Hughes; Able Seamen Mal Kersting and George Tibbits.
49. Wallace, K, p.34.
50. *Ibid*., p.41.
51. This group included POs Tyrrell and Ernie Robinson; Corporal Ron

Bradshaw (RAAF): Leading Seamen Stan Roberts and Ben Chaffey; Stokers Clive Henry, Allan Axton and Dallas Pascoe; AB Eric Hurst and Ord Seam Max Jagger.

52. Wallace, K, p.36.

53. *Ibid.*, p.38.

54. Lieuts Lloyd Burgess and Gordon Black; Sub Lieuts Ray Barker, Bill Roberts, John Martin; Warrant Officer Claude Woodley; Yeoman Neil Biddel: SBA Ernie Noble; Dick Ryan, Turner, Telegraphist Peter Nelson; Stoker Gordon Dvorak.

55. Wallace, K, p.56.

Eleven

1. Charles, Joan (Asplin). Letter, 1 July 2004.

2. Nordish, Beryl, (Millerick). Interview, 19 August 2004.

3. Mathew, Mary, Interview, 1 July 2004; Mathew, Sheila, Interview, 5 July 2004. George Mathew would survive the war as an Acting Telegraphist.

4. Noyce, Bob. Interview, 9 September 2004.

5. McCarrey, Les. Letter, 22 August 2004.

6. *Ibid.*

7. McGovern, Frank, Interview, 15 January 2008.

8. Elix, Ruth (Banks), Letter, 22 June 2004.

9. Madge Private Family Papers.

10. Letter to Jean Justelius for Rockdale Municipal Patriotic and War Fund, 23 March 1942, Justelius Private Family Papers.

11. Stening, Malcolm, Interview, 25 August 2004.

12. *Sydney Morning Herald*, 18 February 1942 and 29 December 1941.

13. In official notices, newspapers and many early publications, the number was given as 682, there were, however, 681 onboard.

14. Letter, 6 July 1941, Justelius Private Family Papers.

15. Letter, 15 March 1942, Justelius Private Family Papers.

16. Justelius Private Family Papers.

17. Letter, 15 March 1942, Justelius Private Family Papers.

18. Vanselow Private Family Papers.

19. McGovern, Frank, Interview, 15 January 2008.

20. Gray, 'Digby', oral history.

21. Bancroft, A and Roberts, R.G. *The Mikado's Guests: a Story of Japanese Captivity*, Patersons, Perth, 1945, p.9.

22. Gee, A 'Elmo' in Gee, M, p.173.

23. AWM 07/0788, Johnson, Ross and Johnson, Anne, 'Experiences of A.V.'Jock' McDonough during WWII 1939–1945', Canberra, p.35.

24. Rivett, Rohan. D. *Behind Bamboo: An Inside Story of the Japanese Prison Camps,* Angus and Robertson, Sydney, 1947, pp.74–75.

25. Stening, Malcolm J.L. *The Class of 35 at War*, Naval Historical Society, Sydney, 2002, p.90.

26. Gray, 'Digby', Oral History.

27. Chattaway, Frank. 'HMAS Perth, The Gallant Ship, "Fight and Flourish", unpublished account of AB Frank Chattaway', Private Family Papers, p.19.

28. *Ibid.*

29. Bancroft, A and Roberts, R.G, p.11.

30. McGovern, Frank. Interview, 15 January 2008.

31. This number varies widely between memoirs and secondary sources; from 600 to 1620.

32. Stening, M, *Class of 35 at War*, p.144; Interview, 25 August 2004.

33. Johnson, R and A, p.35.

34. Adam-Smith, P, p.281.

35. McGovern, F. Interview, 14 October 2005.

36. In 1950 he was re-buried in the Dutch War Cemetery, Batavia.

37. Lasslett, F, *War Diaries*, pp.27–28.

38. *Ibid.*, p.32.

39. During my 2006 interview Fred, with a grin, asked me to tell Charlie Wray, 'I forgive him'.

40. Lasslett, F. Interview, 25 August 2006.

41. Bancroft and Roberts, p.17.

42. There is some confusion of the date, whether it was Monday 13 April or Wednesday 15 April 1942.

43. Bancroft, A, and Roberts, R, p.19.

44. Like most statistics, this number differs in primary and secondary sources. The number could have been 2,000.

45. MP150/1/0, 567/201/17, National Archives, Melbourne.

46. Mason, Fred. Interview, 28 June 2005.

47. *Ibid.*

48. Toovey, E. Interview, 19 August 2004.

49. Christie, R.W. 2/29 Association, Interview, 30 August 2004.

50. Nolan, Kevin *Neither Hero Nor Coward: The War Diaries of Sgt Kevin Nolan*, 2/2nd Pioneer Battalion, Bingham, Victoria, 1997, p.98.

51. Bancroft, A and Roberts, R, p.23.

52. Toovey, E, p.27.

53. The 131st would become known as 'The Lost Battalion' because information as to their whereabouts was not received by United States authorities until 1945.

54. La Forte, Robert S. & Marcello, Ronald E. (eds.) *Building of a Death Railway: the ordeal of American POWs in Burma,1942–1945*, Scholarly Resources, Wilmington, USA, 1984, p.93.

55. Bancroft, A, and Roberts, R, p.29.

56. *Ibid.*, pp. 31–32.

57. Murphy, A. Interview, 4 August 2004.

58. Bancroft, A, and Roberts, R, p.32.

59. Bee, W, p.43.

60. Dawes, Gaven. *Prisoners of the Japanese: POWs of World War II in the Pacific*, William Morrow, New York, 1994, p.170.

61. Gee, M, p.217.

62. Chattaway, F, p.4.

63. Charles, Robert H. *Last Man Out*, Eakin, Texas, 1988, p.42.

64. *Ibid.*

65. McKie, R, p.115.

66. The sail resided in the Anglican chapel at HMAS *Cerberus* for decades until it was presented to the Australian War Memorial.

67. Wallace, K, p.56.

68. *Ibid.*, p.57.

69. There is some disparity in the spelling of town names through various memoirs, furthermore current Indonesian spelling is often different from 1942. Accuracy has been attempted by comparison of various published and unpublished versions and selecting that most used.

70. Wallace, K, p.65.

71. This is a composite of Willis, J, MSS1036, AWM; Knight, H. CPO, PR87/049, AWM; McKie.

Twelve

1. Johnson, R and A, p.36.

2. Chattaway, F, p.28.

3. Hall, Leslie. G. *The Blue Haze: Incorporating the History of 'A' Force Groups 3&5 Burma–Thai Railway 1942–43*, Harbord, NSW, 1985, p.64.

4. Bancroft, A and Roberts, R, p.47.

5. Hill, H, p. 93.

6. Bee, W, p.50.

7. Lynes, T, p.27.

8. Boyle, James. *Railroad to Burma*, Allen & Unwin, Sydney, 1990, p.49.

9. Bancrofft, A and Roberts, R, p.47.

10. La Forte, R, and Marcello, R, p.93.

11. Rivett, R, p.133.

12. Campbell, Gavin. Email, 2 April 2008. They would meet up later in the jungles of Burma and spend valued time together, particularly talking about 'what we would do after we got out'.

13. Lasslett, F, p.62.

14. *Ibid.*, p.63.

15. The spelling of this 'hell ship' and others differs between POW accounts. It is also written as *Maubusi Maru, Maebasi Maru.*

16. Toovey, E, 'For the Duration', p.37.

17. Rivett, R, p.142.

18. Following the war Nagatomo would be hung for his acts of inhumanity against POWs.

19. Whitecross, R.H. *Slaves of the Son of Heaven*, Lake&Ashes, Sydney, 1953, pp.45–57.

20. Toovey, E, 'For the Duration', p.40.

21. Dawes, G, p.184.

22. McQuade, in Gee, M, p.247.

23. Toovey, E, p.43.

24. *Ibid.* Toovey says it was 'Dillinger' who killed O'Donnell.

25. Richards, R, p. 162.

26. Hall, L.G., p.147.

27. Richards, R, p.108.

28. This group boarded the *Dai Nichi Maru.*

29. Bee, W, p.53.

30. Adam-Smith, Patsy. *Prisoners of War: From Gallipoli to Korea*, Penguin, 1992, p.444.

31. Parkin, Ray. *Into the Smother*, Penguin, Victoria, 1993, pp.18–19.

32. The number was 328 but Parkin was told the estimate was 309.

33. Ebury, Sue. *Weary: The Life of Sir Edward Dunlop*, Penguin, Victoria, 1995, p.369.

34. *Ibid.*, p.371.

35. *Ibid.*, p.372.

36. 'Dunlop's Thousand' was believed to be 950 when it left Java, 82 were admitted to Changi hospital.

37. *Ibid.*, pp. 372–373.

38. Like many details this number is given differently by various authors. Parkin says five, Knight gives the number as fifteen and the official *Loss of Perth* file written by Thode give the number as a different 15. The names have been compiled from a variety of records, particularly service cards.

39. Parkin, Ray. *Out of the Smoke*, Hogarth Press, London, 1960, p.36. Unfortunately within Parkin many of the biographical details, ages, MacDonald described as a 'Scotsman', are in error. Details here taken from RAN Service cards.

40. *Ibid.*, p.17.

41. Foster, Frank. *Comrades in Bondage*, Skeffington, London, 1946, p.68.

42. Copy of a talk titled 'The Moji Maru Incident' given by 'Buzzer' Bee, private papers of AB Fred Skeels.

43. In some documents it is suggested that the original Ross/Hawkins party numbered 50.

44. Boyle, J, p.142.

45. Hill, H, p.100.

46. Whiting, B, p.126.

47. Bancroft, A and Roberts, R, p.77.

48. Nolan, K, p.178.

49. McQuade, in Gee, M, p.247.

50. Hall, L.H., p.128.

51. Richards, R, p.146.

52. Toovey, E, p.47.

53. Chattaway, F, p.39.

54. Richards, Rowley. *A Doctor's War*, Harper Collins, Sydney, 2005, p.145.

55. Skeels, F. Interview, 17 January 2008.

56. Bee, W, p.52.

57. Rivett, R, p.212.

58. Daws, p.223.

59. Hartley, Peter. *Escape to Captivity*, London, 1952, p.96.

60. Gray, Peter. Letter, 26 June 2004.

61. Gee, M, p.222.

62. Chattaway, F, p.7.

63. Bancroft, A, and Roberts, R, p.86.

64. Richards, R, p.158.

65. Chattaway, F, p.38.

66. Chattaway, F, p.39.
67. 3DRL/6741, Mathieson, J.K.W. Chaplain, Australian War Memorial, Canberra.
68. Hill, H, p.105.
69. Chattaway, F, p.9.
70. *Ibid.*
71. Lynes, T, p.37
72. Mason, Fred. Interview, 28 July 2005.
73. Hill, H, pp.108–109.
74. Dunlop, E.E. *The War Diaries of Weary Dunlop*, Nelson, Australia, 1986, p.195.
75. PR 85/192, Rockey, John., Australian War Memorial, Canberra.

76. *Ibid.*, p.109.
77. Richards, R, p.162.
78. Hill, H, p.112.
79. *Ibid.*
80. Payne, A, p.128.
81. Parkin, R. *Into the Smother*, Penguin, Victoria, 1963, p.177
82. *Ibid.*
83. Toovey, E, p.48.
84. Gee, M, p.188.
85. *Ibid.*
86. Trimble died 9 December 1943 and was buried in Grave 29, Nike Cross Road (131-kilo), Thailand.

Thirteen

1. *The Mercury*, 9 July 1942.
2. Australian newspaper unknown, 21 March 1942, courtesy Dr Murray Stokan, 10 June 2005.
3. Chaffey, Athol, Letter, 31 May 2004.
4. Hall, E.R. 'Bon'. *The Burma–Thailand Railway of Death*, Graphic, Victoria, 1981, p.98.
5. Mathieson, K.
6. Toovey, E, p.52.
7. McQuade, J, in Gee, M, p.246.
8. Payne, A, p.126.
9. MP1185/9 567/201/82. Lowe, Ralph. LtCdr. Report, 1945, National Archives, Melbourne.
10. McQuade, J, in Gee, M, p.250.
11. Hall, E, p.105.
12. *Ibid.*, p.131.
13. *Sydney Morning Herald*, 25 April 1991.
14. Japanese figures concluded this took the removal of 3 million cubic metres of rock and 4 million cubic metres of earthworks. 688 bridges were built with a total length of 14 kilometres. Statistics from Dawes, G, p.217.
15. Skeels, F. Interview, 16 February 2008.
16. Hall, L.G, p.300.

17. 6,318 British, 132 Americans and 2,490 Dutch.
18. Hill, H, p.111.
19. *Ibid.*
20. Gee, M, p.180.
21. Parkin, R, in Gee, M, p.205.
22. Gee, M, p.189.
23. *Ibid.*, p.190.
24. *Ibid.*, p.180.
25. *Ibid.*, p.190.
26. Hill, H, p.117.
27. Toovey, E, p.59.
28. *Ibid.*, p. 118.
29. *Ibid.*, p.119.
30. *Ibid.*
31. Toovey, E. Interview, 11 September 2004.
32. Campbell, Gavin. Email 2 April 2008.
33. Chattaway, F, p.41.
34. Toovey, E, p.56.
35. Ibid., p.59.
36. Lynes, T, p.38.
37. Toovey, E, p.59.
38. Bancroft, A and Roberts, R, p.134.
39. *Ibid.*
40. Bee,W, p.73.
41. Lowe, R.
42. Hill, H, p.122.
43. Toovey, E, p.66.

44. Blair, Joan and Clay, Jr. *Return From the River Kwai*, Simon and Schuster, New York, 1979, p.26.
45. *Ibid*.
46. Skeels, Fred. Interview, 6 March 2008.
47. PR87/049, Knight, H. Manuscript, Australian War Memorial, Canberra.
48. Michno, Gregory. F. *Death on the Hellships*, Naval Institute Press, Annapolis, 2001, p.267.
49. The race was held on 5 February 1939. The *Frankston Standard* reported on Friday 10 February 1939, that the race was run from Oliver's Bay jetty to the pier. It began at 2.30 p.m. and that George Morriss 'swimming with a wonderful stroke had the race well in hand' and won in 20minutes 26 seconds. When the race was resurrected in 1998, his cousin, Alf Morriss, donated the George Morriss Memorial Trophy.
50. Morriss, Alf, Letter, 23 July 2004.
51. According to his RAN service card, Morriss died on 9 May 1945. According to Lynette Silver, author of *Sandakan–A Conspiracy of Silence*, he died 29 May 1945. George Morriss' remains were exhumed from a grave marked 'Unknown Soldier'. He was reburied in the Labuan Cemetery. His cousin Alf Morriss travelled to Borneo in 2001 for the unveiling of a new headstone with full naval honours for AB George Morriss. General Douglas MacArthur was supreme commander of the region. An advance party was put ashore less than 30 miles from Sandakan. Allied Command Headquarters were well aware there was a large number of POWs there and in jeopardy. MacArthur chose to keep all resources together for the 'grand gesture' of returning to the Philippines, and by then it was too late for the POWs in Borneo.
52. Blair, J and C, p.73.
53. Richards, R, p.237.
54. *Ibid*.

Fourteen

1. Blair, J and C, p.148.
2. *Ibid*., p.187.
3. *Ibid*., p.218.
4. *Ibid*., p.224.
5. Bancroft in Blair, J and C, p.244.
6. *Ibid*.
7. *Ibid*.
8. Gee, M, p236.
9. Whiting, B, p.132.
10. *Ibid*., p.236.
11. Bancroft, A. Medical documents, Bancroft Private Family Papers.
12. *Sydney Morning Herald*, 18 November 1944.
13. Stoker PO William Frederick Hogman; POs William Milne and John James Samuel Turnbull; Leading Signalman Noel Francis Leslie Jackson; Telegraphists Hugh Alexander Keith and Desmond Godfrey Rix; Leading Supply Assistant Socrates Likiard; Leading Seamen Charles Laurence Bell, Frank Dandridge Johnson, and Reginald Albert Gebhardt; Leading Stoker Alfred Thomas Jones; Stokers Gordon Linsdale Dvorak, Ernest Edward Casserly, Walter Constantine McDonnell, Alexander James Rosevear; Stokers II Frederick James Slattery, Charles Alexander Petherbridge and Lloyd Dudley Bessell; Stoker III Vernon Martin; SBAII Frederick Baird Wright, ABs Francis Clifford Campbell, Rex Sidney Wood Williams, Leslie Alfred Thomas Wilson, Cliff Isaac Winnett, Trevis Mayne Hosking, Lindsay Gordon MacPherson, Richard Denis Maher, Harry Lionel Nagle, John Barr Parks, Frank Edward Ritchie, Raymond John Smith; Ord Seam William Thomas Puldich McCall and Walter James

Johnston. Too often left off lists was Leading Aircraftsman Ernest George Toe, RAAF, a 24-year-old Victorian ex-stores clerk who was a member of the *Perth* RAAF group.

14. Bancroft, A. Medical documents, Bancroft Private Family Papers.

15. Bancroft, A. Interview, 2 May 2004.

16. A daughter died of a brain tumour aged 37.

17. Blair, J and C, p.288

18. Chattaway, F, p.49.

19. Leading Seaman Roy 'Nick' Carter; Acting Leading Telegraphist Fred Spicer; Acting Leading Seaman Allan Hawke; Leading Stoker Wally Sharp; Acting Leading Stoker Allan Thompson; Signalman 'Buzzer' Bee; Bandsman Ron Sparks, Stokers 'Tiny' Savage, Ron Crick, Fred Parke and 'Bert' Simons; ABs 'Chesty' Bond, Colin Browne, 'Spud' Murphy, Frank Chattaway, 'Chilla' Goodchap, Fred Skeels, Percy Bullivant, and 'Clarrie' Glossop; Ord Seam Bruce Strange and Stoker II Normal Lindsay Toulmin.

20. Bee, W, p.95.

21. Chattaway, F, p.55.

22. AWM 54, 1010/4/63 'War Crimes and Trials', Part 2 testimony AB Charles Goodchap, 17 January 1945, Australian War Memorial, Canberra.

23. Murphy, Alec. Interview, 4 August 2004.

24. *Ibid.*

25. *Advertiser*, 16 March 1942.

26. Bee, W, p.101.

27. AWM54 1010/4/143, 'War Crimes and Trials'; testimony of Warrant Electrician Cecil Vowles, Australian War Memorial, Canberra.

28. Dawes, G, p.319. Dawes places it at 100,00 but other estimates have been as high as 200,000.

29. McGovern, Frank. Interview, 10 February 2006

30. Anderson, Nan. Letter, 15 December 2006

31. Tibbets named his aircraft after his mother. The aircraft took off from Tinian, a small island in the Marianas.

32. Whitecross, R.H. *Slaves of the Son of Heaven,* Lake and Ashes, Sydney, 1953, p.235.

33. McGovern, Frank. Letter, 21 February 2008

34. PR87/049, Knight, H. Manuscript, Australian War Memorial, Canberra.

35. Adam-Smith, Patsy. *Prisoners of War: From Gallipoli to Korea*, Penguin, 1992, p.441.

36. McGovern, F. Interview, 24 August 2006.

37. Chattaway, F, p.69.

38. McGovern, F. Letter, 21 February 2008.

39. Davis, G, in Nesdale, Iris, p.223.

40. McGovern, F. Letter, 21 February 2008.

41. Chattaway, Frank. Interview, 29 June 2005. Frank married Nell. She died of cancer and he later married Jan.

42. McNab, Margaret. Letter, 8 September 1945.

43. Vanselow, George. AWM 541010/4/143, 'War Crimes and Trials', AWM, Canberra.

44. Vanselow Private Family Papers.

45. Wallace, K, p.74.

46. *Ibid.*, p.76.

47. Hill, H, p.122.

48. Rye, Alan. Interview, 8 May 2004.

49. Manning, David. Interview, 14 March 2008.

50. Grandfather of test cricketers, the Chappel brothers.

51. Hill, H, p.125.

52. Manning David. Interview, 14 March 2008.

53. Justelius, I. Interview, 27 July 2005.

54. A1838 401/3/38, 'East Indies (Netherlands East Indies) – Search for Survivors of HMAS *Perth*, Australian Archives, Canberra.

55. Australian Commonwealth Naval Board Minutes, Minute No. 119, 28 Nov 1945; No.10, 23 Jan 1946

56. Gwatkin, Ted. Letter, 28 July 2004.

57. Perc separated from wife Thelma and continued to play music. In 1958 he met Margaret, another member of the Tasmanian Symphony Orchestra. They were reunited in 1961 when both were members of the Adelaide Symphony Orchestra. They married but when Perc was considered one of the finest Bass Trombonists in Australia, he was killed in a car accident.

58. Wallace, K, p.80.

59. *Ibid.*, p.81. The Wallace's had four children and 'a long married life' before Linda died of cancer. Wallace married again.

60. Lynes, D, p.52.

61. Lasslett, F, p.173.

62. *Ibid.*, p.186. Fred married Gwen Payne in 1948 and 'enjoyed a happy marriage with four children for 52 years. Gwen died in 2000.'

63. Steele, G. Interview, 27 September 2007.

64. McGovern, F, Letter, 21 February 2008.

65. *Ibid.* Frank and Merle had two sons and two daughters. Merle died in July 2006.

66. Johnson, R and A, p.42.

67. *Ibid.*, p.43.

68. Vanselow Family Papers. Letter 23 September 1945.

69. Gee, M, p.254.

70. Gray, P. Interview.

71. *Ibid.*

72. Gee, M, p.169.

73. Lynes, D, p.53.

74. McCarry, Les. Letter, 22 August 2004.

75. Skeels, F. Interview, 14 December 2007.

76. Toovey, E, p.72.

77. Toovey, E. Interview, 19 August 2004.

78. Mason, F. Interview, 28 June 2005.

79. Thomson, N. Correspondence, 30 May 2004.

80. B503 Y93, HENRY, Clive, National Archives, Melbourne.

81. B503 Y19, BLAND, Robert, National Archives, Melbourne.

82. B503 Y57, DUNCAN, Victor, National Archives, Melbourne.

BIBLIOGRAPHY

Primary sources

Interviews and conversations

Bancroft, Arthur	2 May 2004, 26 August 2006
Bateup, John	18 August 2004
Bee, Edith	2 May 2004, 26 August 2006
Chaffey, Dorothea	17 August 2004
Chattaway, Frank	29 June 2005, 14 December 2007, 17 January 2008
Christie, R.W.	30 August 2004
Fuller, Norm	2 May 2004, 26 August 2006, 10 January 2007
Green, Gary (Millerick)	30 July 2004
Hayler, Basil	24 August 2006
Harper, Lewis	31 July 2004, 5 March 2005

Harper, Sydney and Barbara	2 May 2004, 30 July 2004
Houser, Bob (Noyce)	17 August 2004
Jarrett, John	4 March 2005
Justelius, Isabel	17 June 2004, 25 July 2004, 27 April 2005, 14 October 2007
Kirkmoe, John	3 July 2007, 4 November 2007
Lasslett, Fred	9 August 2004, 25 August 2006, 14 December 2007
McGovern, Frank	14 October 2005, 24 August 2006, 14 December 2007, 15 January 2008
Madge, Warren	16 August 2004, 26 August 2004
Manning, David	24 August 2004, 29 June 2005, 19 January 2008, 14 March 2008
Mason, Fred	25 August 2004, 28 June 2005
Mathew, Mary (Hine)	1 July 2004
Mathew, Sheila	5 July 2004
Morriss, Alf	30 July 2004
Murphy, Alec	4 August 2004, 25 August 2005
Nordish, Beryl (Millerick)	19 August 2004
Noyce, Bob	9 September 2004
Parkin, Ray	2 July 2004
Priadko, Pam (Elwood)	17 August 2004
Roberts, Roy	2 May 2004, 30 July 2004
Rye, Alan	8 May 2004
Skeels, Fred	2 May 2004, 14 December 2007, 17 January 2008, 16 February 2008, 6 March 2008
Steele, Gordon	24 August 2006, 27 September 2006, 7 October 2006
Steele, Nell	27 September 2006
Stening, Malcolm	25 August 2004
Stening, Warwick	19 August 2004
Stokan, Murray	10 June 2005
Thomson, Nell	2 May 2004, 2 July 2004
Tibbets, Janice	17 August 2004
Triffitt, Syd	24 August 2006, 7 October 2006
Toovey, Ernie	19 August 2004, 11 September 2004
Woods, John	26 July 2004
Wray, Charlie	19 March 2004, 19 December 2007

Correspondence and email

Anderson, Nan	15 December 2006
Bancroft, Arthur	15 May 2004, 27 June 2004
Bateup, James	20 August 2004

Biddel, Stella	22 June 2004
Campbell, Gavin	7 March 2007, 29 November 2007, 26 February 2008, 6 March 2008, 2 April 2008
Chaffey, Athol	31 May 2004
Charles, Joan (Asplin)	1 July 2004
Cooney, Judy	1 June 2004; 3 July 2004
Elix, Ruth (Banks)	22 June 2004
Elwood, Michael	16 June 2004
Crick, Trevor	13 June 2004
Gowling, Mary (Banks)	14 June 2004
Gowing, Jenny (Tranby-White)	19 August 2004
Gray, Peter	26 June 2004
Green, Gary (Millerick)	8 September 2004
Green, Joyce	3 July 2004
Gummow, Lillian	16 June 2004
Gwatkin, Ted	21 June 2004, 28 July 2004
Hancox, Lorraine (Crick)	22 June 2004
Harper, Syd & Barbara	1 July 2004
Hayler, Basil	9 August 2004, 15 September 2006, 22 November 2007, 3 January 2008, 18 March 2008
Hosking, D	21 June 2004
Jarrett, John	20 February 2004
Kirkmoe, John	14 June 2004, 14 July 2004
Laugher, Jack	5 July 2004
Laugher, Pat	7 September 2004
Lohrisch, Bruce	22 June 2004
Manning, David	2 February 2008
McCarrey, Les	22 August 2004
McGovern, Francis	10 February 2006, 21 February 2008
Mason, Fred	29 September 2004
Morriss, Alf	30 June 2004, 23 July 2004
McCosker, Dennis	17 August 2004
Mynard, Jean	11 August 2004
Nordish, Beryl	23 September 2004
Partington, Margaret	20 July 2004, 9 July 2005
Priadko, Pam (Elwood)	22 July 2004
Reid, Tony.	13 March 2008
Roberts, Griffith, 'Robbie' & Verna	21 May 2004
Skeels, Fred	20 August 2004, 16 February 2008
Sneyd, Marlene	22 June 2004
Stratford, Graham	30 June 2004
Stuart, Athol	26 June 2004

Thomson, Nell	30 May 2004
Triffitt, Sydney	14 October 2006
Toovey, Ernie	22 August 2004
Townsend, Irene	2 July 2004
Vanselow, Don	7 January 2005
Wade, Heather (Absalom)	9 June 2004
Wray, Charlie	7 August 2004

Unpublished papers

Bancroft Private Family Papers.

Chattaway, Frank. 'HMAS *Perth*, The Gallant Ship, "Fight and Flourish", account of Ord Seam Frank Chattaway', Private Family Papers.

Gray, Peter. Imperial War Museum tapes; copied by AWM; Correspondence, 26 June 2004.

Hayler, Basil. 'The Bygone Years', Unpublished Autobiography, Private Family Papers.

Kirkmoe, Don. Diary, Kirkmoe Private Family Papers.

Madge Private Family Papers.

Mellish Private Family Papers.

Reid Private Family Papers.

Spurling, Kathryn. 'Life in the Lower Deck of the Royal Australian Navy, 1911–1952', unpublished PhD thesis, UNSW (ADFA), 1999.

Spurling, Kathryn. 'The Women's Royal Australian Naval Service (WRANS): A Study in Discrimination', unpublished MA thesis, UNSW (ADFA), 1988.

Steele, Gordon. Diary, Steele Private Family Papers.

Stokan, Private Family Papers.

Toovey, Ernie. 'For the Duration', unpublished manuscript, Toovey Private Family Papers.

Author unknown. 'Reflections of a Lower Deck Man', Navy History Directorate, Canberra.

Vanselow Private Family Papers.

OFFICIAL RECORDS

National Archives, Adelaide

D2048 3128237 'Prisoners of War, Japan, Navy.'

National Archives of Australia, Canberra.

A1838 401/3/38, 'East Indies (Netherlands East Indies) – Search for Survivors of HMAS *PERTH*'.

A2684/3 1074, 'Provision of RAN Personnel for the RN'.

A461/9 N337/1/5 ATT, 'Recruits for the RAN'.

A4624 'Ledger of HMAS PERTH, Quarter ending 31 December 1940 and Quarter ending 31/6/1941.'

A5954 (A5954/69) 518/16 'Navy – fire on HMAS PERTH, 22/10/41–4/12/41'.

A5954/1 39/4, 'Sheddon Papers'.

A5954/69,303/4, 'Review of RAN War Effort and Activities to 20 October 1943'.

A6769 Series, 'RAN Officers Records'.

A6770 Series, 'RAN Sailors Records'.

A7112 2, 'Reports from contact and enquiry teams, Part 2 (Investigations into fate of personnel of HMAS *PERTH*)'

National Archives, Melbourne

B503 Y19, BLAND, Robert.

B503 Y57, DUNCAN, Victor.

B503 Y93, HENRY, Clive.

MP150/1, 567/201/41, 'List of POWs who died in Thai camps'.

MP150/1, 567/201/106, 'Report on survivors from HMAS PERTH-name of those in POW camps in Thailand and Burma and those who died'.

MP981/2001, 452/201/714, 'Incident on 4 August 1939'.

MP1049/5, 1951/2/96 'HMAS MacQuarie – search for HMAS PERTH survivors'.

MP1185/8, 1932/2/220, 'Loss of HMAS PERTH'.

MP2049/5, 2944/2/199. 'Officer commanding Australian personnel Thai POW Branch 5, Burma, Major RAE L. J. Robertson, written Bangkok, 12 September 1945'.

Australian War Memorial

AWM07/0788 'Experiences of A.V. 'Jock' McDonough during WWII 1939–1945; transcribed by Ross Johnson from recordings made by Anne Johnson during the 1980s with some historical additions.'

AWM54 505/10/10 Part 1 'Movements Actions and Subsequent Loss of HMAS PERTH, Report on Health of Ship's Company of H.M.A.S. PERTH Prior to and After Sinking'.

AWM54 505/10/10 Part 2 'Naval Historical Section – Documents relating to the loss of HMAS *Perth* in 1942 and the subsequent internment of officers and ship's company in Cycle POW camp, Bandoeng, Java'.

AWM54 1010/4/9 War Crimes and Trials.

AWM54 1010/4/30 War Crimes and Trials – Affidavits and sworn statements: includes statement by 19592 Leading Seaman RJ Carter.

AWM54 1010/4/39 'War Crimes and Trials – Affidavits and sworn statements: includes statement by 18755 Cunningham, J. Chief Petty Officer.'

AWM54 1010/4/63 Part 2 'War Crimes and Trials – Affidavits and sworn statements: statement by B 3093 Goodchap, Charles Arthur. Able Seaman'.

AWM54 1010/4/143 'War Crimes and Trials – Affidavits and sworn statements: statements include Vowles, C.V and W925 Vinney, J.W. Able Seaman RANVR' .

AWM76 'Official Historian 1939–1945 War – biographical files – HMAS PERTH'.

AWM78 202/2 'HMAS PERTH Reports of Proceedings'
AWM78 292/3 'HMAS PERTH Reports of Proceedings (war diary) (includes
    Roll of Honour,1941–45)'.

PR88/051	Anderson, W
PR88/211	Arthur, John
PR90/161	Baker, Keith
MSS1576	Bracht, William Henry
PR03136	Branford, Leonard
PR90/116	Chattaway, Francis
MSS1226	Clifford, Leslie. Signalman
3DRL/6478	Cooper, James Duncan. Able Seaman
PR91/106	Fitzgerald, William T.E.
PR88/110	Flynn, John
PR84/012	Goodwin, D.R.
PR83/205	Hamilton, Gerald E. Able Seaman
MSS1530	Hatton, Alex
MSS1483	Hill, H.J. Able Seaman
MSS1502	King, Norm, Chief Petty Officer
PR 87/049	Knight, Harry, Chief Petty Officer
PR/161	Diary PERTH War Diary
PR01167	McCartney, Sydney
PR01554	McQuade, John Chief Petty Officer
3DRL/6741	Mathieson, J.K.W.Chaplain
PR87/029	Murphy, Alec
PRO0186	Nation, Andrew, Stoker
PR87/098	O'Brien, Francis
PR 02023	Poy, Roy
PR00105	Risley, H
PR 85/192	Rockey, John Thomas George. Chief Petty Officer
MSS 1106	Willis, Jack R.E. Chief Petty Officer
PR 87/185	Willis, Jack R.E. Chief Petty Officer

Newspapers

Advertiser, 16 March 1942
Argus, 13 April 1938
Argus, 30 April 1938
Argus, 22 April 1938
Advertiser, 16 March 1942
Daily News (WA), 2 December 1982
The News (SA), 22 October 1945
Sunday Sun (NSW), 30 March 1941
Sydney Morning Herald, 29 December 1941
Sydney Morning Herald, 18 February 1942
Sydney Morning Herald, 18 November 1944

Sydney Morning Herald, 25 April 1991
The Mercury, 9 July 1942

Secondary sources

Adam-Smith, Patsy. *Prisoners of War: From Gallipoli to Korea*, Penguin, 1992.

Admiralty, (Tactical, Torpedo and Staff Duties Division), *Battle of the Java Sea*, Battle Summary No.28, Published November 1944.

Allbury, A.G. *Bamboo and Bashido*, Hale, London, 1955.

Attiwill, Ken. *The Rising Sunset*, Hale, London, 1957.

Bancroft, Arthur. 'H.M.A.S Perth Survivors, Prisoners of War 1942–1945', Naval Historical Society of Australia, Monograph No.32, Sydney, 1991.

Bancroft, A and Roberts, R.G. *The Mikado's Guests: a Story of Japanese Captivity*, Patersons, Perth, 1946.

Bee, W.A. Bill. *All Men Back All One Big Mistake*, Hesperian, WA., 1998.

Blair, Joan and Clay Jr. *Return from the River Kwai*, Simon and Schuster, New York, 1979.

Boyle, James. *Railroad to Burma*, Allen & Unwin, Sydney, 1990.

Bulcock, Roy. *Of Death But Once*, Cheshire, Melbourne, 1947.

Burchell, David. *The Bells of Sunda Strait*, Rigby, Adelaide, 1971.

Charles, Robert H. *Last Man Out*, Eakin press, Texas, 1988.

Clark, Hugh V. and Burgess, Colin. *Barbed wire and bamboo: Australian POWs in Europe, North Africa, Singapore, Thailand and Japan.*

Clark, Hugh, Burgess, Colin & Braddon, Russell. *Prisoners of War (Australians At War)*, Time-Life Books, Sydney, 1988.

Coast, John, *Railroad of Death*, Tingling, London, 1946.

Dawes, Gaven. *Prisoners of the Japanese: POWs of World War II in the Pacific*, William Morrow, New York, 1994.

Day, David. *The Great Betrayal: Britain, Australia and the Onset of the Pacific War 1939–42*, Angus & Robertson, 1988.

Department of Veteran Affairs, *Laden, Fevered, Starved: The POWs of Sandakan North Borneo, 1945*, Looking Glass Press, Canberra, 1999.

Dower, John. *War Without Mercy: Race and Power in the Pacific War*, Faber & Faber, London, 1986.

Dunlop, E.E. *The War Diaries of Weary Dunlop*, Nelson, Australia, 1986.

Ebury, Sue. *Weary: The Life of Sir Edward Dunlop*, Penguin, Victoria, 1995.

Gee, Margaret. *A Long Way From Silver Creek: A Family Memoir*, self-published, NSW, 2000.

Foster, Frank. *Comrades in Bondage*, Skeffington, London, 1946.

Gill, Hermon G. *Australians in the War, 1939–1945, Series 2, Navy*, Vols 1 and 2, Australian War Memorial, Canberra, 1957 and 1958.

Frame, T.R, Goldrick, J.V.P and Jones, P.D. (eds). *Reflections on the Royal Australian Navy*, Kangaroo, NSW, 1991.

Hall, Leslie G. *The Blue Haze: incorporating the history of 'A' Force Groups 3 & 5. Burma–Thai railway, 1942–1943*, Harbord, NSW, 1985.

Harrison, Kenneth. *Road to Hiroshima*, Rigby, Adelaide, 1966.

Hartley, Peter. *Escape to Captivity*, Dent & Sons, London, 1952.

Hill, Harold J. *Wind Tracks On The Water*, WA, 1992.

Hill, J.R.(ed). *The Oxford Illustrated History of the Royal Navy*, Oxford, New York, 1995.

HMAS *Perth* Survivors Association, Western Australia, *50th Anniversary, Battle of Sunda Strait, Java, 28th February–1st March, 1942.*

Jones, T.M. and Idriess, Ion. *The Silent Service*, Sydney, Angus & Robertson, 1952.

Kinvig, Clifford. *Death Railway*, Pan/Ballantine, 1973.

La Forte, Robert S. & Marcello, Ronald E. (eds.) *Building of a Death Railway: the ordeal of American POWs in Burma, 1942–1945*, Scholarly Resources, Wilmington, USA,1984.

Lasslett, Fred. *War Diaries*, Brolga, Victoria, 2006.

Lynes, Ted. *One Sailor's War,* Manning, David, Ord Seam story, Goodenia Rise, Ballarat, 1999.

McCormack, Gavan and Nelson, Hank (eds) *Burma–Thailand railway: memory and history.*

McIntyre, W.D. *The Rise and Fall of the Singapore Naval Base, 1919–1942*, MacMillan, London, 1979.

McKie, Ronald. *Proud Echo*, Angus & Robertson, Sydney, 1955.

Michno, Gregory F. *Death on the Hellships*, Naval Institute Press, Annapolis, USA, 2001.

Morrison, Samuel Eliot. *History of the United States Naval Operations, Vol. 3, The Rising Sun In the Pacific*, Little Brown, Boston, 1947.

Naval Historical Review, March 2004, Sydney.

Naval Historical Review, June 2004, Sydney.

Nelson James K. *The Mediterranean Diary – The HMAS Perth in the Mediterranean Sea, 24th December 1940 to 12 August 1941,* self published, 2002.

Nesdale, Iris. *Spin me a dit!* self published, 1984.

Nolan, Kevin. *Neither Hero Nor Coward: The War Diaries of Sgt Kevin Nolan, 2/2nd Pioneer Battalion*, Bingham, Victoria, 1997.

Norris, Roy. *A Cook's Tour: HMAS Perth's Mediterranean War 1941*, Naval Historical Society of Australia, Sydney, 2005.

Payne, Alan *HMAS Perth,* Naval Historical Society, Sydney, 1978.

Parkin, Ray. *Out of the Smoke*, Hogarth Press, London, 1960.

Parkin, Ray. *Into the Smother*, Hogarth Press, London, 1960.

Parkin, Ray. *The Sword and the Blossom*, Hogarth Press, London, 1968.

Parry, A.F. *HMAS Yarra*, Naval Historical Society of Australia, Sydney, 1980.

Richards, Rowley. *A Doctor's War*, Harper Collins, Sydney, 2005.

Rivett, Rohan. *Behind Bamboo*, Angus & Robertson, 1946.

Roberts, Rowland G. *Age Shall Not Weary Them*, Patersons, Perth, 1942.

Roberts, Rowland, and Bancroft, A. *Mikado's Guests: a story of Japanese captivity*, Patersons, Perth, 1945.

Robinson, Frank, and Hall, E.R., *Through Hell and Bomb Blast*, Robinson, Tasmania, 1982.

Stening, Malcolm. J.L. *The Class of 35 At War*, Naval Historical Society, Sydney, 2002.

The Australian Naval Aviation Museum, *Flying Stations: A Story of Australian Naval Aviation*, Allen & Unwin, 1998.

Thomas, David. S. *Battle of the Java Sea*, Deutsch, London, 1968.

Van Oosten. F.C. *The Battle of the Java Sea*, Naval Institute Press, Annapolis, USA, 1976.

Wall, Don. *Heroes at Sea*, self-published, Sydney, 1991.

Wall, Don. *Sandakan, Under Nippon: The Last March*, self-published, NSW, 1997.

Wall, Don. *Singapore and Beyond: The Story of the Men of the 2/20 Battalion*, NSW, 1985.

Whiting, Brendan. *Ship of Courage: The Epic Story of HMAS Perth and Her Crew,* Allen& Unwin, NSW, 1994.

Walker, Allan S. *Clinical Problems of War,* Series 5 (Medical) Vol 1. of *Australia in the War of 1939–1945*, Australian Government, Canberra, 1952.

Wallace, Sydney. Leading Seaman Telegraphist Air Gunner. *Sunda Strait: The Last Day of Summer*, Drawquick, Sydney, 2007.

Waterford, Van. *Prisoners of the Japanese in World War II: statistical history, personal naratives, and memorials concerning POWs in camps and on hellships, civilian internees, Asian slave laborers, and others captured in the Pacific Theatre,* McFarland, Jefferson N.C., 1994.

Whitecross, R.H. *Slaves of the Son of Heavens*, Lake & Ashes, Sydney, 1953.

Winston, W.G. *The Ghost That Died At Sunda Straits*, Naval Institute Press, Annapolis, 1984.

Other books by the author published by New Holland Publishers:

A Grave Too Far Away: A Tribute to Australians in Bomber Command Europe, 2012.

Abandoned and Sacrificed. The Tragedy of Montevideo Maru, 2017.

HMAS Canberra: Casualty of Circumstance, 2008.